BRONWEN ASTOR

Peter Stanford is a writer and broadcaster. His previous books include *The She-Pope*, an investigation into the medieval legend of Pope Joan, and biographies of Lord Longford, Cardinal Basil Hume and the Devil, the last of which was made into a major BBC TV series. He writes and reviews regularly for the *Independent*, *Independent on Sunday* and *Sunday Times* and has been a panellist on various popular BBC series including 'The Moral Maze', 'Vice or Virtue' and 'Futurewatch'. A former editor of the *Catholic Herald*, he co-presented the Channel 4 series that accompanied his book *Catholics and Sex*. He is chairman of the disability charity ASPIRE, and lives in London with his wife and children.

Further reviews for *Bronwen Astor*:

'A superb biography . . . He has unravelled a complicated story quite brilliantly and taught me all sorts of things that I did not know . . . Stanford tells the tragic Stephen Ward story in a way that I find totally convincing . . . [Bronwen's] own love story with Bill is beautifully told here.'
LORD LONGFORD, *Literary Review*

'Stanford's respectful biography is well-written, conscientious and thorough, and he shows a good sense of place and period, convincingly recreating the post-war fashion world, the social scene at Cliveden, the London of the 1950s and 1960s, as well as the bickering and barminess of Bronwen's eccentric Christian communities.'
SELINA HASTINGS, *Times Literary Supplement*

'Stanford gives a meticulous account of the Astors' part in the Profumo affair . . . There is much in Stanford's biography that shallow people can deride. Many passages may be incomprehensible or embarrassing to non-Christians. Those who distrust psychotherapy will find their misgivings confirmed. Yet time and again, Stanford's interviewees speak of Bronwen Astor with generosity. Their gratitude vindicates ▮▮▮▮▮▮▮▮▮▮▮▮▮▮▮▮▮.'

▮▮s, *Independent*

'More intimate in tone than most such works are ... The author is required to cover a wide terrain: Pugh's war-time, middle-class upbringing, the glamorous life of a girl model in the 1950s, a celebration of wealth and being recruited into the Astor clan, then on to the seamier side of politics and ultimately, on to the wilder shores of unconventional religious faith ... For many, the best part of Stanford's book will be his account of how an ugly duckling transformed herself by sheer willpower into the leading model of her generation.' ANTHONY HOWARD, *Sunday Times*

'The life of Bronwen Astor is one that demands a movie. Until then Peter Stanford's biography will more than suffice. Her version of the events at Cliveden during the 1960s is told with candour and honesty.' *Women and Home*

'With Bronwen Astor's cooperation, her biographer has set out to straighten the record, homing in on the two lies which destroyed her husband's reputation ... Stanford manages a lively enough account of Bronwen Pugh's hugely successful career as a model.' SUSANNA RUSTIN, *Financial Times*

'This moving and interesting book is about many things, but I carry away from it an impression of a woman with guts as well as beauty and a faith whose power helped her to survive tragedy.' MONICA FURLONG, *Church Times*

Bronwen Astor

HER LIFE AND TIMES

Peter Stanford

HarperCollins*Publishers*

HarperCollins*Publishers*
77–85 Fulham Palace Road,
Hammersmith, London w6 8jb

www.**fire**and**water**.com

This paperback edition 2001

9 8 7 6 5 4 3 2 1

First published in Great Britain by
HarperCollins*Publishers* 2000

ISBN 0 00 638859 0

Set in PostScript Monotype Bembo by
Rowland Phototypesetting Ltd,
Bury St Edmunds, Suffolk

Printed and bound in Great Britain by
Omnia Books Limited, Glasgow

To Mary Catherine Stanford
1921–1998
whose love and nurturing is behind
everything in my life and whose loss
will always be unbearable

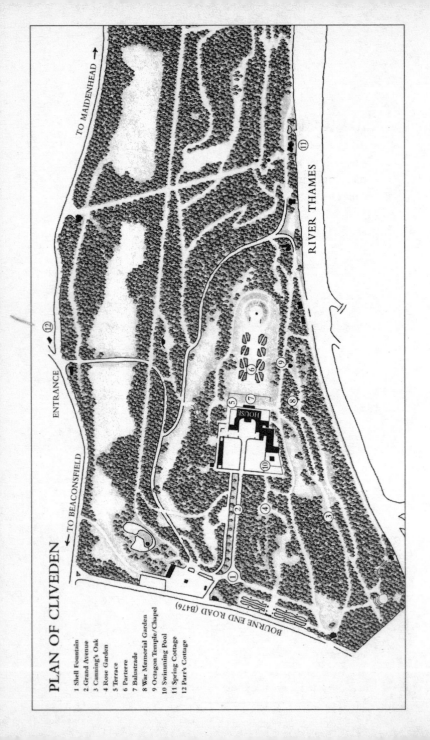

PLAN OF CLIVEDEN

1 Shell Fountain
2 Grand Avenue
3 Canning's Oak
4 Rose Garden
5 Terrace
6 Parterre
7 Balustrade
8 War Memorial Garden
9 Octagon Temple/Chapel
10 Swimming Pool
11 Spring Cottage
12 Parr's Cottage

TO BEACONSFIELD

TO MAIDENHEAD

ENTRANCE

HOUSE

BOURNE END ROAD (B476)

RIVER THAMES

Contents

List of Illustrations

Acknowledgements

This book has been written with the help, support and encouragement of its subject, Bronwen, Viscountess Astor. It is not, however, a ghosted autobiography. Bronwen has seen the manuscript and made suggestions as to how it might be improved. There are views in it which she has found painful and which we have discussed fully, but she has accepted my freedom to come to such conclusions. With such a relationship of trust and openness between subject and writer it is surely possible, despite what is often claimed, to write an honest and revealing biography of a living person.

The book tells the story of her life, which has been fascinating, diverse and often conducted in the public eye, without giving undue emphasis to the one episode with which she is most associated. However, the Profumo scandal is a part of her story and she was, during the book's preparation, often in two minds about whether it was wise to relive those events. Repeatedly she urged me to take my time in the writing, hoping to postpone the date of publication.

Since she has spent the years since the scandal 'keeping her head down', as she puts it, her ambivalence is understandable. Far stronger, however, is her desire that the truth should finally be told about her own role and that of her late husband, Bill Astor, in the affair that is held up as a turning point for Britain in the twentieth century. At the time, they remained resolutely silent despite all the rumours, gossip and innuendo about them. She has maintained that silence ever since.

Now that their daughters have grown up, however, Bronwen feels that at a distance of almost four decades the facts can be set out calmly and without the hysteria and hype that has long been associated with the name Profumo. A generation of adults has now grown up who do not even recognise the word.

In such a climate, the events of the early 1960s can finally be put into some sort of perspective. Part of that perspective is to show that there is very much more to Bronwen Astor than her supporting role in a sixties sex scandal.

So she has kept faith with the project and made whatever papers, letters, diaries and documents I asked for available to me from her unique and hitherto unpublished archive. She even directed me towards people she knew would not have a good word to say about her.

There are still, she once told me in an unguarded moment, those who were happy in the early 1960s to be her houseguests at Cliveden who today cut her dead when they meet her at parties. It was said not as a complaint, or even as part of her agenda for this book, but mentioned over tea one day, when my tape-recorder was turned off, in connection with a party she had just attended. Whether these cold-shoulderers believe that she was in some way responsible for bringing the Profumo debacle into her husband's famous home, or that as a former model she is no better than a brazen gold-digger clinging to her title (she now rarely uses it), or whether perhaps they are now simply too embarrassed to look her in the eye after they abandoned her and her husband at the height of the scandal, she doesn't know. And since they do not speak to her, she will never find out. Perhaps this book may throw some light on why this pariah status persists so long after the events which created it.

My thanks go to the following, who have been generous with their time and memories of Bronwen Astor and her world: Kenneth Armitage, Joan Astley, Philip Astley, Viscount Astor, Bridget Astor, the Hon. David Astor, the late Hon. Hugh Astor, Robert Balkam, the late Ron Barry, Jane Bown, Margaret Braund, Dom Bruno of Parkminster, Pamela Cooper, Lady Cottesloe, Joy Darby, Michael Davys, Lady de Zulueta, the late Father Richard Frost, Princess Galitzine, Flora Glendon-Hill, Lord Gowrie, Melicent Hart, Nicky Haslam, Sir Reginald and Lady Hibbert, Peter Hope-Lumley, the late Diana de Wilton, Svetlana Lloyd, Lord Longford, Romana McEwen, the Hon. Gerard Noel, Mary Quant, Mandy Rice-Davies,

Kenneth Rose, Father Emmanuel Sullivan, Christine Tidmarsh, Molly Tomsett, Claus von Bülow and Bella Wells. Viscount Astor has also given his permission to quote from his late father's archive.

Rupert Allason, Martin Harrison, Sir Ludovic Kennedy, Jamie McCaul, Bernard Nevill, Alice Rawsthorn and Derek Wilson have all given guidance in researching the background to some of the events covered in this book. Invaluable assistance was provided by Michael Bott and Frances Miller at the Astor archive at Reading University Library, Anthea Palmer of the National Trust, Sara Branch at Coleg Merion Dwyfor, Mr Evans, archivist at the Welsh Guards, Julie Ellen at Central School of Speech and Drama, Stuart Johnson at Cliveden Hotel, Emily Naish, archivist at the British Medical Association, and C. M. R. Rider, archivist at the Inner Temple. I must mention especially Kate Sullivan of the Welsh Political Archive at the National Library of Wales, who gave up considerable amounts of her own time to make good my lack of knowledge of Welsh. My thanks, too, to my editor Richard Johnson, my copy-editor Sophie Nelson, and my agent Derek Johns. Cathy James patiently transcribed the tapes of my many hours of conversation with Bronwen Astor. And my wife, Siobhan, as ever, kept me on course in this as in all things with her love and her interest.

THE ASTORS

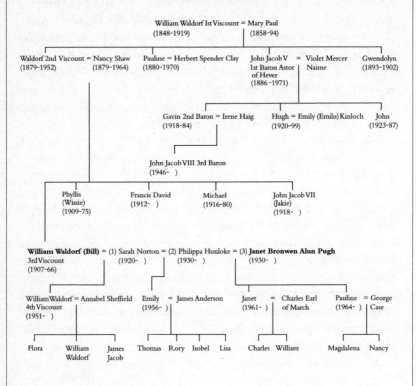

William Waldorf Ist Viscount = Mary Paul
(1848-1919) (1858-94)

Waldorf 2nd Viscount = Nancy Shaw
(1879-1952) (1879-1964)

Pauline = Herbert Spender Clay
(1880-1970)

John Jacob V = Violet Mercer Naime
1st Baron Astor of Hever
(1886-1971)

Gwendolyn
(1893-1902)

Gavin 2nd Baron = Irene Haig
(1918-84)

Hugh = Emily (Emilu) Kinloch
(1920-99)

John
(1923-87)

John Jacob VIII 3rd Baron
(1946-)

Phyllis (Wissie)
(1909-75)

Francis David
(1912-)

Michael
(1916-80)

John Jacob VII (Jakie)
(1918-)

William Waldorf (Bill) = (1) Sarah Norton = (2) Philippa Hunloke = (3) **Janet Bronwen Alun Pugh**
3rd Viscount (1920-) (1930-) (1930-)
(1907-66)

William Waldorf = Annabel Sheffield
4th Viscount
(1951-)

Emily = James Anderson
(1956-)

Janet = Charles Earl of March
(1961-)

Pauline = George Case
(1964-)

Flora | William Waldorf | James Jacob

Thomas | Rory | Isobel | Lisa

Charles | William

Magdalena | Nancy

THE PUGHS

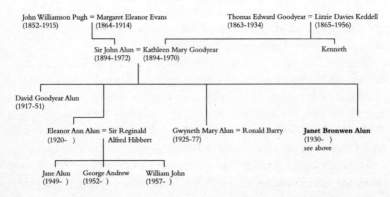

John Williamson Pugh = Margaret Eleanor Evans
(1852-1915) (1864-1914)

Thomas Edward Goodyear = Lizzie Davies Keddell
(1863-1934) (1865-1956)

Sir John Alun = Kathleen Mary Goodyear
(1894-1972) (1894-1970)

Kenneth

David Goodyear Alun
(1917-51)

Eleanor Ann Alun = Sir Reginald Alfred Hibbert
(1920-)

Gwyneth Mary Alun = Ronald Barry
(1925-77)

Janet Bronwen Alun
(1930-)
see above

Jane Alun
(1949-)

George Andrew
(1952-)

William John
(1957-)

Prelude
Cliveden, Berkshire, 1999

'Lady Astor's back.' In the silence of the main hall at Cliveden, now a hotel, this snippet of understairs gossip hangs for just a second in the air, then disappears before I can catch the intonation. Excited? Nervous? Indifferent? Puzzled? Simply reading the guest list for lunch? Does the cleaner, waitress or under-manager responsible for this sotto-voce broadcast even know which Lady Astor she is talking about?

Cliveden, this most famous − and twice this century notorious − of English stately homes, is today a shrine to its most celebrated inhabitant, Nancy, Lady Astor, the first woman to take her seat in the British Parliament. That was back in 1919, but in the timeless opulence of the wood-panelled hall decades and even centuries merge. In such a self-consciously impressive place, it is hardly a challenge to imagine the redoubtable Nancy sweeping in, all long skirts, fur collars and button boots, barking at her servants in the Virginian drawl that she never lost after almost a lifetime on the British side of the Atlantic, and greeting the houseguests assembled for one of the gatherings of what was mistakenly labelled the 'Cliveden set' of Nazi appeasers in the late 1930s.

Yet the Cliveden visitors' book was far more eclectic than that. In the 1910s, 1920s and 1930s kings, prime ministers, world leaders and Hollywood stars came for the weekend to Cliveden to be entertained by this witty, sharp and unfailingly direct woman. Edward VII, Franklin Roosevelt, George Bernard Shaw, Mahatma Gandhi and Charlie Chaplin all fielded Nancy Astor's barbs and bouquets over feasts in the ornate French dining room which once graced Madame de Pompadour's château near Paris. Joseph Kennedy,

American ambassador to London in the 1930s, brought his brood to stay at Cliveden, linking across decades and thousands of miles one Camelot with another.

As if on cue, Lady Astor arrives. Not Nancy but Bronwen, her successor as mistress of this Palladian mansion which peers down imperiously from its hilltop over the Thames. As she comes through the main doors, she hesitates for a beat before she meets my eyes and walks over to the plush but anonymous hotel settee near the open fire. Later, when more relaxed, she admits that she had stopped in a lay-by near the main entrance to collect her thoughts and pray so that she could walk calmly into her old home. 'I always used to do it before I lived here and was visiting – as a preparation to face my future mother-in-law.'

Nancy and Bronwen, both Lady Astors, overlapped for less than four years. Bronwen arrived in October 1960 as the third wife of Nancy's son and heir, Bill. Nancy died in May 1964. Theirs was neither a long-lived nor a close friendship. They could hardly even be described as friends. Bronwen sought to placate her mother-in-law, who was unfailingly critical of everything she did. In her declining years Nancy was not the force she had once been, her wit extinguished and replaced by a certain brutality. Living mainly in London in exile from Cliveden, which she only visited by invitation, she grew bitter and resentful.

Bronwen's treatment was not unique. Nancy had never been keen on any of her daughters-in-law: she resented them for usurping her place in the lives of her five sons. Strangely, for one whom history acclaims as a female pioneer, she took a perverse delight in making the lives of the women close to her a misery and virtually driving many of them to divorce. And she was particularly cruel to the women Bill, the third Viscount Astor, chose as her successors as chatelaines of Cliveden – though she did once grudgingly admit to her biographer Maurice Collis that Bronwen was 'the best of the bunch'.

None of the other guests lounging in deep armchairs and sofas scattered around near the carved stone fireplace could have guessed from Bronwen's demeanour that Cliveden had once been her home. Yet for all her self-effacement in the simple navy blue trouser suit she is wearing, there is an undeniable something about Bronwen Astor. Even in her late sixties, she still turns heads just as surely as she did when, in the 1950s, after a spell as a BBC television presenter, she became the public face of one of the most distinguished Parisian fashion houses.

Bronwen Pugh – her maiden name – was the forerunner of today's supermodels and in her time was just as much a headline-maker and a household name as Kate Moss, Elle MacPherson and Claudia Schiffer are now. She was muse to Pierre Balmain at the height of his fame. He couldn't pronounce Bronwen so he called her Bella and told the world that she was one of the most beautiful women he had ever met.

Some faces only last a season. Time and fame take their toll. But Bronwen Astor still has it. 'It' is something to do with the combination of her height (just under six foot), her bearing (purposeful, haughty, distant) and a certain freedom from conventional restraints. There is, Balmain believed, a Garboesque quality about her. And then there are her eyes – greeny blue, piercing, wild and Celtic, set in a long, elegant, bony face, framed now by strong, wavy grey hair.

Our preconceptions of models today are of visually stunning but empty-headed women. The gloss was taken off Naomi Campbell's attempt to write a novel when it was revealed that the text had been put together by a ghost-writer. In that sense, a vast gulf separates contemporary fashion superstars from Bronwen Pugh – or 'our Bronwen', as the press dubbed her, turning her into a mascot as potent as the Union Jack or the national football team. 'Our Bronwen leaves them gasping', the *Daily Herald* reported proudly from the Paris fashion shows in 1957.

Being a 'model girl', a phrase she prefers to the word model, which in her time carried a tawdry undertone, was never more than a distraction – 'tremendous fun', as she invariably puts it. By day she worked with Balmain – or a distinguished procession of designers from Charles Creed to Mary Quant who chart the transition from one fashion epoch to another. But in her spare time she was devouring spiritual and psychological writings like the Russian P. D. Ouspensky's *The Fourth Way* (published in 1947), which explored new ways of thinking about consciousness, or the books of the

French Jesuit and palaeontologist Teilhard de Chardin, who brought Christianity and science closer together than perhaps any other authority this century.

The contrast between Bronwen's two worlds could not have been greater – one to do with a skin-deep worship of the body and the creations that cover it, the other probing deep and complex matters concerning the mind and the soul. It made for a curious and ultimately untenable double life. A career in the most material of worlds thrived while her mind was fixed on spiritual concerns. Perhaps that accounted for the distant look that Balmain recognised.

The inter-relation – indeed often competition – between these two elements dominates her life story. She loved her husband in a conventional way but also felt guided towards him by God. At Cliveden she was pulled in opposite directions, acting the chatelaine of a great house but unable for the most part to talk of her inner life even to her husband. Occasionally someone would reveal him- or herself to be on a similar wavelength. Alec Douglas-Home is one name she recalls, but usually she preferred to keep quiet. Only in more recent times has she found fulfilment as a practising psychotherapist and a devout, sacramental, if otherwise unconventional Catholic.

It is not until she settles down next to me on the sofa that Bronwen allows herself a proper look around the Cliveden hall. 'The tapestries are still the same,' she says, gesturing with those eyes at three great wall-hangings that face the main entrance. 'But everything else is different. New.' She strokes the sofa arm. Her tone is almost casual. Almost. 'It was all sold, you see. Each of Bill's brothers got to choose a picture and I took some things for my new home, but everything else was sold.' Her life with Bill went under the hammer – 2,000 lots snapped up by eager collectors.

On Bill's premature death in 1966 – from heart failure brought on by the strain of his public disgrace as, allegedly, a player in that landmark of the sixties, the Profumo scandal – the Astor trustees, acting on behalf of Bronwen's stepson and Bill's heir, then a minor, decided to relinquish the lease on Cliveden. They handed it back to the National Trust, to which Bill's father had bequeathed it in 1942. In August 1966 Bronwen Astor and her two daughters, aged four and two, left Cliveden with unseemly haste. In the thirty-three years since, she has only been back inside twice.

When I was a small child I used to have a recurrent nightmare. My parents would move out of our family home and other children would take over the nooks and crannies, hiding holes and secret places in the garden that were properly mine. I would be hiding behind the hawthorn hedge watching them play on my lawn, put their toys in my cupboards, climb the narrow stairs to my playroom, take my cup and saucer out of my special cupboard in the kitchen. They would spot me and ask me to join them. I didn't know how to respond. I always woke up at that stage.

The dream was never realised, but it took me years to recognise that memories are more than bricks and mortar. For Bronwen Astor, the scale is increased tenfold – she was an adult; this was her marital home where she spent five and a half years with the man who was the love of her life; and Cliveden is considerably grander than my suburban house.

After Bill's death she had hoped to stay on for at least part of the year, so that her children and her stepson, who had lived with them at Cliveden, could remain together as a family; but she was informed by the trustees that she had to leave. It was a traumatic time. 'For many years,' she says, 'I couldn't bear to come here, but now it is like looking in on another person's life.'

Again there is that ability to withdraw to another level of consciousness. I sense she is watching herself disinterestedly as she did on the catwalk as she wanders around the grand entertaining rooms that lead off the hall – rooms where once she played hostess to Bill's friends from the worlds of politics, international charity work, racing and society. 'I trod a tightrope,' she recalls. 'I tried to live a life among people who came from a different class to me but also to remain who I was. The class system was much stronger then. There was a distaste – always in the background. I was not upper class. My husband' – and her laugh banishes a darker memory – 'didn't like the way I said "round". He used to try to teach me to say "rauwnd".'

Her diction, though, is perfect. As a young woman she trained at the Central School of Speech and Drama as a teacher. However much she makes herself sound like Eliza Doolittle, her upbringing

was solidly middle class, the privately educated daughter of a Welsh
county court judge. Indeed, Lord Longford, an old friend of both
Bill and Bronwen Astor, is fond of remarking that, such was her
poise when greeting him at Cliveden, his practised eye always took
her for the daughter of a duke.

The wool-panelling of the library has been treated, she notices,
to make it lighter. She stands close and sniffs it. Amid the formality
of a smart hotel it is a curiously relaxed gesture, as if this is still home.
Yet one of the smells that she associates with Cliveden has gone.

Outside the window of what was once her drawing room – now
the hotel's dining room – she points out the metal cups set in the
balustrade around the terrace that looks out, in Cliveden's most
celebrated view, onto the Thames as it meanders down to London.
'We used to put an awning up there and eat out in the summer.'

It must, I suggest, have been like living in a huge museum cum
art gallery. Even the balustrade had been brought by Bill's grandfather
from the Villa Borghese in Rome. 'My first impression, I think, was
that it was all very cosy. It sounds strange now, but all the rooms
lead off the hall and off each other and Bill had a flair for making
them, well, cosy.'

Bronwen took on not only Nancy Astor's title but her study too.
Nancy, a southern belle, had called it her 'boudoir'. As Bronwen
leads the way in, she is halfway through a sentence when she notices
a group of hotel guests talking and sipping coffee in there. She pulls
up short and turns to leave but one woman calls out in a proprietorial
way: 'Do come back, dear. There's a wonderful view you should
see.' For a moment Bronwen looks ill at ease. She knows the view
only too well. She smiles nervously, as if a fly is about to land on
her face. It is the closest she comes to any display of emotion.

Upstairs a footman shows us into her old bedroom – again
inherited from her mother-in-law. 'THE LADY ASTOR ROOM' the
plaque on the door announces. A copy of John Singer Sargent's
portrait of a youthful Nancy on the wall makes plain which Lady
Astor is being commemorated. Bronwen Astor, for all the fame that
surrounded her when she arrived at Cliveden, does not merit a
mention. Her period here, you feel, is regarded as something best
forgotten.

Yet on the day of her marriage to Bill a press pack every bit as large and insistent as that which hounded Diana, Princess of Wales, had camped out at the pub that faces the gates of Cliveden in the hope of getting a glimpse of its heart-throb, 'our Bronwen', as she married her lord. The previous night, tipped off that a ceremony was in the offing, they had chased her, her mother and father across London in a taxi until the cabbie had somehow given them the slip. It was another of those headline-grabbing matches – supermodel marries one of the richest men in the world, even though he was old enough to be her father.

'When I arrived here, I didn't change a thing,' Bronwen says, walking past the chambermaids, who are making the bed. 'It was the way Bill wanted it. It was like *Rebecca* and I was the second Mrs de Winter. I literally didn't move an ashtray – apart from here and in the boudoir. And even then it was a friend of Bill's – John Fowler – who helped me.' She says the name as if I should recognise it. When I stare back blankly, she adds: 'You know, Colefax and Fowler. Wallpaper.'

I was two when the Profumo scandal that destroyed Bill and Bronwen Astor's life hit the headlines in July 1963. 'Steamrollered' is the word Bill's younger brother David, celebrated editor and owner of the *Observer*, uses to describe their experience at the hands of the popular press, society gossips and erstwhile establishment friends. It all began in Cliveden's swimming pool on a hot weekend in July 1961, when War Secretary Jack Profumo and Soviet official Yevgeny Ivanov frolicked with Christine Keeler, watched by her mentor Stephen Ward. During the Cold War a British minister sharing a girl of ill-repute with a Russian agent had major security implications.

When it leaked out, the sex and spy scandal cost Ward his life, Profumo his career and heralded the end of Harold Macmillan's government. To the list of victims should also be added Bill and Bronwen Astor. Advised by his lawyers to maintain a dignified silence as allegations of orgies at Cliveden abounded, Bill saw his health was destroyed and he died of a broken heart in March 1966, his reputation in tatters. He is one of the forgotten victims of Profumo. He was labelled a seedy playboy, an adulterer, a coward who abandoned Ward in his hour of need in court, and a fool. He became the symbol, however mistakenly, of a world of lascivious ministers and aristocrats with double standards, who, in the mock-Edwardian Macmillan era, had lectured the public on morals while in private hosting poolside romps and attending sado-masochistic parties.

When Keeler's sidekick, Mandy Rice-Davies, was told in court during Ward's trial for living off immoral earnings that Lord Astor denied ever having been sexually involved with her, she chirped up: 'He would, wouldn't he?' It earned her immortality and damned him for ever. It has been Bill Astor's most enduring public legacy, though Rice-Davies's own detailed account of the assignation soon unravels.

In May 1999 the *Independent* newspaper, in a profile of one of the 'accidental heroes of the 20th century', described Christine Keeler as having been 'procured for Lord Astor's Cliveden set'. There was no 'set' and Bill Astor was not a man to procure women. Yet the myth is apparently set in stone.

John Profumo redeemed himself by good works among the needy of the East End of London. For Bill Astor, whose philanthropy was on a vast but almost invariably 'no publicity' basis and who played a central role in the founding of such inspirational international bodies as the British Refugee Council and the Disasters' Emergency Committee, there was no such redemption.

Though cleared of any guilt by Lord Denning's subsequent enquiry into the affair, Bill Astor died feeling himself a social leper. Almost four decades on, it is hard to understand what he and Bronwen were meant to have done wrong, what crime it was that brought such vilification on their heads. The most that can be said about them was that they were too indulgent of Stephen Ward, allowing him to live in a cottage on the Cliveden estate and thereby giving him some kind of respectability. 'I warned Bill about Stephen,' Bronwen recalls. 'From the first time Bill introduced us, I didn't want him at my dinner table.' Bill agreed to that but, tragically, did not recognise the deeper unease behind his new wife's demand and so continued to see Ward elsewhere.

For a man who believed the best of most people, it was a small sin. However, those who had been happy to accept Bill and Bronwen's lavish hospitality before they heard the rumours of high jinks at Cliveden decided that there was no smoke without fire and shunned them. Bronwen recalls being cut dead at parties and grand gatherings at race tracks, while the writer Maurice Collis, a regular guest at Cliveden, recorded in his diary after a weekend there in 1965: 'The house was completely empty, the great hall without a soul and nobody coming or going. The silence and emptiness were somehow ominous.'

Unlike most political scandals, the Profumo affair has outlasted the avalanche of headlines, the court case and the ministerial resignations. It has even outlasted most of its principal players. And it lives on in the public imagination as a watershed in the 1960s, the turning point between the stuffy, buttoned-up and sometimes hypocritical post-war world and the more liberated age of the Beatles, the King's Road and the pill. In 1988 the film *Scandal* brought the whole business to a younger audience. Visitors to Cliveden today still make for the swimming pool rather than the classical treasures that adorn the house and grounds.

Part of that enduring Profumo myth has been to degrade Bronwen Astor. To the list of victims of the affair should also be added her name, as well as those of Bill Astor's four children, the youngest just two when her father died.

In the film Bronwen is all pouts and shopping trips funded by Bill, an upmarket version of Keeler. 'Keeler used to call herself a model,' Bronwen says, 'and I think at the time some people, some of our friends even, didn't know the difference between a model and a model girl. And Stephen [Ward] at the very end, when he was desperate, started telling people that he had introduced Bill to me even though I had never met him until I came to Cliveden.'

It is a slur that still riles Bronwen. In July 1963 *Paris Soir* published her photograph alongside Keeler's as one of the women Ward was supposed to have trained to secure rich husbands. Once implanted in the public consciousness that idea has refused to go away, despite the evidence. In *Honeytrap*, a 1988 best-seller by Anthony Summers weaving a Cold War espionage drama into the Profumo scandal, Bill Astor is described as having been introduced to Bronwen through Ward's good offices.

After lunch we wander through the grounds. Though it was many years before she could face coming back to the house itself, Bronwen used to return occasionally to see Frank Copcutt, the head gardener who stayed on when first Stanford University and later the hotel took on the lease of Cliveden from the National Trust. And there was her husband's grave – next to those of his mother, father and grandfather in the Cliveden chapel, an octagonal temple, lavishly decorated with mosaics, set away from the house. 'I used to come back there regularly on anniversaries, but I don't feel the need now. Bill's spirit isn't there. It's . . .' And she gestures as if to mean everywhere.

'I think I'd like to be buried in Jerusalem. It's at the centre.' Her remark comes out of the blue. Initially I'm not entirely sure what it means but Bronwen Astor, I begin to realise, sometimes moves on a different plane from the rest of us. For one thing she talks unembarrassedly about God in everyday conversation. And then every now and then she throws down a line and you have to seize it. I struggle to take my chance – Jerusalem is more a state of mind than a city. For 5,000 years the Old City has had a legitimate claim to be at the centre of the world. The Islamic Dome of the Rock sits on the spot where Abraham almost sacrificed Isaac, where Muhammad ascended to heaven on a white horse, where the Jews built their Temple, and where Christ died and rose from the dead.

Bronwen has made me think, stretched me. I like that, her capacity to say startling things, her involvement in exploring the frontiers between body, mind and spirit. She is an adventurer who attracts others on to her treks. She has come a long way since her days at Balmain.

After Bill's death she moved with her two young daughters to a eleventh-century manor house in what feels like a hidden valley outside Godalming. It has not been a conventional widowhood. Free to live her life on her own terms, she converted to Catholicism in 1970 – 'it was an odd thing for an Astor to do because my mother-in-law hated Catholics'. For four years she ran a charismatic Christian community at her home, open to all comers. Few of her friends and acquaintances had realised that while working as a model or welcoming friends to Cliveden she had been on a secret spiritual journey – 'most people would look puzzled if you mentioned God' – so they were horrified to discover that Bronwen had suddenly 'got God'. They tried to warn her and feared that, in her grief, she was being sucked into what to them had all the signs of a cult.

The community had its crazier moments, she now realises, and its collapse perhaps saved her from further exploitation. Her fellow members had wanted her to give up the remaining trappings of her former life – like the chauffeur or the housekeeper. 'They meant nothing to me, but I was determined that I was going to bring my girls up as Bill would have wanted, as Astors.' The spiritual and material once again clashed.

Yet for Bronwen the whole community experience was a great liberation, the first of several subsequent attempts which ultimately gave her life a coherence. After the community was wound down, her spiritual exploration became less public – though she did, in one grand theatrical gesture, hire the Royal Albert Hall in 1983 for a prayer meeting.

Later she trained as a psychotherapist and has achieved a distinction in her chosen field that has attracted eminent academic institutions like the Religious Experience Research Centre at Oxford University. Her appointment as chairman of its support body emphasises how far she has travelled since her days on the Paris catwalk.

Her own spiritual life is now at the heart of each and every day. She prays for half an hour in her private chapel, reads the scriptures and attends communion as often as possible. She is permanently aware of the presence of God, feels close to Him and guided by Him, and she carries with her a spiritual air. She is shy of the word usually employed to describe such people – mystics. In the Christian tradition mystics are the great and the good of the church – John of the Cross, Teresa of Avila, Julian of Norwich. Bronwen is not in their league. In secular terms the word 'mystic' carries with it overtones of 'Mystic Meg', stargazers and fraudulent eccentrics on Brighton Pier.

If mysticism is stripped of its trappings and seen as something unusual but not unheard of in everyday Christians, the mark of those who have had some direct revelation from God, then she is undeniably a mystic. No priest or religious who has come into contact with her has ever doubted her sincerity.

Yet in spite of these spiritual blessings, that sense of injustice, for herself and for her late husband and his children, has never gone away. With her daughters married, she has finally decided to talk about her own part in the scandal of the century in a final effort to set the record straight.

Our walk round the garden at Cliveden is almost over. The door to the swimming pool hasn't changed, she remarks as we go through. The pool, however, is smaller than it was on that fateful weekend in July 1961 when Profumo, Ivanov and Keeler met. The reduction is somehow appropriate since the pivotal event of the Profumo scandal was scarcely, for any of the participants, of earth-shattering importance. Only later was it blown out of all proportion as a result, Bronwen now believes, of a complex and profoundly evil conspiracy.

Her own memories of the weekend are mundane. 'It was very hot and we came over from the house on the Saturday night with the guests and found Stephen Ward and some of his friends here. It was nothing. And then on the Sunday, some of the other guests – Ayub Khan, the President of Pakistan, was here and Lord Mountbatten – wanted to go down to the stud and I remember looking in on the pool, seeing Jack and Bill and thinking, "Oh well, they're all enjoying themselves, that's fine, I can go."'

Two years later this weekend took on serious political implications. The papers were alleging that all manner of odd and perverse activities were going on, while the Astors' friends took care to avoid the pool and Cliveden itself. Teams of photographers in helicopters were flying over the house at all times of the day to try and snatch that visual shot that would prove that Bronwen was running a house of ill-repute. Trapped inside with her child and her ailing husband, she was under siege.

'You only have to look to see it couldn't have been true,' Bronwen says, a note of indignation in her voice as she points to a row of windows overlooking the pool. 'Taylor the groom and Washington the butler lived there with their families. Nothing could have gone on with them so close.' Her tone is one of bemusement. After all these years she is still puzzled as to how the whole affair got so out of hand.

We head back to her car. When she lived here, a chauffeur was forever at her beck and call. Guests' vehicles would be taken off to

Cliveden's own garage, valeted, polished and filled with petrol, ready for the journey back to London. Bill's fortune and generosity with it meant that Cliveden operated in a style and on a scale that had not been seen in other grand country houses in England since 1939. With his disgrace that life came to an end. Bronwen's Cliveden was almost the last in the line of the great stately homes.

She is suddenly and unexpectedly overtaken by an air of sadness as she prepares to leave, but I sense it's not for the house or the lifestyle. After so long, it is not even to do with the unhappy memories attached to the second half of her period here. It is for the things she lost in those years – her husband, her reputation. 'It seems like another life now,' she sighs, adding, almost with relief, 'finally.' And with that Lady Astor takes her leave.

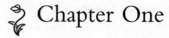 Chapter One

There is no present in Wales,
And no future;
There is only the past,
Brittle with relics

R. S. Thomas, *Welsh Landscape* (1955)

Exiles have curious and sometimes contradictory attitudes to their 'fatherland'. Often the first generation to leave retains a strong emotional bond with all they have abandoned, but for some, depending on the reasons for their departure – adventure, economic necessity, education – return or even nostalgia is out of the question. They develop an antipathy to the past and determine to be assimilated into their new culture and society by virtue of rejecting the old. In succeeding generations, of course, such attitudes can be reversed: children or grandchildren of unsentimental or ambitious exiles may over-compensate for their parents' or grandparents' abandonment of the family 'seat' with romantic notions about their roots which also offer a means both of rebellion and of self-definition. A place with which their physical connection is tenuous becomes crucial to their psychological and spiritual identity.

Because of the bland image of the plain old English – repressed, over-polite and concerned only with what the neighbours will think – many of those born in England explore family links with Ireland, Wales and Scotland in order to appear more exotic. In economic terms, they have, like as not, embraced the values and assumptions of their generally more prosperous English homeland, but in their more rhetorical moods they celebrate their Celtic and Gaelic roots in exiles' clubs and sporting societies, harking back to something that has been irretrievably lost.

The Pughs fit loosely into this pattern in their attitude to Wales.

They were and are proud to be Welsh. They regard it as a defining feature in their make-up. Yet by the time Janet Bronwen Alun Pugh was born in 1930, the family link back to Cardiganshire was wearing distinctly thin. It accounted for just 50 per cent of their bloodline since their mother, Kathleen Goodyear, was solidly English. And even their father Alun – after whom, in a spirit which now seems oddly egotistical, Janet Bronwen Alun, her two elder sisters Eleanor Ann Alun and Gwyneth Mary Alun, and her brother David Goodyear Alun were all named – had been raised in Brighton, studied in Oxford and worked in London.

For the early and middle sections of his career as a barrister Alun Pugh, who had two native Welsh parents, defined himself as Welsh. Since this period coincided with the time of his most influential and hands-on involvement with his children, he passed this self-image on whole and undigested to them and it remains with his two surviving daughters to this day. Only towards the end of his working life, when his increasingly successful career as a judge offered an alternative means of defining himself, did his enthusiasm for all things Welsh mellow.

So when his youngest daughter was seven, Alun Pugh placed her on a stool and invited her to choose between her first two Christian names. Did she want to be called Janet, to the ear more English, though it was in fact chosen to mark a Welsh godmother, or the more unusual, Celtic Bronwen? Given her father's predilection, her decision was inevitable. 'I got the impression,' recalls the family's nanny, Bella Wells, 'that Mrs Pugh wasn't that happy about it, but Mr Pugh was delighted. She was always Bronwen after that.'

Though her formal links with Wales have since childhood been few and far between, Bronwen Pugh in her days at the BBC and later on the Paris catwalks was habitually referred to as the 'Welsh presenter', 'Welsh beauty' or 'Welsh model girl', as if she returned every evening to a mining cottage in the valleys. And outside perceptions reflected both what she had learnt as a child and, more significantly, since the two became inseparable, what she felt in her heart – that her Welsh roots had shaped her personality. 'It's made me a bit manic, I think,' she says. 'One minute you're up a mountain and the next you're in the valley. And romantic. The Welsh are great romantics. We have a tremendous feeling about everything. We're moody, contemplative and passionate.'

This is, of course, a caricature of the Welsh, a snapshot of a national state of mind that ignores those who are cynical, outgoing and level-headed; but in the same way that, with our deep-rooted prejudices, we ascribe a love of fair-play and propriety to the English and dourness and attachment to money to the Scottish, it is legitimate to draw the parallel.

Alun Pugh's parents had both been born in Cardiganshire, two thirds of the way down the west coast of Wales, in the middle years of the nineteenth century. It was and remains a predominantly mountainous, rural, Welsh-speaking area, one of the few strongholds of the language outside the north. It was also very poor. On the eve of the First World War *Welsh Outlook*, a 'journal of social progress', described Cardiganshire as 'this shockingly backward county', bottom or near bottom in every measurement of public health in terms of deaths of mothers during childbirth, stuttering, rotten teeth, ear defects, blindness and mental handicaps. A bastion of Nonconformity – in 1887 there were riots in the Tywi Valley against payment of the tithe to the established Anglican Church in Wales – it was also for much of the nineteenth century the victim of an unholy combination of a booming birthrate among poor families and some of the worst excesses of heavy-handed, absentee English landlords. The result was that Cardiganshire became a place from which exiles set off on newly built railways in search of work in the industrial valleys and port towns of South Wales or further afield in England, America and even, from the 1850s onwards, in Y Wladfa Gymreig, the Welsh colony in Patagonia in southern Argentina.

John Williamson Pugh came from the small port of Aberaeron. His family were poor and he left school in his early teens, was apprenticed to a local brewery, then worked on a sailing ship under his uncle, David Jones, and only began to follow the ambitions that led him away from Wales at the age of twenty-two, when he attended teacher training college in Bangor, in the north, becoming a schoolmaster at Ponterwyd in 1875. The classroom was in this era a means of escape from drudgery for many ambitious and bright young men of humble origins, but John Pugh found it too limiting. He aimed even higher and in his late twenties obtained a place to train as a doctor at the London Hospital in Whitechapel, qualifying in 1886 at the age of thirty-four. His first post was at Queen Adelaide Dispensary in Bethnal Green, in the heart of the poverty-stricken East End, but three years later he moved to Brighton, where he joined a prosperous general practice.

Pugh's wife, Margaret Evans, came from Llanon, another port town, six miles north of Aberaeron. They did not meet in Wales, though their shared background must have attracted them to each other when their friendship blossomed at the London Hospital. Where John Pugh's upbringing had been characterised by a struggle to get on, Margaret Evans's was dominated by tragedy. Her family were more prosperous than the Pughs, but her mother died when she was just three and she was brought up, along with her sister Catherine, by her aunt Magdalen and her husband, Daniel Lewis Jones, a general merchant. When Magdalen also died young and her husband remarried, the two girls did not get on with their step-aunt and so packed their bags and headed for London. Catherine's health soon broke down and she returned to Wales, where she died aged just twenty-one. Margaret stayed on alone, and eventually trained at the London Hospital as a nurse.

However, it was not until three years after John Williamson Pugh arrived in Brighton that the couple married. Their long courtship was a result no doubt of Pugh's desire to establish himself, but it meant that his bride was already thirty-one when she gave birth to a son, John Alun, on 23 January 1894. He was always known by his second name. It was a difficult birth and the Pughs had no further children.

Despite their new-found prosperity, Dr Pugh never forgot where he had come from and had a reputation for treating those who, in pre-National Health Service days, could not pay. And at home the family spoke Welsh, though Alun's knowledge of what he came to regard as his native tongue remained inadequate until he settled down to study it as an adult.

The Pughs' attachment to Wales had its limits, not least in their decision to settle in Brighton and not back in Cardiganshire. They were part nostalgic exiles but part also assimilators, embracing their new world and choosing, when it came to education for young Alun, the very English minor public school Brighton College.

He was both a keen sportsman and a talented student who won a scholarship to read history at Queen's College, Oxford – not Jesus, bastion of the Welsh. His best friend at both Brighton College and Queen's was Kenneth Goodyear, the son of a wealthy accountant from Bromley in Kent. As their friendship developed Goodyear introduced young Alun Pugh to his sister Kathleen, a strikingly tall, fair, blue-eyed but shy beauty. They fell in love.

There was some disquiet from T. Edward Goodyear, Kathleen's father and a man with ambitions to be Lord Mayor of London, about Alun Pugh's relatively humble forebears, but in spite of such reservations the couple married in Brighton in 1915 when both were twenty-one. Alun Pugh – he was throughout his adult life always referred to by both names, even by junior members of his staff, with the result that the 'Alun' and the 'Pugh' were linked by an imaginary hyphen – had been admitted to the Inner Temple as a pupil in April the previous year, but the First World War was underway and soon after their marriage, in July 1915, like nearly every young man of his generation, he joined up. He went to Bovington Green Camp at Marlow in Buckinghamshire, close to Cliveden, home of the Astors. He chose the Welsh Guards. Kathleen volunteered as a nurse.

In August 1915 Kenneth Goodyear, who was a conscientious objector, was killed in France behind the lines after serving in Gallipoli as a stretcher-bearer. The effect on his parents was devastating and their attention was ever more focused onto Kathleen, their one surviving child. Second Lieutenant Alun Pugh went out with the Prince of Wales Company of the Welsh Guards to join the British forces in France in February 1916. Seven months later, on 10 September, having already seen many of his colleagues killed in the stalemate of trench warfare, he was badly injured in the knee by a sniper's bullet at Ginchy during the Battle of the Somme. It left him in pain and with a slight limp for the rest of his life, but he owed his survival to his sergeant who, after Alun Pugh had fallen back into the trench, bent double as he carried him on his shoulders to the first aid post. Another officer, wounded at the same time, had been passed back along the trench, but his injured body had appeared above the parapet and was riddled with bullets.

A lengthy convalescence with his young wife and grieving in-laws at Rothesay, their home in Bromley, saw Alun Pugh soon on the mend, but the psychological damage caused by his injury was long-lasting, according to his daughter Bronwen, and affected his whole family: 'My father felt very fortunate still to be alive, but also guilty too. So many of his friends had been wiped out.' It gave him – and by association his children – a determination to do what seemed right, to live their lives to the full, regardless of the restrictions of convention, class or social mores.

Today Alun Pugh would have been diagnosed with post-traumatic stress disorder, but in the aftermath of a world war ex-soldiers simply had to get on with rebuilding their lives. The trenches did, however, remain a painful and sensitive memory for him. While his eldest and most direct daughter Ann questioned him about his experiences, drawing him out on the subject, Bronwen felt inhibited about raising what she saw as a taboo. 'I've always been bad about asking people important questions. I wait to be told. I knew there was something but it went unmentioned. I grew up thinking that the silence meant it had been so terrible that there must have been fighting in the street or something.'

His wartime trauma left Alun Pugh with a profound distrust of anything German. He would not, for instance, have Christmas trees, which he saw as a German custom, imported via Prince Albert. There would be one at the Goodyear house in Kent, where the Pughs spent 25 December, but it was only when Bronwen went to live at Cliveden that, reluctantly, having inherited her father's prejudice in this as in many things, she had to put up with a tree.

That wartime experience also made Alun and Kathleen Pugh – like many others of their generation – determined in the aftermath of the conflict to re-evaluate the assumptions they had made before its outbreak. They already had one child – David born in 1917 – and Kathleen had lost a baby the previous year. While the couple, following Kenneth's death, would eventually come into the Goodyears' substantial fortune, there was the question of finding a job and financing a home. Alun Pugh resumed his career in the law and was called to the Bar in June 1918, eventually specialising from chambers in Harcourt Buildings in Inner Temple in workman's compensation claims.

He found a house in Heathhurst Road in Hampstead, just off the wide-open spaces of the Heath and in the shadow of the house of the poet John Keats – his last London home before he left for Italy and a premature death. Hampstead, then as now, was a favourite place for writers, artists, academics and free-thinkers, though in the 1920s, with its villagey atmosphere, it had acquired little of the smart, expensive image of more recent times.

However, as a place where the normal constraints of the strict class system then prevalent elsewhere did not apply so rigidly, it suited the Pughs. 'I think my parents decided to live in Hampstead,' says their daughter Ann, 'as a gesture of defiance because then it was a rather way out sort of place. Certainly my mother's parents would have regarded it as an odd choice.' In that period of post-war optimism, Alun Pugh was searching for an identity that tied together his life before the conflict and his experiences on the battlefield. Increasingly he hit upon Wales as the linking thread, having used his convalescence to brush up on his sketchy knowledge of the Welsh language.

Perhaps the comradeship he had felt in his Welsh Guards battalion, which lost an estimated 5,000 men in France, gave Alun Pugh a sense of belonging to something – the Welsh nation – that had in his parents' home seemed of little more than sentimental importance. Perhaps also it was a reaction to the death of his father and mother who, having struggled so hard to find prosperity and happiness, died comparatively young within months of each other in 1916 without being able to enjoy the fruit of their efforts. In one sense, though, their deaths may have allowed Alun Pugh to explore roots that had, during their lifetime, been regarded with ambiguity.

It was undeniably a romantic quest. His parents had travelled far – socially, geographically and economically – from Cardiganshire. They had bought their son an English education and his knowledge of Wales was limited to holidays, relatives and family folklore. A public school educated, Oxford graduate had little in common with the relatives who remained in Cardiganshire. Yet Alun Pugh was also a practical man. He did not seek merely to wallow in nostalgia for his parents' homeland, he wanted to do something of substance that would establish his own bond with it.

In his work as a barrister Alun Pugh developed a reputation for working on Welsh cases, especially those involving coalminers. Bronwen recalls frequent visits to Paddington Station to wave him off on, and greet him from, the train to Cardiff, Swansea and beyond. He sought out the company of other Welsh exiles where he practised in Inner Temple – it had and has a sizeable contingent – and he became a member of the Reform Club, bastion of Welsh Liberalism and favourite haunt of its epitome, David Lloyd George. He was also a pillar of the London Welsh Association.

These were little more than affordable gestures for a man whose career at the Bar was already taking off. At the dawn of the 1920s, however, he saw a more tangible, though risky, chance to make his mark by joining the largely academic and middle-class movement campaigning to protect and preserve the Welsh culture and language by all available means.

The most charismatic figure among Alun Pugh's new-found friends was Saunders Lewis, like him a son of the Welsh diaspora, born of Welsh parents on Merseyside. Lewis was a visitor to the Pughs' Hampstead home. Once when he stayed the night, Bronwen gave up her room and moved in with her sister. Her father, she recalls, told her that she should always be proud that Saunders Lewis had slept in her bed. She should 'never forget'. Among the family's most treasured possessions was a copy of Lewis's *Braslun o Hanes Llenyddiaeth Gymreig* – a history of Welsh literature, published in 1932. It had been inscribed by Lewis to his friend Alun Pugh in gratitude for his work on behalf of their people.

Lewis's long-term contribution to the nationalist revival was huge, though often in his lifetime he suffered spells of disappointment and marginalisation. 'The dominance of Lewis,' writes D. Hywel Davies in his history of Welsh nationalism, 'from 1926 to 1939 was such that his name and that of the nationalist movement had become almost interchangeable.' A poet, dramatist, historian and teacher of the Welsh language, he was heavily influenced as a young man by Ireland's political struggle to break free from Britain and the literary renaissance that ran in parallel. His political ideas – authoritarian and

tinged with religion – owed much to the radical conservatism of
Charles Maurras's *Action française*.

Lewis was the most prominent member of *Y Mudiad Cymreig*, the
Welsh Movement, a society founded in Penarth in January 1924,
and the following year, at the National Eisteddfod, threw his lot in
with *Plaid Genedlaethol Cymru*, the National Party of Wales. The
aim, Lewis said, was 'to take away from the Welsh their sense of
inferiority . . . to remove from our beloved country the mark and
the shame of conquest'.

Alun Pugh endorsed this manifesto enthusiastically and would
often provide legal help to the fledgling party. In 1930, for instance,
he sat on a committee of London Welsh with the former Liberal
MP John Edwards, which advocated that Plaid should campaign for
Wales to be given dominion status within the British empire – treated
as if it were equal, free and self-governing like Canada or Australia.
Five years later Alun Pugh was again called on to advise whether
teachers who took part in the pro-Welsh protests organised by Lewis
could face disciplinary action by their employers. There could be,
he concluded in July 1935, 'no martyrdom with safety'. It was a
message that was to become increasingly relevant to his own involvement with Plaid.

Those living in Wales able to speak Welsh were in steep decline.
Their numbers fell in the decade to 1931 by over 5 per cent, to just
35 per cent of the population. Only 98,000 – out of a total population
of 2.7 million – used Welsh as their first language at that time. If
Plaid successfully but slowly began a reversal in this trend – pressing
for the Welsh language to be given more prominence in schools and
the new broadcast media – in the political field the party was for
many years a failure.

In part this was because it insisted on members breaking all links
with existing political parties, including Lloyd George's Liberals, still
dominant in rural Wales, and Labour, now controlling the southern
valleys, and with the Westminster Parliament. Hence it had no effective environment in which to operate and gain influence. In part
too it was brought about by the extreme political philosophy that
Lewis mapped out as Plaid's president between 1926 and 1939. The
Welsh, he argued, echoing other inter-war utopian schemes like Eric

Gill's distributist guild, had to reject both the capitalism that was destroying the valleys and towns of the south and the socialism offered by the growing Labour Party. Lewis's own third way – what he called *perchentyaeth* – dreamt of 'distributing property among the mass of the members of the nation'.

The president's own unpredictable personality also weakened the movement he headed. His decision to become a Catholic in 1932 alienated many in Plaid's naturally Nonconformist constituency. Yet it was a typically bold Lewis gesture that won Plaid international attention in 1936 and put Alun Pugh's devotion to the cause to the test. Lewis's firebomb attack on an RAF training base near Pwllheli on the Lleyn peninsula caused outrage. The 'bombing school', as Lewis dubbed it, represented for him British military imperialism in Wales.

For Alun Pugh this was a crucial moment. As a member of the Bar, he could not but deplore breaking the law. Yet as historian Dafydd Glyn Jones has argued, the fire was 'the first time in five centuries that Wales had struck back at England with a measure of violence . . . to the Welsh people, who had long ceased to believe that they had it in them, it was a profound shock.' Such an awakening was what Alun Pugh had been yearning for.

Already before the 'bombing-school' episode, the strain between the different elements in Alun Pugh's life had emerged in his letters to J. E. Jones, a London-based teacher and Plaid's secretary. 'The time has come,' he acknowledged in March 1933, 'for us to have secret societies to work for Wales – two sorts of societies – one of rich supporters to give advice to us without coming into the open, and the other of more adventurous people willing to destroy English advertisements that are put up by local authorities.' For all his bravado and implied association with the second group, Alun Pugh's role was largely confined to the first, as a later letter to Jones in June 1934 testifies when he offers to make a loan to the party.

In the following month he sent some legal advice to Jones but insisted that, if it were used, 'don't put my name to it'. In March 1936 he was urging Jones or 'someone else' to write a letter to *The Times* on 'some other burning issue', but was obviously unwilling to do so himself. The possibility of compromising his position at the

Bar was already exercising his mind. Yet in the same month he told Jones that he was lobbying Lloyd George, through a contact of Kathleen Pugh's, to give public support to Lewis, who had already embarked on his fire-bombing campaign.

In responding to Lewis's arrest and trial after the attack on the bombing school, Alun Pugh took a big risk. He gave the defendant legal advice – the case against him and two co-conspirators was transferred from a Welsh court, where the jury could not reach a decision, to the Old Bailey, where the three were sentenced to nine months. 'Thank you very much,' wrote J. E. Jones to Alun Pugh in September 1936, 'for your work in defending the three that burnt the bombing school.' Alun Pugh clung to the fact that Lewis was advocating violence against public installations, not individuals or private property, but it was a difficult circle to square, his heart ruling his head and potentially posing a threat to his career. His solution was, it seemed, to put different parts of his life into boxes – Wales, the law and, separate from both, his family.

'As a small child,' recalls his daughter Ann, 'I used to be terrified that we would have a knock on the door at three o'clock in the morning and it would be the police coming for my father because he was part of it. There was an attack on a reservoir in the north that supplied Liverpool. The Welsh nationalists were indignant that Welsh water was being piped to England.'

Alun Pugh's relationship with Lewis underwent further strains with the coming of the Second World War. Lewis's insistence that it was an English war and nothing to do with the Welsh offended Alun Pugh's sense of patriotism and ran counter to his own determination to contribute as fully as his injury allowed to the war effort. The detachment of Alun Pugh from active involvement in the Welsh cause gathered pace in the post-war years: his appointment as a judge reduced his freedom for manoeuvre and also crucially provided him with an alternative source for self-definition to his Welsh roots. Yet a link endured through Lewis's two decades in the wilderness following his defeat by a Welsh-speaking Liberal in a by-election for the only Welsh university seat in 1943, subsequent splits in Plaid about tactics, and on to the great nationalist and Welsh language surge of the 1960s.

However, in the early days there was a strong contrast between Alun Pugh's middle-class enthusiasm in London and the custom, in many primary schools in the valleys in the 1920s and 1930s, of placing the 'Welsh knot' – a rope equivalent of the dunce's hat – over the head of any child caught speaking Welsh. Practical as many of Alun Pugh's concerns were for Wales, they were tinged with idealism. He could afford his principles and time off to attend Plaid's most success-ful innovation of the period – summer schools. Others, at a time of record unemployment, could not.

The reality of events on the ground is demonstrated by the fate of *Ty Newydd* (New Cottage), the house in Llanon where Alun Pugh's mother had grown up with her aunt and uncle. It was be-queathed to him some time after the First World War and later he in turn gave it to Plaid Cymru on condition that it was used only by Welsh-speakers to further the cause. Within a short period of time it was being used, according to Ann, by 'all and sundry'. The fact that he gave a valuable property to the cause – and not to his family – is evidence, she feels, of the extent to which he could separate his obligations to one or the other in his head and discard the conventional route of leaving such an asset to his children. Yet there were deep ambiguities in Alun Pugh's attitude: he insisted that a plaque commemorating his son David, who had by that time died, had to be erected in the house before it could be handed over to Plaid.

If he placed each of his responsibilities into separate categories, Alun Pugh never failed to convey the importance of their Welsh roots to his children. 'We were always very conscious that we were different from most people,' Bronwen recalls. 'Primarily it was because we were Welsh, but other things led from that. We were taught to be classless, apart from the class system, and our parents encouraged us to look at things differently. The general atmosphere in our family was not rebellion but revolution. It's a subtle difference. Outwardly you conform, but all the time you are doing things and thinking things in a different way from others.' When later she found herself in the class-ridden world of Cliveden, this alternative side of her upbringing gave her the resilience to withstand those who would judge her on the basis of her parents' income and social standing.

At home Alun Pugh's conversation over breakfast every morning was always in Welsh. The children became adept at remembering the right word for bread or butter or milk. Sunday worship would often be in the Welsh chapel, though later the Pugh became more solidly and conventionally Church of England. And when it came to schooling, Alun Pugh decided – despite his wife's reluctance – to send their daughters to boarding school in Wales.

The Pugh children fell into two distinct duos, based on age and emphasised by their names, one pair solidly English, the other ringingly Welsh. David and Ann, thirteen and ten respectively when Bronwen was born, formed one unit, while their new sister and five-year-old Gwyneth were another. In 1926, with the help of Kathleen's parents, the Pughs had purchased an empty plot of land in Pilgrims Lane two streets away in Hampstead and built a larger house. Number 12 still stands to this day, a suburban version of a gabled country house in Sussex vernacular style, with leaded windows and a formal garden sweeping round the house and down the hill towards the Heath.

Alun and Kathleen Pugh had intended to have no more than three children. Bronwen was not planned. Her parents decided the baby was going to be a boy. They even chose a name – Roderick. Two girls, two boys would have made for a neat symmetry, but there was a more particular reason. David, already away at boarding school, was proving a sickly child, undistinguished in his academic work, poor in exams, unable to participate in sport, underdeveloped physically, mentally and emotionally. At the age of sixteen, Bronwen recalls, he was still insisting that a place be set at the dining table for his imaginary friend, Fern. The contrast with Ann, three years his junior and a robust, practical, natural achiever, could not have been greater. Even if it had not been their original intention, circumstances meant that the Pughs, unusually for the time, made no distinction between their treatment of their son and his sisters. All three girls were encouraged to be independent and to think about careers.

Janet Bronwen Alun was born on 6 June 1930, delivered by caesarean by the family GP in the Catholic hospital of St John and St Elizabeth in London's St John's Wood. Her early years were dominated by Frederic Truby King, the New Zealand-born Dr Spock of the 1920s and 30s. Kathleen Pugh followed the methods he advocated in books like *The Feeding and Care of Your Baby*. Baby Bronwen was on a strict regime of four-hourly feeds, with nothing in between. Picking up the child and cuddling it was not recommended by Truby King in case it encouraged spoiling or over-attachment. 'A Truby King baby,' the master wrote of his own methods, 'has as much fresh air and sunshine as possible. The mother of such a baby is not overworked or worried, simply because she knows that by following the laws of nature, combined with common sense, baby will not do otherwise than thrive.'

Kathleen Pugh was certainly not overworked since the bulk of practical child care fell on the family's nanny. In spite of their progressive ideas, the Pughs – in line with the middle-class norms of the age – maintained a full complement of domestic help: a maid, a nursery nanny, a cleaner and a part-time gardener. When Bronwen was three, Bella Wells was taken on to look after her, leaving Kathleen Pugh free for most of the day.

Bronwen was not, her sister Ann recalls, a particularly attractive child. 'She was all eyes, teeth and pigtails. When she was about four, she went off on her bicycle with my mother and when they came back my mother was very upset. Bronwen had had a bad fall. She had managed to pull the muscle at the side of her eye. It left her with a squint which later had to be corrected by surgery, but she still wore glasses.' There were as yet few signs of her future career on the catwalks. She had to wear a patch over one lens of her glasses to strengthen her eye muscles and later she wore braces to pull her protruding teeth back into line.

She was also, Ann remembers, infuriating. 'She was always very lively. She'd hide behind the door in the dining room and then when you went in for lunch leap out and say boo! Or else she'd be crawling under the table tickling your feet. She was always on the move, dressing up, play-acting, getting over-excited.' Bella Wells's memory is of a very determined three-year-old. 'On the first day I arrived I took her out in her pram and she just kept saying, "Now can I get out? Now can I get out?" She wanted things her own way.' One of Bronwen's greatest delights as a small child was to watch the fire engines going down Hampstead High Street, bells ringing and lights flashing. Her earliest ambition was to be a fireman. It appealed to the theatrical side of her nature. 'There was the drama of it all, I suppose, and that thing of rescuing people. It must always have been a part of my psyche.'

While Bella Wells was devoted to her charge, mother and daughter had from the start a difficult relationship. Kathleen Pugh's regret at not having a boy was explicit and was overlaid by personal frustration. She had wanted to find something challenging to do outside the home but Bronwen's arrival delayed the day when she could seek once again the sense of self-worth that she had enjoyed as a volunteer nurse during the war. She was an intelligent woman: to her husband's breakfast-table lessons in Welsh she would add her own questions to the children on mental arithmetic. They all learnt early how to keep accounts of how they had spent their pocket money.

Kathleen had finished school at sixteen and, with her staff leaving her with too little to occupy her time in the Hampstead house, she grew bored and occasionally, Ann remembers, impatient with her youngest daughter. Though she had forward-thinking ideas about women's choices – she had her own car at a time when two vehicles in the family was unusual – Kathleen was by nature a reserved and private person. She mixed with neighbours but had few close friends among them; she found some of the more academic residents of Pilgrims Lane intimidating. She warned her youngest daughter against Dr Donald Winnicott, an eminent child psychiatrist (and the greatest critic of the Truby King method of child-rearing) who lived in the same road, for fear, Bronwen suspects, 'that he might carry out some strange experiments on us'.

Rather than her reserve throwing her back on her role as a mother, however, it appeared only to exacerbate Kathleen Pugh's restlessness. Sometimes she could be fun. She taught her youngest daughter to fish – a hobby Bronwen pursues with gusto to this day in the salmon rivers of the Scottish borders. 'We started off one holiday in Suffolk with a simple piece of string and a weight. You threw it in and waited to see if you caught anything. I must have been six when I caught an eel and I was so pleased.'

Another treat was to raid the dressing-up box with Kathleen or put on a play in the drawing room. Again there was a theatrical element. Their mother was a woman, her daughters recall, who liked, indeed expected, to be entertained by her children; she could grow exasperated if they failed to perform. Yet any frivolous side to her character was strictly rationed. She had an unusual and occasionally cutting sense of humour and for the most part, despite all the Pugh's progressive ideas, was for Bronwen a rather Victorian figure, distant and dour. She had had a strict Nonconformist upbringing and passed aspects of it on to her children. She would remind them of phrases like 'the Devil makes work for idle hands' and circumscribed their lives and her own with peculiar self-denying ordinance like never reading a novel before lunch. Her favourite children's book was *Struwwelpeter*, a collection of often brutal, gloomy moral tales about such character as 'poor Harriet', who was punished for her wrong-doing by being 'burnt to a crisp'.

'My mother was, I now realise, not very child-orientated,' says Bronwen. 'I found being with her agony. There was one terrible time when Gwyneth and my father were both away and I had to be with my mother on my own for two weeks. I can only have been six or seven at the time, but once I realised what was happening, I went into a catatonic state. She had to call the doctor. I just sat unable to move for three hours. I was in such a state of shock at the prospect of two weeks on our own. Now it sounds like nothing but then it was a lifetime.'

Siblings experience their parents in different ways and while Bronwen found her mother a cold, distant figure, Ann remembers an entirely separate person with great affection. 'My mother was not a cuddly sort of person but she was kind and caring.' Such a divergence of views is not uncommon in brothers and sisters, depending on their temperament and their position in the family. Parents who are strict with their older children, perhaps daunted by the serious business of forming young minds and possibly, at an early stage in their careers, anxious over material matters, become indulgent, relaxed mentors to their younger children, self-confident in their behaviour and sometimes cushioned by greater financial resources. In Bronwen's case there was certainly more money around when she was a child and Ann retains the distinct memory that her youngest sister was spoilt and indulged. Yet Bronwen was also aware of a new anxiety in Kathleen Pugh – her desire to break out of the confines of being a stay-at-home parent, which contributed to the temperamental clash between mother and daughter.

Kathleen's difficult relationship with her youngest and most independent daughter reflected her tense dealings with her own mother, Lizzie Goodyear, who lived on in her Bromley house to the age of ninety-one, surviving her husband by twenty-two years. 'My mother was scared of my grandmother,' says Bronwen. 'I used to be taken to tea when she had to go and visit her mother as a kind of distraction. Out would come the silver and the maid and the cucumber sandwiches – the complete opposite of the way my mother ran our house. So it was wonderful for me but I sensed my mother was terrified.'

Bronwen's picture of the house in Pilgrims Lane as one that was lacking in warmth is also qualified by Bella Wells, the nanny. 'There was no hugging or kissing or anything like that. But then not many people would do that then.' Much later, in an academic paper she wrote 'Of Psychological Aspects of Motherhood', Bronwen reflected obliquely on her own experiences: 'Assuming the child is wanted from the moment of conception – and many of us are not – and is the right gender – again, many of us are not', the mother's love, attitude and behaviour are 'more fundamental to the child's early formation than that of the father'.

Her perceptions of the absence of that love from her own mother left a deep scar. 'I could entertain her – go shopping with her, do the crossword – but she made me feel like a thorough nuisance. I'm still always apologising for being a nuisance. I try to stop now that I know. I had my handwriting analysed recently. "Oh, but you're still running away from your mother," the graphologist told me. Even now!'

What love she felt – and therefore returned – was all to do with her father. As she grew up, Bronwen knew from an early age that she did not want to be like her mother. 'I remember deciding, when I was quite young, that I was going to be more graceful than my mother. She never made the best of herself. She never wore make-up and her hair was cut in an Eton crop like a boy.'

Alun Pugh, by contrast, was his daughter's hero – indeed the hero of all his daughters. 'We were all devoted to our father,' says Ann. 'I can remember as a girl walking down the High Street in Hampstead with him and saying, "What would you do if the house caught fire? Who would you save?" and being heart-broken when he said, "Your mother, of course."' He was, she recollects, a charmer, but part of that charm lay in the fact that he was so seldom at home; his work often took him away and he was unpredictable in his hours. He brought an excitement but also an uncertainty to the home with his eccentricity and sense of adventure. He would have great enthusiasms that were utterly impractical. At one stage he decided it would be fun to keep silk-worms and make their own clothes. So Gwyneth and Bronwen made cocoons out of old newspaper and hung them from the ceiling, but when the worms began to produce silk the little hand-spinner their father had made could not cope with the output. 'It had closed-in ends, so you couldn't get anything off it,' says Bronwen. 'It was typical of my father, this do-it-yourself-and-have-fun-doing-it mentality, but then never to finish it off. He had lots of imagination and was terrific fun. When he emerged from his study at home, the atmosphere would change at once. But he was totally impractical.'

When he was a student, Alun Pugh had made a jelly in a teapot, thinking it would make an interesting shape, but then he couldn't get it out. It is a useful symbol for most of his schemes. When he imported hives of bees into the garden, he eventually had to abort the project because his wife grew allergic to their sting, though he did manage to make some mead and plenty of honey.

Like Kathleen, Alun Pugh didn't go in much for hugging and kissing, but as a substitute he took a keen, almost zealous, interest in his children's progress, forever pushing them to do better and be the best. When Bronwen was twelve she was taken to see Roy Henderson, then a celebrated voice coach. He said she had a pleasant voice and good pitch, and suggested lessons, but when he made it clear she would never sing solo in the great concert halls of the world, Alun Pugh decided against. 'You do something to get to the top or you don't bother at all,' is how his youngest daughter sums up the prevailing attitude.

Singing had been something Alun Pugh associated with his

mother, who reputedly had a beautiful voice and played the harp, with her son accompanying her on the piano. Bronwen was also told that physically she resembled her paternal grandmother and this may have contributed to a special closeness between father and daughter that compensated for the alienation between mother and daughter.

With Ann and David away at school, Bronwen and Gwyneth developed an enduring bond. The two would get up to all sorts of mischief and it was Gwyneth who was Bronwen's chief source of fun in the house. 'She was always inventing things,' Bronwen remembers. 'Once when she was ill in bed, she spent hours building this elaborate system of pulleys and string so that we could send each other messages from bedroom to bedroom. Or she would devise complicated games where she would be the captain and I would be the boatswain. I was always saying, "Ay, ay, captain," to her. She was in charge.'

The five-year age-gap with Gwyneth meant that the youngest Pugh sibling often had to while away many hours on her own or with her nanny. There were friends in the neighbourhood and cycle rides around the carefree streets of Hampstead, but going to school just before her fifth birthday came as something of a blessing. St Christopher's was a Church of England primary on the way down Rosslyn Hill from Hampstead into central London. Though the Pughs retained their links to the Welsh chapel, their ordinary practice of religion had become increasingly Anglican. (When he joined up with the Welsh Guards in 1915, Alun Pugh had claimed to have no religious affiliations at all.)

Bronwen's reports suggest a model pupil, with hints at future interests. From her earliest days she did well at recitation, and was praised in April 1936 as 'a useful leader of the class'. She joined a percussion band that same year and the only blot on the landscape was her problems with an unusual addition to the otherwise standard curriculum, Swedish drill, where she 'sometimes lacks control'. At the end of summer term 1937, aged seven, she was put up two classes – into a group where the average age was fourteen months above hers – on account of her excellent progress. She made the transition effortlessly, save for occasional blips in arithmetic – 'must try to be more accurate' – and painting – 'is inclined to use too pale colours'

(both spring term 1939). By the time of her final report from
St Christopher's, her card was littered with 'very goods' and adjectives
like 'appreciative', 'careful', 'neat' and 'musical'.

She did not return to the local school that autumn. War had
broken out in September and her parents decided to send her early
to join her sister Gwyneth at boarding school in Wales. The two
older Pugh girls had gone at the age of twelve, but in view of the
anticipated threat to London by German bombers and Alun Pugh's
own ambitions to join the war effort, it seemed sensible to pack
Bronwen off to the comparative safety of north-west Wales and close
up the house in Hampstead. It appeared to Bronwen Astor at the
time like an awfully big adventure, but later she came to see 1939
as a pivotal moment in her childhood, the end of an age of innocence
and plenty and the start of a period when she was continually without
the things and people she needed to sustain her.

At the age of seven Bronwen had been invited by a school friend
to a birthday party in Bishops Avenue, a leafy street of very large
houses in Hampstead, known today as 'Millionaires' Row'. 'Until
then I had thought that our house was big, but this was so much
bigger than anything I had seen,' she recalls. 'It even had a swimming
pool, all the things you were supposed to want. Immediately I felt
very uncomfortable there. It seemed so cold and unwelcoming.'

She joined in with a game of hide and seek in the garden but 'I
was suddenly aware that I was standing totally alone. Everyone had
disappeared and a voice spoke to me and said, "None of this matters.
None of these things. Only love matters."' It was, as she now
describes it, 'a flash of understanding, that the beautiful house, the
lovely garden were not as important as what I had experienced, love.
There was a tension in this family that I had felt. It was not a happy
home.'

She did not mention the experience to anyone. 'I knew it was
God because it was said with such authority. My father would say
prayers at night and I think he probably had a mystical streak. We
would go to church on Sundays, where my mother would enjoy
singing the hymns, but it never occurred to me to mention it to either
of them. I thought it was something that happened to everyone. I

wasn't frightened, but reassured. It highlighted love for me as the most important thing, as my lodestar.'

Sixty plus years on, without any independent confirmation, it is impossible to verify the details of this incident. However, its broader significance is all too clear. Though she didn't know it at the time, this was the start of what Bronwen later came to map as her spiritual journey and the first glimpse, however fleeting, of a capacity within her to experience and react to feelings, tensions, fears or pain in a physical way.

ꙮ Chapter Two

The land of my fathers? My fathers can keep it.

Attributed to Dylan Thomas (1914–1953)

The old Dr Williams' School building has the look of a neglected North Country nunnery, its wide gables sagging down over grey stone walls blackened with age, its windows positioned high off the ground to shut out the prying eyes of the world. Next to the road out of Dolgellau to Barmouth and the North, it is now part of a local sixth-form college, but a weather-beaten plaque over the main entrance recalls its history. ENDOWED OUT OF THE FUNDS OF THE TRUST FOUNDED IN 1716 BY THE REVD DANIEL WILLIAMS DD, ERECTED BY PUBLIC SUBSCRIPTION IN 1878. Williams, a wealthy Welsh Presbyterian minister, had wanted to promote primary education in Wales, but once the state took over such provision in the early 1870s, his trustees had redirected their funds to secondary education and established Dr Williams' School.

Today there may be new tenants and the Welsh Dolgellau has replaced the Anglicised Dolgelley (or Doll-jelly, as the boarders here in the 1930s and 1940s called their host town), but the bleak backdrop to Dr Williams' has altered little over the centuries. The Wnion river flows into the Mawddach, which widens as it leaves its mountainous hinterland and sweeps out towards the Irish Sea and the sandy beaches of Barmouth and Fairbourne. On both sides of the estuary are rolling hills dotted with isolated farms. Towering above everything else is the vast, bleak, greyish-green lump of Cader Idris, its peak shaped like a horse's saddle.

For some, notably the eighteenth-century painter Richard Wilson, this was a lyrical and romantic landscape to be celebrated, but after the familiar, crowded, urban environment of Hampstead, with its trees, buses and tamed Heath, north-west Wales must have seemed an alien territory to nine-year-old Bronwen Pugh. This empty and usually rain-swept wilderness was a day's journey by train from London. A specially designated coach for Dr Williams' girls took her, chaperoned by her older sister Gwyneth, now one of the seniors at the school, plus other boarders, from the capital up to Ruabon Junction, over the border from Shrewsbury, where they changed on to a now abandoned branch line which snaked through the mountains before descending to the coast via Dolgellau. At the station – now a second-hand clothes shop – they were met and then marched uphill the mile or so to the school building. Trunks had been sent on ahead. Each girl brought only a small overnight bag. It was a spartan start to a spartan life.

The Pughs were remarkably relaxed about their young daughters undertaking what to any parent today would seem an epic and dangerous voyage. At least Bronwen had an older sister with her who knew the ropes. When Ann first went to the school, her mother accompanied her for just half the journey and then left her in the care of the guard. Independence was learnt at an early age. Parental visits to the school were permitted just once a term and often only their mother came. During the war years, even these dried up. Though Kathleen Pugh had initially put up some opposition to shipping her daughters off to north-west Wales – she would have preferred a more standard girls' boarding school at Felixstowe – she bowed to her husband's wishes and the couple, as ever, presented a united front.

The distance from London was so great that any term-time trips back to the capital were out of the question. During the war years Wales was Bronwen's principal home. Though her father had drilled her Welsh roots into her, young Bronwen had little other experience of the country than that gleaned over a Hampstead breakfast table. Family holidays, in deference to her mother's wishes, had been taken on farms in Suffolk or at Bognor with Bella Wells.

To describe Dr Williams' as 'home' would be to create a false impression of comfort. It was cold, often damp and the food was no better than adequate. Wartime shortages meant a restricted and mea-gre diet in the communal dining room. 'On Fridays, the cook would always produce something the girls called "lucky dip",' recalls

Margaret Braund, a member of staff from 1944 to 1948. 'It was basically bread and butter pudding but with whatever else was left over and lying round the kitchen – bits of sandwich, sausages, even a nail once, I think. They hated it and it was truly awful.'

Each day pupils changed seats and eventually table to a predetermined pattern to ensure that they all mixed, under strict supervision. 'It was regimented,' Ann recalls, 'but for me at least it afforded a sense of confidence because you always knew what was going to happen.' Boarders slept in six- or seven-girl dormitories – or 'dormies' – and were again regularly moved round to prevent schoolgirl crushes. Some of the seniors were housed off site in *Pen-y-Coed*, a building halfway up the hill that faces the school. It was also home to the younger members of staff and therefore had a more relaxed atmosphere.

Sickness was dealt with robustly – a good gargle of Dettol was regarded as enough to put most ailments right. Morning bell rang at seven. There was a quick wash in cold water, with baths strictly by rota once a week. And then on with the uniform. For summer there was a navy tunic, a green and white striped blazer, with green poplin blouse and straw hat; for winter, the same blazer but a green viyella blouse and navy blue velour hat. (The straw hats reputedly were excellent for sifting for gold in the streams around Dolgellau, home then to one of Britain's few gold mines.) At the weekend it was a thick velvet or shantung green dress, depending on the season.

The Pughs were all put in Cader house, one of the six groupings into which the 300 or so pupils were divided. There were rules, with order marks for good behaviour contributing to honours for one's house. And there was little indulgence. 'No magazines or comic papers are to be sent to girls at school,' stipulated a set of rules sent to the Pughs in 1939, 'with the exception of the *Girl's Own* paper and *Riding* and *Zoo*. Permission must be obtained from the headmistress for any other magazine which parents may think suitable.' The handbook went on to specify that only fawn socks would be allowed, no heels, no garters and no fur trimmings on coats, which must be navy gabardine, lined and waterproof, in deference to the prevailing climate.

The school stands apart from the town. Today it is simply an accident of geography, but in Bronwen's day the distance had a symbolic value. Town and gown were separate. Dolgellau has long been a bastion of the Welsh culture and Nonconformity. With its winding, narrow streets and grey local stone houses, it was one of the first constituencies to return a Plaid Cymru MP in 1974. Even back in 1939 it was represented by one of the rump of self-consciously Welsh Liberal MPs who followed Lloyd George to the bitter end. The neo-classical Salem Chapel of the Presbyterian Church of Wales, high on the hill above the tiny shopping centre, is still larger and better attended than the squat Anglican church of St Mary's.

It was to St Mary's, however, that the English boarders from Dr Williams' trooped each Sunday for morning service. Alun Pugh may have wanted a Welsh education for his daughters, but despite being in Wales, endowed by a Welsh benefactor and including Welsh language lessons on the curriculum plus a Welsh hymn and an offering on the harp once a week at assembly, Dr Williams' was effectively a little bit of England in exile. 'In those days it was as Welsh as any suitable school for us could have got,' estimates Ann, 'but that wasn't saying a great deal.'

In line with its charitable purposes, in addition to its boarders like the Pughs, Dr Williams' admitted a number of local day girls – around 20 per cent of the total – but these locals remained marginal to the ethos of the school. They were mainly Welsh-speakers – several from hill farms high above Dolgellau – and outside of lessons tended to stick together. Displays of Welsh patriotism were rare enough to merit a special mention. When Bronwen enrolled as a girl guide in November 1942, she told her father: 'I hope this will console you N'had,* we are having a Welsh dragon on our shoulders to show that we are Welsh guides and not English.'

Most of the teachers and boarders came from across the border, the majority of the latter from well-to-do Midlands families, attracted by the school's reputation as quietly progressive. If it was not particularly Welsh, Dr Williams' did have a name for enlightened attitudes. When Bronwen arrived, its character had been moulded for many years by headteacher Constance Nightingale, who was herself drawn

---

* She always used the Welsh form of 'My father' in letters.

to Quaker ideas and who had established a regime with no corporal punishment and none of the decorum, deportment and decorating lessons that dominated many girls' boarding schools at this time. She aimed to turn out young women with self-confidence and self-awareness, not debutantes. Persuasion rather than force ensured the smooth running of Dr Williams' and the pupils, in an age when marriage and children were still regarded as the pinnacle of female ambitions, were encouraged to excel in whatever field attracted them – academic work, sports or, if they wanted, domestic science. The atmosphere was not competitive. There was, for example, no attempt to draw up 'class positions' at the end of term to denote the cleverest in the form and to encourage competition.

The curriculum was comprehensive, from scripture to science, Welsh to gardening. What time was left over between prep and lights out at nine was filled with uplifting talks by local worthies and travellers, occasional plays and, on special occasions, gatherings in the headmistress's private quarters to listen to the wireless. At weekends it was sports – Dr Williams', in another progressive gesture, spurned lacrosse in favour of cricket, but embraced the more traditionally female netball, hockey and tennis – guide camps, accompanied walks or bicycle rides along the river from Dolgellau out towards the sea at Barmouth and Tywyn, or up to Cader Idris, and finally, on Sunday evenings, letter-writing to reassure anxious parents.

Bronwen's first letter home was short, stiff and bland. 'We've arrived. Here is a picture of our dormy. I can't think of anything else to say but I'll write soon.' Looking back now, with her psycho-therapist's training and the benefits of hindsight, she believes she was in shock at the alien world that had greeted her. Gwyneth Pugh revealed how the staff allowed her to break her young sister gently into school life by putting them in the same 'dormy' for the first few nights. Then they were separated and Bronwen put with girls nearer her own age, though she was the youngest in her form by two years. 'I was told that Bronwen was to go to Trem [the junior school],' Gwyneth wrote home, 'so I packed all her things and she went off. So although Bronwen is at school, she is quite O K.'

Big sister was still hovering in the background the following Febru-ary, mentioning to her parents that she had been doing Bronwen's knitting for her. The same letter displayed a touch of exasperation: 'Bronwen told me the other day that she had lost David's Christmas present. So I went up to her dormy, opened the drawer at the top and there it was. "Oh, I never looked in there" was the bright remark.' She was forever losing things.

Gwyneth's 'big sister' attitude is emblazoned on the page of a letter Bronwen wrote home in November 1942. 'G is in sick-wing. In fact she has been since Monday. It's her heart again and she's been working too hard,' the youngest Pugh reported. 'I don't know what she means by this. She's a bit potty,' her older sibling scrawled across the offending section. Yet, heart trouble afflicted Gwyneth for most of her adult life and precipitated her early death.

Realising that leaving home and going off to boarding school at such a tender age could be an emotional wrench the Pughs attempted to provide their last-born with other companions – Thomas and Doreen, two rabbits, substitutes for the family cat, Lancelot, who had been left behind. Both survived only a few short weeks in Dolgellau, but it wasn't entirely down to the inclement weather. 'This is, I think, the reason for Doreen's dying,' nine-year-old Bronwen told her parents. 'Last weekend it was absolutely pouring with rain and I hadn't got an umbrella, so I didn't go to feed them. And on Monday at break when I went to see Thomas and Doreen, she was dead.' Thomas followed soon afterwards.

Though having Gwyneth around was a comfort and deepened the lifelong bond between the two, being the third Pugh girl to pass through Dr Williams' had its drawbacks. 'I was always compared with my older sisters and found wanting,' Bronwen remembers. 'We were all three head girls. I was made to feel that I was made head girl simply because my sisters had been before me. My father came to give away the prizes when I was head girl and I remember him saying, "All my three daughters have been head girl here. Some are born great, some achieve greatness and some have greatness thrust upon them." That last one is the category I came into and I felt put down again. My sisters were better at everything.'

Being seen as part of a package, not as an individual, was part of the reason that Bronwen – or 'Pug' as she was known to her form-mates – came to feel trapped within the walls of Dr Williams'. She could never wait to get away from its confines. Her letters suddenly became upbeat and almost frenzied as the end of term approached and were full of references to the landmarks in the build-up to departure – One Glove Sunday, Cock-Hat Sunday, Kick-Pew Sunday. When the weekly countdown was almost complete, it turned into a daily task of crossing off days by means of the name Jack Robinson. It worked like an Advent Calendar. On each of the final twelve days, he lost one letter.

Another source of unhappiness was finding herself in a form of much older girls. In July 1942 the head wrote to the Pughs to suggest that Bronwen be kept down a year. 'I cannot put it down entirely to her work which reaches a fair average, but she is the youngest in the form and in many ways is much more immature than the others . . . She is very childish still in her outlook and frequently in her behaviour.' The transfer went ahead, but even then she was still a year younger than most of her classmates. In retrospect, Bronwen believes there was more to the head's verdict than academic concerns. 'I don't think my temperament fitted in at the school. Yes, there was certainly immaturity. The others were all older. But I think what she was also getting at was that I had this sense of enjoyment and fun – still have it – this ageless enjoyment that people can find very disconcerting.'

Staying down a year did, however, bring about an immediate improvement in her academic performance, though still teachers felt that she was falling short of full effort and dedication. 'An able pupil who can do really well when she wants to,' her English mistress commented in the summer of 1943. 'Bronwen can do very good work but at times is too easily distracted,' echoed her arithmetic teacher in autumn of the same year. 'Must try to be tidier and less noisy,' the head summed up in autumn 1944. Towards the end of her career at Dr Williams', however, her marks and the accompanying appraisals changed. 'She is acquiring dignity and a sense of responsibility,' the head concluded at the end of 1945.

Reading Bronwen's letters home, all carefully dated and preserved by her father, it is hard to imagine that she was anything but uproariously happy at Dr Williams'. They are full of stiff upper lip, sporting triumphs (she was in every team and captain of hockey), gusto and good cheer. 'We were all trained not to complain,' she says now. 'Remember I was a Truby King baby. I was trained from the start to be self-contained and self-controlled. If you complained you were told to go away and not bother people. There was no giving up and so you repressed it and cried yourself to sleep.' Subsequent research on the effects of Frederic Truby King's methods bears out her memory. In a paper in the *British Journal of Psychotherapy* Gertrud Mander identifies 'a grin and bear it ethos', 'a deep sense of being unacceptable and unlovable' and even 'an on-going depressive under-current' as the hallmarks of a Truby King baby. By encouraging mothers to subject their children to a rigid regime and concentrating in a Victorian way on physical well-being, Mander writes, Truby King's 'own fateful contribution to infant care' was erroneously to assume that in a healthy body mental and emotional equilibrium would naturally follow.

Dr Williams' was not, however, a universally bleak experience. Occasionally something excited Bronwen's interest. In October 1941, little suspecting her future fame, she told her parents: 'Yesterday there was a lecture about clothes and the person was called Miss Haig and the head chose twelve manekins [sic] from the sixth form and dressed them up in various costumes and in different centuries. There were lanterns slides as well, and we started from the time when people began to wear clothes to 1939. It was very good and some of the manekins looked frightfully funny.'

The school was in the process of change in Bronwen's first years there. The benign and enlightened Miss Nightingale retired and was replaced by Miss Orford, a thirty-five-year-old ex-civil servant from England.

There's no nonsense about her [Gwyneth wrote home in May 1940]. She knows what she wants and she's getting it. She scares me stiff. She comes into prayers in the morning and swooshes round the door so that her gown, which she wears all day, flies right out. Then she strides across the stage and stares round and everyone feels sure that she is going to pounce on them for something. At last she says 'Good-morning'. With a question mark at the end and everyone sort of breathes a sigh of relief.

Margaret Braund confirms the aura of authority that surrounded Miss
Orford. 'She was very shy and could therefore appear cold. I remember she used to slip in and sit at the back of my drama classes and
even if I hadn't seen her or heard her come in, I'd know she was
there. The girls' behaviour would change completely. They would
freeze.'

Once Bronwen fell foul of Miss Orford and it nearly cost her
her school career. A typically impulsive midnight feast on the hillside next to the school, consisting only of a couple of oranges and
a biscuit, became a major incident when the escapees were caught
in the act by a monitor. Miss Orford wrote to the Pughs saying
that Bronwen was lucky not to be expelled. 'Please don't be too
cross,' the culprit wrote home in November 1943, 'as this is the
first hot water that I have really been in, and one has to do it
sometime during school life or else you will be thought an awful
prig.'

Alun Pugh's reaction, though, was not a standard parental rebuke
and reveals much of the attitudes he passed on to his daughter. If
you're going to do this sort of thing, he warned her, make sure you
don't get caught. Such advice might equally have applied to his own
links with law-breaking extremists at the same time as continuing
his career at the Bar. Moreover, he went on, why weren't you the
ringleader? 'I found this marvellously liberating,' she says. 'I remember it so clearly. It had never occurred to me before to be the
ringleader. I was the youngest and I just followed.' The rebel in
Alun Pugh's heart was reaching out to his youngest daughter.

It was not ultimately Miss Orford – or her sporty successor, the
cricket-playing Miss Lickes – who turned Dr Williams' from con-
finement into a nightmare. It was the war. Bronwen's childhood and
adolescence were dominated by the Second World War. Cut off
from her parents, denied the only familiar surroundings she had
known when her father and mother went off to work in Lancashire
and shut up the family home in London, she felt herself virtually cut
adrift.

Her father's knee injury meant that active service was out of the
question for him, but he was still young enough in theory to qualify
for call-up, which in 1941 was extended to men up to fifty-one. He

was determined to serve King and Country. In a national emergency his particular loyalties to Wales, Plaid Cymru and Saunders Lewis were forgotten. Lewis urged the Welsh not to fight, saying the conflict had nothing to do with them. Alun Pugh, however, was ready to take up his rifle, or its non-military equivalent. Early in the war he obtained a post as legal adviser to the Ministry of Pensions in the port of Fleetwood in Lancashire. He could not bear to be a barrister while everybody else of his age was fighting and so accepted the substantial pay cut involved and moved north.

Kathleen Pugh also found an outlet for her frustrated energies. In the first war she had been a volunteer nurse. In Fleetwood she managed the Ministry of Pensions' canteen, one of thousands of egalitarian outlets set up by the authorities to provide cheap, nutritious food at a time of shortages. In place of the house in Pilgrims Lane, which was left empty, the couple moved around from one set of unsatisfactory digs to another. When Bronwen came home in the school holidays, it was initially to the Lancashire coast.

The journey from Dolgellau to Fleetwood on trains crowded with men and women in uniform, through stations prepared for air raids, scared her. 'I think my greatest nightmare of the war was getting lost because they removed all the signs from the stations. At first I had Gwyneth with me, but there were journeys I made on my own, changing two or three times, with no signs, clutching my gas mask and lots of smog. I was petrified of getting lost and never being found again.' When she arrived, there was little to celebrate. 'Fleetwood was a ghastly place,' she remembers. 'I have terrible memories of it. They celebrated something called Wakes Week and we were put out of our digs to make way for holiday-makers. We were literally on the pavement with nowhere to go. We ended up staying in a hotel until we could find other digs. As usual it was up a dark, dank staircase, two or three rooms at the top of a house. It was such a come-down. I remember dreaming of a big house with lots of space.'

'Bronwen found herself in a very strange environment in Fleetwood,' says her sister Ann. 'We were known by the locals as southerners because we spoke with a different accent. And we felt foreign. It wasn't meant cruelly, and because I was older, I had a great time going to the Tower Ballroom in Blackpool. But because

Bronwen was younger and my parents were so busy, I think she felt abandoned.'

A greater blow than the physical hardship was the loss of the security that had hitherto surrounded her childhood. During the summer before she went off to school her father took her on a bus trip around the centre of London, pointing out monuments and buildings 'because they will probably be bombed and this will be your last chance to see them'. The effect of such a message, when combined with being sent off to a boarding school in a strange environment and losing your home, must have been profound. And because Alun Pugh's income fell dramatically, his youngest daughter suddenly began to notice money. Until the war she had always taken for granted the fact that the family was well-off, able to afford all the things she needed. Now the budget was squeezed, so much so that Ann Pugh had to delay going up to Oxford.

'I couldn't imagine there were people who had more than us,' Bronwen says. 'Obviously there were – the Astors for instance – but I was totally ignorant of that. Then the war came and there was no money because my father had given up his career and lived on a tiny salary in digs and we had to go and eat where my mother worked – rice puddings and awful food. They were meant for the poor. And we had been dragged down to that. I felt it as a humiliation.' Her reaction to new hardships emphasises how little she enjoyed or even comprehended the war period. Its privations came at a difficult time in her life. She was too old to be oblivious to the greater threat. Children under ten write of seeing the whole thing as one long adventure. Yet neither was she old enough to get caught up in the war spirit, the comradeship, the sense of doing your bit in a vast community effort. She had all the worry, without enough real insight to put it into any context, and none of the excitement of broadening horizons experienced, for example, by her sister Ann, who was conscripted.

Hitler's strategy towards Britain was two-fold – to bomb it into submission from the air and to starve it into surrender at sea. Over half of all foodstuffs in the pre-war period had come into the country by ship. If the aerial policy made relatively little impact on Bronwen's life, the maritime blockade drove her to despair as her empty stomach ached. Rationing was the order of the day: marrow or carrot jam spread on stale bread was sometimes all that was on offer for tea at Dr Williams'.

Sleepy and safe Dolgellau managed to work itself into a fever about the war. In June 1940 the girls from Dr Williams' took part in an air-raid practice. 'We had to go down into the basement in single file and in silence from our forms,' the weekly letter home detailed, 'and the Head said that we had got to get down in four minutes – the whole school of 300 girls. It was an awfully queer siren.' Later there were air-raid practices for boarders in the middle of the night. The drills were a sensible precaution though predictably, given the town's location, it entirely escaped the attention of German bombers. The nearest to a raid was when an American plane crashed several miles to the north.

Sometimes the elaborate preparations for eventualities that were extremely unlikely to befall Dolgellau left Bronwen and her contemporaries fearful but bemused. In October 1942 they all went to Sunday morning service wearing their gas masks. 'What a sight we looked,' twelve-year-old Bronwen reported home. 'I wish I'd got a proper gas-mask case because I've still got that cardboard thing and it's all come to pieces. You see it's all very muddling, but I'm sure G[wyneth] will explain better than me about this gas attack. There are some people who are attacking some other people somewhere and some girl guides are running messages to somewhere from somewhere.'

As the war passed Dolgellau by, the pupils of Dr Williams' were determined to do their bit, even if they had no clear idea of what war entailed, but their active service stretched no further than evenings of knitting scarves for 'our lads' in the army or watching Ministry of Information films about how to disarm a German. There were collections of spare toys for 'bombed-out children'. When Bronwen played Nerissa in a school production of *The Merchant of Venice*, the townsfolk were given a rare invitation over to Dr Williams', with their ticket money raising £5 for the RAF Benevolent Fund. Town and gown for once had common purpose.

The war did change Dolgellau's landscape. Various schools were evacuated out there and a group of children from Birkenhead, a target for the bombers because its port worked hand in hand with neighbouring Liverpool, took up residence nearby. And there were American soldiers stationed in the area who paid particular attention to the teenage girls on their doorstep. In March 1943 Bronwen, showing the first signs of impending womanhood, wrote excitedly of one of the older girls at the school being greeted by a chorus of wolf-whistles when a military truck overtook her on her bicycle.

North-west Wales was also considered a safe place to detain prisoners of war – far away from the continental coastline and any hopes of escape or liberation. In September of the same year Bronwen recorded an encounter with the enemy while on a school walking trip at nearby Bala Lake. Her oddly neutral tones reveal a lingering bemusement about the issues at stake in the war:

> We saw a very nice-looking Italian prisoner, who was working in one of the fields. By the way we see tons of them round here. Anyway down we got and went to talk to this prisoner. We talked in very bad French, and he seemed to understand. Anyhow he answered. He had been captured in Tunisia and he liked Mussolini and Hitler, but hated Churchill. He was a fascist. He didn't like Wales. He said in a very strong Italian accent 'Wales, rain, rain, rain, but Italy sun, sun, sun!'

The mixture of childish mantras and glimpses of the conflict in the adult world is revealing. More wholeheartedly positive was her response to a British war hero and family friend who dropped in to take her to tea on his way to Barmouth. Major-General Sir Francis Tuker, a senior figure in the Gurkhas, had been at school with Alun Pugh and had visited the family home on several occasions. Thirteen-year-old Bronwen had developed something of a schoolgirl crush on him, which he played along with by calling on her at Dr Williams' in 1943. 'He came in a small army van, raised awfully high from the ground by big wheels,' she told her parents. 'There were three soldiers in the car with him, one driving.' The link endured. In February 1946, towards the end of her time at Dr Williams', he answered one of her letters. 'He didn't actually say much,' she reported, 'except that he would be stuck in Calcutta through the summer and that it was already "beastly hot".'

Dr Williams' itself certainly got caught up in the national mood of patriotism and swept Bronwen along. She described an armistice service in a letter home in November 1943. She was one of a number of guides there, but the head had refused to allow them to carry the Union Jack. 'Everybody,' Bronwen raged, 'thinks it is disgusting. Not having a Union Jack on Armistice Sunday because "it isn't done", goodness. We all feel jolly hot about it.'

However, for Bronwen, the privations of a wartime childhood greatly outweighed any excitement. Her biggest problem was the absence of food. 'For me the war was one long hell,' she says. 'It got worse and worse and worse because the food ran out, the clothes ran out, there were shortages of everything, then rationing. I was always hungry. I felt I never had enough to eat.' And even when plates were full, it was 'lucky dip' or its equivalent that was on offer. 'Dinner,' she wrote to her parents in November 1940, 'consisted of soup with bits of raw celery floating around and huge chunks of carrots also floating around like corks, then a pudding something like a terrible bright yellow blanc-mange with a few prunes also floating round, then two mingy little biscuits.' The hunger pangs were so extreme at times that she felt moved to steal food from the school dining room. The headteacher caught her with her hand in the biscuit tin and stopped her sweet ration for a fortnight.

Hitler's maritime cordon quickly affected the nation's eating habits. Churchill's Food Minister, Fred Marquis, later Lord Woolton, was by Christmas 1940 advocating a wholesale change in diet to meet the new circumstances. 'It is the duty of all grown-up people to do with less milk this winter,' he advised through the columns of the *Daily Express*, 'so that children and nursing mothers can be sure of getting as much as they need. Oatmeal, one of the finest foods for giving warmth and energy, is a "must" for growing children.' With a blithe ignorance of the eating likes and dislikes of youngsters, he continued, 'they will probably like it as oatcakes. Encourage your children to eat baked potatoes, jacket and all. Carrots are an important protective food. Most children love carrot,' he suggested hopefully, 'when it has been washed, lightly scraped and grated raw into a salad or a sandwich.'

Children were encouraged to abandon their sweet tooth in favour of carrots by the example of night fighter ace, 'Cat's Eye' Cunningham. His ability to dodge German anti-aircraft guns and repel the Luftwaffe's 1940 blitz on London was put down in official propaganda to a rabbit-like love of carrots, which enabled him to see in the dark.

A taste for salad, Woolton ordered, must be inculcated at once. 'Salads and vegetables are what [your child] needs almost more than anything else, so teach him to like them as early as you can. You will find that many children, when they can't cope with a plateful of green salad, will enjoy it when it's well chopped up between slices of wholemeal bread.'

With even adult rations pegged to tiny quantities – three ounces of bacon per week, two of cheese, two of tea, eight of sugar and four of chocolate and sweets – a spot of recycling was required, Woolton advised, to fill empty young tummies. Apple cores, his department proposed, could be turned into 'delicious and very health-giving drinks' by boiling them in water.

In this regime of bitter tastes and recycled waste, the chocolate that Bronwen and many other children craved became a rare treat. 'For the duration of the war,' the head of Dr Williams' informed parents, 'fruit and chocolate may be sent to individual girls but they must be handed in to the matron who will keep them and distribute them at the proper time. The school does still have regular, though limited, supplies of chocolate which the girls can buy, but no girl who has sweets or chocolate of her own may also buy school chocolate.' When the pooled resources were shared out on high days and holidays, Bronwen's joy knew no bounds. 'It's Freda's birthday today,' she wrote in February 1945. 'We are all looking forward to this afternoon as she is having a DOUBLE birthday table with Maureen Oates. Yum, yum! We are going to stuff and stuff and *stuff*!!'

Sometimes she ended up caught between her patriotic duty and her rumbling stomach. In December of the same year she told her parents: 'the head-girl of the Mount School, York, has written a letter to the head-girl of every other boarding school to ask if anybody would give up their 4 ounces of extra Christmas chocolate to send overseas to France etc. I think it is an excellent idea and everyone here who has got some is sending it.' Goodness carries its own reward, but the following month her sacrifice of chocolate was repaid.

'Have you had any bananas at home yet?' she enquired in January 1946. 'Some kids have brought a few back with them and so I have tasted them once again. It was a thrilling moment.'

If the food shortages got worse before they got better, there was some relief at the end of 1941, when the Pughs returned to London from Fleetwood. 'What marvellous news,' Bronwen wrote. 'I jolly well hope that the war will be over by the Easter hols so that we can go to London.' It wasn't, of course, but at least holidays were once more in a familiar location, though the house in Pilgrims Lane now also provided shelter for refugees, who gave the increasingly adult Bronwen some idea of the realities of the war on the continent. 'I remember in particular one Jewish woman, a Miss Seligman. She spent all her time in tears. And there were two Dutch refugees. They had survived on a diet of tulip bulbs.'

The return to London also brought her face to face with what war was about. 'Later there were doodlebugs and it was horrendous. You would go up the High Street and these things would come flying over and you would be petrified. You would wait for the engines to cut out and just hope that they had passed you by. Everyone was so exhausted and bad-tempered that they got angry with you all the time.' Hampstead is on a hill and from her bedroom window she would watch the East End of London being bombed – just the destruction that her father had predicted in 1939.

The contrast between north-west Wales, where war was experienced at second hand, and Hampstead was huge. It was as if Bronwen was dipping in and out of the conflict, almost an adult in London but still a child in the safety of Dr Williams'. She was back in Dolgellau for VE Day, 8 May 1945. The school worked itself up into a state of great excitement, with the head deciding on a special treat – two extra days' holiday. 'Isn't that marvellous,' she wrote home girlishly, adding with a note of regret, 'anyone who can get home and back in a day is allowed. For the rest of us, she is going to try to provide something special, which will of course include the flicks.' In the event, there was also a one-off trip to the circus.

Already by 1944 some aspects of life had begun to return to normal. Alun Pugh was appointed a county court judge of Norfolk in May. He was to prove popular with the barristers who appeared before

him, a benign man with firm principles and old-fashioned values
when it came to domestic disputes. In the Inns of Court they even
put together a short verse to celebrate him:

> Love, said His Honour Judge Pugh,
> Should act on a couple like glue.
> Making birds of a feather
> Stay flocking together
> Just as they do in the zoo.

If it restored the family's material prosperity to pre-war standards, it
did mean once again leaving the house in Pilgrims Lane so soon after
returning to it. The Pughs kept it on, but made Norwich their main
base. Bronwen was, however, full of delight. 'Hurray! Congratu-
lations! I haven't seen it in the papers yet. We haven't had *The
Times*, only the *Daily Telegraph*, and I can't find it in there. Anyway
practically all the school knows and it was the topic of conversation
wherever I went.'

In June 1945 she passed her basic school certificate – the equivalent
of current GCSEs. Like her sisters before her, she stayed on at Dr
Williams' to study for her higher certificate – A levels – but her
patience with constantly trailing in the wake of Ann and Gwyneth
had reached breaking point. Like many younger children – particularly when their older siblings are of the same sex – she had long
felt eclipsed. At Dr Williams' was born her lifelong determination
to chart her own course – if possible in the opposite direction to
that chosen by Ann and Gwyneth. This meant that some of her
natural abilities – in academic work, for instance – were cast aside,
or at least marginalised, since they were shared strengths with her
sisters, in favour of talents that she considered unique to her, notably
her delight in performing.

Having passed her school certificate, she found herself at what,
with hindsight, can be seen as a crossroads in her life, for much of
what she did subsequently flowed naturally from her decision to
reject the path already well-trodden by her sisters and enthusiastically
advocated by her parents. 'I think,' she recalls, 'they had in mind
that I would go to Oxford and become a teacher. My father told
me I would make a good headmistress.'

By 1947, however, she had set her heart firmly and finally against going up to Oxford. The additional term it would entail to prepare for the Oxbridge examination was not the real problem. She stayed on after her highers anyway because she was still a year younger than most of her class. In that extra year she was appointed head girl. It was meant to be for a whole year and, having said no to Oxbridge, she set about learning French and Latin but she became increasingly unhappy as her relationship with Miss Lickes broke down. The head-teacher, who had succeeded Miss Orford in September 1945, was obsessed with stamping out overly intimate friendships between girls and ordered Bronwen to devise a quasi-military campaign to achieve this end. Her head girl realised that it was a pointless exercise, doomed to failure, and that many of these illicit passions were in any case quite harmless. It was taking a sledge hammer to crack a nut.

Headteacher and head girl clashed again when Miss Lickes insisted that Bronwen sleep in the main school. All previous head girls had been allowed to sleep in the separate and more relaxed house on the hillside above Dr Williams' with their fellow sixth formers and younger members of staff. Bronwen was outraged and lonely. After just two terms, she left.

'If I don't get Higher,' she had written in January 1946, 'and I don't honestly see how I possibly can, with two languages at which I'm no good, I don't think it's much use going to Oxford because even if I got in, I would most probably be sent down or some-thing awful.' There is an obvious lack of self-confidence – especially since she later passed all the exams she predicted she would fail – but her reasoning was more complex. 'It was probably a mistake,' she now acknowledges, and she often mentions her lack of formal academic qualifications. 'But I was so fed up with always being compared with my sisters. Although I did in the end get my Latin matric and I could have got a place, I decided to go to drama school instead.'

Towards the end of her school career Bronwen came under the influence of Margaret Braund, a young drama teacher who had just qualified from London's Central School of Speech and Drama. 'She was a very gawky schoolgirl,' Braund remembers, 'very tall, quite uncoordinated and really not very attractive. She used to stoop to try and compensate for being so tall, she had pigtails, wore glasses and had a slight cast in her eye.'

Bronwen had done a great deal of singing at school, and had played Little Buttercup in a production of Gilbert and Sullivan's *HMS Pinafore*, but she had never thought seriously about drama as a career. After a while Braund realised that there was something about this awkward adolescent girl and decided to give her a chance by casting her as the lead in a school production of George Bernard Shaw's *Saint Joan*. 'The rest of the staff all said I was mad, that she would make a fool of herself, but slowly she became less inhibited, began to move more easily and – although I only realised this later when she became more religious – brought out the spiritual side of Joan very well.' *Saint Joan* was Bronwen's proudest moment at Dr Williams'. It made her consider drama as a career. 'I think before I arrived,' says Margaret Braund, 'that she had nurtured some ambitions to be a singer. She had this rather romantic idea of being a great opera diva, but her voice had been strained in one of the school musicals and that had taken away her confidence. And then along came acting and her success in *Saint Joan* and it made such a difference to her that I suggested she apply to Central.'

To Alun Pugh his youngest daughter's new-found delight in acting was of secondary importance. 'He came to see me in *Saint Joan* and when I asked him afterwards what he had thought of it and my performance, he told me that he was prouder of the speech I'd made as head girl at prize day.' Yet despite his disappointment, and after talking to Margaret Braund, he gave way and agreed to pay her fees at Central if she got a place. At least she would be living back in the family home at Hampstead, where he could keep a watchful eye on her potential student excesses; his career had now moved on with his appointment in 1947 to Marylebone County Court. Having brought up his daughters to be independent and strong-minded, it would have been inappropriate and out of character now to try and force Bronwen's hand.

It was not that, at this stage, she had a burning ambition to tread the boards, or emulate the film stars she had glimpsed during her occasional trips to Dolgellau's tiny cinema. She had no strong vision of a career or what she wanted to do with her life. Her strongest

motivation was largely negative – to break the mould of the trinity
of Pugh sisters by doing something entirely different. And perhaps
those feelings of not being the longed-for son – overlaid by the
strains of a wartime childhood – had made her, in a more positive
way, determined to strike out on her own. Her parents, after all,
had responded to growing up during the First World War with a
similar resolution to overturn conventions.

She had no blueprint, just an unbending conviction that she
wanted to be left to her own devices. Planning has never been one
of her strengths. Subsequently she has come to recognise, in the
various life-changing decisions that she made as if on a whim, the
influence of what might be called a guiding spirit or guardian angel.
She may not have seen it at the time, but she is sure with hindsight
that it was there.

Formal religion had played little role in her life at Dr Williams'.
In July 1940, when the whole school caught a bad bout of flu, she
was writing, 'we are all in quarantine. Three cheers there is no
church tomorrow.' As she grew towards adulthood, she rejected the
conventional practice of Christianity. Yet separate from, and indeed
unconnected to, church-going and the God who presided over lifeless
recitals of prayer and hymns, there were, she recalls, glimpses of a
spiritual dimension, removed from routine attendance in the pews.

After her first brush with something 'other' at a seven-year-old's
birthday party, she continued in her school years occasionally to have
experiences for which she could find no rational explanation. 'As a
teenager, I was having these extraordinary experiences of nature. I'd
be on a walk with my school friends and quite suddenly there was
no one there. It is like an explosion. And it left me with this wonderful feeling of being at one with everything. You're not looking at
the sunset, you're part of it. Something clears in your mind and you
understand something of the reality of nature.' Had she then consulted the literature of Christian mysticism, she would have found
parallel accounts of an overwhelming sense of oneness with the natural world and divined a clue as to what she herself in a small way
was experiencing. Yet there was no one who could point her in the
right direction and such exotic and generally Catholic spiritual raptures had no place in the conventionally Protestant and pointedly

practical world of Dr Williams'. 'I tried making a remark about it, wondering if the others I was with felt the same things, but no one said anything. Up to then I'd assumed everyone was the same. When I realised they weren't, I felt very isolated.'

In July 1945 fifteen-year-old Bronwen Pugh went with a group of girl guides from Dr Williams' to spend a week camping at Maidenhead next to the Thames in Berkshire. A mile or so up river at Cliveden, a wedding had just been celebrated. William Waldorf Astor, the thirty-eight-year-old eldest son and heir of the second Viscount Astor and his formidable MP wife Nancy, had married the Honourable Sarah Norton, twelve years his junior, daughter of the sixth Baron Grantley and a descendant of the playwright Richard Brinsley Sheridan. While the girl guides cooked beans over a camp fire and got up to schoolgirl pranks, 'Bill' Astor was away in the States introducing his new bride to his wealthy American relatives before returning to set up home near Oxford and pursue his own political career.

The gulf in age, class and experience between Bill Astor and Bronwen Pugh in 1945 could not have been greater. For her part, she did not even register from her campsite the existence of Cliveden, the stately home that fifteen years later was to become her home.

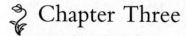 Chapter Three

It is vital to realise that we have come through difficult years
and we are going to face difficult years and to get through them
will require no less effort, no less unselfishness and no less work
than was needed to bring us through the war.

Clement Attlee, broadcast (1945)

The Central School of Speech and Drama boasted an impressive
London address – the Royal Albert Hall of Arts and Sciences on
Kensington Gore. This circular, red-brick and terracotta landmark,
with a capacity of 10,000, had since its opening in 1871 doubled as
a giant concert hall and a conference centre. This dual purpose suited
Central well, for the school not only had use of various conference
rooms and a mini-theatre back stage but also had access to the main
auditorium at various times during the day.

As a stage from which to learn voice projection, the vast arena
was unparalleled. It was also, past pupils recall, a baptism of fire. The
infamous Albert Hall echo thwarted many of their best efforts and
was only cured much later in 1968, when the decorated calico ceiling
was replaced by the giant suspended mushroom diffusers that still
hover incongruously over the auditorium today.

Most of Central's stage work, however, took place in a small
theatre housed above one of the four great porticos that lead into
the Albert Hall. There were other movement rooms and a lecture
theatre, with the school's canteen and additional teaching rooms
housed down the road on Kensington High Street. Being part of the
life of the Albert Hall had many fringe benefits for the students, not
the least of which was the chance, outside hours (and occasionally,
playing truant, when they should have been in lectures), to relax in
the stalls and watch and learn as a procession of musical and theatrical
stars rehearsed for their evening performances. When the habit

became too popular and threatened to interrupt lessons, the principal, Gwynneth Thurburn, would send a note to the absentees in the stalls, telling them that any classes skipped would have to be made up out of hours. It usually prompted an exodus, for Miss Thurburn's word went unchallenged at Central.

She had taken over in 1942 from the founder, Elsie Fogerty, and it was her dynamism during her long reign until 1967 which transformed Central into an internationally renowned drama school and ultimately saw it move away in 1957 from the Royal Albert Hall to bespoke premises in the old Embassy Theatre at Swiss Cottage. Admittance was by interview and audition with 'Thurby', as she was known to staff and pupils. She could appear very stern, recalls Margaret Braund, Bronwen's drama teacher at Dr Williams', a graduate of Central and later a tutor there, 'but she was also very kind, very understanding and knew in a minute what students were or weren't capable of achieving.' As well as a stage course, Central also offered three-year diploma courses for speech and drama teachers and for speech therapists. Thurburn believed all three to be of equal merit. 'There is something,' she once wrote, 'uniting everybody in this school – actors, teachers, speech therapists. For me it certainly is the voice, being the centre of all communication.'

Though the recommendation from Miss Braund may have helped Bronwen in her interview, she would not have got in unless Gwynneth Thurburn had spotted some talent in her. With hindsight, Margaret Braund believes it may have been Bronwen's voice. 'Her voice had a very pleasing quality, and it was very flexible. She had grown quickly into a good actress but it is her voice that stands out in my memory.' All three courses at Central were officially on a par, but it was the actors' diploma which carried most glamour. The eighteen-year-old Bronwen Pugh nursed ambitions to be on the stage, but she applied instead for the teachers' course.

Part of it was a lack of confidence. She may have shone in the small pond of Dr Williams' school productions, but was unsure how her credits from rural Wales would fare when placed alongside a string of leading roles in cosmopolitan youth theatres. Though physically now an adult, there was still a legacy of immaturity from her sheltered school years and her treatment as the baby of the family.

And there was also a vulnerability about her that at this stage of her life was linked to that immaturity, but which remained ever after, even when she had learnt about the world in sometimes the cruellest ways. Fear of rejection, of being among people who do not want her there, has been one of the strong emotions in her life, a practical weakness set against and sometimes curtailing another of her enduring qualities, her willingness to strike out on bold, unexpected and often criticised paths with an unshakeable belief that she is somehow being guided from above on a predetermined spiritual journey.

Many of her rivals for one of the coveted places on the Central actors' course, she believed, would have been living and breathing the dream of treading the boards from the cradle, while she had come late and not entirely wholeheartedly to the idea. It was for her less a vocation, more a cross between an alternative to Oxford, something to do, a gesture of defiance and a way to be different from her sisters. Moreover, she lacked the firm parental support that might have given her, at an impressionable age, the confidence to opt for acting. Alun Pugh, whom she looked up to above all others, who taught her that if you do anything you must be the best at it, may have agreed to pay the two pounds, six shillings per term, but there was little of the instinctive sympathy for his daughter's choice that would have greeted a decision to apply to Oxford. He had his youngest daughter down to succeed as a headmistress, so the teachers' course was at least a compromise between her option and his.

There was a further complicating factor – one that was to haunt Bronwen throughout her professional life. The Goodyear genes made for tall women and all the Pugh girls were giants. Gwyneth was just over six foot, her mother and two sisters just under. So Bronwen was deemed by the standards of the day too tall to be a successful actress. Even in later, more tolerant times tall actresses like Hollywood star Sigourney Weaver have struggled to find female leads (she was sidelined into science fiction), but back in the 1940s anyone over five foot six faced a bleak future. Leading men had to gaze masculinely down on their petite feminine charges – women like Celia Johnson, Olivia de Havilland and Audrey Hepburn. Actresses approaching six foot would find it impossible to persuade casting directors of their merits. Of Bronwen's generation, only the well-connected and extraordinarily talented Vanessa Redgrave – for whom she was once mistaken while on a plane – became a star despite her height.

And the slight cast in her eye, corrected by surgery in childhood but set to return at various stages of her life, also counted against her in the theatrical world of the 1940s and 1950s. Though today actresses like Imogen Stubbs have won acclaim despite having a squint, four decades ago it was considered an insurmountable obstacle to success on the stage.

Bronwen was unusually realistic for an eighteen-year-old about her own talent – or lack of it. It was as if simply being at Central – rather than Oxford – was enough for her. 'I think that great actresses succeed because they can let go of themselves and become totally someone else. I think that even at that stage I knew myself well enough to know that I couldn't do that. Obviously later there was an element of letting go in being a model girl, but then it was not about taking on another character. It was simply letting go. I could go half the way, but I was too self-conscious to be an actress.'

Perhaps the final deciding factor was the encouragement of her mentor, Margaret Braund, who was also pushing her towards the teachers' course. 'It was not that I didn't believe in her as an actress. It was rather that I knew she was an intelligent girl and one who would need academic stimulus. You got more of that in the third year of the teachers' course. For the first two it was virtually the same as the stage course, but in the third year the teachers did subjects like psychology and phonetics. And I also thought that she would make a good teacher. She had imagination and ideas and she could inspire others if she wanted to. Though at this stage she was still quite young for her years, she was quite mature in her dealings with others.'

After decamping from Dolgellau a term early, she spent the spring and summer of 1948 in Hampstead – part of it acting as housekeeper to her father while her mother packed up their home in Norfolk. Alun Pugh and his youngest daughter also went off together for a motoring holiday in Europe. The stated reason was so that Bronwen could practise her skills as a driver there. She was at the wheel most of the time and although driving on the opposite side of the road might not be considered as the best preparation for the British test, she nevertheless passed with flying colours on her return. 'We were always taught that getting your driving test was as important, if not more important, than getting your highers. It made you mobile and therefore independent. Being independent was the big thing.'

The real purpose of the trip to the continent, however, was to revisit some of the battlegrounds where Alun Pugh had served in the First World War. Father and daughter did not get as far as the trenches or the graveyards. When it came to that point, he couldn't go on. 'He wanted to try, but he couldn't face it. He didn't talk about it at all. I was just there.' The silence that seemed to encase the details of her father's wartime trauma persisted, but Bronwen became even more acutely aware of the pain it continued to cause him. Perhaps Alun Pugh chose his youngest daughter as his companion on this trip precisely because he knew that she – unlike her more assertive older sisters – would not press him to discuss topics that were difficult for him. She was content simply to let him be.

That summer between school and college Bronwen had her first romance. It was a short-lived, shared but unspoken passion, more an early and tentative stepping stone in her own emotional development than any significant pointer to her orientation. She fell for a girl of her own age, the daughter of Major-General Sir Francis Tuker, the Gurkha chief who had inspired her as a schoolgirl with his visits to Dr Williams', his letters from the front and his tales of bravery. Joan Tuker, the same age as Bronwen, lived on the family farm in Cornwall and the two met up several times that summer. Undoubtedly some of the awe with which Bronwen regarded Sir Francis was transferred on to Joan. 'I put her on a pedestal and just gazed adoringly at her. She had wonderful eyes and blonde hair. I think it was the first time I realised what romance was, that I began to understand how love could develop between two people, that I had had those feelings for anyone. It lasted six months and was reciprocated, but then I think we simply grew apart, me with my life in London and she down on the farm in Cornwall. We had nothing in common really.'

Joan was, like Bronwen, a third daughter and the two shared

similar frustrations about how they were simply expected to be like their successful older sisters. Bronwen compares their friendship to that of Sebastian Flyte and Charles Ryder in Evelyn Waugh's *Brideshead Revisited*, a stage both were going through on the road to adulthood. 'By the end, I knew I wasn't a lesbian. If anything it was like a practice before I entered a world where there would be men of my own age.' They lost touch but, soon after leaving Central, Bronwen heard that Joan Tuker had died tragically young of a brain tumour.

Bronwen started at Central in September 1948. For the first term all three groups – actors, teachers and therapists – had classes together. The focus was on the voice, under the guidance of Cicely Berry, later head of voice at the Royal Shakespeare Company. 'They'd tell us to come in in trousers and we would lie down on the floor and relax with lots of oohs and aahs,' recalls fellow student Diana de Wilton, 'and then the teacher would say something like, "Think of a sunny day in the country," and we'd all have to concentrate our minds on our feet and then work our way slowly up to our necks.' On another occasion they went off to visit the mortuary at the old Royal Free Hospital in Islington to inspect the lungs of dead bodies so as to understand how to breathe and project the voice.

There were twenty students on the teaching course. It was predominantly female, with just three men. Among the acting fraternity, the star of the year was the young Virginia McKenna, later to appear in *Born Free* and *A Town Like Alice*. It was the slight, elegant, conventional McKenna who was regarded as the great beauty of the set. Although the intake in 1948 was unusual in including some older students – recently demobbed from the forces, their education delayed by the war – the atmosphere at Central was less like a modern-day university and more an extension of school. The timetable was rigid, free time scarce and a well-ordered, disciplined and slightly parsimonious feel pervaded the whole institution, radiating out from Gwynneth Thurburn's office. 'It was always vital,' she recalled of this early period of her principalship, 'that if we were to keep going, we should not waste a pennyworth of electricity or a piece of paper, a habit that has become ingrained in me. If we had not kept to Queen Victoria's remark – "We are not interested in the possibility of defeat" – we should probably not be here today.'

The controlled environment of Central was then for many of its younger students a transition point between the childish world of school and adult society rather than a straight transfer. There were, of course, new departures from school life, among them famous names on the teaching staff. The playwright Christopher Fry was a tutor, as was Stephen Joseph, later to be immortalised when Alan Ayckbourn helped fund a theatre named after him in Scarborough. One of the most distinguished voice coaches at Central was the poet and essayist L. A. G. Strong, by chance an old school friend of Alun Pugh. He would take each of his pupils to lunch on nearby Kensington High Street each term. He regarded them as adults and treated them accordingly.

Yet the freedoms now associated with student life barely existed for Bronwen and her colleagues. In part it was the prevailing social mores of the time. After the wartime blip, these had settled down into more traditional patterns. More influential was the precarious economic state of Britain. It was a grey and serious world, with only Labour's initial radical fervour for a centralised, managed economy to set people aglow. When that ran out, along in August 1947 with the American loans that had shored up the British economy, rationing bit ever harder, shop shelves were empty and pessimism set in. The great winter crisis of 1947 was the prelude to Bronwen's arrival at Central. It was one of the coldest on record, and the mines could not supply the power stations so electricity rationing was instituted. There were fines for switching on a light outside prescribed hours. The lack of housing – some half a million homes had been destroyed during the aerial bombardment of Britain – loomed large in many lives, with endless waiting lists even for temporary 'prefabs'. Many despaired of ever reaching the top and between 1946 and 1949 1.25 million Britons emigrated to Canada, Australia, New Zealand and Southern Rhodesia.

Basic foodstuffs remained restricted until 1954 – one egg a week, three ounces of butter, one pound of meat. And clothes were bought by coupon until 1949. While Christian Dior's 'New Look', launched in Paris in early 1947, captured the public imagination, its long skirts and flowing lines harking back to an earlier age of plenty, young women in Britain had to make do with dull and utilitarian garments purchased with coupons. Even Princess Elizabeth struggled to acquire the 300 coupons needed for the Norman Hartnell wedding dress she wore when, on 20 November 1947, she married Philip Mountbatten in Westminster Abbey.

Bronwen, liberated at last from the green and blue ensemble of Dr Williams', did not let the post-war restrictions constrain her from developing a style of her own. On a limited allowance from her father and faced by the absence of choice in shops, she turned to dress-making with the grey satin and pink lace she could scramble together. The boat neckline was in vogue, worn without sleeves. 'It must have looked so drab, I've never had any idea about colours, but I thought it was the most marvellous thing in the world.'

In contrast to most, she was once again privileged – not only in her freedom to attend the decidedly un-utilitarian environment of a drama college, but also economically. The differentials that had been eroded in the Pughs' life by war were restored. When she turned twenty-one in June 1951, her last month at Central, she received the then considerable sum of £1,000 as her part of her maternal grandfather's will. It enabled her to buy her first car – a convertible Morris Eight – and later to move out into her own flat, a radical departure in the early 1950s for a young, attractive, unmarried woman of her class. Usually flying the nest only took place when the parental home was being exchanged for the marital one, but the Pughs, anxious as ever that their daughters should be independent, raised no objections. Bronwen may not have moved in the same world or same league as her contemporaries among the blue-blooded debut-antes who were still being presented at court, but she led a cushioned, privileged and in many senses thoroughly modern life.

For her student days and beyond, though, Pilgrims Lane remained home. She would take the tube in each morning and return every evening. Relations with her mother, never close, became at least more relaxed. Kathleen Pugh had been appointed a magistrate on the local bench. Whatever frustrations she had felt in the pre-war years at her own lack of a career were thereby assuaged and she began to resent her youngest daughter a little less. Gwyneth, working as a journalist for a farming magazine after completing her degree at Oxford, continued to be close to Bronwen, but after a short career as a sub-editor, in 1949 Ann married Reginald Hibbert, her boyfriend from Oxford, and followed this bright, high-flying diplomat overseas on a Foreign Office career that culminated in his appointment as British ambassador in Paris in 1979 and a knighthood. Constantly abroad, Ann was largely absent from her younger sister's life in the decades ahead.

In 1950, when Bronwen was just twenty, tragedy struck when David Pugh died of cancer at the age of thirty-three. He had served in the ranks in Germany during the war, but as ever his record had disappointed his parents, who would have liked to see him an officer. His marriage – to a Welsh girl on St David's Day 1943 – should have pleased his father. It was by all accounts a happy union, but again the Pughs harboured reservations, suspecting that Marion Pugh was chasing what she supposed to be her in-laws' wealth. After his demobilisation, David Pugh was dogged by ill-health and in 1949 cancer was diagnosed in his groin. Further tests revealed that it had already spread all around his body and within a couple of months he was dead. 'It shattered my parents,' says Bronwen. 'He had never been the son they wanted. He had an unusual mind. He had perfect recall, could remember telephone numbers, facts and figures, but he could never pass exams. He was weak, sickly and highly strung. When he died there was such remorse, especially when they realised the reasons for his illness.'

A post-mortem revealed that David Pugh had a small foetus inside his ribs. During her pregnancy Kathleen Pugh, doctors suggested, had originally been carrying twins, but the fertilised ovum had not divided into two as it usually does. Instead David had absorbed his twin. It is a very rare, but recognised medical condition, though usually it is discovered soon after the surviving twin is born.* The Pughs believed that it could have explained David's ill-health and physical weakness. It also cast an interesting psychological light on

---

* In a recent similar case in Egypt, reported in British medical journals, a sixteen-year-old builder went to see his doctor with severe stomach pains. An X-ray revealed a swollen sac pressing against his kidneys and containing his unborn twin, a seven-inch long foetus, weighing more than four pounds. It had a head, an arm, a tongue and teeth. Like an incubus it had been surviving inside the sixteen-year-old, feeding off him.

his insistence, even into his late teens, on having a place set at table for his imaginary friend 'Fern'.

For Alun and Kathleen Pugh, the tragedy of their son's premature death left a lasting scar. Ann Hibbert remains convinced that the grief her mother felt damaged her health and eventually contributed to the stroke she suffered many years later. For Bronwen, though, David's death, while regretted and mourned, was something she could recover from. The age difference between them had meant that the two had never been close. However, the loss of her brother may have had one lasting effect on her life. Alun Pugh had made no secret of his ambitions for his children. His son had not satisfied him. His eldest daughter had chosen marriage and a supporting role over a career of her own. Gwyneth was happy taking a back seat. Bronwen's natural ambition – apparent but carefully reined in as she went to Central – may have been sparked by the desire, in some way, to make good her beloved father's disappointment.

Bronwen soon fell in with a crowd at Central. She made up a foursome with fellow students Diana de Wilton, Erica Pickard and Joan Murray. They were an oddly symmetrical quartet – two tall, two short, two fair, two dark. While they all came from middle-class backgrounds and shared a similar sense of humour and a youthful determination to be frivolous whatever the gloomy national outlook, the four had contrasting but complementary characters. Diana de Wilton was a reserved, unconfident, convent-educated Irish Catholic from Tunbridge Wells, brought up by adoptive parents, while Joan Murray, small, witty and outgoing, had a Scottish father and French Jewish mother. It was Erica Pickard, however, who was the pivot of the group. The other three all regarded her as their special friend. Bronwen Pugh, even as a student, still lived in the shadow of others – her sisters, the glamorous Virginia McKenna and, within her own circle, Erica.

In Erica – as with Joan Tuker – Bronwen was again drawn to the third of three daughters, though this time there was no hint of romance in their friendship. And like Bronwen, Erica was trying to break the family mould. Her two elder sisters had become doctors. She was determined not to follow in their footsteps. There was, friends remember, something compelling and unusual about Erica. For a start, her family lived in Geneva, where her father taught at the university. She had spent the war years in America and that experience also contributed to her standing out from her peers.

'She arrived with this American preppy look,' Diana de Wilton remembers, 'skirts and jumpers and blouses with little collars. We were all still in twin set and pearls, though under Erica's influence we soon changed. And she was freer in thought, much more adult. I'd been to a convent where there was no freedom of thought, but Erica would take me to Quaker meetings "to broaden my mind". I used to worry that I was committing a sin.' Erica also had a more mature attitude to men than her three friends – all of them straight out of protective all-girl schools. 'She was freer in her thoughts about boys and sex and those things,' says Diana de Wilton. 'Not that any of us were in any way experienced, but she was just less buttoned up. We tried to follow her lead.' While the other three all lived at home, Erica enjoyed the freedom of her own flat in Golders Green, shared with one of her sisters.

All four – with the possible exception of Erica Pickard – were naive and unworldly in their dealings with men. For Bronwen there would be great romantic crushes that faded before the man in question even realised she was interested. If he then made a move, she would already have passed on to another equally unrequited passion. Men, in general, were regarded as desirable but optional and often little more than a subject of amusement. Alun Pugh's efforts to introduce his daughter to eminently suitable but sensible young barristers across the dining table at Pilgrims Lane therefore failed to move her. 'They would always be saying, "Well, what about so-and-so, there's nothing wrong with him?" One of their candidates became known to us all as "poor Smith" because he was always wanting to take me out and I wasn't interested. It wasn't that I didn't want romance, but I had no wish for anything serious, let alone thoughts of marriage.'

Despite being a young eighteen in many ways, she had a clear and unfashionable view that life had to be about more than marriage and settling down. 'We had men friends, but they were never intense partnerships at all. We'd often swap boyfriends between the four of us. And then we'd drop them really just because we felt like it. It was all very innocent and casual. We were far too inhibited for it to be anything more serious. There was no pill so you didn't have sex. Nice girls like us didn't do it for fear of what might happen. If you did then it would be the person you intended marrying and I wasn't thinking about marriage at all.' Only later did her father tell her that she had left a trail of broken hearts in the Inns of Court.

Outside hours, the four young women would head off to the coffee bars and salad counters that were just starting to open up in the capital. There they would bury their heads in fashion magazines, planning what dizzy dress-making heights they would aspire to over the weekend with whatever they could get on coupons, though Bronwen now recalls that she invariably looked tatty. In the evenings they frequented the West End theatres – half a crown in the gods and then a long walk home. Laurence Olivier was a particular favourite of all four, while the link with Christopher Fry through Central got them into the first night of his celebrated verse play *Ring Round the Moon* at the Globe in 1950.

Otherwise there were parties, though Bronwen was twenty before she stayed out all night – at a sleepover at Joan Murray's. 'My parents were never strict, but if I was going to be late I'd tell them where I was, whom I was with and when I would get back. I always made sure that I was there on time.' She began smoking, more because it was the done thing than through any overwhelming addiction, and enjoyed the occasional drink, though seldom to excess. Though she had ambitions to be a free spirit and mould-breaker, the Pughs' youngest daughter gave her parents few sleepless nights.

The four young friends would often congregate at Pilgrim's Lane. On one occasion Alun Pugh took his youngest daughter and her friends to court for the day. 'We had asked him something about the law,' says Diana de Wilton, 'and he had then decided we should see what goes on at first hand. He was a very kind man, and charming too, but he could still be a little bit frightening. I remember him asking me what books I liked to read. I was only nineteen and shy and said, "*Rebecca*". "Oh," he said, "can't you think of anything better than that?" I felt so ashamed.'

The unspoken assumption all through the course at Central was that it would lead to a career in teaching. Towards the end of the final term there was a tour of Home Counties' schools, with the students producing and performing *Companion to a Lady*, *The Harlequinade* and the obscure *Second Shepherd's Play*. Bronwen's role was mostly on the production side.

After passing her final examinations and getting her diploma in June 1951, she turned her mind to finding a job. A selection of vacancies was displayed on the school noticeboard and she got the first post she applied for – at Croft House School, Shillingstone, in Dorset. That enduring lack of planning again played a part in her life for, had she made any preliminary enquiries, she would have realised it was a place to be avoided. Croft House was an odd set-up, run in their home by an eccentric, elderly couple, the Torkingtons, known to their disgruntled staff (for reasons that are now obscure) as Caesar and Pop. Miss Pugh's classroom was in a greenhouse.

The pupils were all girls and had originally come to Croft House to keep the Torkingtons' own daughter company as she was educated at home. It had subsequently grown in size but lacked any strong guiding principle beyond keeping its young ladies occupied during the school term. It was certainly not an outstandingly academic environment. When any girl passed her school certificate, it was announced at assembly and everyone clapped in surprise and awe. Such an achievement was something out of the ordinary. More often than not, a pony club rosette was all a girl had to show for five years at Croft House.

To her surprise, Bronwen found she enjoyed teaching. Or she enjoyed working with individual pupils. In front of a class full of disgruntled and unmotivated girls, however, she soon realised that her father's ambitions for her to be a headmistress were misplaced. 'My classes ended up uproarious, with me laughing almost as much as the girls. Since as well as teaching drama and voice, I was also their form teacher, I was summoned by the owners and asked to explain my behaviour. They asked how I was going to punish my class. When I suggested one idea, they countered with another. On my plate at the next meal time was my notice.'

Bronwen had lasted a year, by which stage she had become one of the longest-serving teachers. The Torkingtons had a habit of falling

out with their staff over money, discipline or their unorthodox
but dogmatic approach. Throughout the year she had managed to
keep one foot in Dorset and one back in London, shuttling between
the two in her car. Though Joan Murray had married the future
television and film director Christopher Morahan straight after leaving Central, Bronwen, Erica and Diana would head off in search of
adventure.

Once they motored up to Oxford to visit Nigel Buxton, an
undergraduate there who had previously been lodging at the house
in Pilgrims Lane. Through Buxton, later a successful journalist
and travel writer, they were able to taste a little of the Oxford social
scene that Bronwen had rejected as part of her decision to go to
Central. It led to invitations to summer balls next to the Cherwell
and even to Bronwen making such good friends at Oxford that
in the summer of 1952 she joined some of them for a holiday in
Europe.

When he had been lodging at Pilgrims Lane, Buxton had caught
Bronwen's eye and she had developed quite a crush on him, but by
the time she visited him at Oxford her romantic thoughts had, as
ever and girlishly, moved on. He, however, was now keen on her,
as he confided to Diana de Wilton, but the object of his ardour was
now unobtainable. 'It was typical of me at the time,' Bronwen now
says. 'I was so very impatient.'

Bronwen spent the Christmas of 1951 in Geneva with the Pickards.
She and Erica both admitted to each other that they were disappointed by teaching and feared that they had drifted, unthinkingly,
into a career that held little enjoyment for them. So, together, they
dreamt up a route to adventure. With their heads buried in fashion
magazines, the solution was obvious – be a model girl. It is now a
standard teenage fantasy, but in the early 1950s it was an ambitious
plan because the status of the model girl was still somewhat dubious.
When, in the middle of the nineteenth century, the first mannequins
had appeared in Paris, they were little more than glorified shop girls.
Certainly it was not a career any bourgeois family would consider
suitable for its daughters. 'At the beginning of the century,' the
designer Pierre Balmain wrote, 'mannequins were not accepted in
society . . . they were often girls of easy virtue who dined in private

rooms at Maxim's and were slow to take umbrage if followed in the Rue de la Paix.'

Later, however, in the early years of the twentieth century, the advent of the Gibson girls added a new veneer of respectability to the profession. Named after the society artist Charles Dana Gibson, these big-busted, pinch-waisted young women, all with classical hour-glass figures, first featured in his work and later achieved national celebrity as the epitome of feminine beauty. The original Gibson girl – and the artist's wife – was Irene Langhorne, whose younger sister Nancy was Lady Astor and who therefore became Bronwen's aunt by marriage. Through Gibson, Irene Langhorne turned the archetypal southern belle into the icon of young American women for almost two decades.

Until the Second World War a slightly seedy pall had continued to hang over the whole business of modelling, especially in Europe, with many of its practitioners rumoured also to be dispensing sexual favours. Only in the late forties and fifties did it become a desirable thing for a well-bred girl to do. This was first and foremost a commercial development. Those selling couture clothes realised that their customers were well-to-do and respectable women who would respond to seeing the garments they were about to purchase shown off by a young woman of the same class and background as themselves.

So Bronwen and Erica were among the first generation of young women able to read in fashion magazines of the glamorous but squeaky-clean lives of well-born and thoroughly upright models like British-born Jean Dawnay or the Americans Dorian Leigh and Suzy Parker, both immortalised by the celebrated fashion photographer Richard Avedon. These women were fêted as stars and role models in the Hollywood mould. As Dawnay herself put it, in Paris in this period modelling 'became an accepted profession, whereas before it was looked down upon as something into which men put their mistresses'. Dawnay, a household name in the early 1950s, set the seal on the new-found respectability of modelling when she married into the European aristocracy and became Princess George Galitzine.

In Erica Pickard's case there was sufficient charisma and conventional good looks to make a career in modelling more than a pipe dream. 'She had a lovely face, wonderful features and she was always slim,' Bronwen remembers. 'The only thing that marred her was her teeth. They crossed over slightly but we decided they could be sorted out.' In Bronwen's case, though, aspiring to be a model was a radical departure. She certainly had a theatrical side that liked performing, but only three years earlier she had lacked the confidence even to try for the actors' course at Central. And up to this point there had been no hint that either she or anyone in her family regarded her as a great beauty.

Quite the opposite, her former nanny Bella Wells remembers. The orthodox line in the Pugh family remained that Ann was the beauty and Gwyneth the clever one, with Bronwen lost in a no man's land between the two. Yet there was an obvious appeal in modelling for a young woman who had grown up feeling herself unwanted and who had therefore spent a good deal of energy in encouraging, cajoling and forcing her parents to 'look at me'. This was attention-seeking turned into an adult profession.

Erica's encouragement was crucial. According to Bronwen, 'We never thought it would work, but we would look at the model girls in the magazines, look at ourselves and I would say, "You could do that," to Erica, and then she would say to me, "And you could too." It was a game, but slightly more than that – a challenge.' Erica made Bronwen believe that her wild eyes and strong bone structure could be assets for a model girl, but the same problem that had blocked her path as an actress – her height – also made it seem unlikely that she would succeed in a world where short women were the most highly prized. (Dawnay, for example, was a petite, curvaceous blond.) And there was also the issue of her squint.

Diana de Wilton was another who could see beyond such eventually minor details to glimpse an unconventional beauty in Bronwen. De Wilton in particular was struck by her mannerisms. 'She had this way of standing and walking. She had poise. When I look at our student photographs she had a way of placing her hands and turning her head that I now see made her a natural for modelling.'

Back in London after the Christmas break, Erica and Bronwen might well have forgotten their dream had they not read of a competition for budding model girls in *Vogue*. It was a diversion, but, bored by their everyday lives, they went at it wholeheartedly and had their portfolios made up by a high street photographer in Kensington. It was, they knew, a million-to-one shot, and their number did not come up. Modelling was put to one side and there it might have remained but for a tragic accident which changed the course of Bronwen's life.

Soon after Easter 1952 Erica Pickard was standing on the open platform of a London bus when it swung round a corner. She was reaching over to press the stop bell and lost her grip. She fell out on to the pavement, cracking her skull against the curb as she tumbled. She was rushed to St Bartholomew's Hospital in a coma. Her friends and family kept up a vigil at her bedside, but three days later she died at the age of just twenty-two.

'It had a devastating effect on all of us,' says Diana de Wilton. 'I can only liken its effect on our group to the effect of Princess Diana's death on the whole nation. We were used to older people dying, but when someone young, someone you know dies, then you realise your own mortality for the first time.' For Bronwen it went further. It thrust her overnight into adulthood and precipitated a complete re-evaluation of her life and beliefs.

She was distraught. Of the four friends, she and Erica had grown the closest in the year after leaving Central. 'I went to the funeral at Golders Green crematorium. When the coffin disappeared behind the screen, I heard this unearthly scream. It took a while for me to realise that it had come from me. I had to go back to school to teach straight away afterwards. One day, six weeks later, at tea I saw this piece of cake on my plate and couldn't remember taking it. That's when I realised I had been on auto-pilot. It was as if I had suddenly come round from concussion.'

Physically it may only have taken her six weeks to get over the shock, but the mental turmoil caused by Erica's death was to remain with her for many years, pushing her ever more in on herself as she struggled to work out what the tragedy had meant. 'I hadn't realised that death could be so sudden. I'd lived through the war. I knew that people died. Yet Erica's death changed everything.'

In coping with her grief, Bronwen turned naturally to the Pickard family. They clutched her to their bosom and tried to persuade her to take over Erica's London flat in Golders Green and to apply for Erica's job as a way of escaping the horrors of Dorset. She was reluctant, unwilling to step into the dead girl's shoes at this vulnerable moment. She had fallen out with the Torkingtons and, if she was to stay in teaching, would need to start looking for another job. Yet she wasn't sure teaching was for her. She liked one-to-one encounters but hated the classroom. And at least at Croft House School the timetable had been relaxed. Elsewhere the very sides of teaching she disliked the most – the discipline, the regimentation – would loom larger.

More broadly, Erica's death focused her attention on the monotony of her day-to-day life. Was this how she wanted to spend her time here, however long or short? If she died tomorrow, would she feel fulfilled? Or was she in danger of falling in, after a brief period of rebellion, with the plan mapped out for her by her own family?

She knew she had to make a decision but was unsure which way to turn. The catalyst came from an unexpected quarter. She was invited to dinner by her old tutor from Central, L. A. G. Strong. 'I said the usual thing, "Why this, why Erica, what now?" And he said, "Why did she choose you as her best friend?" And it was as if a light was turned on. As we talked I mentioned our idea of being model girls. I began to realise that one way to cope with Erica's death was to follow that dream. She had given me the courage and confidence to try it, she had made me think it was possible. It wasn't so much that over dinner I thought, "Oh yes, I can be a model girl"; it was that he set me thinking about what inner qualities she had recognised in me and what I should now do with them.'

Much later she was to realise that living out their daydream was a form of grief therapy, a way of blocking out the unanswerable questions that had suddenly descended on her after Erica's death. Ultimately it was those questions that initiated Bronwen's conscious spiritual journey, for the loss of her friend touched directly – as no event in her hitherto short life had – on the spiritual dimension that she had long been aware of, but which she had kept carefully hidden away and separated from her student friends and her family. 'I think my father realised, though we never talked about it. And Gwyneth. But my mother and Ann had no inkling and even if they did, they would have had no sympathy.' To this day Ann remains resolutely sceptical about Bronwen's religious experiences.

Bronwen had taken tentative steps to reveal this inner dimension to her friends, knowing that she could no longer keep it bottled up. Leading a double life was, she came to see, unsatisfying. Some of her crowd had been unreceptive. Others had noticed but could not follow it up. Diana de Wilton, for instance, vaguely noted Bronwen's tendency, whenever performing a passage for voice-training at Central, to choose something spiritual, like a Gerard Manley Hopkins poem. Yet she was never taken into Bronwen's confidence.

On the surface there were few other clues. As a student Bronwen drifted away from any sort of formal church attendance. What she had experienced, she convinced herself, had little to do with organised religion. But with Erica it was different. 'From the very start, all my insights into this parallel world had been about love – "Only love matters" is what I had heard that first time at the birthday party when I was seven. And it was so painful when Erica died, that I thought I had to stop loving. But equally I knew I couldn't harden my heart. For a while I just shut down. That was my way of coping.'

And she might have remained 'shut down', closed to this other world, perhaps for ever, had not her meeting with L. A. G. Strong prompted her to follow her heart. Having a go at modelling became a small part of what was ultimately a wider liberation and discarding of conventional restraints that helped to form her later self. It was the outward sign that something had changed within her, but she did not know quite what for another eight years. Modelling gave her the space to find out.

Although hitherto she had had little inclination for books, after Erica's death Bronwen became an uninhibited and often daring reader, working her way through a constant stream of sometimes enlightening and some disappointing texts – history, fiction, science, religion, psychology. Occasionally in the course of her life she has come across a book that has changed the way she thinks or opened up another perspective. Having, by her own choice, missed out on a university education, she has taught herself through books.

She was introduced to the writings of Georgei Ivanovitch Gurdjieff (1874–1949) and his sometime disciple Peter Demianovitch Ouspensky (1879–1947). Both had died recently and she was directed to them, casually, by someone she met at a party. 'You can imagine what I was like at parties then, very intense, always wanting to talk about ideas and only interested in people if they had something interesting to say.'

In the late 1940s and early 1950s among a younger generation of readers reacting, it has subsequently been suggested, to the recent world war with an abnormal degree of introspection and an over-eager and sometimes naive search for alternative paths, Gurdjieff and Ouspensky achieved the sort of cult status later enjoyed by Indian mystics in the sixties. They were, for Bronwen and many others in that period, a revelation and a first introduction to psychology.

Both were Russian, though Gurdjieff had Greek parents. Both were fascinated by the occult and experiments to prove that magic had an objective worth. But their enduring influence – certainly in Bronwen's life – was their emphasis on the need for each individual to develop psychological insights in order to grow into a new state of higher consciousness. Such insights, she came to believe, could bridge the gap between her everyday world and the spiritual world she had glimpsed.

About Gurdjieff himself opinions were divided, even in his life-time. His supporters – who included the New Zealand-born short-story writer, Katherine Mansfield – regarded him as a prophet and philosopher without equal. Kenneth Walker, a writer who was one of many who were drawn to the Institute for the Harmonious Development of Man in Fontainbleau, described its leader as 'the arch disturber of self-complacency', but the press at the time and historians subsequently have judged Gurdjieff less kindly. R. B. Woodings, the distinguished chronicler of twentieth-century thought, sums him up thus: 'His ideas are not original, his sources can be readily traced and the movement he stimulated was obviously part of reawakening of interest in the occult in the earlier part of this century.' However, Woodings is in no doubt about the impact of Gurdjieff. 'Whether charlatan, mystic, scoundrel or "master", he exercised remarkable authority charismatically over his disciples and by reputation over much wider American and European circles.'

Ouspensky – for nine years until 1924 Gurdjieff's self-appointed 'apostle' – was no less popular and now enjoys a little more academic credibility. Again he inspired a cult-like following, based on his estate at Virginia Water in Surrey, but he had a sounder grasp of philosophy than Gurdjieff and had studied both mathematics and Nietzsche before dabbling in the occult and theosophy, the belief system promoted in the late nineteenth and early twentieth century by his fellow Russian Helena Blavatsky and her American associate, Henry Steele Olcott, which embraced Hindu ideas of karma and reincarnation.

And it was Ouspensky who made the greater impact on Bronwen. His *The Fourth Way*, published soon after his death in 1947, brought together many of the ideas he had relentlessly explored in his lifetime. It introduced Bronwen to eastern thought, which she found considerably more attractive than Christianity, and it described in detail his 'system' for greater self-knowledge and enlightenment. 'The chief idea of this system,' he wrote, 'was that we do not use even a small part of our powers and forces. We have in us, a very big and very fine organisation, only we do not know how to use it.' The idea, then, was to study oneself, following Ouspensky's guidance.

This ranged from the mundane to the enlightening to the foolish. 'We are divided,' he claimed, 'into hundreds and thousands of different "I"'s. At one moment when I say "I", one part of me is speaking, at another moment when I say "I" it is quite another "I" speaking. We do not know that we have not one "I", but many different "I"'s connected with our feelings and desires and have no controlling "I". These "I"'s change all the time; one suppresses another, one replaces another, and all this struggle makes up our inner life.'

To a young, impressionable woman who felt herself torn between the material and spiritual parts of her life, such ideas appeared attractive. She had already realised that she had two apparently contradictory impulses pushing her forward. One was the outgoing, fun-loving, meet-any-challenge, sporty side that was now drawing her to modelling. The other – a legacy, she was sure, from her Welsh ancestors – was driven by a solitary, contemplative, inward-looking instinct that made her want to run away from the world, curl up in a ball and search through books and thought for an answer to why Erica had died in such a tragic way. Ouspensky helped her at least to recognise these two faces within herself and gave her clues as to their origins.

When later he talked about the 'negative emotions' bequeathed by childhood and parents and the need to confront these in order to move to a higher level of consciousness, Ouspensky was speaking directly to Bronwen's own experience, but it would be a mistake to imagine that she became any sort of convert to his cult. She was enthusiastic about her introduction to psychology and to discussions of levels of consciousness – Ouspensky declared there were four – and she was heartened to know that others too were struggling with the sort of questions she had hitherto tackled in secret and largely alone, but Ouspensky was simply a starting point.

In the light of her subsequent determination to combine psychological insights with organised religion – though of course at this time she was a lapsed Anglican – Ouspensky's antipathy to belief should be noted. Despite borrowing from eastern and western religious creeds, Ouspensky boasted that his system 'teaches people to believe in absolutely nothing. You must verify everything that you see, hear or feel.' And some of the conclusions to which he took initially attractive ideas appeared ridiculous, even to one as inexperienced and naive as Bronwen at that stage. His theories about the effect of earthly vibrations on the mind and his peculiar mathematical tangle, 'the ray of Creation', ascribing numerically quantified 'forces' to a series of worlds (which themselves were listed from one to ninety-six) must have been difficult for even the most avid follower to swallow.

Yet Ouspensky and Gurdjieff initiated a search for a complementary psychological and spiritual framework that has since dominated Bronwen's life. In her student days and as she took her first faltering steps into the adult world of work, the two principal elements within her and hence in her story began to unravel – the spiritual and the material. At the same time as she was setting her sights on the flimsy, fun and throwaway world of model girls, with their jetset lifestyles, headline-grabbing antics and aristocratic suitors, she embarked on a lonely and often painful journey to understand her own psyche and soul.

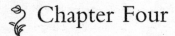# Chapter Four

> One of the many reasons why it is difficult to make a start as a
> model is that, although the photographers and fashion houses
> are crying out for new faces, when it comes to the point none
> of them want to take the risk of trying out a new girl while she
> is still green.
>
> Jean Dawnay, *Model Girl* (1956)

The fashion world recovered more quickly than most industries from
the dislocation of the war. In Paris in February 1947 Christian Dior's
'New Look' thrilled critics, buyers and public alike. 'It's quite a
revolution, dear Christian,' remarked Carmel Snow, reporting for
Harper's Bazaar, at the unveiling of Dior's dramatic, narrow-waisted,
low-cut, very feminine and distinctly nostalgic collection, harking
back, some experts said, to the hour-glass silhouette of the 1890s.
'Your dresses have such a new look. They're quite wonderful.'

Snow had coined a phrase to emphasise Dior's break with the
drab, austere and utilitarian style of the war years, symbolised by his
abundant use of material after a period in which it had been severely
rationed. Dior, Snow claimed with some truth, had done more,
however, than simply create a style. 'He has saved Paris as Paris was
saved in the Battle of the Marne.'

For there had been doubts expressed about the French capital's
ability to regain its pre-war dominance of the fashion industry, notably with American buyers. Certainly during the war years Paris had
lost its crown when Hollywood brought together fashion and film
to make New York's Seventh Avenue the place to be, but the
transatlantic clamour that followed the launch of the New Look –
Olivia de Havilland and Rita Hayworth were amongst the Hollywood
stars who rushed to place orders – ensured that Paris was back at the
top of the tree. Pierre Balmain, Jacques Fath and Cristobal Balenciaga

all contributed to this pre-eminence; by 1950 they had been joined by Pierre Cardin, two years later by Hubert de Givenchy. But it was Dior who reigned supreme.

In so far as Paris entertained any European rivals, they were Rome and Florence, where designers like Capucci, Pucci, Simonetta, Fabiani and Galitzine were admired, if not held in quite such global high esteem as Dior and his near neighbours. In the fashion industry, London remained something of an enigma. It considered itself as good as, if not better than, Paris and certainly looked down on the Italians. Throughout the 1950s the universal penchant amongst Europe's designers for classically English tailored evening dresses and tweed suits as part of an exaggeratedly aristocratic look contributed to London's self-assuredness. But the irony was that the driving force behind this English look was Paris, which took the safe lines coming out of London – 'knights' wives clothes', as they were sometimes unkindly labelled – and turned them into something special.

The traffic was, in reality, two-way. London had been touched by the shock waves that issued forth from Paris with the New Look. Like the rest of the fashion world, it followed Dior's lead. Yet it did so in moderation, sticking to its own particular style and developing its own innovations – like coloured furs. Jean Dawnay, who worked with the top designers on both sides of the English Channel before she retired as a model girl in 1956, sums up the subleties of the battle with an anecdote. While working at Dior, she was sent as one of a small team to show some of the house's latest designs at the French embassy in London. The clothes had a strongly English look. To acknowledge his design debt to his hosts, Dior decided that his designs should be made up in British tweeds and worsteds. According to Dawnay, the gesture backfired when the flowing dresses she had worn in Paris overnight became stiff and ungainly when made from home-spun cloth. They did not move with her body but stood out in counterpoint to it. Only the most formal suits and evening dresses translated well. 'The English designers catered almost exclusively for the smart English families,' says Dawnay. 'If they were having a ball or a coming-out party, they would go to Hardy Amies for a dress and so on. It was very insular, had its own standards and was rather dismissive of anywhere else.'

The global commercial reality, as Bronwen Pugh embarked on her career as a model girl in 1952, was that London, for all its pride and introspective one-upmanship, remained very much a stopping-off point for American buyers on their way to the main market, Paris. It wasn't until several years later that Mary Quant and Alexander Plunket Greene launched their Bazaar shop on Chelsea's King's Road and revolutionised London's standing. As yet their particular new look was nothing more than the dream of fashion college students.

For a decade and a half after the war the London market was dominated by twelve names who joined forces in the Incorporated Society of London Fashion Designers. Worth, Norman Hartnell, Charles Creed, Neil 'Bunny' Roger, John Cavanagh, Digby Morton, Ronald Patterson and Hardy Amies were among the best-known stars in this galaxy, each putting on two shows a year – in January and July – where they unveiled their couture collections. Below them was a layer of younger designers, the Model House Group, who made their living by adapting last year's couture house creations from Paris. And then there were the ready-to-wear houses, from smart names like Jaeger through to high street chains like Richards Shops. The days of the big names doing anything other than making individual items to order for a wealthy, predominantly older clientele had not yet dawned.

The timeless, upper-crust English quality of the designs of Amies or Hartnell, their appeal for a female audience looking for sensible suits for a weekend's shooting in the country or a frock for a presentation at court, chimed well with the era. After the grey years of Labour centralisation of the economy, the election of a Conservative government in 1951 heralded both an end to rationing and a welcome return to some of the pleasures of pre-war days. London was loosening up. Taking their lead from the young Queen Elizabeth II on her accession in 1952, women who followed fashion aspired to a classical simplicity that mirrored the dress codes of the landed classes at play.

This was what the satirist and social historian Christopher Booker has described as 'the strange Conservative interlude of the fifties':

By the summer of 1953, the glittering coronation of a new young queen, marked in a suitably imperial gesture by the conquest of Everest, was a symbol that during the years of hardship the old traditions had been merely sleeping. People were once again dressing for dinner and for Ascot . . . Debutantes once again danced away June nights on the river, to the strains of Tommy Kinsman and the splash of champagne bottles thrown by their braying escorts. Unmistakably British society seemed to be returning from a long dark night to sunnier and more normal times.

It was a time when government and electors alike convinced themselves that Britain was back where it had been in 1939. 'It's just like pre-war' was the phrase on everyone's lips – before Suez, economic reverses, angry young men, the Lady Chatterley trial and finally the Profumo scandal destroyed the illusion and ushered in the new, brutal and classless world of the 1960s. In this interval a particular sort of upper-class conduct, confidence and style were the dominating social and cultural goals. Harold Macmillan's governments, containing such a heavy contingent of peers that on paper they seemed like pre-1914 administrations, contributed to the process. The look that Bronwen Pugh came to embody – aristocratic, detached, elegant – reflected the general mood and had an emblematic quality.

The London fashion world did have one up on Paris in that it had adopted the American system of agents for model girls. In the States Eileen Ford, the godmother of model agents, had built up her agency from scratch in 1946, representing two of the most important US models of the decade, Suzy Parker and Dorian Leigh. In Paris such innovations were not allowed for fear that they would become little more than glorified escort agencies, but in London they advertised in the phone book and were run by outwardly frightening but often benign men and women who provided the respectability and parental-style security that ushered middle-class girls like first Jean Dawnay and later Bronwen into the profession.

With her teaching career behind her and her heart set on fulfilling the frivolous dream she had shared with Erica, Bronwen went about getting herself on one of the agency's books. The first name she tried was Pat Larthe. Dawnay, trail-blazer in the new wave of post-war British models, provided an uncomfortable picture in her autobiography of Larthe's working methods. At the dawn of her career, Dawnay, like Bronwen almost a decade after her, had nervously presented herself at Larthe's office in London's Covent Garden only to find ten other hopefuls in the waiting room, clutching their portfolios and fiddling with their hair.

When she was finally summoned into the inner sanctum she was greeted by a tough, theatrical woman, sheltering behind a vast telephone-laden desk. 'The interview was short and humiliating. I showed Miss Larthe my pictures. She barely seemed to glance at them before telling me I was too ordinary, that modelling was the toughest, most soul-destroying profession in the world, and that girls who had far more than I in the way of looks and figure got nowhere.' Dawnay was reduced to tears. That appeared to be Larthe's intention, perhaps – to take the most charitable option – calculating that it was better if it was done by her now rather than by someone else further down the line. Having destroyed the younger woman's self-confidence, she could then appear her protector. She took Dawnay under her wing, directed her first to favoured photographers, then got her bookings at the less glamorous end of the market – shows at Scarborough hotels – and finally helped her to make the leap to the top London houses.

Bronwen's first impression of Larthe was equally unfavourable. 'I just turned up in her office and said, "I want to be a model." She looked at me and said bluntly, "You're too tall and you squint."' Most hopefuls would have turned and walked out. A few months previously so would Bronwen, but in the aftermath of Erica's death she clung to the idea of modelling as her salvation. She could not afford such dramatic gestures when Larthe potentially held the key to success. 'Then Pat asked me to walk across the room and I must have done something right. She said she wouldn't put me on her books, but she'd teach me how to be a model.'

Bronwen accepted this less-than-overwhelming offer without a second thought. She and another hopeful would turn up after hours at Larthe's office every evening for a week. First they were instructed on walking in the correct way. You had to place one foot exactly in front of the other and swing your hips – 'but not all that sashaying they do today,' says Bronwen. 'We had to be "ladylike but exaggerated".' Then there was some good old-fashioned practice with books on the head to improve balance and poise.

Equally important was the correct form for the catwalk – not then usually a raised platform but simply a walkway between rows of chairs ending in what was and remains known as 'the cheese' or 'le fromage' because of its resemblance to a slab of Camembert. To succeed as models, according to Ginette Spanier, the great Parisian couture house directrice of the 1950s, girls had to 'swish their bottoms and stretch their legs out straight in front like a race horse, pirouetting at corners as though dancing an old-fashioned waltz.'

Other evening sessions covered make-up – at which Bronwen was a novice. At that time model girls were expected to turn up with their own shoes and do their own hair and make-up. Then there were hints on showing clothes off to best advantage – 'wearing a jacket off your shoulders, that sort of thing'. And finally, another taste of the outwardly more buttoned-up 1950s, there was the etiquette of taking off and putting on clothes quickly, discreetly and demurely.

As Pat Larthe had spotted, nature had given Bronwen a spectacular walk. The lessons may have given it a little more polish, but it remained highly individual and one of her most devastating assets, something that was to make critics, designers and men sit up and take notice of her. Eugenia Shepherd, fashion doyenne of the *New York Herald Tribune*, later described her as that 'husky, Welsh mannequin' who 'drags a coat down a runway as if she had just killed it and were taking it to her mate'.

The same openness that had made her a quick learner when Margaret Braund had fashioned St Joan out of a gawky schoolgirl at Dr Williams' helped her to digest Larthe's lessons in double-quick time. Despite her progress, at the end of the week Bronwen still found the agent adamant that she would not take her on. Her squint and her height would make her too hard to place. The current vogue was for petite girls with the gamine 'little boy look' – Jean Dawnay, its epitome, was five foot five and a half – rather than lanky, bony, long-legged women like Bronwen, who came in at just under six foot.

Yet once again, Bronwen displayed a remarkable single-mindedness. She couldn't do much about her height, but the squint

was easily cured. Raiding her savings, buoyed up by financial assistance from her parents, she went back to the surgeon who had treated
her as a child and he operated once more on the lazy muscles behind
her left eye. After a couple of weeks' recuperation she was out
knocking on the agents' doors once more. Her friends marvelled
at her perseverance. 'I remember being full of admiration for her
confidence and more so her resilience,' says Diana de Wilton. 'I just
kept thinking I know I couldn't have done that and that the very
first time someone said no, I would have given up. But it was a new
Bron. She wasn't in the mood to be put off.'

Those same attributes also enabled her to ride out her family's
reaction to her decision to throw in teaching and try her hand at
modelling. The Pughs were not frivolous people and the news that
their daughter wanted to abandon her career in the classroom and
spend her money on what must have seemed to them like a hopeless
whim cannot have been easy to swallow. First she had refused
Oxbridge. Then she had gone to drama school, but just when it
finally looked as if she was back on the rails, working as a teacher,
here she was giving it all up. They could not understand her motivation and she, still in shock over Erica, could not explain it – to them
or even to herself. However, the Pughs were not so heavy-handed as
to express their disappointment that she had abandoned what had
been her anointed role. Indeed, whatever their misgivings, they
helped her pay for her eye operation. They had taught their daughters
independence, had deliberately avoided giving them either gender
or class stereotypes, and realised that they were now reaping what
they had sown. They may even have understood on some unspoken
level, that modelling – like dressing-up and acting before it – fitted
in with Bronwen's penchant from earliest days for eye-catching gestures, the 'look at me' syndrome that she puts down to feeling
insufficiently wanted as a child.

According to Bronwen they were relaxed but qualified any support
with the hope that she wouldn't come to regret her decision. Her
future brother-in-law, Ron Barry, soon to marry Gwyneth, felt it
went further: 'I think that they regarded Bron as a bit of a mad-hatter
after she turned to modelling. They didn't understand what made
her want to do it, but eventually they were very proud of her. Their

only concern, and this was mainly later when her name was in every newspaper, was about all the people who were going mad about her and the endless partying. It was an entirely foreign world to them. They were still doing the quiet Hampstead life.'

Gwyneth was the most enthusiastic, applauding her younger sister's nerve and, with an instinctive understanding of Bronwen, suspecting the real cause of her crusade. Very tall and skinny, with none of Bronwen's new-found poise and self-confidence, Gwyneth suffered from poor eyesight and generally bad health as an adult, caused by heart problems; she wore heavy glasses and came to see her own body as a burden. The prospect of her extrovert little sister celebrating hers prompted her to express unselfish pride and encouragement. Gwyneth, her older sister Ann says, had already settled into a pattern where 'she lived much more of an inward life. Bronwen was a much more open, outgoing sort of person.' As a judgement from within the family, it shows the extent to which Bronwen kept that other side of her, the inward-looking, contemplative and, she believes, Celtic-influenced melancholy, well-hidden.

Too much can be made of the point since Ann was, of course, overseas with her new husband when she learned of Bronwen's career change. 'When I heard, I just laughed. I found it terribly hard to imagine why anyone would want to be a model.' The oldest and youngest of the Pughs' daughters had by this stage recognised that they were, despite a strong physical similarity, chalk and cheese. 'I never felt Ann was envious of me, or me of her. We had both simply chosen very different lines of work and she couldn't understand why anyone would want to do something so unacademic as modelling.' If her goal since arriving at Dr Williams' had been to follow a radically different path from her sisters, then Bronwen had finally and flamboyantly succeeded.

The only member of the Pugh clan to express outright disapproval of her boldness was her Goodyear grandmother down in Kent. To this Edwardian matriarch, the whole business of modelling seemed tawdry and she would have preferred her grand-daughter to give it a wide berth. A strict teetotaller, she once remarked to Ann of Bronwen's career as a model girl: 'I know that she lives on gin and sandwiches.' However, she had little influence in such matters, even if it was partly a legacy from her late husband, given to each of his grand-daughters at twenty-one, that was allowing Bronwen to pay for the surgery on her eye and Pat Larthe's course of lessons as well as to support herself until the hoped-for job offers came rolling in.

At first, on her return from Dorset, Bronwen shared a rented flat at 44 Harley Street with Diana de Wilton. Later she moved into her own place, first a small mews flat, and later in nearby Hyde Park Square, her home until her marriage. 'I remember noticing,' Diana de Wilton says, 'not out of jealousy but curiosity how my room was always tidy and I would emerge from it looking plain. But Bron's looked like a bomb had hit it, and then she would emerge looking lovely, immaculately dressed.' She was developing her own style and her own, individual look, emphasising her Celtic eyes with her choice of colours and making the most of the aristocratic bearing her height, poise and strong facial bone structure gave her.

Eventually Bronwen persuaded the agent Peter Hope-Lumley to take her on his books. He was not quite so daunted by her height as Pat Larthe. And he was more successful at persuading his clients to take a chance on this unusual model girl than Jean Bell, the severe headmistress-type who had represented Bronwen for six months but failed to find her a single job. She had suffered numerous rejections; she was either too tall, too inexperienced, too unphotogenic, or not thin enough. 'She just stood out,' Hope-Lumley now says. 'She was very exceptional. It was not only that she was much taller than the other models and had this air of distinction. There was something different in the way she walked. She was very good-looking rather than pretty.' It is an observation reinforced by the interior designer Nicholas Haslam, then a youngster working on *Vogue*. 'When you saw Bron, you wouldn't say, "Oh, what a pretty girl," you'd just say, "Wow!"'

Even with Peter Hope-Lumley, there were setbacks. When her modelling career was slow to pick up and things got tight, she gave private elocution lessons to make ends meet, taking on anyone from businessmen who wanted to make more effective presentations to shy schoolgirls with dreams of the stage. Had Bronwen's eyes not been so determinedly fixed on the goal of modelling, fearing that without it she would simply collapse into a chasm of grief, she could have been persuaded to quit. It was as if Erica was still with her, pushing her on.

In an effort to help Bronwen, Diana de Wilton introduced her to a family friend, the owner of Mary Lee's, a smart women's clothes shop in Tunbridge Wells. The lowest rung on the ladder of modelling was to work as a shop model in the provinces, showing off the usually uninspiring ready-to-wear collection. It wasn't quite what Bronwen had in mind, but she realised she had to start somewhere. Only Mary Lee's said no. She did not fit their preconception of what a shop model should be. The idea, they explained, was that their models would show their customers what they would look like in the clothes. Bronwen was more likely to intimidate run-of-the-mill Tunbridge housewives than persuade them to open their cheque books.

She had the last laugh. Those with more imagination eventually came to share Hope-Lumley's instinct that there was something attractively unusual in her. Her first big booking came along – to show off Bunny Roger's celebrated 'tea dresses' at Fortnum and Mason's on Piccadilly. Roger was an extraordinary character who recognised the extraordinary in his new model girl. One of three sons of a wealthy Scottish industrialist, none of whom married, preferring each summer to share an isolated house in Ross-shire, the camp and laconic Roger had tried his hand as a costume designer in Hollywood before opening his first showroom as a couturier in London's Great Newport Street in 1937. After the war he had reopened in Fortnum and Mason's, where he was famed for his floaty, summery chiffon dresses, made for an English lawn to complement scones, croquet hoops and men in boaters.

As well as his two main shows each year, Roger would use model girls to display his dresses in the restaurant at Fortnum's, where they wove their way in and out of the tables as potential buyers took tea. Roger was impressed with his latest recruit and soon she was promoted to his main shows. Kathleen Pugh came to see her daughter in action and might have blighted her career by telling the couturier, with characteristic bluntness, never to put Bronwen in shocking pink again, but Roger liked strong-minded, even abrasive women. At his parties in London he would greet guests dressed as Norma Desmond, Marlene Dietrich or Lana Turner.

Soon Hope-Lumley was getting her more bookings – mainly ready-to-wear collections at shows at the fashionable stores like Simpsons, Harrods and Woollands on Knightsbridge. There would be a short fitting the week before to select which clothes would look best on which model girl, and to make any necessary adjustments to fit their shape. And then came the show itself.

The fashion director at Woollands, Martin Moss, became quite a fan. His wife, the distinguished *Observer* portrait photographer Jane Bown, was then just starting out on her own career, but recalls the impression Bronwen Pugh made on her when they worked together. 'She was very tall and very flamboyant. You remembered her. I think it was because she looked so well-bred and almost above what she was doing.' There was also, according to both Bown and Hope-Lumley, a certain detachment about Bronwen that made her stand out. 'She was always very professional,' he says, 'but you did sometimes get the impression she regarded modelling with a certain detached amusement. She was somehow apart.'

Bronwen was undoubtedly beginning to have fun, living a life that satisfied both her desire to be different and, as her reputation grew and her name began to be noticed, that Pugh determination to be the best at whatever she did. Yet the detachment that Hope-Lumley noted – and which was later to become so much a part of her legend on the catwalk – sprang from an innate appreciation of the absurdity of what she was doing. It was, to use one of her favourite descriptions, 'a game of dressing-up' and had to be set against the spiritual journey on which she had tentatively embarked in private and in solitude with her reading and interest in psychology.

The two made odd bed-fellows, each distracting her from the other, but each reflecting what were at the time contradictory sides of her character. Ultimately they couldn't coexist. Bronwen knew there was something more to achieve than showing clothes to wealthy women, but she hadn't worked out quite what. Logically she should have given up one or other – thrown herself into modelling wholeheartedly and unreservedly, or abandoned her new career and gone off to study the mind or live in a convent, though at this stage she had still not made a direct link between her inner journey and organised religion. But she was not – and is still not – a conventionally logical creature, being given to great enthusiasms, surges of energy and often a lack of rigorous analysis. She was both driven from within *and* felt herself being guided from outside. So the contradictions remained, though ironically it was her very ambiguity about modelling that helped to lift her above the crowd.

She was able to step back from the first flickerings of acclaim in London in 1953 partly because she resolutely refused to believe it when designers, writers or even suitors told her that she was beautiful. She remains convinced to this day that they were simply mistaken. 'I think I just gave the impression of beauty. I knew I didn't have perfect features. And it was only later when I came to regard what was inside me with any sort of approval that I could see myself as in any way potentially beautiful. But perhaps already I was projecting it before I knew I had it.'

It is a point echoed by (Lord) Grey Gowrie, then a young man, later a Conservative minister and chairman of the Arts Council: 'When I saw her on the catwalk, I knew I was seeing a star. She was not just good-looking and wearing good clothes, she brought a strange emotional power to what she did. At that time models could express themselves more dramatically and with less inhibition when they showed clothes. There were fewer openings, fewer cameras, less of a mass market and only a handful of clients who encouraged them to be original. With the benefit of hindsight I realise that even then Bronwen's feelings were running deeper than most models' and that this – perhaps unconsciously – shone through.'

When a couturier or a fashion writer hailed Bronwen as a great and unique beauty, however, she would choose instead to believe what she had always been told at home – that Ann was the beautiful one, Gwyneth the clever one, and she somewhere in between, habitually as she grew older playing the clown to jolly her parents along. As the clamour grew, what she had once regarded impatiently as a family put-down became a treasured source of sanity. Most of the hullabaloo about 'our Bronwen' in the press would only come later. When she had made a name for herself in Paris, the top English couturiers lined up to design clothes for her to wear in their twice-yearly shows. In her early days she had to be content with a diet of ready-to-wear at the big stores.

Occasionally she would find herself in decidely down-beat locations that were far removed from any fashion magazine account of a model's glamorous life. She was once booked for a provincial tour with *Vogue* pattern books. She and her fellow model girls had to parade about in front of audiences in Manchester and Leeds in swimsuits and shorts, giving a commentary about how good each design was to wear. 'It was nothing like those awful swimsuit parades you used to get in Miss World. We were well covered up. It was *Vogue* pattern books, after all.' Even so, Bronwen didn't find it odd wearing revealing clothes in public. 'People were just looking at me. They didn't know who I was. Now I have learnt you have to have your mind, body and spirit together. Then they were entirely separate. It was as if I wasn't there.'

Christine Tidmarsh, who later shared a flat with Bronwen in Paris, first met her when they both turned up at a fire station to do a show. 'There were about forty other models and before walking into the audience, they wanted us to slide down the pole. We refused. It was all so badly organised. And badly paid. And the clothes were terrible. I remember we both ended up sending up the clothes – just by the way we showed them. You couldn't take them seriously.'

Sending up the creations she wore would later become part of Bronwen's repertoire – a characteristic that came to the attention of Bill Astor – but in her early days it required a confidence that she had not yet developed or a willing accomplice like the mischievous Tidmarsh. Bookings were still sporadic. She never took a holiday in case she missed an opening that could lead to her big break. If she was going to do modelling, her upbringing had taught her she must do it in a professional, focused and career-minded way. The Pughs were not dilettantes.

Weeks would go by without anything, then jobs would come one after another. She was prepared to take on anything, including posing for the artists who would produce the hand-drawn advertisements for fashion stores that were popular at the time. It was poorly paid and involved several days of standing like a statue for five hours at a stretch. Show models in general were notoriously badly rewarded, though with the advent of agents and the professionalisation of their trade the rewards improved. The best money was to be made as a photographic model, though some regarded working for the camera and not an audience as a lower form of life. The big names in London at the time were Cecil Beaton (who never took to Bronwen and later declined Bill Astor's invitation to photograph her after her marriage on the grounds that her nose was too ugly), Baron* and, especially in Bronwen's world, John French of the *Daily Express*, a tall, elegant, almost military man who did much, along with his features editor, Harold Keeble, to make the British models he photographed into household names via his newspaper.

Although he trained freer spirits like David Bailey and Terence Donovan, French himself played the role of old-fashioned gentleman with the models he shot. This approach was reflected in his pictures which have, to modern eyes accustomed to provocative poses, a chaste, overly formal air. However, this was the code of the times, not only in photography but in the wider world. The look for women was prim and proper. Debate in studios revolved around how far apart the model's feet could decently be, while knees were always, photographer Norman Parkinson later remarked, 'bolted together'.

The fifties did, however, see the first flowering of a more modern style of photography. In comparison to the sixties, when more natural-looking poses came in, fifties fashion photography still appears all art and artifice, grand-looking ladies in austere settings rather than the gamine Twiggy or Jean Shrimpton with their fresh faces. Yet in the fifties the statues came to life, with a subtext of sex and flirtation introduced into the fashion image. Instead of static poses, fifties photographic models were asked to act, to bring the image to life.

It was a trend that Bronwen was later to embrace in her subtly alluring work with photographers, but for the time being, though a favourite with the fashion store managers, she was never the photographers' first choice. As fashion historian Charles Castle has written of her, 'whilst she was supreme on the catwalk, photographers found her doe-eyed looks and angular proportions too exaggerated for

---

* Baron Nahum, always known only by his first name, a society figure of Italian ancestry, close friend of Prince Philip and devotee of dancers.

readers of *Vogue* and *Harper's Bazaar* who could hardly identify with the individuality of this exceptional model.'

Only in the last years of her career did Bronwen begin to have photographers queuing up to work with her. Her one hit in these early days was a booking with Baron to do a lingerie advertisement. These were regarded with some suspicion by most model girls and as slightly degrading. But Baron was a big name, always in the papers on account of his close friendship with Prince Philip. So Bronwen accepted. It was not a happy assignment. She found the playboy photographer a little too eager as she posed, and he never tried to book her again.

Of the big names, the only one to pay particular attention to Bronwen in her pre-Paris days was Charles Creed, best remembered today for his perfume Tweed. Famed at the time for his tailoring and his tweed suits, he gave her her break into couture collections, recognising that his designs and her shape made a natural partnership. 'I had got broad shoulders and the height to carry them off. I was quite flat chested, tall, low-hipped, and had proportionately a long back and a long front.' Next to shorter, petite, buxom models, she gave Creed's classical look an added drama and impact.

Creed may have given her a start, but he also managed to break her ribs. A tall, strong, well-built man of great enthusiasm and exuberance, he once picked her up and swung her round to celebrate the end of a show. So powerful was his grip that she heard her bones crack. Suitably bandaged, she turned up the next day for work.

More often than not Bronwen would return in the evenings and at weekends to her flat, to her old college friends, or to Pilgrims Lane, but model girls were regularly invited along to first nights. The fashion world and its stars at this time were not generally well-known to the public. Only a handful would become household names. For the most part – in London at least – it was an enclosed world where designers and top model girls would be known to a small audience who were their customers – wealthy, often titled, usually older people who could afford couture clothes. And within that narrow orbit business and pleasure would go hand in hand. So there would be invitations, parties, the chance to mix with a social elite.

It was all new to Bronwen. She had not been part of the debutantes' world. She was in her early twenties and in the first flush of success and for a while enjoyed the life that went with her work. There were occasionally clubs – like the 400 in Leicester Square, Les Ambassadeurs (or Les A's) in Hamilton Place, Milroy, Edmundo Ros's Coconut Grove or Esmerelda's Barn in Knightsbridge. Sometimes one of the posse of what Bronwen calls 'stage door johnnies' would persuade her to accompany him to these expensive and exclusive places, but it was a rare indulgence. A larger presence in her diary were parties. 'I remember going with Bronwen to a party just behind Liberty's,' says Nicholas Haslam. 'She was so tall with very white skin, arched eyebrows and very dark hair. There was this ungainly elegance about her. She was sublimely inelegant. Everyone turned and looked at her. I think that I was a little bit in love with her.'

Haslam, who is gay, was one of Bronwen's favourite escorts to such occasions. He was, simply put, safe. Though she was flattered by the attention, she quickly learnt to regard the entreaties of wealthy, famous and titled older men with a certain caution. 'I was always avoiding people because often I simply felt way out of my depth. Modelling meant that I met people I would not normally meet. You have to understand that in those days the class structure was still very much in evidence.' Equally she was aware that many of the men who courted and flattered her had wives and families at home and had a certain expectation of a model in their mind. 'The model girls I mixed with socially were terribly above board. We were really rather prim in retrospect. There were one or two girls on the fringes of modelling who perhaps took things further, but if we suspected that about them, we had nothing to do with them.'

Attitudes in some circles in London had not yet caught up with the changing face of modelling and the influx of respectable, middle-class girls. As Jean Dawnay once reflected, 'if a scandal or a divorce is reported [in the papers], more often than not a model seems to be involved – an unfair reflection on the trade and the really serious members of it. Most of the girls mentioned just call themselves models for want of a better name.' The risk of naive young women being taken in by those with only a minimal interest in their day jobs was an ever-present one, as agent Peter Hope-Lumley was acutely aware.

'It could be a seedy world and it was really women like Bronwen who induced daughters of well-off or middle-class families to do this wicked thing called modelling. Even when Bronwen was starting, it would still be common for photographers to chase the girls round the studio and try to seduce them.'

Bronwen quickly learnt another trick when it came to nights out. Trust other women in the same position. 'It was a case of who you knew. Most models got married young and then would have dinner parties where you would be introduced to their husband's friends. In those days it was a very small society and everyone seemed to know everyone else.' Yet she didn't want to shut herself off. She was unsure how to judge, given her new-found success, if people liked her for who she was or for who they imagined she was. 'I would find myself talking to people at parties in the rather intense way I always talk to them and then they would say come to dinner. And then they would say come to bed. And I'd say no thank you very much. I was constantly trying to weave my way through without falling into the traps on the way, remaining true to what I felt inside. And of course the life I was leading meant that the traps were everywhere.'

The social scene that she became part of embraced all sorts of characters, many honest, straightforward and, like Bronwen, simply out to have a good time. The Chelsea Set, with their smart backgrounds and Bohemian attitudes, were just getting going in south-west London around the hitherto unfashionable King's Road. Bronwen attended the Chelsea Arts Club Ball and candlelit parties at Crowther's, the storehouse of antique statuary at Syon Lodge, west London. Elsewhere there were famously flamboyant MPs, academics, businessmen, minor royals and members of both the British and European aristocracy. Not all regarded beautiful young model girls simply as potential mistresses. Indeed, many went on to make them their wives, adding to the new-found respectability of their vocation. Jean Dawnay became Princess George Galitzine, Anne Cumming-Bell, the Duchess of Rutland, Anne Gunning, Lady Nutting, and Fiona Campbell-Walter, Baroness Thyssen.

Another face in this world was Bill Astor, who had succeeded his father on his death in 1952 to become the third Viscount Astor, but although Bill Astor enjoyed partying – using his London house on Upper Grosvenor Street as a base – his main interests in this period were elsewhere and he did not come across Bronwen Pugh until some years later. Just as she was making a name for herself, he was going through an unhappy divorce from his first wife, Sarah Norton; two years later he married Philippa Hunloke, a young stage manager in the theatre who was related through her mother, Lady Anne Holland-Martin, an old family friend of the Astors, to the Prime Minister, Harold Macmillan.

'In a year, I thought I had done it all.' By the autumn of 1954 Bronwen had reached the summit of the London modelling scene, starring in the annual show put on for Queen Elizabeth, the Queen Mother, by the top couturiers and organised by the great socialite Lady Pamela Berry, daughter of the former Lord Chancellor F. E. Smith and wife of the owner of the *Telegraph* titles. The prospect of several more years going through the same annual cycle did not appeal to her. She was growing bored with the game and restlessness had set in once again.

In November 1954 the newspapers were suddenly full of the news of the appointment of the 'Welsh girl' and well-known model, Bronwen Pugh, as the new face of the BBC. It was not a description they had invented, but one that Bronwen had given of herself. Her awareness of her Welsh roots, of being somehow an outsider in English society, had become by this stage acute.

BBC presenter Sylvia Peters, who along with Mary Malcolm, McDonald Hobley and Peter Haigh shared the task of sitting each night in full evening dress in the studio and linking the programmes, was leaving to have a baby. Bronwen had been given a six-month contract to replace her. She had answered an advertisement and ended up in front of Clive Rawes, who was head of presentation, to discuss details of her background as an elocution and drama teacher and her modelling credits. Though she had begun to make a name for herself, that interview was the true beginning of her national celebrity, which lasted a decade until her self-imposed exile in 1966.

All the popular press reported at length on her new job and, professional, polite and theatrical to the end, she told them what she thought they wanted to hear. So *Empire News* quoted her to the effect that she had become a model because she was teased by her sisters about her hair. Perhaps it was shorthand for explaining her drive to move out of their shadow. As part of a wholesome description for the same paper of the Pughs' family life, Bronwen 'revealed' that her greatest joy was listening to her judge father and her magistrate mother debate legal cases over the dinner table. Elsewhere it was similarly light, frothy and fanciful stuff, playing up her outgoing side and keeping her contemplative self carefully under wraps. The *London Evening News* had her down as a fluent Welsh speaker who smoked and drank in moderation and refused to diet because 'it makes me too melancholy'.

Press interest did not end with profiles. At the end of November the *London Evening Standard* was running a competition – first prize £5 – for the best bit of advice to give "our Bronwen" on her first appearance on screen. That was scheduled for 8 December 1954 and it took on national significance. 'Millions will see Bronwen today,' announced the *Daily Mirror* sub-title beside a photograph and, in block capitals, GIRL WITH TWINKLING EYES. It was a far cry from the days when Pat Larthe had told her that her eyes would stop her being a model girl.

Bronwen's first task was to announce an international football match between Scotland and Hungary. She did not bring the home team any luck – they lost 4–2 – but the next day her reviews were glowing. Clifford Davis in the *Daily Mirror* was in raptures. 'The most beautiful face that ever presented a television programme came on the screen yesterday,' he wrote. Sylvia Peters and her colleague, Mary Malcolm, were, Davis said, eclipsed. 'Bron's style on screen was very ladylike,' Diana de Wilton recalls, 'but with good diction. She was like an earlier version of Angela Rippon.'

Where today the BBC's continuity readers are unseen, in 1954 their forerunners were national stars. With television in its infancy – a second, commercial channel was not launched until the following year – the face that linked programmes was a key feature of the schedules for viewers and, for the technical staff, a welcome stand-by in case all else failed. Theirs was often the only face that viewers grew accustomed to seeing. BBC Television News, hitherto merely a voice speaking over pictures, did at this time experiment with two presenters in vision – the young Richard Baker and Robert Dougall – but they had to keep their eyes down on the piece of paper in front of them in case they should ever be judged to have given even the merest hint of editorial judgement.

Broadcasting did not start until around 6 p.m., so two or three nights a week Bronwen would come in at five, read her fan mail (she had to answer every letter as part of her contract) and then learn her lines for the evening ahead. There was no autocue. 'You announced the programmes as if you were opening a garden party,' she recalls. 'I sounded like a vicar's wife. And the thing was often breaking down, so you had to fill in with chat while either your face or a potter's wheel showed.' On Saturdays there were football results to read – to the great delight of her ex-nanny Bella Wells – and there would be occasional appearances in other programmes.

Overnight celebrity and the size of her post bag did not, however, go to Bronwen's head. 'The reviews were amazing, but I knew that they were not something to be taken at all seriously. And if I showed any sign of doing so, my family soon brought me down to earth. It was just like modelling. I was having fun rather than doing a proper job.'

Fame certainly didn't make her rich – her salary was small. It was treated lightly by her family – though her father kept a cuttings book of all her reviews. He was secretly proud of her. She herself knew that her triumph was hollow. 'Succeeding at the BBC was just like being captain of hockey at school – an achievement but an empty and meaningless one.' At first, however, the novelty of it all carried her merrily along. And at the age of twenty-four, it is thrilling constantly to be stopped in the street. 'It was like being in a play all the time. I would accept invitations to open fêtes at the drop of a hat. The best part was being able to meet interesting people. Doors just opened. Up to then my life had been very enclosed and very shut away. Finally I felt I was getting somewhere where I could meet people with good minds.'

One of the more significant contacts she made during her time at the BBC was Sir Mortimer Wheeler, the mustachioed, Terry-Thomas-like archaeologist who became a household name on the panel of the popular game show *Animal, Vegetable, Mineral*. The thrice-married sixty-year-old, known to his friends as Rik, invited her down to Maidstone Castle to join in an archaeological dig. He became an informal and fatherly mentor, taking her to good restaurants that were beyond her pocket and discussing literature and ideas with her. 'He was horrified how little I had read and it was he, more than anyone, who directed me away from straightforward spiritual books and into reading the classics. He started me on Thomas Hardy and I think I read them all in the end. He also recommended *Moby Dick*. Over dinner we would discuss the novels. It was part of a process of getting to know myself better and making myself think.'

Reading also became a kind of therapy for Bronwen, her one way of confronting the questions Erica's death had raised. Modelling enabled her to put them out of her mind, but in her quieter moments, through books, she began to come to terms with her sense of loss and what it told her about life and a divine presence.

Bronwen's detachment from the trappings of celebrity proved to be a blessing for, at the start of September 1955, out of nowhere the BBC announced that after nine months it was letting her go. Sylvia Peters was back from maternity leave and would be reclaiming her place on the team of presenters. Bronwen, unaware of the news which was being announced to the public, was busy signing autographs at the *Radio Show* in central London when someone told her what had happened. Her fifteen minutes of fame had ended. Without the BBC behind her, the celebrity appearances soon dried up, but not before she had made her debut in a commercial for the fledgling ITV as a houseproud young woman alongside comedian Charlie Drake as a window-cleaner discovering the joys of Windolene. She also made a brief appearance in a Norman Wisdom film as a haughty announcer at a fashion show.

It was a high-profile cameo. Wisdom was Britain's best-loved and most popular entertainer at the time, but such work was only a diversion. Though occasionally an American model had crossed over into films – Lauren Bacall being the best-known example in the 1940s – there was no well-trodden path to follow. When Suzy Parker and Dovima had appeared in the 1956 film *Funny Face*, starring Audrey Hepburn as a model, they were playing themselves. The model-actress was, on both sides of the Atlantic, a much later phenomenon.

Bronwen's route back to modelling was effectively blocked by the fact that her face was now, thanks to the BBC, too well-known for a British audience. As her agent discovered when he tried to get her erstwhile fans among the couturiers and fashion store managers to book her, the feeling was that potential buyers would be too busy trying to spot Bronwen Pugh the announcer in the line-up of model girls to concentrate on the real business at hand – buying clothes. Model girls had to be anonymous and for that Bronwen's agent suggested she would have to try her hand in Europe.

Chapter Five

Les anglaises, elles ont tant de chic.

M. Donati of Christian Dior, *London Evening News*, 28 July 1958

The end of 1955 and the start of 1956 was one of the lowest points in Bronwen Pugh's professional life. She had tasted success, financial independence and public acclaim. It hadn't gone to her head. She knew that modelling and being the face of the BBC did not come close to personal fulfilment. Neither had they made the pain of the loss of her closest friend, Erica, any easier to bear. Yet her recent experience of celebrity had changed her life. It had opened up her horizons, given her self-confidence, introduced her to people she would not otherwise have come across. However much she may have told everyone that she was simply in modelling for fun, she had made it her career and as such treated it seriously and profession-ally. To be informed at the age of twenty-five and after little more than two years of work that she was virtually unemployable was disheartening.

Her agent's suggestion that she should head for the continent was daunting, though Mortimer Wheeler, among her friends, encouraged her to take the risk so as to broaden her horizons. Her grasp of foreign languages was, however, almost non-existent and her knowledge of Europe was limited – one trip with friends from Oxford and another with her father. The mid-1950s, for all Britain's resurgent prosperity, was still not a time of mass travel to Europe. Moreover, she had developed a close circle of friends in London and was reluctant to leave them behind. And, for all their foibles, she had grown used to living with her family close at hand. Her father and Gwyneth in particular were vital to any sense of equilibrium she had achieved, a counterbalance to the frivolous world of modelling. Being an inde-pendent career woman was fine as long as Pilgrims Lane was only a brief car journey away. To take her agent's advice would be to embark on a truly solitary and, given the dangers she had already noted, almost nun-like life.

However, she could see no alternative. She was not about to admit defeat in her chosen career and settle back into the pre-selected option of schoolteaching. So she kept on her flat in London, but bought an open-ended return air ticket to Italy and set off to see if the streets were paved with gold. 'I literally wandered round Rome with my portfolio. It wasn't even a portfolio. It was a little piece of folded paper with two or three photographs, my statistics, height and measurements. It was a dreadful time, very lonely, but by then I had got used to doing things alone.'

As chance would have it, she quickly found a photographer in Rome who spotted her potential. Scrimali – only ever known by his surname – saw that same unusual quality that had made Pat Larthe, Bunny Roger and the BBC sit up and take notice. He asked Bronwen to accompany him – with his girlfriend as chaperone – to the fashion shows in Rome and then to Florence's Pitti Palace (Milan was still establishing itself on the European calendar), where he photographed her in the latest clothes from the Italian fashion houses, couturiers like Fabiani and Simonetta or Roberto Capucci. Their look was more modern and less classical than anything she had worn in London. Shorter skirts in bright pinks, greens and yellows worn with low heels contrasted with her long bones, white skin, greeny eyes and the red hint in her brown hair – augmented by artificial colour. If not exactly tailor-made to emphasise her best qualities as a model, the Italian couturiers' designs did at least give her another opportunity to stand out. She was hailed by the Italian press as the epitome of an English rose, though she tried in vain to explain the distinction between England and Wales, Anglo-Saxons and Celts.

Scrimali posed a new challenge for Bronwen, who felt that in London she had never quite mastered being a photographic as opposed to a show model. Her early attempts had seemed ordinary and stiff, too obviously posed, without any hint of the irony she later brought with her exaggerated gestures. Photography was also the more lucrative end of the modelling world. Some top American photographic models earned as much as $300 a day working with

Vogue. While Italian rates for someone unknown outside Britain were considerably lower, they did enable Bronwen after just six weeks to return to London in funds and with several more jobs lined up in Italy and in Germany.

She returned to Rome with Katherine Edwards, a model she had met on the English circuit, and the two shared very basic lodgings. Bronwen had hoped for companionship in work, but Edwards was less successful in getting bookings and soon found an alternative to modelling in Roman society. Bronwen would work long hours each day to make money, her career and a reputation. Then, just as she was getting in, Edwards would be off out to parties with a sprinkling of Italian royalty and plenty of European aristocrats as well as, she told her flatmate in shocked tones for both were innocent in such matters, drink and drugs. The invitation to join her was always there, but Bronwen declined.

'It never really appealed to me. She did keep asking me along, but I needed my sleep so as to be ready for work the next day. We did spend the occasional evening in together, but otherwise I would work late with photographers – they often liked to shoot you after the day's shows – or else I'd go to a restaurant and read my book. I suppose I was lonely, but there was plenty of life going on around me.'

She thus missed out on the world immortalised four years later by Federico Fellini in his celebrated study of a playboy hack, *La Dolce Vita.* Only rarely during the several periods she spent in the Italian capital did she end up on a date. 'I remember sitting sideways on a Lambretta, clutching the man around the waist, thinking, I'm not sure about this. We went to a restaurant on top of a hill overlooking Rome and I was wined and dined. It was so romantic. But then when we got back to Rome, he made it clear what he wanted and I made it clear it wasn't on. That was it. I never saw him again.'

It was all too reminiscent of the London social scene but with the inevitable approach and rebuff played out against a Mediterranean sunset. Whichever European city she was in, men's expectations of models were the same. 'I was very down. Here I was at twenty-six and my thoughts were inevitably turning to marriage, but I wasn't meeting anyone. I was always looking for a Prince Charming to come and sweep me away, but I was in the wrong world for that.

The people who did try to sweep me away, I wouldn't have dreamt of marrying.'

At least Italy offered frissons of out-of-hours excitement. Other jobs took her for six weeks to work for the couturiers Gehringer und Glubb in a war-damaged and divided Berlin, where she ended up boarding with a kindly but narrow-minded German family. 'In Italy it was all drama. In Germany, even though I was working for what was considered the top house, you were a drudge, a clothes horse, and that's all there was morning, noon and night. In Italy the clothes were beautiful. In Germany they were dull.'

In Berlin there was photographic work again – with an acclaimed young photographer called Charles Wilp, who went on to make a name for himself on the international stage. But Bronwen's peripatetic life was taking a toll on her energy, her body and the sense of inner calm she had been drawing from her inner journey. Her weight dropped to nine stone. She cut down on liquids as the simplest and fastest way to keep her weight down. At just under six foot, she had that waif-like quality so fashionable in 1990s supermodels like Kate Moss.

It was a stark contrast to her situation just a few months before, when she had been the toast of the BBC. If her dismissal had come as a shock, the work that followed in Rome and Berlin left her flat and depressed. However little worth she placed on being recognised in the street, to go from that to being a clothes horse in Germany could hardly be counted as a promising career move. To do so when you were still grieving and searching for a sense of your own identity was doubly hard.

This period of loneliness and introspection did eventually bring dividends. 'I don't think that inner spiritual strength comes out of the blue,' Bronwen says. 'You have to work at it, spend long periods contemplating, facing adversity. And I was certainly examining my own navel at this time, but I did have this feeling that I needed to be alone, to think things through, to experiment with praying or reading or whatever I was doing at the time. Erica's death had shocked me into isolation.'

She was also very determined. While she realised that modelling was not the be-all and end-all of life, her other career options were few – she could simply go back to teaching and hope to find a kindly headmaster to marry. And like many other women who have had to fight to claim the right to a career, she knew that working very hard, being single-minded and, as a consequence, tolerating a degree of loneliness were par for the course. That Pugh ambition was nagging away in the back of her head. Rome, Florence, Berlin were also-rans on the fashion map. Making it there meant nothing. If you're going to do something make sure you're the best or don't bother, her father had often told her. And in European terms Paris was the best. Armed with a much-expanded portfolio, she set off for the French capital to see what the great couture houses would make of her.

First stop was Balmain at 44 rue François Premier, just off the Champs-Élysées. Though Christian Dior was King of Paris, Pierre Balmain and Cristobal Balenciaga enjoyed royal status. Balenciaga, who trained as an architect, was celebrated in the trade for his innovation and the timeless quality of the clothes he designed. It was said that he led in terms of style and the others followed but made more noise about it. 'Balenciaga was so special, so unusual, that it is hard to categorise him,' says Bronwen's friend, former model girl Svetlana Lloyd. 'Balmain would dress fashionable women beautifully. Dior's clients did not have to be pretty or have a good figure. His clothes were built to make good any lack, to rearrange the anatomy, to deliver the vision Dior had of the dress worn by a woman who happened to be paying for it.'

Pioneer of the 'jolie madame' style, a delicate and sophisticated cut for society women, Balmain's reputation was founded on precious furs, extraordinary hats, sumptuous embroidery and classical lines in his trademark suits and evening dresses. These were tailor-made for Bronwen's strengths – her height and her haughty bearing on the catwalk. Balmain's assistant, the Danish-born designer Erik Mortensen, spotted it at once. He asked her to walk and was impressed by her unorthodox technique. It spoke of distinction, austerity and nonchalance. 'Bronwen never did the standard model's walk,' says Svetlana Lloyd. 'At first she tried but mainly she just did her own thing with big easy strides. It looked perfect on her because of her height. It gave her this air of great aristocracy and great indifference and always created a sort of gasp from the audience.'

Though Mortensen was impressed, he could not make the decision alone. First he turned to 'Madame', Balmain's elderly but elegant grande-damish mother, who until her death in 1957 oversaw the business side of her son's couture house. Madame was against. Bronwen wouldn't sell clothes, she argued, because she looked so unlike anyone likely to be buying them. Most of the other model girls were short, petite and blond. This woman with height, brown hair and big hands was no good, said Madame. Lined up against Mortensen was another powerful voice in the house of Balmain, Ginette Spanier, the assistant directrice. Though later an enthusiastic convert to Bronwen's special qualities, she was initially implacably opposed. 'When she first walked along the podium she looked like something from a cartoon by Charles Addams . . . sleep-walking, almost falling over her long feet.'

In the end it was Balmain himself who made the decision. He was then in his mid-forties and at the height of his powers. Almost totally bald, with a fleshy face, arresting eyes and a pencil-line moustache on his upper lip, he was a curious, often contradictory man whose enthusiasms were hard to predict. The product of a pious household in Haute-Savoie, all his life he enjoyed having priests around him. Yet he worked in an industry short on morality and restraint. Having trained as an architect, Balmain turned to designing and originally worked as a *modelliste*, or stylist, alongside Christian Dior at Lucien Lelong, celebrated in pre-war Paris for the simplicity and elegance of his designs.

As the war ended Balmain and Dior considered a joint business venture, but Dior got cold feet, leaving his friend to set up alone in the unwelcoming climate of Paris in 1946. Balmain's mother sold some of her jewellery to fund him. He made a moderate splash – 'Pierre Balmain opened his own house,' reported Bettina Ballard of American *Vogue*, 'with a small and charming collection that allowed the press to leap on him as a discovery' – but nothing compared to the wave of adulation which greeted Dior eighteen months later. Balmain had little of his former colleague's showmanship or business acumen and was, in fashion industry terms, always the bridesmaid, never the bride. The irony was that the much-trumpeted Dior New Look, the antithesis of severe wartime designs, was very similar to

Balmain's own softly contoured earlier collection. It was simply that Dior's timing and presentation was such that he touched a nerve.

Though gay in his private life, professionally Balmain had an unusual love for tall women. Bronwen was irresistible. He hired her on the spot. 'Everyone thought he had gone mad,' Spanier wrote in her autobiography. 'But he was right. She had something. She inspired him.' There was only one problem, Balmain explained in his flawless English. He could not pronounce Bronwen. Henceforth, he decreed, she would be known as Bella.

Popular culture has a short memory and the cult of the supermodel is today treated as if it were a new phenomenon. Yet throughout this century the top models of their era have been stars. All that has changed has been the financial rewards that go with the work and the balance of power in the industry. In the 1950s model girls were paid buttons. At the height of her fame Bronwen earned around £10 a week. Though freelancers, once they worked for one house, they remained loyal to that couturier. Today's lavishly rewarded top models work for different designers at every fashion show. What remains constant is the public interest in top models. From the thirties onwards they have been household names. The most successful have always been known by their first names – Alla and Victoire, Christian Dior's muses, and later Twiggy and Iman. All are written about in the press; playboys surround them like hungry flies.

Though in London in the 1950s the model girls had brought a new-found respectability to their profession, in Paris even the top couturiers were prone to blur the line between modelling and prostitution. Dior would occasionally find his models in bordellos which he visited because, he said, though gay he was fascinated by the atmosphere there. Victoire's background was rumoured to be less than salubrious. 'The girls became models and clients,' writes historian Michael Gross. 'They knew men with money. They'd go to Cannes, Monte Carlo and Deauville for dirty weekends. They had to have their suit from Chanel, their cocktail ensemble from Dior, their evening dress from Fath.'

The risks in Paris were not just from those out to exploit models. Some of the women themselves were expert exploiters, keen to find themselves security and a well-funded alternative to work. Another model at Balmain when Bronwen was there regularly arrived for work in the chauffeur-driven car provided by her wealthy and married Italian film-star boyfriend to ferry her from their suite at the Georges V, Paris's smartest hotel just round the corner. Equally many of the most successful models damaged their health to stay at the top of their profession. Carmen dell'Orefice, signed up in 1946, at the age of fourteen, on an American *Vogue* contract, was so thin that all her dresses had to be pinned at the back. When this was made public, the magazine arranged for her to have injections which precipitated the onset of puberty. When her curves then began to appear, they lost interest. Nancy Berg, a contemporary of Bronwen's, has described how she did not sleep for a decade because of a 'red liquid called the "doctor"', a drug which she took to keep her thin and put her on a high. Even the level-headed Jean Dawnay gave up modelling in 1956 after a spell at Dior 'because it was killing me. My waist had shrunk to sixteen inches and I knew I couldn't keep it up.'

And though the Paris fashion world had all the trappings of glamour, it was, for most models, a hard slog. There were long days spent almost entirely on one's feet. Often there would be physical exhaustion, as another English name of the period, Christine Tidmarsh, recalls of her days at Dior. 'You read now about these supermodels jetting around the world first-class, being picked up at airports in limousines. We were lucky if we got taken on the plane from Lympne to Le Bourget over the English Channel. It was usually trains and heaving your own bags.'

Balmain, according to the fashion historian Jean-Noël Liaut, favoured two distinct types for his models. 'On the one hand were the "young girls" whose elegance was cheeky and impish. On the other there were the women of the world.' The greatest of the usually blonde young girls had been Praline, who in the late forties and early fifties was the tempestuous star of the house. Her humble roots (she was the daughter of a bus driver), her flamboyant lifestyle off the catwalk, and her unsuccessful attempt to break into Hollywood made her a household name in France. The Greek tragedy of her life came to an end in 1953 with a car crash and unleashed a national wave of mourning in France.

On Bronwen's arrival, Praline had been replaced but never eclipsed as head 'young girl' by Marie-Thérèse, the embodiment of the 'jolie madame' look which was the mainstay of eleven Balmain collections between 1952 and 1957 and which spawned a successful perfume launched with the same name in 1953. Marie-Thérèse was one of the stalwarts of the house until her retirement in 1962. She and Balmain were more than employer and employee. She would stay with him at Bon-Port, his country house at Croissy, or his villa on the island of Elba, and accompany him to the opera or grand receptions.

The 'young girls' always made up the majority of Balmain's team of eight house models. They would carry the more standard designs. Yet from the start he lavished particular creative attention on unusual and eye-catching '*mannequins mondials*' or 'women of the world'. It all began, fashion historian Guillaume Garnier has suggested, when Balmain employed as model girls a number of well-born eastern European women who found themselves in Paris, and came to a peak in the years immediately after the Second World War. One of the first was Elizabeth Grabe, who would take a break from showing his designs to greet her close relative Grand Duchess Helen of Russia with a ritual profusion of kisses. Another was Dan – or Baroness Danita Dangel – who had fled her native Poland when the Germans invaded in 1939. 'I have to work,' she once told an interviewer. 'I like clothes, I detest couture, but I have to do something.' Such was Dan's standing at Balmain that she alone of his models would dare to question the couturier's designs. Bronwen's own background may have been more humble and less troubled than these women, but she followed in their footsteps in the couturier's eyes.

She did not, however, get off to a very promising start. Her first show, the traditional dress rehearsal before the main opening for staff and a few long-standing customers, was greeted with icy silence. Her unconventional walk, her height and her habit of striking exaggerated poses – necklaces held out at strange angles from her body, her back arched, her head thrown back, just a flicker of an ironic smile on her lips – left her audience unsure how to react. Yet Balmain's faith in his Bella did not waver. For her first introduction to the public he picked out something guaranteed to emphasise her unique qualities. It was, he recalls in his autobiography *My Years and Seasons*, 'a long evening dress in a cloud of silk chiffon scarves printed with huge, dark flowers. The ensemble had been christened "Nemesis" and when Bronwen stepped forward proudly, her eyes fixed on the far distance and thoroughly determined to have her revenge on the doubters, she possessed a tragic beauty.'

Her name was made in that moment. There were still those who questioned her but, as Balmain himself remarked, 'it is better to be a talking point than to create only indifference.' After that first show Bronwen exerted a muse-like hold over the designer. 'He would, as with others, design clothes on me – often quite literally – draping material around me. Or sometimes he would draw something, have it made up in the workroom and then he would call me up.' The toile – a prototype made of sharp and scratchy ecru-cotton – would then be fashioned into something devastating as 'Bella' stood before the couturier.

According to the art historian Sir Roy Strong, the fashion designers of the later part of the twentieth century have been creating 'mobile sculptures on the human body' – which echoes the way in which Balmain worked with all his model girls. 'There are two sides to a mannequin's work,' the couturier wrote. 'The public sees her displaying the dress in the most majestic manner, but during the weeks of its creation, she had had to "live" the successive versions of the dress until its most perfect expression has been found. Sometimes simply by standing still she helps to create and she must always keep to herself her personal opinion of the dresses she wears.'

Yet with Balmain and his Bella, it was not simply that he hung a masterpiece on the easel that was her body. There was interplay in the creative process between the two, which was acted out in the 'grande dame' character that she became on the catwalk. Balmain encouraged her to play his Greta Garbo. 'He gave me my type. One day he said, "You are my Garbo," and he sent me off to see Garbo as Marie Walewska at the cinema to study her. I came back, made my make-up paler, plucked my eyebrows into a thin arc, put on more lipstick and false lashes and emphasised the impression of being detached.' The result was spell-binding. 'Very tall and incredibly slim,' Balmain wrote of Bronwen, 'she walked with long easy strides, her arms motionless against her sides. In her big light-coloured eyes, there was a complete absence of expression and ignorance of what was happening around her. She had a habit of slightly disarranging her hair as she entered the salon, giving herself a nonchalant air that is a sign of supreme English elegance.'

Though she had turned her back on acting when she opted for the teachers' course at Central, Bronwen was now blurring the distinction between modelling and acting, not simply giving clothes an elegance, drama and coded sexual frisson like most models of the time, but forgetting herself and creating a personality – quite at odds with her real self – on the catwalk. To the Garbo blueprint she also added humour, the wry smile, the ironic gesture with her hand, but it was her air of being above the fray – '*housse*', as the French described her at the time, borrowing an adjective used for thoroughbred race-horses – that marked her out. 'Bronwen always looked like a princess,' recalls Svetlana Lloyd, 'or at least what everyone expected a princess to be.'

Balmain was inspired by her shape. He created long, tubular dresses and coats for her with clear simple lines and no attempt at *décolletage*. They would be topped off with the angular hats which were part of the Balmain trademark. His suits were impeccably cut and he would finish off the austere evening gowns he made for her with furs. Typical was a dress called 'Grande Duchesse', a sheath of fine, violet satin with an eye-catching embroidered top, long gloves and a purple and gold skull cap, covered in gauze, in which she posed for the photographer Tom Kublin in 1957.

When later Balmain came to write his memoir it is significant that in his chapter on his special mannequins, he describes in detail just two women – first Bronwen and then the legendary Praline. All the others – even his beloved Marie-Thérèse – merit only a sentence. Together Praline and Bronwen epitomised the two sides of Balmain's genius – the former the more conventional, elegant look that became the *jolie madame*, and Bronwen his more adventurous, romantic side, in whose creations luxurious simplicity and restraint combined to evoke a formal 'traditionally feminine' style that belonged to the early years of the twentieth century.

Balmain was not a man for bold and ever-changing statements.

Continuity was his watchword and his often difficult relationship with the press came about partly because he resented their insatiable appetite each January and July in his shows for something new and eye-catching. 'Fashion is not planned,' he retorted. 'It must impose itself on the designer. We cannot sit down and decide to create longer skirts. New trends in clothes are not just plucked out of the air.' This belief in an almost mystical power of creation was most in evidence with his mysterious, elusive Welsh mannequin.

Yet when Balmain did want to cause a stir, he would also turn to Bronwen. Asked in 1958 to take part in a gala for Bastille Day, 14 July at the Ambassadeurs in Deauville, Balmain designed three dresses – one red, one blue and one white. The colours of the French flag were emphasised by the jewellery worn by each model to match her dress. Marie-Thérèse and Barbara, in blue and red, with sapphires and rubies supplied by Van Cleef and Arpels, came on first. Then Bronwen was carried on in a sealed, bejewelled box by four stewards. Balmain walked forward, unlocked the doors and flung them open. Bronwen emerged, covered in diamonds, her dress finished off by a white fur, her dark hair, as ever, messed up in a display of patrician indifference. She stood as motionless and impassive as a Greek statue with just a flicker of an ironic smile until 'The Marseillaise' struck up and a firework display began.

As one of the stars of the house, Bronwen enjoyed privileged freelance status. She was only required in Paris for two spells of eight weeks running up to the January and July launches of the new collection. In the interim another house model wore her dresses. Bronwen would arrive a few weeks before the grand unveiling to work with Balmain on designs, have fittings and be allotted her dresses for the show. Then, on the big day, she would capture all glances and all the headlines. For a few weeks she would model the collection daily for the most important customers of the house before handing on her pieces to her understudy and disappearing off to England.

There were some downsides to this arrangement. Balmain would often take a group of his models to show his clothes overseas – to America, to Berlin and, in March 1959, to Thailand at the invitation of one of his greatest admirers, Queen Sirikit. Bronwen never had the opportunity to go on these trips. Yet her schedule – though not unique for the time – still caused some envious looks in the *cabine* or models' room. Bronwen, less than fluent in French, let most of it drift over her head. In between shows she would sit quietly in a corner and immerse herself in Jane Austen, Kipling, Dickens, Tolstoy's *War and Peace* and Dostoevsky's study of good and evil, *The Brothers Karamazov*.

Yet she was aware of the resentment. Some French models felt their territory had been invaded. With around 150 dresses in each Balmain collection and just eight girls showing them, competition could be brutal and the atmosphere in the *cabine* – especially during the two hours of the performance – chaotic and emotional. 'The back-stage scene is a mixture of harem and bathing-box,' Balmain's directrice, Ginette Spanier once remarked.

The Paris fashion shows in the 1950s would make the front page of every major international daily. The British press, with the same chauvinism that now makes them focus – albeit on inside pages – on the success in the capital of fashion of Stella McCartney and John Galliano, quickly took note of 'Bella'. In a January 1957 report headlined OUR BRONWEN LEAVES THEM GASPING, the *Daily Herald*'s Serena Sinclair wrote: 'getting a gasp out of the foreign fashion buyers here is like squeezing a sigh from a sheikh with 40 wives. The model must be a very special type of girl . . . She [Bronwen] floats in like an apparition from another world, eyes glazed and distant, hair parted in the centre and flapping down her forehead, dressed like someone in a Victorian portrait.' Six months later, when Balmain revealed his next collection, the *Daily Sketch* declared that Bronwen Pugh was the 'toast of Paris'. Later, in an interview with the *Sunday Dispatch*, Balmain came out with a remark that he repeated many times subsequently and which has followed Bronwen ever after. There were, he declared, on the basis of his own considerable research, five beautiful women in the world – Greta Garbo, Marlene Dietrich, Vivien Leigh, the singer Lena Horne and his Bella.

Such a comment rises above the commonplace chauvinism of the British papers and even the praise lavished on his current star by her designer. It was not a compliment that Balmain ever paid to Praline. And from the papers' point of view, there were several other English girls in Paris to focus on if they merely wanted to pick out home-grown talent. Even with the retirement of Jean Dawnay, Bronwen emerged at a time when Fiona Campbell-Walter was still turning heads and Barbara Goalen, another tall, unconventional, aloof model girl, christened the 'Got-It Girl' by the press, was on the scene.

From the French perspective, however, the English – or British – contingent was still small enough for its members to be considered exotic. Bronwen's play on her Welsh roots gave her an added mystery since most of her admirers in Paris would have had little idea where Wales was. But however much they were fêted, the British girls never wavered in their strict professionalism, a quality not always associated with their French colleagues. There were agents in London to consult, schedules, punctuality and a clear distinction between work and pleasure. Ginette Spanier came to respect this new style of model girl: there were many vital elements to being a successful model and gradually she recognised them all in Bronwen.

> They [models] must be found beautiful and strange enough to inspire the boss, attractive enough to interest the press and self-effacing enough to satisfy the private customers to whom they act as clothes pegs. Above all they must be healthy. They have to turn up for work every day and take the strain of standing for hours on end, showing dresses. Most mannequins are a little in love with themselves. If they were not, they could never do the job they do, season after season. The applause, the little snippets about them in the papers – these are the only rewards they have.

Spanier was an acute observer, and for all Bronwen's professionalism and detachment, there was enough narcissism in her make-up to keep her coming back for more.

If Balmain was the creative genius behind the house – assisted by his young designer Karl Lagerfeld – then it was Ginette Spanier who controlled everything else. From her desk at the top of the main staircase, she ruled the roost. 'To run a house of haute couture is no light matter,' she wrote in her memoirs. 'I have to give the impression of dignity, calm and indestructibility. Not only to my staff but to the customers who pour in each day. I am able to influence their taste.' The life of the house was, she said, with a characteristically flowery flourish, 'like a tropical ocean. Here swim strange fish, glorious and glowing creatures; here are sharks, savage and peculiar; here are octopi, treacherous and grim, uncoiling themselves upon the unwary visitor.'

Spanier directed the *vendeuses*, who would give each client individual attention. Before the age when top designers produced off-the-peg collections for their own shops and franchised their name to mass-market operators, these customers were the principal source of income for the house. The bigger their celebrity, the more attention Spanier herself would lavish on them. Marlene Dietrich, Claudette Colbert, Josephine Baker, Brigitte Bardot and Queen Marie-Jose of Italy were among those who bought the clothes that Bronwen had modelled. And Balmain also designed for Hollywood's leading ladies – for Rita Hayworth in *The Happy Thieves*, Cyd Charisse in *Two Weeks in Another Town*, Jennifer Jones in *Tender is the Night* and Kay Kendall in *The Reluctant Debutante*.

The house of Balmain was never anything less than polished and elegant in the face it presented to the outside world, but behind closed doors it could be an amusing, camp, sometimes bitchy and self-absorbed environment. 'Once,' wrote Ginette Spanier, 'Bronwen Pugh, with her hair newly done up into heavy fringes, swayed up to Balmain asking him what she looked like. "Like an old, terrible woman sitting in a London pub drinking gin," said Balmain. "Divine." "Oh," said Bronwen, unshaken as she slipped through the curtains, "I thought I looked rather pre-Raphaelite."'

As the show approached, nerves could fray but there was a definite buzz in the air.

> I love the wildness, the elation and perennial feeling of dress rehearsal that means we open tomorrow [wrote Spanier]. I have sometimes stood on the pavement after dark and stared up at the House of Balmain, seeing every floor blazing with lights and the dark shadows of busy women passing and repassing across the unshaded glass. And I have been there the next morning at 5 am to see them still at it. Tired little girls from workrooms with arms full of half-finished gowns. Model girls made up like ballerinas, weeping from exhaustion, surviving on bottles of champagne.

Outside work hours, Paris was swinging. 'They were ten to twelve years of great euphoria,' wrote Pamela Harriman, the 1950s and 1960s socialite who lived in the French capital after her marriage to Winston Churchill's son Randolph broke up. 'We had won the war. We had earned our playtime. We were indulging ourselves. We knew it, but we felt we had a right to indulge ourselves. Dior came out of that indulgence . . . It was a glamorous time.' French culture – its films, its literature, its stars like Piaf and Yves Montand – had an unparalleled international following. And even if the ready-to-wear collections of the Seventh Avenue stores in New York were beginning to undermine the popular perception of Paris's status at the apex of the fashion world, the French still behaved as if they were the only ones who knew how to dress.

Paris's charms were initially lost on Bronwen. 'Paris can be a terribly lonely place,' she told the *Daily Mail* in September 1957. 'I think too that it's a rather sad place. To me it looks as though it was all very wonderful 50 years ago. Now I think the most typical sound of Paris is a sad, cynical laugh.' In a *Picture Post* cover story in April of the same year on how 'Bronwen Pugh takes Paris by scorn', Katharine Whitehorn, later a celebrated *Observer* columnist, reported how Bronwen's 'dirt-beneath-my-feet style of modelling' had made her the queen of the French capital, but how Balmain's star was unhappy lodging in 'a cheap room in a good hotel'. 'Bronwen has not decided whether to stay in Paris,' Whitehorn wrote. 'She has an ambition to set up a Welsh dress house.' Once again there was the element of Bronwen hiding behind an artificial pose, but she was on these occasions being rather more truthful than usual. Perhaps what she was really describing was her own outlook on life, mirrored in the city around her. A melancholy had continued to grip her soul since Erica's death, a fear for the fragility of life, an inability to divine a higher purpose, a certain inherited Celtic introspection and gloom. The intensity of her daily routine during her eight weeks at Balmain left little time for her fun-loving side. That had to wait until she got back to London, her friends and family. In Paris, she lived in a cheap hotel room near rue François Premier and spent her evenings reading and eating very little.

She told the *Daily Mail* that she was studying French. No one who knew her at the time believes a word of it. Her French was always rudimentary. Much more likely was that she had discovered another classic novel that had set her thinking anew. As ever, she was keeping her real self and real interests separate from the public figure who was becoming so regular a feature in the British press. Once again a celebrity, she found the loss of anonymity as disturbing in Paris as it had been in London. 'Suddenly all sorts of people were rushing up to meet you and take you out and you had to be very quick to size them up. Most of them you wouldn't want to meet. I suppose I became very suspicious, even paranoid.'

She was rescued from going mad by two other English-speaking girls who were working as house models at Dior. Cockney Christine Tidmarsh had already come across Bronwen on the modelling circuit in London. She now shared a tiny flat with Svetlana Lloyd – born of Russian parents in Egypt and schooled in England. There was not enough room for a third permanent flat mate, but for two spells of eight weeks they could squeeze up and benefit from the extra rent. So Bronwen, for the duration of her trips to Paris, moved into the avenue de la Bourdonnais. The small flat, above a porter's lodge, had a great view of the Eiffel Tower. Her room was a cubby hole off the main lounge, but however cramped it was, this bijou Parisian pied-à-terre provided her with the same sort of protection and sanity afforded in London by Pilgrims Lane. Svetlana and Christine shared her view of modelling as a career that was also, in many respects, an elaborate game. 'We all saw the humour of it,' Bronwen says now. 'We couldn't take it seriously. It wasn't a proper job, just something we did for fun and to make money.'

The problem with men was a constant topic of conversation in the flat. All three women favoured what they recognised as a safe and entertaining option. 'At work you had to put up with a certain amount of bottom-pinching and that kind of thing,' says Svetlana. 'There it was homosexual men who were easiest to work with because they didn't do that sort of thing. And as friends outside work, they were uncomplicated.' At Dior, Christine and Svetlana worked with the young Yves Saint-Laurent, soon to be propelled into the limelight by Dior's early death in 1957. At Balmain Bronwen got on famously with Karl Lagerfeld, then training under the master.

So they invited the two young men round to dinner. 'They thought they were coming to a proper sit-down meal,' Bronwen remembers, 'but (a) we had no money and (b) we had this tiny flat with no chairs. So we arranged cushions on the floor. They were polite when they arrived, but taken aback. The French like to dine properly. Karl was principal assistant to Balmain, which meant that one of his dresses might get included in the collection, but most of the time he was feeding Balmain with ideas. I remember so well that he said one day he would be rich and famous. We just laughed.'

The flat resounded most of the time with laughter. Bronwen, banishing her introspection, refused to be serious, though she could lapse into domesticity – 'she was a great one for laying the breakfast table at night,' Tidmarsh remembers – while Svetlana often ended up the good-natured butt of their jokes. 'Bronwen was always laughing', says Svetlana, 'a lovely tinkly laugh, but Christine was the clown. She had us all in stitches. She had a very mobile face and could do marvellous imitations. I was not great at making jokes. Being the youngest, I expect sometimes the joke was on me.'

On evenings out the three flatmates were sometimes accompanied by Karl Lagerfeld and Yves Saint-Laurent to Left Bank restaurants and clubs. 'Karl would dance in an unusual way,' Bronwen recalls, 'and we used to say to him, "What's this dance?" and he would reply, "You wait, this is the modern dance." We'd never seen anything like it.' Surrounded and supported by close friends with a similar outlook on life, Bronwen began to enjoy her time in Paris. She drove herself over from England in her yellow Renault Dauphine and got to know the city better. And she persisted, outside hours, in giving the impression of casual disregard for all the fuss she was causing. 'I can remember the days when Bronwen used to lope in looking like last year's birds' nest, with her hair all over her face and a string bag for shopping,' recalled Ginette Spanier.

This was the real world. Its pleasures were innocent. The three flatmates once went to see a fortune teller. Bronwen, she predicted, would one day be very rich but would end up with little money once more. Struggling to make ends meet on their meagre wages, they laughed off the prediction.

Some evenings, away from the hot-house of Balmain, the three

girls would earn extra money by working for the photographer
Georges Saad, modelling clothes from a whole variety of designers
for the trade catalogue, *L'art et la mode*. On other evenings, though,
there were more formal outings for their employers. The house of
Balmain would send its stars to charity galas and opening nights,
wearing the couturier's latest designs. They were ambassadors for the
collection. After a brief show, they would go and join the dinner
tables of the great and good. It was a new experience for Bronwen.
In London, designers at that time had not recognised the public
relations potential of having beautiful women parade before flash-
guns in their evening dresses and furs.

Balmain's largesse extended further. If one of his stars was going
out on a date with a wealthy or famous man who had contacted her
back-stage at the house, he would insist that she wore one of his
creations. With the fashion houses then so dependent on patronage,
it was a wise investment. So when Bronwen was taken out to
Maxime's by Aly Khan, a celebrated playboy, escort of the most
glamorous models of the day and a friend of her future husband, she
was head to toe Balmain.

Rather more embarrassing was Ginette Spanier's largesse, or more
particularly her attempts to pair off Bronwen with her husband Paul
Emile (or Polly Mill, as he was known to some of the models). To
be sent out on a date with the directrice's husband was a tricky
enough assignment in itself. Then to have to fight off his amorous
advances was a trial. And finally to realise that Spanier not only knew
but, acknowledging that her marriage was a matter of no more than
companionship, was complicit in the arrangement was a shock.

For the most part, however, Bronwen steered clear of dinner
invitations and took the blandishments of her admirers with a pinch
of salt. The adulation being heaped on her by Balmain, reporters
and the endless procession of wealthy men keen to take her to dinner
were all summarily dismissed. 'Yes, I was flattered and if it was
someone famous, I was curious. But I had learnt to be very careful.
You might dine, but you wouldn't get involved. There was a glamorous side to it, but I found it too unsafe.' Svetlana Lloyd echoes this
note of caution. 'The people who wanted to take us out were not
the people we wanted to go out with.'

In Paris, building up to a show, the outside world could seem a million miles away to the three girls in their flat on avenue de la Bourdonnais. The Suez crisis of 1956, pitting Britain and France against Egypt's President Nasser and bringing the eastern Mediterranean to the brink of war, touched them via Svetlana's parents, who left Cairo and took refuge in Beirut. The Hungarian uprising of the same year, ruthlessly crushed by Soviet tanks, made a similar impact because some of Svetlana and Christine's colleagues at Dior had relatives caught up in the conflict. So comfortable did Bronwen grow to feel in her own little world in Paris, that she was tempted to stay there for a greater part of each year. It was a subject that often came up with Christine and Svetlana. But Bronwen's reasoning was straightforward, Svetlana maintains. 'She did not want to lose her roots in England and her friends there, her place among people she knew and understood.' There was also her need for rest. She quickly became exhausted, ending up in hospital in 1958 when her career demands grew too great.

Though a star in Paris, part of Bronwen's allure was the mystery that surrounded her, the exotic Welsh woman who would appear twice a year and turn the house of Balmain upside down. Familiarity, by contrast, breeds contempt. Back in London, life could be lived on her own terms, within parameters she understood and in a language she could speak. Moreover her celebrity in Paris had made her a star back home all over again.

Chapter Six

The believer, who has communicated with his god, is not merely a man who sees new truths of which the unbeliever is ignorant; he is a man who is stronger. He feels within himself more force, either to endure the trials of existence, or to conquer them. It is as though he were raised above the miseries of the world, because he is raised above his condition as a mere man.

Emile Durkheim, *Elementary Forms of Religious Life* (1951)

London was quick to claim the new queen of the Paris fashion world as its own. The British designers who in the past had used Bronwen Pugh only sparingly, if at all, were suddenly convinced that she was the only person who could show their couture collections. And the photographers who had overlooked her in the mid-fifties on the grounds that she was too unusual now couldn't get enough of her distinctive style.

Peter Clark, one of the best-known photographers in London at that time, chose her as his face of the year on his 1958 calendar. With a lighted cigarette in a long black holder, jewels round her neck and wrist, she stared impassively into the lens in homage to Marlene Dietrich. The illusion is all the more impressive when you remember that there were no make-up artists to assist model girls at that time. Bronwen's look was all her own work. A rising and later controversial star, Helmut Newton, begged her as a favour to pose for him as he built up his portfolio. She did, and the results, with Bronwen in a fur hat peering imperiously over a balcony, appeared in *Tatler* in July 1958. But she was later to regret her generosity when Newton, at the height of the debate in the 1970s about his 'White Women' collection of photographs which many regarded as pornographic and exploitative, named her as one of his early muses.

Both *Tatler* and *Town and Country* put her on their covers and in 1959 she was accorded the honour that had hitherto eluded her – the great John French photographed her. In the result, Bronwen, leaning back, glancing over her shoulder with her left arm, white glove reaching towards its elbow, held out at the sort of exaggerated angle that had become her trademark, is simultaneously the alluring temptress and the haughty aristocrat. The pose – provocative, but not too provocative – neatly illustrates the changing style of fashion photography as the buttoned-up fifties gave way to the freer sixties.

The British press followed 'our Bronwen' and her every move. In May 1959 she was unanimously declared 'the queen of London Fashion Week' by the critics. In September she was guest of honour and made a speech at an annual lunch at the Savoy, organised by the Marchioness of Lothian, to hail her as one of the 'Women of the Year' alongside Edwina Mountbatten. And when Balmain came to London in May 1960 to show his collection at Sotheby's auction rooms, Bronwen was acclaimed the hit of the evening as she first trailed a white mink coat with a sable collar after her along the catwalk and then stood, impassive, as Balmain gave a lecture likening her tall, thin shape to the model for a Modigliani portrait which hung on the wall next to her.

Socially, too, Bronwen was in demand. 'There seemed to be so many parties then, small gatherings at people's homes, great big receptions. The Chelsea Set was in full swing.' When her flatmates from Paris, Svetlana Lloyd and Christine Tidmarsh, came back to London for a few days, the three of them would go out and have fun. 'I would save my money and every three weeks come to London for the weekend,' Svetlana remembers, 'to have a good time with boyfriends and parties and everything. You couldn't do that in Paris because French models were considered if not exactly prostitutes then fair game.' Bronwen would go out to supper with old friends like Mortimer Wheeler, and was introduced to new admirers like the actor Christopher Lee and the Duke of Marlborough, who invited her to the Dorchester to dinner. There was the simple thrill of it all. Nothing in her upbringing had involved dining at the best restaurants in London and she was curious to see what they were like. But there was something more. Despite her celebrity, she continued to seek out interesting minds, people with something to teach her, with a perspective on life that stretched beyond photo calls and trophy escorts.

At a party organised by a Polish photographer she met the sculptor Kenneth Armitage, a rising star of the international art world who had won particular acclaim for his work at the Venice Biennale exhibitions of 1952 and 1958. 'I was introduced to a group of models who were at the party. One of them was very sexy, I remember, and then I noticed the tall one. "Who's she?" I asked the photographer. "She's the most famous fashion model at the moment," he told me. We spoke briefly, but afterwards Bronwen had told him she'd like to meet me again. So we did and it was the beginning of a friendship that has continued ever after.

'At first we would meet every month or so – over lunch or dinner. Later when she married it was less frequent. But we were only ever friends. What struck me most about her was her poise – she was not like anyone I had ever met. I was used to more earthy types, art students. You couldn't imagine Bronwen in an art school. She was very correct. You would never think of fondling her, or putting your arm around her, affair or no affair. There was something superior about her. She would talk about writers and we would talk about my work. She was bright, which was unusual for a model, and she used to accompany me to events. I remember having dinner with her, the painter William Scott and Tony Crosland. She was clever and outgoing and fitted in very easily.'

Another artist who was entranced by her was the Scottish painter, later film director, Donald Cammell. In 1957 after meeting her at a party, he asked Bronwen if he could paint her portrait. The finished result, which he gave to her, was not a great success, her austere, angular beauty softened into a Princess Diana-like pouting prettiness, but again Bronwen was attracted to an unorthodox, Bohemian, intense figure with an unusual perspective on the world. A couple of years later Cammell turned his back on painting, claiming it was finished as an art form, and concentrated on film, releasing in 1970 the cult classic *Performance*, hailed by some as the original sex, drugs and rock 'n' roll movie, and starring Mick Jagger, Anita Pallenberg and James Fox. According to Fox, Cammell, who committed suicide in 1996, had a knack for 'pushing people to the edge in terms of knowing themselves and going where they hadn't been before'. It was a quality that had a definite appeal to Bronwen as she struggled to make sense of her own mental journey.

In a professional sense, Bronwen had it all. Modelling was never going to make her fortune, given the rates of pay in those days, but she worked hard and was in demand. She was financially independent. Her career was booming and her national and international reputation growing. She was a household name in Britain.

Yet it was no longer enough. On one level, it was simply a case of the age-old problem of it being easier to get to the top than stay there. 'The fun was going out of it,' she says. 'It was becoming a drudge. I was finding it harder and harder to get motivated and of course I knew that you are only the face for a season or two. Nineteen sixty was approaching and I was beginning to wonder what next. I was twenty-eight and getting on.'

She was mulling over the possibility of going to America, where photographic models were better paid and continued to be in demand until well into their thirties, but the real problem was that mapping out a career blueprint was not her major concern. Modelling had, after all, never been anything but a distraction, a way of dealing with Erica's death and proving herself in the face of her family's expectations. The greater her celebrity, the more she regarded the whole circus that surrounded her as empty.

By what she regarded as a fluke the daydream had come true, but now she knew that the person the audiences and the public were celebrating was not her but their own projection on to her. If they knew that privately she preferred reading Aldous Huxley's *Perennial Philosophy* to attending an opening night, a discussion with an academic to a date with a film star, her fans would have been bemused. Tidmarsh sensed that she was different: 'A beautiful woman with nothing inside is a very dull woman. Bronwen wasn't dull. There was something else about her. She was very private about it, hardly ever talked about it, but I knew it was there.' The epitome of late 1950s glamour was leading a double life, torn between the drama and materialism of her career and the solitude of her spiritual journey. If anything, she was leaning ever more towards the latter as a counterbalance to her fame. Yet ironically it served only to enhance her professional reputation. When, in shows, her detachment led her to strike ever more exaggerated poses, to cast ever more disdainful looks, she was applauded.

The temptation to send the whole performance up with humour became irresistible. Modelling a collection of evening dresses at Courtaulds in Cavendish Square, she and Christine Tidmarsh grew steadily more bored as the various rehearsals dragged on all day. 'Bronwen was sitting in the corner doing some knitting – of all the unglamorous things,' Tidmarsh recalls. 'And when it came to the great dress rehearsal, with just a favoured few in the audience, we thought we might make it a bit funnier. I had this great Zizi Jeanmaire fan which covered my face when I first appeared. I put these big false eyelashes on my upper lip like a moustache, put the fan up in front of my face and walked out into the lights. When I stopped, I dropped the fan and everyone roared with laughter. Then Bronwen appeared, still clutching her knitting. The agent who was organising it didn't find it at all funny. He didn't speak to us for years.'

In April 1959 Bronwen had the bitter-sweet pleasure of returning to her old employers, the BBC, to appear on a special 500th edition of the popular current affairs magazine programme *Tonight*, with Cliff Michelmore and Geoffrey Johnson Smith. The item marked a big mink show at the Dorchester and she appeared wearing a £9,000 pale lavender mink coat. When Michelmore asked her how it felt to wear, no doubt expecting a paean of praise, she announced rather grandly that she didn't much care for mink. 'You see too much of it around.' He was lost for a response.

The truth was that her budget didn't stretch to mink. She only had a three-quarter-length rabbit coat – the cheapest skin you could get – but she had bought it from the smartest furriers in town, Calman Links. Bronwen the model might disparage such luxuries in public; in private she had a taste for them, but insufficient funds to indulge it.

Her particular nonchalant but majestic style on the catwalk might have suited mink, but the London fashion scene was in the first stages of a revolution that was already signalling the end of the era begun by Christian Dior's New Look. John Stephen opened his first shop on Carnaby Street in 1957. Mary Quant's waistless, twenties-style sack dresses and new knee-length short skirts were all the rage down on the King's Road in Chelsea. In a matter of years they would have conquered the world, with even Balmain forced to shorten his lengths and abandon his studied austerity.

That *fin-de-siècle* feel contributed to Bronwen's restlessness. Younger models, like the waif-like Jean Shrimpton, were more in tune with the new designs. Yet her Pugh blood made her go out to meet every challenge. She knew Mary Quant through Chelsea Set parties and when the opportunity came to show the designer's first collection in her new Brompton Road shop, Bronwen, to everyone's surprise, accepted. 'I knew it was a great thing to do her first collection and there was no doubt that she was absolutely dazzling.'

'Bronwen was such a wonderful model,' Quant recalls now, 'that I viewed her with the utmost awe and didn't dare suggest she had a Vidal Sassoon hair cut when she was showing my new collection. Late and minutes before the show she arrived – full make-up and looking sensational with the new Vidal Sassoon cut and showed to ecstatic applause.' If shorter skirts and boots were not quite tailor-made to Bronwen's catwalk persona, she demonstrated that she still had sufficient style and flexibility to carry them off.

One of the star names that Bronwen had met through her work at Balmain was Noël Coward. He was a great friend of Ginette Spanier, who regularly had him to dinner at her Paris apartment. On one occasion, she invited Bronwen along. As 1959 began, Bronwen met Coward again at St Moritz, where he was holidaying and she was showing a collection by leading English designers as part of a New Year's Day event. He invited her for a drink after the show and she met up with some old acquaintances from London, Patrick de Laszlo, a wealthy banker and a friend of Bill's, and Deborah, his wife. They complimented her on her performance. She smiled and thought no more of it.

However, it had been an extraordinary show. 'We had such awful clothes,' she says. 'We were so embarrassed by the collection. They were from England – good designers like Hardy Amies, John Cavanagh and even some early Mary Quant, but they were six months out of date and the audience was sophisticated enough to realise. One model made a mistake and the audience started to laugh.' Emboldened and, in her unsettled state of mind, unafraid to let her professional guard slip, Bronwen led the other girls in gently mocking the clothes they were showing. In an age before cameras were at every major fashion event, such licence was occasionally possible, although the audience's ready and surprised response demonstrated that it was in their experience highly unusual.

'We started making deliberate mistakes to let them know what we thought about the clothes. One girl went on and as she twirled round she had nothing but her petticoat on underneath. Then my zip undid and I screamed and made a big thing of it. It became like a cabaret. The compère, David Wynne-Morgan, was getting more and more het up, which made it funnier and funnier. The audience, thinking that it was all rehearsed as some sort of cabaret, began clapping each mistake.' At the time, the organisers were furious, but in retrospect even Mary Quant sees the funny side.'Bronwen wore a white leather mini-length coat with white fur collar and cuffs and high white boots. But forgetting she had nothing on underneath, she flung the coat open with the most majestic swirl revealing a white crêpe thigh bandage – the most chic spare garter ever seen.'

Bronwen's cabaret performance had made quite an impact on the de Laszlos. So much so that the next day, when they lunched with their old friend Viscount 'Bill' Astor, a regular visitor to St Moritz, they mentioned the model girl cum comedian they had met the previous day. Bill Astor, brought up by a mother who liked nothing more than to send up people and institutions, and a man who valued highly both beauty and a sense of humour, decided that he had to get to know this Bronwen Pugh. He put out some feelers. 'The next thing I knew was a model girl called Margaret Brown met me at a party at Esmerelda's Barn and said, "Bill Astor wants to meet you." I said, "Who is Bill Astor?" And she said, "You know, Cliveden." I didn't. Anyway I said something about my name being in the telephone book for anyone who wanted to call me, and a few days later Bill called. In those days London was very small and it was not odd to be rung. I'm afraid I just thought, Here is another one, and when he asked me to lunch I just said, "Thank you very much, but

I'm afraid I'm not free then." That was always how I dealt with these callers.'

Bill Astor was not used to being put off. Since the collapse of his second marriage he had dated a number of glamorous, successful women. Bronwen's reluctance only made him more curious. So he called three more times. 'Once he asked me down to Cliveden. I think it may have been on his second call. I was very shocked. I told him that I couldn't come because we hadn't been introduced. I didn't realise at the time that he would invite down whole groups of people he hardly knew. I thought it was something more intimate, that he was just another of those rich men that one avoided.'

If there was a particular type of man who appealed to Bronwen, he would combine the good looks of the film star Leslie Howard with a certain vulnerability – what she now calls 'little boy lost'. Since she hadn't met Bill Astor she couldn't judge him on the first count, but when he displayed the second quality, she softened slightly. 'He rang me quite late one evening. He'd just been to a white-tie dinner with the Knights of Malta – he was one of only two non-Catholics to be decorated by them for his work with refugees – and he said that being all dressed up with his sash and medal had given him the courage to call me and risk being told "no" one more time. I agreed to meet him for lunch really just to get rid of him. I made sure I had something to go to straight away afterwards.' Lunch was on a spring day at Bill Astor's London home at 45 Upper Grosvenor Street – a property he had bought in 1935, after his election to the Commons, as a base from which to pursue his parliamentary career. Though he had moved to the House of Lords in 1952 on the death of his father and had all but abandoned whatever political ambitions he once had, he had maintained a well-appointed and well-staffed residence in the capital.

Bronwen's first impressions of her host were mixed. There was something in him that reminded her not of Leslie Howard but of Fred Astaire, slight of build, graceful, precise, full of nervous energy, always moving around physically or in conversation. He was old enough to be her father – twenty-two years her senior, she later discovered. It did not unduly put her off, though, since she had grown accustomed to going out with older men like Mortimer

Wheeler, who continued to act as a mentor to her. And Bill made
her laugh. A shared sense of humour was subsequently the bedrock
of their relationship. 'He had this very quick wit that all the
Langhorne Astors had. It wasn't just that he told funny stories but
he had a funny way of looking at things. The whole lunch was
much more enjoyable than I thought it was going to be, but I still
hurried off to my prearranged appointment and really thought that
was it.'

A few weeks later Bill telephoned to ask her down to Cliveden
for lunch during Ascot Week in June. This was no whirlwind courtship. Still Bronwen regarded Bill simply as a friend. She said yes,
knowing very little of the Astors' annual ritual of lavish parties for
the great and good at Cliveden to accompany the social whirl of
the royal meeting at nearby Ascot. It was only when she got to the
house and drove up its long drive that she began to realise what
sort of world Bill inhabited. It was, she quickly concluded, outside
her orbit. With no interest in horse racing – Bill had a celebrated
stud and several of his horses were running at Ascot – she had not
expected to know any of the other guests, but there were a couple
of familiar faces who reassured her at least that their host was a good
man. She had a pleasant time glimpsing another world, but still felt
no emotional bond towards Bill. The truth was that her heart lay
elsewhere.

At around the same time as the St Moritz show Bronwen had met
a young Welsh psychiatrist, Michael Davys. If ever a man was tailor-
made to appeal to her, it was Davys. They were close in age, passionate about their Celtic roots and their shared experiences of Welsh
patriotism through their parents, and fascinated by the mind. They
had hit it off immediately and Bronwen, for the first time in her life,
at what was then the late age of twenty-eight, fell deeply in love. 'I
was so focused on him, so intent on chasing him that I didn't really
think about Bill.' But there was a problem. Michael Davys didn't
want to be chased. He was keen on Bronwen, flattered even to be
pursued by someone universally regarded as a great beauty. Yet he
had no plans to settle down. 'We are still friends,' Bronwen says,
'and he told me years afterwards that I hadn't given him time. But

Bronwen's parents: Alun Pugh with his wife Kathleen pictured outside Buckingham Palace in 1959 when he received a knighthood.

Chimps' tea party: Bronwen, aged six, on a visit to London Zoo.

The Pugh children: pictured outside their Hampstead home are (left to right) David, Bronwen, Ann and Gwyneth.

Above: Alma mater: Dr Williams' School at Dolgellau pictured in the 1940s.

Left: Soul mate: Erica Pickard, in costume, was Bronwen's closest friend at the Central School of Speech and Drama. Her tragic death in 1952 catapulted Bronwen into modelling.

Right: Continuity announcer: in 1954 Bronwen became the face of the BBC, appearing on screen to link its programmes.

The TATLER

JULY 9 1958

& BYSTANDER — 2/-

Cover girl: Bronwen during her days as one of the big names in the London fashion scene on the front cover of *Tatler* in July 1958.

Star of Paris: as well as containing a lengthy interview about her life in Paris as Balmain's muse, the *Picture Post* had Bronwen on its cover in April 1957.

Balmain's 'Bella': the young English photographer, Jane Bown, later at the
Observer to become the most celebrated portraitist of her age, took this picture
of Bronwen in 1958.

Camera-shy: John French, the doyen of British fashion photographers in the 1950s, was only converted to Bronwen's looks late in the day. This picture, her only one for him, was taken shortly before her marriage and retirement.

Statuesque: Bronwen's height made her a natural, Balmain recognised, for showing to best advantage the tailored English suits that were then so fashionable.

I was in a hurry and in those days I thought whatever I wanted I could have.'

Though she had taken with a pinch of salt the praise that was routinely heaped upon her, being told day in day out that she was beautiful, whatever her own doubts, had undoubtedly made an impact on her self-image and hence on her expectations. She had begun to take on board her own myth. At the very least it gave her self-confidence. So when Michael Davys rebuffed her advances, it was an unexpected and shattering blow. However, the effect of this unhappy love affair went much deeper. It brought to the surface those questions that she had been pondering since Erica's death and the start of her modelling career. Her obsessiveness about Michael, her inability to see that she was overstepping the mark, was a sign, she realised, that she was teetering on the edge of a breakdown. Her inner life and outer life were dramatically out of kilter. The combination of unrequited love and hard work was not only making her painfully thin – her weight continued to drop off her 35-23-36 figure – and prone to bursting into tears; it was bringing her to a crisis point.

'I understood so little at the time,' she says, 'but now I know that when the pressures are building up inside you, when you are fundamentally unhappy but unable to face it, you reach a stage where you either break down or break through. I had got to that point. I knew that I just couldn't cope any more. Michael was not the cause, merely the catalyst who brought a whole lot of other issues to the surface.'

It is a theme she has explored in her subsequent work as a psychotherapist, contributing an essay, 'Of Psychological Aspects of Motherhood' (1990), to a published collection of academic papers. There is just a hint of autobiography when she writes: 'the person in trouble has come to a point of the conflict of contradiction and is unable to hold opposites together. Often one set of opposites is repressed or suppressed in the unconscious but has surfaced and caused confusion in his or her life.'

Since that early other-worldly experience at the age of seven, Bronwen had been acutely aware of another dimension of life. As a schoolgirl there had been moments when she felt an overwhelming oneness with nature but, unable to make sense of the experiences or talk them through with others, she had begun to suspect that there was something wrong with her. Put plainly, she worried at times that she was going mad. Yet she had a very real sense that the world was not as straightforward and – in the light of Erica's death – futile as it seemed. The problem was to integrate in her head her intuitions and her everyday observations.

That was what had started her reading psychological gurus like Gurdjieff and Ouspensky, philosophical tomes and a wide range of fiction, from Jane Austen through Tolstoy to Dostoevsky. What she learned confirmed her suspicion that there was an unknown but potentially huge power in the mind and the human spirit, but she was still far from fashioning any sort of framework, much less understanding or in any way controlling a capacity within her to remove herself from her body, mentally to stand aside and watch herself do something.

So far she had failed to associate what was going on inside her with organised religion or a Christian God. She had abandoned the church-going of her childhood, finding it an empty and soulless routine. However, she began to realise she could not reject the notion of a divine presence. She had known instinctively in that Hampstead garden at seven that she was in the presence of God. It was just that she didn't associate that divinity with the Christian God to be found in churches. She had therefore started to read a little about Buddhism and had been attracted to its beliefs, finding in them some echo of her own feelings, but she still tended to feel isolated in what she had experienced. Occasionally her friends would recognise something unusual in her. Kenneth Armitage, the sculptor, speaks of her in this period as being 'in her own island, in her own soul', but the only person she felt able to open up to was her sister Gwyneth.

'I was once describing to her how I felt when I was showing clothes – that I wasn't really there and could stand aside and watch myself doing it – and she likened it to the experience of some Spanish mystics she had studied at Oxford. "It's a mystical state you're describing," she said, and it was such a relief. Not that I suddenly thought I was a mystic, but it took away that sense of being all alone with this. I hadn't known what was going on. In my reading I'd been trying to find out and here Gwyneth was telling me that there were others.'

This was the first time that Bronwen had made a link between this capacity within her and Christianity. It was still only a tentative step, but the connection, broken since childhood and abandoned in a world where God figured very little, had been remade almost inadvertently by Gwyneth. Mysticism – usually defined as a loving knowledge of God which is born in a personal encounter with the divine – is a well-established though minor tradition within the Christian churches. In the western church it centres around the idea of individuals involuntarily entering into mystical states, leaving the physical world behind and glimpsing God or feeling His presence. That awareness of God remains with the person thereafter. Many of those who have recorded such experiences are ordinary believers, but mysticism is usually associated with a handful of celebrated names. In the twelfth and thirteenth centuries there were schools of mysticism, while later mystics like Meister Eckhart and the nun, Julian of Norwich, had popularised the idea of reaching God through letting things be, or rather letting go of worldly and therefore sinful compulsions.

But it was the Spanish mystics of the sixteenth century that Gwyneth had referred to who had done most to establish their approach as a distinct and respected Christian spiritual tradition. The Carmelite mystic, poet and theologian John of the Cross provided beautifully symbolic and subtly analytical accounts of the human experience of God. The way to God was through the 'dark night', an often perilous journey of faith and love beyond images and thought. He called God 'a ray of darkness'; each believer was transformed by the experience of God's love in an intense and personal encounter into a harmony with Him that was a type of mystical marriage.

It was Teresa of Avila, John of the Cross's great correspondent, who bridged the divide between the psychological world that Bronwen had hitherto been exploring and the religious dimension that Gwyneth was now pointing out to her. Teresa was an incipient psychologist who created categories and images to communicate her subjective, interior responses to the ineffable experience of God – the interior castle, as she put it. She dwelt at length on people's lack of self-knowledge and God's power, as experienced in a personal revelation, to make individuals know themselves better and live their life henceforth in unity with Him. Integral to her type of mysticism were visions, ecstasies and other extraordinary events, but these, she stressed, were just openings to God's love. Gwyneth had made Bronwen aware of such writings, but before she had made much progress in exploring them further, the disarray in her emotional life reached fever pitch.

'It was night-time. Michael had gone away on holiday and I was standing at the bedroom window of my flat and the sky began to move towards me – or me to it. I started to project myself out, out into space and space started moving. It was very frightening. Terrifying. The sky was literally racing past me. I knew it was happening in my mind, but it felt like something physical. I remember thinking I must have it out with God, if it was God that was making this happen, that something had got to happen, that I couldn't go on any more like that. I felt like a puppet on a string, that God had promised me love, told me love was all that matters but now was playing with me, denying me this love with Michael that I wanted. So what was this love? What was God if not love?

'I went to bed to sleep but I began to play a game that I played when I was a child – I thought everyone did and only found out later how unusual it was – of losing consciousness. I used to be put down for a rest every afternoon when I was a child and I was never tired, so I would pretend that I didn't have any feet until I couldn't feel them any more. I used to let it go up to my neck and then I'd stop because I was frightened. And this night that came back to me, but this time I didn't stop at my neck. I felt I had nothing to lose – I was in such a state. I felt that life was not worth living anyway, that I'd be better dead.

'The numbness overwhelmed me. It was terrifying. I can only liken it to what I imagine throwing yourself out of a window is like. Except this time I was throwing my mind out of my body. I had this feeling of falling – like when you feel yourself falling asleep but I was very much awake, and then I was conscious, I know this sounds odd, of my Welsh grandmother, of her presence, urging me to "Go on, go on". I was in terrible pain which was cutting me in half. I thought I was dying, that I had gone out of my mind and now this was it, death. And all the time I was falling down a tunnel like Alice in Wonderland. On either side of it, things were trying to get me, things that I hated, slimy, muddy things that wanted to smother, kill or suffocate me. I kept my arms at my side so as not to touch.

'And then finally I saw the bottom, the light. I knew that if I fell into the light, I'd be safe. It was like falling into a furnace, but not hot at all. It was warmth, light, love, knowledge. It was God. I knew it was God. And every cell of my body went into orgasm. It was like being ravished all over. And I thought, "So this is what God is, God is light, and overwhelming love." There were no longer any distinctions between mental, physical and spiritual and emotional. Love was everything and it was all one. And there was the sense too that God knew me already. To realise that you're known is such a wonderful thing – and to know that you are forgiven, the slate is wiped clean.

'When I came round, I had no idea of whether it had been hours, days, weeks even. But I knew I was thrilled and relaxed, that the burden had been lifted. And almost at once I fell into a deep, deep sleep.'

The sceptical, late-twentieth-century temptation in considering such a detailed description is to suspect the work of the sort of powerful imagination that Bronwen Astor certainly possesses. Yet other writers through history and in various religious traditions who describe mystical experiences of the divine use disarmingly similar language – dropping through a trap door into darkness, the tunnel, the great pain, and finally falling into a sea of sparkling energy where they find oneness with themselves and oneness with a divine presence. Those who bring the Christian God into the picture speak of Him in terms of an ocean of consciousness, or unmanifest energy. 'Suddenly everything made sense,' one contemporary writer, Catherine Lucas, puts it. 'It was like watching the sun sail out from behind a cloud – the light was there all the time, but now I knew its source and everything became more radiant.' Teresa of Avila, too, wrote of entering the light in a physical rapture when she encountered God in the series of mystical experiences that dominated her middle years. 'It is not a radiance which dazzles, but a soft whiteness which, without wearying the eyes, causes them the greatest delight . . . It is a light which never gives way to night, and being always light, is disturbed by nothing.'

There are, essentially, two types of mystical experience, a distinction described by T. S. Eliot in a celebrated lecture he gave at Trinity College, Cambridge, in 1926. 'I wish to draw as sharply as possible the difference between the mysticism of Richard of St Victor, which is also the mysticism of St Thomas Aquinas and Dante, and the mysticism of the Spaniards, which . . . is the mysticism of Crashaw and the Society of Jesus.' The first sort, Eliot pointed out, was classical and ontological – concerned with pure being. The second was more psychological and romantic. Bronwen, from the start, had elements of the first in a cocktail made up largely of the second. In time, however, she would develop a more balanced hybrid.

Some churchmen, trained to discern true mystical experiences from flights of fancy, have listened to Bronwen's description of her spiritual experience that night and are convinced of its authenticity. 'There is a dramatic element in what she recounts,' says Dom Bruno, a Carthusian monk who later befriended her. 'The idea of being ravished by knowledge of God introduces a psycho-sexual element that one has to be wary of. Yet equally it is there in the writings of John of the Cross and in the Bible in the Song of Songs'. Teresa of Avila too introduced an erotic edge into her account of her encounters with God's angel. 'In his hands I saw a long golden spear and at the end of the iron tip I seemed to see a point of fire. With this he seemed to pierce my heart several times so that it penetrated my entrails. When he drew it out, I thought he was drawing them out with it and he left me completely afire with a great love for God. The pain was so sharp that it made me utter several moans: and so excessive was the sweetness caused me by the intense pain that one can never wish to lose it, nor will one's soul be content with anything less than God.'

The only real way of judging claims about mystical experiences, according to Dom Bruno, is to look at the life of the person afterwards. 'In Bronwen it seems to me that she lives with and is influenced by the close presence of God on a daily basis, that she is conscious of this and cooperates with it, and that you can see the inner vitality of the Holy Spirit about her. They are things that are impossible to capture on film or in a portrait, or even in writing, but you can both discern them or their absence in the person.'

Yet set against any such endorsement is the fact that medical science has long denounced descriptions of mystical experiences as the signs of a pathological state, bordering on madness. They are often dubbed 'primary delusions'. Even the Christian church has been suspicious of them as potentially influenced by anti-Christian forces. And philosophers have argued that ecstasy is immoral, contrary to nature and a renunciation of human liberty.

'The next day,' Bronwen remembers, 'I woke up and I felt that it was my birthday. I had a totally new outlook. That feeling lasted for at least three weeks – total ecstasy and excitement. The first thing I did that morning was go to my bookshelves and pull out a book of Dylan Thomas's poems which until then had been incomprehensible, and then T. S. Eliot, and suddenly I could understand everything that I hadn't been able to understand before. It was as if suddenly I could read French.'

Again this has direct parallels in Christian writing – the gift of tongues, given to the apostles by the risen Christ in the New Testament so that they could preach to people whose language they did not speak, is the most obvious example. And the books that Bronwen names fit neatly with her own preoccupations at this time. The theme of acceptance of the unknown, humility before a greater, divine and mystical force, is one that appears in both Thomas and Eliot. Having fought against any recognition of this for so long, having tried to fit it into some clear and logical pattern, Bronwen found that her own spiritual experience had unlocked for her the meaning of their words.

Though Thomas wrote much that is accessible – his play *Under Milk Wood*, for instance – elsewhere, especially in his poetry, his imagery can be dense, psychological, Celtic and mystical; it can be approached only on an instinctive level. His *Eighteen Poems*, published in 1934 and influenced by surrealism, is wild, romantic and difficult. One critic, Martin Dodsworth, has written of Thomas's 'impossible endeavour to utter a magically transcendent truth'.

Certainly his immersion in the Celtic twilight would have appealed to Bronwen's growing attraction for the identification with her own Welsh forebears. When, around this time, she began a journal of her inner thoughts, which she kept up only intermittently over the next decade, she wrote out on the opening page a quote from the Preface to *Under Milk Wood*. 'The Welsh are difficult even for themselves . . . deeply emotional but sternly self-controlled except on important occasions, distrustful of one another, hostile to strangers, thrifty because of poverty, secretive because of pride, melancholy because joy is dangerous, hard-working but without the German complacency in labour for its own sake, sensuous but puritan . . .'

In his combination of philosophy and eastern and western religious traditions T. S. Eliot had an obvious attraction for Bronwen at this transitional point in her life. She had already been moving from the psychological insights of her early reading towards Buddhist and Christian ideas in the days immediately before her spiritual experience. The *Four Quartets* charts a spiritual journey, with Eliot both distilling his own experiences – the four places he describes all had a special meaning for him – and assessing human insignificance and powerlessness when faced with eternity. He mixes Buddhist-influenced concepts of reaching the place of knowledge by the way of not knowing with an acknowledged and – for Bronwen appealing – debt to Christian mysticism and Teresa of Avila.

Initially Bronwen's instinct in trying to understand what had happened to her was to turn towards Buddhism. Despite Gwyneth's advice she still held the God of her childhood at arm's length. 'Straight away I saw a book that I had picked up on Zen but never understood. And I began to read that and read about the oneness of everything and I decided that I had had what Buddhists call an enlightenment experience – "satori". I thought I was a Buddhist. For a few months I thought I was a Zen Buddhist.'

If she struggled to find a way of explaining the transformation, she couldn't mistake its fruits. 'I had changed totally from negative to positive. The outside world was all right as it was, but inside I suddenly saw everything in a completely different light. That has stayed with me. Of course at the time I had no idea what had happened, only its results – a feeling of fulfilment, of in-dwelling love, of compassion, of inner healing. It has taken me years to realise, through reading and praying and meeting people who have had similar experiences of the Holy Spirit. You get a feeling of being totally at one with everything. You are part of it. You are not looking at it, but you are actually the sunset as well. And something clears in your mind and you understand something of the reality of nature, and you feel at last that you are a drop in the ocean, of one mind with the universe. It was not until I had this experience that I suddenly was inundated with love.'

The pain she had felt on her descent down the tunnel, she came to believe, was not a splitting apart, but a welding together of her different and previously contradictory parts, healing the pain of Erica's death. Likewise the sensation that washed over her at the bottom of the tunnel was her experience of a power that knew her, could act through her, but was a mind, an intelligence beyond anything she could comprehend. This concept of overwhelming love, of some kind of preordained plan which managed to reconcile past and present, grief and happiness, the material and the spiritual, gave her a pattern into which to fit the peaks and troughs in her life up to then. 'I had been trying to find my path, trying to fix on this beam of love since I was seven and it wasn't happening. It had driven me to a pitch of despair and then suddenly it was there with me. It was as if every cell in me, once it had been ravished by that warmth, was now "determined". There had been peaks of experience before, but now I had reached the plateau and would be fixed there. Each cell now knew what it was meant to be. I had been turned inside out, fixed on to God and on to a purpose of life.'

The experience had left her joyful, full of spontaneity and overflowing with energy. It also enabled her to face up to what had been negative in her life up to then – her feeling of being unloved. 'That is all part of inner healing. With the growth of the ego in each of us, we develop so that we cannot integrate both the good and the bad in ourselves, so we shut off the bad, deny it is part of us. But we have to come to terms with it if we are to unblock our energy.' When Davys returned from holiday, she turned to him as a friend and as a psychiatrist for a psychological explanation of what had happened to her. 'He tried to explain it with his psychiatric training.

He thought I was close to being psychotic, which I probably had been before the experience, and that I was looking for a meaning for the experience. The spiritual aspect was not something that he could grasp completely.'

The problem, however, was to know what to do with her experience, how to apply it to her everyday life. 'When you are filled with this feeling of light and power, you want to tell people but they just thought I was either stupid or nutty. I'd go round singing, laughing, being jolly, but I had to learn to contain this gift, this fountain of energy, to use it constructively and not let it dribble away.' Her need for acceptance and understanding once more thwarted, Bronwen began again her solitary, contemplative search through books to find a context for what had happened to her. Leafing through the Sunday papers, she saw a review of a book called *The Phenomenon of Man* by a little-known French Jesuit, Pierre Teilhard de Chardin, with an introduction by Sir Julian Huxley, an eminent writer of the period on religion and science. She went out at once and bought a copy. What caught her eye immediately was Teilhard's assertion that 'co-extensive with the without, there is a within'; in other words, that the world had inner meaning and that one's inner thoughts and one's outer reality had to be in harmony. At last she had found a soulmate, albeit one who had died four years earlier.

It was through Teilhard that Bronwen came to see her experience in Christian terms. It was a slow and gradual process over a period of years, but Teilhard was the key. In 1912 he had had the first of several mystical experiences of his own which had parallels with her own revelation. He described it as dying and being reborn in the Lord, as a Pentecost experience – in the sense that at Pentecost the apostles had realised the divinity of Christ, the incalculable breadth of His power and their own mission as His instruments.

The enrichment and ferment of religious thought in our time [he had written in the 1920s], has undoubtedly been caused by the revelation of the size and the unity of the world all around us and within us. All around us the physical sciences are endlessly extending the abysses of time and space and ceaselessly discerning new relationships between elements of the universe. Within us a whole world of affinities and inter-related sympathies as old as the human soul is being awakened by the stimulus of the great discoveries. And what has hitherto been dreamed rather than experienced is at last taking shape and consistency. Scholarly and discriminating amongst serious thinkers, simple or didactic amongst the half-educated, the aspiration towards a vaster and more organic one, and the premonitions of unknown forces and their application in new fields, are the same and are emerging simultaneously on all sides. It is almost a common-place today to find men who, quite naturally and unaffectedly, live in the explicit consciousness of being an atom or a citizen of the universe. This collective awakening, similar to that which at the same given moment makes each individual realise the true dimen-sions of his own life, must inevitably have a profound religious reaction on the mass of mankind, either to cast down or to exalt.

The echoes in such passages of Bronwen's own search, her own experience and her own attempt to reconcile her sense of the divine with a material world won her round at once. The poetic and dra-matic tone of Teilhard's prose held a great appeal for her. Here was a man far removed from the Christian church of her upbringing, who could describe an experience of God in a way that mirrored her own mystical experience.

Teilhard's lifelong interest had been in effecting a reconciliation between science and religion over the question of the origins of the universe. A geologist and paleontologist, he was ahead of his time in his church, where science continued to be viewed as the enemy of God. While he had a strong academic following, efforts to explain his theories to a wider audience always ran the risk of caricature – a lecture in the States in 1936 made headlines in the *New York Times*, with Teilhard dubbed 'the Jesuit who believes man descended from the apes'. Such coverage invariably raised hackles amongst his superiors and Teilhard, throughout his working life, kept his head down. Academic posts were denied him by Rome and he had to endure long periods of exile to China and America plus censorship of his writings in order to remain true to his vocation as a priest. 'He was a mystic, you see,' says Bronwen. 'He could see a greater purpose and if people in the church were awful to him, he wouldn't have thought of leaving the priesthood. He would just have known that they didn't understand.'

By 1959, however, the tide within Catholicism was turning in Teilhard's favour. A new Pope had been elected in 1958 – John XXIII – and in 1962 he summoned the Second Vatican Council with the express aim of 'aggiornamento', opening a window on the modern world. Teilhard's admirers – men like the Dominican theologian Yves Congar – were among the leading reformers at the Council and the influence of his philosophy can be detected in some of the most significant documents to come out of the three-year gathering, notably the encyclical *Lumen gentium*, the constitution of the church.

Bronwen discovered Teilhard just as he was posthumously receiving credit for his pioneering work, and at a time when his books and essays were finally being published in translation. *The Phenomenon of Man*, written in the early 1940s while he watched the world at war from China, was a summary of his vision of humanity, covering all its biological, sociological and mystical aspects. His own religio-scientific philosophic system linked Darwinian ideas of evolution with Christian concepts of a creator God. Divided into four sections – pre-life, life, thought and survival – the book's message was that the universe is a single, evolving organism, started by God, continuing in God and ending in God, in which everything is linked with 'germs of consciousness' existing in the smallest particle of 'brute matter'. Here was a way of explaining Bronwen's own conviction that she was 'a drop in the ocean, one with the mind of the universe' and increasingly 'one with a personal God'.

Energy, both human and abstract, which had been a key part of her own revelation, was central to Teilhard's thought and he identified two sorts in the on-going evolutionary process – tangential or measurable energy in terms of winds, heat or light, and radial or psychic energy which the human species uses to bring measurable energy from disorder to order. The scientific, the philosophical and the religious were all bound in to this theory, since both types of energy were ultimately God-given and God-directed.

However, the greatest force of psychic energy, Teilhard wrote, was love. Again it was as if he had read Bronwen's mind and was commenting directly on her own mystical experience. As his biographers and disciples Mary and Ellen Lukas put it:

Men would, he believed, learn in time to care for one another, and even be willing to sacrifice their individual interests for the great 'self' of mankind, in the certainty that their mutual co-operation could only individualise them further. When this attitude became common, Teilhard held, the psychic temperature of the conscious world would reach a new incandescence. Men, individually and collectively, would naturally turn inwards on themselves in search of union with a Being more living and more conscious than they were themselves. And such a Being could only be that mysterious force which lay at the heart of reality from the beginning – the point of incandescence and personal passage to which Teilhard gave the code-name Omega.

Bronwen knew the mysterious force and on that night in 1959 she had experienced her own moment of incandescence, but until she read Teilhard's book she had not made any firm connection with the Christian God. Now she knew that she could be a Christian and true to herself. She could combine the faith of her upbringing with the insights of her adult life and no longer had to turn to eastern religions for an explanation. Moreover Teilhard's determination to combine the spiritual with the material found a ready echo in her own search to reconcile her life, with its professional successes and personal disappointments, with what she came to recognise, through his writings, as mystical experiences of the divine. Reading his words convinced her finally that she was not going mad, while his openness to psychology and science in general chimed neatly with her developing appreciation of her own psychic and psychological potential.

The combination of her spiritual experience and her discovery of Teilhard brought about a profound change within her. When modelling, she felt freer and happier. 'When I look at pictures of me from that time I can see the detachment had gone. My inner conflict had gone. I was at peace with myself at last.'

It was at this point that she heard again from Bill Astor. He invited her to lunch in August. 'I was trying not to appear any different and most people hadn't noticed, but he immediately said, "You've changed, what is it?" So I talked to him about it. I didn't go into details because I still didn't really understand myself, but he listened and tried to understand. It didn't matter that he didn't. He had recognised that I had changed.' She had been waiting for a sign and here it was, from a totally unexpected source.

He called her again soon afterwards. Over dinner, he produced a diamond brooch. 'It was one of those assumed proposals. I knew if I accepted the brooch, I accepted him.' She still had feelings for Michael Davys: though his reaction to her mystical experience had been cold and rational, a part of her continued to believe that if she gave him sufficient time, they might still marry. She had even gone so far as to propose to him, only to be told that he was not at a stage in his career where he could contemplate marriage.

The two men in her life emphasised the different sides of her character. To marry Bill would throw her into a world where her party-going, fun-loving, extrovert side – what one friend once called 'the jolly hockey sticks Bronwen Pugh' – would be satisfied. To wait for Michael would be to yield to the solitary, contemplative, Celtic side of her nature, the part that made her withdraw when people mistook her friendship for more and made her hold herself aloof. What tipped the balance in Bill Astor's favour was her spiritual revelation. 'It all fitted. Outwardly it was very appropriate – model girl marries millionaire. Others had done it before. And inwardly it was appropriate because I could not turn away from Bill's love without turning away from God's plan for me, and also because Bill knew his Bible inside out. He was a very spiritual person. He may have turned his back on Christian Science* but he had been brought up with firm religious principles and he now was Church of England.'

Yet on the surface it was an unlikely match – a man so much older, twice married, with two children, whose lifestyle and expectations were completely foreign and indeed intimidating to Bronwen. For all her love of partying, she had no idea how to run a large house, let alone one of the most famous stately homes in Britain. She knew, too, that people would suspect her motives and query her suitability in a world peopled by ex-debutantes. Yet the element of caricature went much deeper. Part of her persona as a model girl was the haughty aristocrat, the grande dame. By marrying Bill she would be playing the role in real life as chatelaine of a stately home.

* Espoused by his mother, Nancy.

But it was just a role. It was not her natural inclination. She knew – on the basis of her success as a model – that she could probably do it well, but to outsiders it would merely confirm a certain, mistaken view of her.

Yet she couldn't explain to anyone – not even Bill – the confusion that was going on in her head and her heart. 'When I knew Bill was going to ask me, I thought, God, I don't particularly want this. But I realised that when Bill had said that he had recognised that something had happened, it was a sign. I would rather have had someone of my own age who had not been married and who had a simple life. I was hoping for that. I knew that it was all about love and there was Bill who thought he was unloveable. This was what God wanted me to do. That's why I said yes. After you had had a sense of this overwhelming love, you don't fall in love again because you realise that falling in love is a projection of yourself. It is finding something in the other person that you don't realise you have got. Once you've got this thing, once you feel directed by someone or something other, by an overwhelming love, you love everybody and in that sense you could be married to anybody.'

Bronwen's spiritual high did not sweep away all her doubts, however. Her friend Kenneth Armitage remembers discussing with her over lunch the pros and cons of marrying Bill Astor. His own view was that she should go ahead, but again she could not explain what was pushing her forward. Though he had an inkling of her spiritual beliefs, he too made the obvious link between the duchess of the catwalks and the future viscountess at Cliveden. 'It seemed to me that there was something very right about the marriage,' he says. 'She was used to being photographed, to dressing up in fancy clothes and she would have to do all of those as Bill's wife. And Cliveden was not a normal house. It had its own tinge of theatre for Bronwen to play up to.'

From Bill's point of view there was one very concrete problem. Divorce in those days was a lengthy process and he was still legally married to his second wife, Philippa. Until the technicalities had been sorted out, Bronwen insisted that they tried to keep their plans a secret. Her main concern that any news of her forthcoming marriage shouldn't interfere with her work. Such was her status with the press that she knew she would never have a minute's peace once they heard she was marrying a wealthy viscount. Bill agreed and saw the need for caution, but his enthusiasm for his wife-to-be was such that sometimes he found it hard not to give away his feelings. Even if they did not know about the planned marriage, friends soon noticed that the couple were seeing a lot of each other and that Bill Astor was noticeably happier than he had been of late. Nicky Haslam recalls taking Bronwen to a glittering party in Syon Park, 'but once we had made an entrance, with everyone turning to look at her, we sat down and Bill Astor was at our table. Their eyes met and they danced all night. I used to think that I was the one responsible for introducing them, but then I learnt the truth.'

'Bill was always talking about Bronwen to me,' says Joy Darby, his secretary at the time, 'about how wonderful she was and I used to see her letters pouring in and his pouring out. But at first she didn't come to Cliveden that often. He kept all her letters in a secret hiding place behind one of the panels in his study. He felt he was very lucky. He kept trying to give her the earth, but she just wasn't interested in his money.'

When they were apart Bill deluged Bronwen with letters. In March 1960 he wrote to her in Paris: 'the luxury of communicating with you is so great that having spoken to you at nine fifteen, written to you at ten fifteen, here I am at one forty five starting again. I would never have dreamt that at 52 I could be so gloriously, violently helplessly happy.'

Though many of his old friends when they later learnt of his attachment to Bronwen assumed that he was simply a rich man seeking a trophy wife and finding one in a woman hailed as one of the world's great beauties, Bill's letters to her tell another story. It was not her looks that had bowled him over. Indeed, on the one occasion that he came to see her model he was rather disconcerted at the distant, slightly dishevelled look she favoured. 'I got a shock,' he wrote to her after seeing her on the catwalk, 'as I had always imagined you at work as lovely and gay, and I was knocked off my emotional perch when you looked cold and aloof.' He mentioned in particular his dislike of the top-knot in which she had gathered her hair.

'The extraordinary thing about you,' he wrote in the spring of 1960, 'is that your mind has survived the chicken chatter of the *cabine* for so long, remaining lively, enquiring, intellectual and deep. That really is amazing as whatever the virtues of your sex and your profession, a lively intellectual life is not one.' In another equally ardent communication he continued the theme: 'It is you I love, not your face, your figure, your legs or your glamour, but the basic Bronwen the person.' This he defined as 'your sweetness, integrity, humour, daftness, intelligence, affection, practical ability, lunatic fancies, and your capability to give and receive love – and inspire it'.

Bill found it hard to conceal the source of his new-found happiness from those closest to him. Early on he introduced Bronwen to his old friend Zara, Lady Gowrie, who lived in Parr's Cottage, one of the properties on the Cliveden estate at his disposal. She was in poor health and Bill used to visit her every week. 'Zara's letters were full of Bill's latest romance – with Bronwen Pugh,' writes Pamela Cooper, Lady Gowrie's daughter-in-law. 'Zara called her "The Pencil" in a not very flattering tribute to her wonderful legs and shape.'

Zara Gowrie's grandson, then a student at Oxford, now Lord Gowrie, often spent weekends at Cliveden and saw a complete change in the Bill Astor who had acted as a mentor to the younger man. 'My grandmother saw at once that Bronwen was genuine. Bill was suddenly bubbly and looked so happy. And she had real energy. "Come on, let's do this, let's have fun," she used to say. She was so much better for him than one of those conventional upper-class wives whose main concern is who to invite back to dinner next Tuesday. In time Bron had to do a bit of that too, but she gave him back a feeling of being alive.'

On Bronwen's part Grey Gowrie detected great tenderness towards Bill. 'She had and still has a certain instinctive gravitation towards lame ducks. I don't mean that in a patronising sense. Bill was highly intelligent and remarkable in many ways, but he lacked self-belief.' And he, like other friends, saw that despite their differences something clicked between them. To casual enquirers, Bronwen would always say that what attracted her to Bill Astor was his sense of humour and his charm. There was a strong element of dodging the question about this response, which avoided touching on much deeper, more complex motivations, but there was also a hefty dose of truth. 'They had this enormous shared sense of humour,' recalls Christine Tidmarsh. 'Bill was a terribly funny man in an innocent, practical joker sort of way. And Bronwen's humour was always very physical, jolly jokes. They just went together.'

'We clicked in a way which was remarkable,' Bronwen remembers. 'I am not very amusing but I am very light-hearted. If people take me too seriously, but at the same time don't take me seriously enough, I can't bear it. Bill got it absolutely right. We both appeared to make light of things, but we were both rather serious people in principle.'

Gradually Bill began to introduce Bronwen to his family and then to include her in parties and gatherings at Cliveden, though all the time refusing to answer any questions about marriage. In January 1960 the writer Maurice Collis records a dinner at Cliveden with the Commander of the American fleet, Admiral Robert Dennison, Lord Granley, Bill's ex-brother-in-law, Wilfrid Blunt,* Zara Gowrie and 'Bronwen Pugh, the dress model and daughter of the County Court judge of that name'.

> The rumour that there exists an understanding between her and Bill may have substance. Her expression is charming. She told me that old Nancy Astor had spoken nicely to her. Perhaps there is an engagement there. Bill even asked me what I thought of her and I said I had been struck by the look of humanity in her face.

Another fan of Bronwen's was Joan Astley, who had been a friend of Bill's since 1943, when she was working for British Intelligence in Cairo; she met her while staying at Cliveden one weekend as Bill's guest. 'My first impression of her was how quiet she was. I suppose I might have been a little frightened of her, this great beauty that I had read about in the papers. But as soon as I talked to her, I saw she was both genuine and had common sense. At last someone with common sense at Cliveden, I thought. Because Bill did have this side to him, the charming fifth-form boy who would never quite make it to be a prefect.'

---

* Art master at Eton and brother of Anthony.

Until they were married Bronwen did not, however, spend a great deal of time at Cliveden. Discretion mixed with a reluctance to immerse herself in such an imposing and regimented world. She would meet Bill in London or at a small cottage she rented on an island in the Kennet near Newbury, where she could indulge her passion – learnt from her mother – for the characteristically solitary pursuit of fishing. Her sister Gwyneth and her husband Ron Barry once joined them. 'I remember doing the washing-up with Bill one evening,' says Barry. 'He said it was the first time he'd ever done it in his life. Bron brought that sort of normality to his life.'

Despite the couple's circumspection, the rumours grew. They even reached the ears of Bill's formidable mother. A few months later Collis was again at Cliveden to celebrate the publication of his biography of Nancy Astor. Bill had just returned from several weeks in New York attending to family business matters there. Lady Astor asked Collis about the rumours of Bill's plans to remarry. Collis admitted he knew nothing but added, 'the rumour is very strong. Michael Westropp, the vicar of Cookham, mentioned it to me when I dropped into the churchyard to see the daffodils. He spoke as if it was certain and deplored it, feeling that Miss Pugh was much too young, a disparity that is alleged to have bedevilled the second marriage.'

Lady Astor, a possessive mother who was never by instinct keen on any of her sons' choice of partners, shared the vicar's misgivings. She opposed the principle of Bill marrying again. Maurice Collis recorded in his diary in May 1957 a conversation he had had with her. 'We spoke of the disaster of Bill's second marriage and she said that she hoped very much that no reconciliation with Philippa would take place. "But perhaps he had better not seek a divorce as he will only marry a third damn fool." Like many women of her generation, Nancy Astor regarded models as little better than prostitutes chasing rich men. She finally met Bronwen when Bill brought her to his mother's London flat. They apparently got on passably well, but some time later, at a Cliveden weekend gathering, Joan Astley witnessed Nancy making public her disdain for Bronwen. 'Nancy Astor made some terribly cutting remark to her like, "Oh, Bill must be just another of your boyfriends," implying that she was a tart. And

Bronwen was marvellous. She did not bat an eyelid. She just laughed back. She had her own dignity.'

Nancy Astor's was not the only voice urging Bill to rethink. His second wife's well-connected relations held him responsible for breaking her heart and seized on the sight of him courting a model girl to ridicule him as an old fool and denigrate Bronwen as a gold-digger with ideas above her station. Lady Dorothy Macmillan, Philippa's aunt, made clear her disapproval when she later met Bronwen. 'We had heard the unkind gossip about Bronwen,' Lord Gowrie remembers. 'In those days it wasn't in the papers as now, it was in what people called society. "Model gets her millionaire." But you only had to see them together to know at once that such a judgement was wrong.'

Among Bronwen's circle, most could only see the inner calm that had descended on her and assumed it was the result of her relationship with Bill. They had no idea of her spiritual experience. There were also anxious voices. The most direct was Billy Wallace, a rich bachelor, best known as an escort of Princess Margaret. He knew Bronwen socially and took her to one side when there were rumours of her involvement with Bill Astor and warned her not to marry him on the grounds that he was a 'child-snatcher'. The phrase referred to Philippa, who was only twenty-five, compared to Bill's forty-eight, when they married in 1955.

Bill had something of a reputation as a playboy, though it was much exaggerated. In the gossip of gentlemen's clubs, where it was deemed perfectly normal for a chap to have a wife and a mistress, and not unusual if the two women knew about and tolerated each other, a separated man who lived alone but sought female company could quite feasibly be judged louche without anyone sniffing a whiff of hypocrisy. If he chose as his companions women who were not well-born, it would be assumed he was having a roll in the gutter. In an age when divorce was still uncommon and carried with it a certain moral stigma – in 1955 Princess Margaret herself was prevented from marrying her great love, Group Captain Peter Townsend, simply because he was a divorcee – Bill Astor's track record of one divorce and one pending, plus the nasty taste that had been left following the rapid break-up of his second marriage to a much younger woman, led some to suggest that he had a problem with long-term relationships and preferred casual sexual liaisons. It was, his friends insist passionately, malicious innuendo, spread by old men with too much time on their hands and too little experience of women.

'There had been a few girlfriends who had come up for weekends after the failure of his second marriage,' recalls Grey Gowrie, 'and some of them were not very genuine in their affection for him, but I always think of Bill as more vulnerable and childish than over-sexed, a man for pillow fights and romping, not some kind of sex maniac.' With his secretary Joy Darby, an attractive unattached young woman who often used to dine alone with him in the library at Cliveden on quiet evenings, Bill Astor was a model of propriety. 'He was lonely, he was charming and he used to tease me a lot. But he didn't flirt and he certainly never made any improper suggestions.'

Despite his evident joy during their long, secret engagement, there were moments when Bill did let the sceptics get to him. 'Gwyneth and I went to Cliveden before they were married,' says Ann Hibbert, 'and Bill asked if he could have a quiet word with me. He and I went into his study and he said, "Do you think I should marry Bronwen?" I just said, "It's up to you, Bill." I got the sense that he was never sure of anybody, that he was surrounded by bloodsuckers, people after his money. I assume that was what was on his mind about Bronwen. What he thought I would answer I just can't imagine. I think he did love her.'

Fear of failure and a self-protective instinct were just part of it, however. Bill Astor simply could not believe his luck. It was as if he thought he might one day wake up and find it had all been a dream – as he made clear in a letter he wrote to Bronwen while he was travelling on business in the West Indies.

I cannot on reflection get over the fact that I'm wildly in love with you. I've really only had two 'grande passions' – a Russian girl in China and a French girl in the Middle East. And I felt that after all my buffetings it would never happen again. And it has – to you who I meet by fate and are not my type, 22 years younger – and I'm mad about you and live in a mixture of bliss and worry that it may all vanish. I love you more and wonder how to do it.

He also speculated about her feelings: 'It seems to me you have never had the complete love of anyone and been able to love anyone who can return your love. Am I right? Well, I go on loving.' Her inability at this stage to explain her own emotional processes to her soon-to-be husband was perhaps responsible for introducing a note of doubt into his mind. 'So poor Miss P, reflect on what you have on your plate – a passionate, jealous, eccentric, opinionated, loving, rich, occasionally economical, bossy, self-centred yet attached, priggish, lewd, under-sexed, over-sexed, high-minded, low-minded, middle-aged Spaniard.* Can you bear it? It's heaven and hell and will be heaven.'

* One version of the Astor family history suggested that they were originally from Spain.

Chapter Seven

There was at Cliveden a family ghost ... The ghost was a
dynastic image that implied that the Astors, moving north and
east across Europe from Spain, had, as landlords of New York,
became a family immune to the ordinary problems of life, aloof,
high-minded, gifted, a little misunderstood, a two-dimensional
spectre that had no reality in the world of flesh and of men.

Michael Astor, *Tribal Feeling* (1963)

Bill Astor, on first acquaintance, seemed to have everything going
for him. A multi-millionaire with homes in London, Scotland, Ireland and the United States, as well as the celebrated Cliveden on the
Thames in Berkshire, he had been born into the most sumptuous
and affluent family environment that Edwardian Britain, then at the
height of her imperial power, had to offer. In America – where he
would spend just a few weeks each year at his flat in the 'family
hotel', the Carlton House – he was listed as one of the richest men
in the country on account of his substantial stake in the family trust
which owned several blocks of central Manhattan.

While he did not have a matinée idol's chiselled features, women
found something endearing about him. 'He was a nice-looking man,'
says Gloria, Lady Cottesloe,* 'but if you didn't know he was a
multi-millionaire, I suspect some girls wouldn't have looked twice.
Once you talked to him there was something very genuine about
him. He had no airs and graces.' Joy Darby, his secretary for much
of the same decade, remembers his eyes. 'They were a lovely brown.
He was balding but there was something very appealing about him.'

Yet the Bill Astor who was courting Bronwen was also, she quickly
came to realise, a deeply unhappy man. The failure of his second,

* Gloria Dunn, a friend of Bill's from the fifties who later (in 1959) married Lord
Cottesloe, politician and patron of the arts.

and very brief, marriage to Philippa Hunloke was only the immediate cause. With a disparity of more than twenty years in their ages, the couple had rushed into it, he on the rebound, and it had ended almost before it began. He was left profoundly lonely and deeply depressed after a second broken marriage and often spoke to friends of how much he missed his baby daughter Emily, who had gone with her mother when she left Cliveden. However, the melancholy mood that had engulfed him for much of the latter part of the 1950s had much deeper roots.

A bequest from his paternal grandfather – the man who turned his back on America and brought the Astors to Britain in the 1890s – had made Bill, at the age of twenty-one, independently wealthy. He had lived well and spent freely ever after. He came of extraordinary stock. His father's family had, in just over a hundred years, transformed their fortunes, first through fur-trading and then through property; having come to America as penniless European immigrants, they had become one of its grandest families. They could trace their ancestors back to Baden in Germany in the early seventeenth century, but spent a fortune trying to create a more elaborate ancestry back to Spain or Italy in the Middle Ages. His mother, a Virginian who grew up in relative poverty until her charismatic but feckless father Chillie – pronounced 'Shilly' – Langhorne finally got lucky in her teens, was the flamboyant Nancy Astor, the first woman to take her seat in the House of Commons. Though she had retired from Parliament in 1945 and was, by 1959, beginning to lose her formidable mental powers, she remained one of the most famous figures in the world.

The Astor millions meant that Bill continued to live alone at his main home, Cliveden, in almost unparalleled style. Bronwen's suitor had a chef, an assistant cook, a butler, a valet, two footmen, two secretaries, sixteen gardeners (half of them paid for by the National Trust), two stable men, a housekeeper, three housemaids, two chauffeurs, two carpenters, a handyman, a laundry maid and a sewing maid to service his needs and those of the house guests he entertained every weekend in 'the season' to assuage the loneliness, plus the many who attended the succession of charitable events that kept him busy in between. In 1957, for example, he had welcomed the Queen,

Princess Margaret, the Duke of Kent and Princess Alexandra into his home when he had played host at a coming-out ball for Daphne Fairbanks, daughter of his friend the actor Douglas Fairbanks Junior.

Bill Astor was one of a dying breed of British aristocrats who lived in the same style as their pre-war parents and grandparents. For many of his neighbours and peers, the ending of the Second World War had come as a rude shock. Labour had won a landslide victory in 1945 on the back of promises to replace privilege and social hierarchy with a more egalitarian society. Denis Healey, the future Chancellor of the Exchequer and Labour deputy leader, had dismissed the upper classes in a celebrated radio broadcast as 'selfish, depraved, dissolute and decadent'. Such sentiments, when allied with Labour's economic programme, had put an end to many of the great houses.

In the rhetoric of the egalitarian post-war world, the idea of working as a servant to the local aristocratic family had lost much of the cachet it once had, while the establishment of the welfare state and nationalisation had been funded by high levels of taxation on the rich. Death duties alone had risen to a peak of 80 per cent, leaving many inheriting heirs unable to keep up the family seat without selling off huge tracts of land or priceless art works. Evelyn Waugh's prediction, in the preface to his 1945 novel *Brideshead Revisited*, that the ancestral seats of England would disappear like monasteries in the sixteenth century, had proved prophetic.

Old families, like the Marquesses of Hertford at Ragley Hall in Warwickshire, had moved out of what they judged uneconomic houses. Some had torn down their abandoned homes. Between 1945 and 1955 400 ancestral piles had been demolished. At one stage they had been coming down at the rate of one every five days. Those families that had remained in residence resorted to desperate measures to make ends meet. At cash-strapped Stapleforth Park in Leicestershire, Lord Gretton drove paying customers around his estate in miniature trains on a specially constructed railway.

The Astor fortune that Bill had inherited from his father in 1952 may have been substantially reduced by such punitive taxation – and by the spendthrift tastes of his parents over half a century – but it still consisted of £2 million in UK assets alone (£50 million by 1999 standards), plus its bedrock, the Manhattan property portfolio. If his reserves had fallen, as the Astor family biographer Virginia Cowles puts it, 'from the peaks of superabundance to the mundane valleys of mere affluence' in the post-war period, Bill Astor still had more than enough resources to avoid the indignities of other aristocrats. He once told his friend Grey Gowrie that it cost him £40,000 to run Cliveden in 1965 alone, a sum which when translated to today's rates totals over £1 million.

His late father, the second viscount, had handed Cliveden over to the National Trust in December 1942 and established a substantial endowment to support its upkeep, but the family still retained control of White's Place, the dairy farm on the estate, plus the Cliveden stud, which housed their racehorses. And the Astors had the right to occupy the main house for as long as it suited them.

Bill's grandfather had purchased Cliveden in 1893 from the Duke of Westminster for $1.25 million. It had been designed by Sir Charles Barry, architect of the rebuilt Palace of Westminster, in Italian baroque style. The rectangular main building, completed in 1850, was topped by a Latin inscription composed by Prime Minister Gladstone himself. It had brought the first viscount little joy, however, his beloved wife dying soon after they moved in. In 1906 he gave it to his son Waldorf and his American bride Nancy as a wedding gift. They filled it with five of their own children – Bill, born in 1907, Phyllis (known as Wissie) in 1909, David in 1912, Michael in 1916 and John Jacob (Jakie) in 1918 – plus Bobbie Shaw, Nancy's son by her first brief marriage. They turned it into one of the most celebrated and occasionally notorious political salons of history in the 1920s and 1930s, with the journalist Claude Cockburn coining the phrase the 'Cliveden set' to describe what he believed – on balance wrongly – to be an organised circle of appeasers of Germany seeking to influence the great and good as they gathered round the Astors' dining table.

Yet with Nancy's retirement from front-line politics and the sub-sequent estrangement between her and her husband that was only partially mended by the time of his death in 1952, the social whirl of Cliveden had slowed down considerably in the late forties and early fifties. Bill had spent that twilight period living at his own house in Oxfordshire, but he had returned to Cliveden on inheriting the title, intent on reviving the traditions of his youth. This modest return to the entertaining of the pre-war years reflected the climate of the late 1950s and the resurgence of aristocratic influence and self-confidence under the Conservative government of Harold Macmillan.

Yet Bill himself was on the periphery of such circles. The establishment had always regarded the Astors with suspicion as a self-made 'new money' American dynasty, like the Rockefellers, Vanderbilts or Morgans, which had washed up on British shores. There remained a question mark over whether Bill was, to use a modern phrase, 'one of us' as far as the ruling classes were concerned. Neither his grandfather, his mother nor his father had been, of course, but Nancy, as Lord Gowrie puts it, 'had the force of personality to sweep all before her. Bill didn't have sufficient self-belief for that. He worried too much about what people thought of him. He was conventional to the degree of not escaping the conventions of upper-class society at the time but they certainly didn't fit him like a glove.'

His parents had delighted in their own independence of belief, buttressed by Christian Science, the almost primitive form of Christianity founded by Mary Baker Eddy in the nineteenth century. First Nancy and later – somewhat reluctantly – Waldorf joined her disciples and turned their back, as Baker Eddy had insisted, on conventional medicine. They included their children in this, and hence a minor heart condition that Bill suffered as a child went untreated, causing many problems in adult life. Bill's parents flaunted their unconventional religious beliefs almost as a matter of principle, but he had rejected them in favour of a more modest though devout Anglicanism. Though such a rejection was, he believed, crucial to his sanity, it contributed to the absence of the evangelical fervour in him that so marked out his mother. His instincts were conformist and pragmatic, though the combination of the legacy of suspicion with which his parents had been regarded and his own consciousness of living up to their reputation meant that he habitually stood apart from the world that had so consumed Nancy and Waldorf Astor. 'Bill had had since he was a young man an interest in the Far East and there was,' Grey Gowrie remembers, 'something almost Buddha-like in his apartness.'

His estranged second wife was Lady Dorothy Macmillan's niece and the recriminations that had surrounded the end of that marriage had only further reduced whatever standing Bill had in the Prime Minister's eyes. Where Macmillan had been happy to come to Nancy Astor – he had a home near her seaside retreat at Sandwich – to discuss his own marital problems, he had no time for her son and whatever political ambitions he harboured.

With his inherited wealth, there had been no need for Bill Astor ever to contemplate working, but such an abdication would have horrified his puritan parents. They had taught him that money brought with it public obligations. Once a conventional upper-class education at first Eton and then New College, Oxford (where he just missed a first), was complete he worked first on Lord Lytton's League of Nations enquiry into the Japanese incursion into Manchuria on the Chinese mainland – an experience that sparked a lifelong interest in the Orient – and later, in 1933, in the unemployment division of the National Council for Social Services. His parliamentary career had started well but quickly faltered. An effective platform speaker, he had won East Fulham back from Labour for the Conservatives in 1935 against the national trend and had risen rapidly up the ranks of junior office before the Second World War despite suffering a terrible teasing from fellow MPs on account of his formidable mother, then one of the most significant players in the Commons. When he had taken an unpopular stance in a speech, a heckler demanded that Nancy give him a good spanking. His closest links had been with Sir Samuel Hoare, one-time Foreign Secretary and an arch-appeaser of Hitler. As a political patron, Hoare had quickly become a liability when he was exiled, once war broke out, to be ambassador in Madrid.

Bill Astor had seen service as a naval intelligence officer in first Lebanon, then Jerusalem and finally at Ismailiya on the Suez Canal. On his return to Britain in the autumn of 1942, however, all his plans and assumptions about his future in public life had fallen apart before his eyes. In political terms, the tag of appeaser had proved hard to live down. Even though his mother had been amongst the Tory rebels who voted Neville Chamberlain out of office and installed Winston Churchill, the association of the Astor name with discredited ideas of appeasement had remained strong. Bill had been sharp enough on his return from active duty to see that the political climate was changing. Labour had come of age as part of the coalition government, while the Beveridge report on the welfare state offered the promise of a more equal society when peace came. Bill's instincts – like those of his parents – inclined towards social reform, and to that end he had been a founder member in October 1943 of the Tory Reform Committee which, unlike most of the Conservative Party, supported implementation of the report. As well as the principle of the matter, he had seen that rejecting Beveridge would lead to disaster at the polls.

Nancy's name had also been on the writing paper, but by this time she was rapidly and erratically becoming more right wing in her tendencies and was soon denouncing Beveridge and his plans for the 'farewell state' – to the horror of her husband, who had managed to persuade her to stand down at the 1945 election, though she had subsequently refused to accept his view that her judgement had gone and had blamed and punished him until his death for her exile from political power. The Labour landslide of 1945 had taken her old seat in Plymouth and had also claimed Bill amongst its victims. East Fulham had reverted back to Labour. Though he had remained politically active, he had failed by a handful of votes to be re-elected in 1950 at Wycombe, near Cliveden, and had to wait until 1951 to return as its Conservative MP. After six years away from the political mainstream, however, he had only one year to re-establish himself before his father's death moved him to the House of Lords.

Soon after his return from the front in 1942 he had suffered another blow when Cliveden was handed over to the National Trust. Despite the press release announcing the decision, which added that it had been made 'with the full approval of Mr William Waldorf Astor MP . . . who has returned from the Middle East with reinforced faith in the future of the country', another part of Bill's inheritance had effectively been removed. His future role at Cliveden was altered – though, as his son, the current Viscount Astor, points out, 'it was only the house and 250 acres of garden and woods, not the whole estate. In terms of making a difference to his life, it was only irritation with the National Trust.'

However, his most eagerly awaited prize from the family vault of treasures had been control of the family newspaper, the *Observer*. As the eldest son he had always assumed that this would one day be his and would provide him, whatever the vagaries of political fortune, with a national platform and corresponding influence. He had been closely involved at the paper for several years, writing articles, backing its independent stance, defending in letters to friends unpopular positions taken in editorials. When it had questioned the conduct of the war, Bill had written proudly, 'We are like Saint Athanasius "contra mundum".'

Yet at the end of 1942, with little or no warning, his father had passed him over in favour of his brother David when handing on the *Observer* to the next generation. Waldorf had come to believe that if the *Observer* was to take an independent position, above political party, then David, with his highly developed and highly individual philosophy, would be a more suitable custodian than Bill.

David habitually stood apart from his siblings, not least because he had, in his twenties, made a clean break with his mother, regarding her attempts to direct the lives, loves and intellects of all her sons as intolerable. He rarely visited Cliveden and, like his father a painfully shy man, avoided the socialising and posturing of Nancy's flamboyant 'court'. He brought to the *Observer* a modern variation on nineteenth-century radicalism, combining liberalism in the broadest sense of the word with a willingness to needle the political establishment and, on occasion, to oppose it over its most cherished beliefs and schemes.

If David had parted from his mother, he had grown, in the late 1930s and early 1940s, increasingly close to his father Waldorf, in whose gift, ultimately, the editorship of the *Observer* lay. Both Waldorf and David – unlike Bill – belonged to the high-thinking, plain-living school and both adopted what David himself later called 'a Liberal-Conservative attitude' in contrast to Bill and Nancy's instinctive Toryism. Sensing perhaps that the end of the Second World War would not see a return to pre-conflict Conservative hegemony, Waldorf decided that David represented the future.

Waldorf Astor, though publicly overshadowed by his famous wife, was a formidable, though austere and often distant figure within the domestic environment. His life was directed by a distinct puritanism

– what his son Michael called 'a conscientious form of Lutheran orthodoxy'. Michael later wrote of his father:

> The measure of his success in life, in my opinion, cannot be judged only by the 'good' and constructive things that he did, of which his record is modestly impressive, so much as in the quality of his struggle to think and where necessary to act independently of inherited belief, which was not for him easy because the pattern of his childhood had been restricted, formalistic and rigid; and he was by nature a man of classical rather than romantic mould, a respecter of institutions rather than a rebel.

After the disappointment of losing his Commons seat in 1919, when he succeeded to his father's title, Waldorf had devoted himself to a life of public service, believing that the wealth and position he had gained by an accident of birth should be used to the greater good of society. It was a creed that for most of Nancy Astor's political career in the Commons united the couple, but with the onset of war she became increasingly reactionary in her sentiments, launching into repeated attacks on state socialism. It caused a public rift with Waldorf (George Bernard Shaw, Nancy's great correspondent, once referred to Waldorf Astor as 'that commie'); he believed that his wife was losing her judgement, and became increasingly close to David and therefore distanced from Bill, who seemed to share his mother's right-wing sympathies.

In some respects, however, it had been a caricature of Bill's views. Though his instincts were entirely conventional for a man of his background, he was not without a radical edge. His stout defence of the concept of empire in the war years, for example, was counterbalanced by an early appreciation of the danger of racism. He had denounced it in the early 1950s in, for the time, impeccably progressive terms. 'If missionaries are going to be encouraged to take a bigger part in Kenya so that people can get the benefit of the Christian religion,' he had told his fellow peers, 'it behoves the Europeans to give an example of that religion by abandoning practices such as the colour bar which are wholly incompatible with Christianity.' Later he had savaged the bar on women taking seats in the Lords in the period before the introduction of life peerages in 1958. 'To oppose their admission to the Lords,' he said, 'would make the House absurd in the eyes of the country.' And he had been one of the first and most enthusiastic advocates of the Common Market.

Indeed, it could be argued that, though perhaps in 1942 it had been less apparent, Bill had turned out both politically and personally very like his father, both of them shy, patrician, charitable, farseeing and compassionate men. That realisation must have made his exclusion from the *Observer* all the harder to bear. Though he continued to work conscientiously as a director under David, he remained hurt by his treatment, too generous openly to resent his brother, but complaining privately in 1943 to his friend Thomas Jones, a socialist professor of economics, that his younger sibling had 'a complete ascendancy . . . over Papa' and later that his father 'had seldom asked my views on any political subject . . . although he often sends me his which are often David's in origin'.

Sidelined at the *Observer*, Bill had never quite recovered any sense of direction in his work and fell back on the more conventional pleasures of a wealthy man in what we would now call his middle youth. Though much was later written giving him an exaggerated reputation as a playboy to rival his great friend, the Prince Charming of the international jet set, Aly Khan, Bill, like many of his contemporaries, had simply in these grey post-war years enjoyed having fun – at the racetrack, skiing in St Moritz, playing polo, shooting pheasants, riding with the Whaddon Hunt near Cliveden, fishing at his property in Scotland or partying in London. There was an element of rebelling against the rather joyless Christian Science-inspired moral code of his upbringing – Nancy Astor was a teetotaller who taught her children the Bible every morning – but also of a hankering for the social pleasures of his youth without any of the political overtones which had subsequently served him so ill. While sitting in the desert during the war, he had written of a dream he had had of Cliveden:

I can hardly believe that it ought to be Ascot Week, with a big party at Cliveden: tennis and riding in the morning: and all the girls in their best dresses and men in grey top hats fixing on buttonholes and sprays of flowers in the hall at 12 and the cars all lined up and

the Royal Procession and Father's colours on the course and polo
in the evening and swimming and all the rhododendrons out and
for once my parents forgetting politics and giving themselves over
to social joy! I hope so much that I won't find a new order when
I get back: I enjoyed the old order so much.

When Bronwen met him he had been and remained a regular
attender in the backwater of the Upper Chamber, where he spoke
occasionally with passion on national issues. But, compared to his
earlier days, he had become a dilettante. Alongside the platform a
national newspaper would have afforded him, the Lords was a small
compensation prize. At the time of the Suez crisis, for example,
David, as editor of the *Observer*, had clashed with the government
over the wisdom of confronting Egypt. His apparent lack of patriotism had made him a national talking point. Even his younger brother
Jakie, who had recaptured his mother's old Plymouth seat in 1950,
had caused a splash by making similar comments in the Commons.
But Bill, in the Lords, echoing his younger brothers' misgivings on
the proposed invasion, had gone largely unnoticed, save among several establishment diehards for whom his words had merely confirmed
their prejudice that he was at heart a rich American. As a boy at
Eton, he had once suffered the indignity, his friend and contemporary
Lord Longford reports, of being held upside down out of a window
by fellow pupils in the belief that his pockets were full of money.

That savagery remained, so that while David's defiance of convention had made him hero of the left and had helped create the distinctive profile of the *Observer*, Bill's rebellion, Maurice Collis reported
in his diary in January 1957, had simply led to him 'being cut in
London', albeit by a small group of right-wing patriots. However,
the whole Suez episode had had a further indirect result for Bill
Astor. Harold Macmillan never forgave his old friends the Astors for
their opposition to the government. 'Mac never spoke to David
Astor again and denied Nancy Astor a [life] peerage as a result,' the
current Viscount Astor reports.

For all its shortcomings, however, the Lords was perhaps a more
congenial setting for Bill's developing temperament than the elected
chamber. 'I was really rather glad to leave the Commons,' he told a

later interviewer, Lucy Kavaler, author of *The Astors* (1966). 'As I have high blood pressure, I found that it was just too much.' From the early 1950s onwards he suffered from problems with his heart that often left him drained of energy and curtailed what had been until then a very active sporting life. He had not, however, abandoned all hope of some sort of sinecure office to satisfy his continuing instinct towards public service. A colonial governorship was once mooted, but it had come at a time when he was in the pit of his depression, without a wife to act as his consort, and hence he had refused. For the most part, though, his craving had been well-known but never satisfied. The leading politicians of the day were happy to enjoy his hospitality at Cliveden, but they had never felt the need to give him anything back. Indeed they had simply been encouraged to ask for more – borrowing his house in the late 1950s for Foreign Office-led peace talks on Cyprus.

By 1959 his brothers had all made some sort of mark – David at the helm of the *Observer*, Jakie as an MP and Michael, first as a pioneering television producer and now on the way to recognition as a writer and artist – but Bill, at the time of his meeting with Bronwen, was still struggling. He lived in his brothers' shadows. 'He was in some ways the cleverest of Nancy Astor's children' says his friend Lord Gowrie. 'He was thoughtful, intelligent and very funny, but he could also be vacillating and indecisive. His relationship with his mother was a very difficult one and had left him without her strength of character.' Certainly, by his own admission, Bill lacked application. In a letter to his mother in March 1947, he wrote: 'when I take a lot of trouble over my work, I nearly always get cursed. When I don't, I nearly always get praised. That fact has always diminished my respect for my teacher.'

'All the Astor boys were very spoiled,' Grey Gowrie recalls, 'but you got the sense that they had all enjoyed the experience except Bill. He was like the schoolboy who had missed out on the treat.' Frank Longford goes further. 'Bill was a person people were not very kind about. They seemed to enjoy telling stories against him. It may have been envy – that he had a great inheritance and came from a very rich family. Particularly when he was young, he had a way of flaunting his wealth. I once rode against him in a point-to-point at

Oxford. He had a 2,000 guinea horse for the occasion and I had a 30 shilling one.'

The inhibiting and defining factor in Bill's life until he met Bronwen had been his relationship with his mother. She was, some of his friends have remarked, the great curse of his life. Unlike his brother David, who turned his back on Cliveden and removed himself from her orbit – though the effort caused him a minor nervous breakdown – Bill Astor never quite broke the umbilical cord. It was not that his mother had ever smothered him with affection and love. Rather the opposite. But a part of him remained throughout his life the child trying to catch her eye and failing. He was clever enough to recognise the problem, but had never up to the time of his proposal to Bronwen been quite strong enough to deal with it. He had remarked more than once that in order to maintain any close relationship with his mother, he had first to kill his love, but he had habitually given her one more chance.

'Mr Billy was frightened of her,' Nancy's long-serving maid Rose Harrison wrote. 'He would turn white when she came into the room.' 'I always thought,' Bill's cousin Hugh Astor★ remarks, 'that I was fortunate to have Aunt Nancy as an aunt and not a mother. She could be quite a bully.' All her children suffered the inconsistencies of her affection. When she put her mind to it she could win small children round like no one else. 'My mother's gaiety,' Bill's brother Michael wrote, 'acted like magic with small children, her own or anyone else's. It was thrilling and contagious. She enjoyed the whole game of turning everything into farce or making fun of the awe-inspiring things of life which was what every child prayed for.' Yet in an instant she could turn. 'There was no question that she enjoyed reducing single children to tears as much as driving them, en masse, to a frenzy of excitement,' her great-nephew James Fox has commented.

With her own children, that cruel streak was more often in evidence, though in her own mind it was the product of maternal love. 'So far as her children were concerned, ' John Grigg, Nancy's godson and biographer, has suggested, 'the harmful effects of . . . possessiveness were aggravated by a good deal of neglect. Nancy was too busy

---

★ Second son of the first Baron Astor of Hever, Bill's father's brother.

to see very much of them, but when she did see them she tended to be overpowering.' Another biographer, Christopher Sykes, who dedicated his book to Bill Astor, believed that she was able to do two opposite things at once. 'There was never a person of more contradiction than Nancy. She had in greater or lesser extent the opposite of all her qualities. She could be fanatic, she could be extraordinarily broad-minded; she could be cruel, she could bring comfort as no one else was able to; she could be foolish, she could be remarkably intelligent; she could be tyrannical, she could be humbly self-critical.'

Of all her children, Bill had suffered most from this unpredictable but remarkable woman. His position had been complicated by the fact that, though he was heir to the Astor fortune and title, he was not Nancy's first-born. Before she met Waldorf Astor en route by boat between New York and London in December 1905, Nancy Langhorne had briefly been married to a rich young Bostonian, Robert Shaw, by whom she had a son, also called Robert but known to his family as Bobbie. Though he lived at Cliveden and was treated by Waldorf as if he were another Astor, Bobbie Shaw was very much his mother's creature, the one among her brood whom she adored unreservedly and who could answer her back with impunity and without fear.

When she felt that the rest of the family was against her – a regular occurrence in this combative household – he was the child to whom she turned, sure of support. When she was exasperated by Waldorf and the society in which he immersed himself, she would retreat into her room with Bobbie and lock the door. Her love for her husband was a pragmatic one, a meeting of minds, not a great passion. Bobbie was a part of her and only her, and she would forgive him anything (including a prison term for what is now called cottaging). When she ranted and railed about the Astors, he would agree. 'I think you're right about the Astors,' his step-brothers remember him saying to their mother with just a hint of a smile, 'I think we should go back. You get out my little sailor's suit and we'll go back to America.'

'In his own perception,' James Fox writes, 'Bobbie understood that this domination of his life by his mother had its origins in

Nancy's trauma and loneliness in Virginia after her divorce, and her insecurity in England before her second marriage when she never let him out of her sight; he was for ever associated with these painful emotional experiences which had bound them like twins.' Yet it was Bill who would one day inherit his father's house, his father's title and, along with the Astor brothers, the family fortune. Bobbie would get nothing as of right. 'If Bobbie suffered from an excess of (unwise and misapplied) mother-love,' John Grigg estimates, 'Bill suffered no less acutely from the lack of it. He deserved better . . . He had distinct ability.'

The family nanny, Frances Gibbons, who was left in day-to-day charge of the Astor children while Nancy and Waldorf pursued their political careers, had a theory about Bill's difficult relationship with his mother. In Nancy's first years at Cliveden, Gibbons said, she had been overwhelmed by the scale and social conventions of life there, exhausted by childbirth and mentally out of control. It is indeed well-recorded that until 1916 she was a semi-invalid, spending the greater part of each day in bed until she discovered Christian Science and it 'cured' her. Her son Michael later wrote of these early years of her marriage that 'psychologically, intellectually, as well as in terms of possessions and worldly success, she [Nancy] had swallowed more than she could digest.'

Developing that theme, Gibbons claimed that, as part of her feeling of displacement, Nancy came to believe that her children born in this period – principally Bill and his sister Phyllis, known as Wissie – were not really her children. They were as strange and alien to her as life at Cliveden and English society. It was only, Nanny Gibbons used to say, when Nancy saw David (born in 1912) walking like a Virginian that she believed he was her son.

In a letter to her own sister Phyllis, Nancy Astor wrote soon after Bill's birth: 'Oh Phyl, if I die, keep Bobbie from them [his father's family]. It is my last will and testament. Don't bother about the new baby, but look after Bobbie.' It could be argued that she was sure the Astors would take care of Bill, but she elaborated in another letter to Phyllis. Bill was not, she wrote, 'so nice as Bobbie was', nor would he 'grow up as handsome'. Many years later she had softened somewhat but the undervaluing of Bill was still there. 'Oh

Phyl, they are wonderful children, David so robust, Wis so winsome and Bill all a companion should be, but Bobbie has my heart.'

That early experience of rejection forged a lifelong bond between Bill and Wissie. Of all his siblings he was closest to her, but where Wissie had in adulthood developed a more balanced relationship with her mother – a riding accident as a young woman which threatened her with paralysis brought them closer – Bill's desperate craving for certainty about his mother's love survived the end of childhood unrequited. It is painfully evident in his earliest surviving letters to her, written when, as a young man of twenty, he was touring the world at his parents' behest as part of his political education. In the letters he is constantly trying to impress her, doing and saying the sort of things that he saw amused her in life. He mixes political with social observations, flattering those who he knew stood higher in her affection than him and rounding off with professions of his own love. If there is a chance he adds a dash of piety to appeal to her Christian Science sense of duty to the unfortunate.

In July 1927 he was in Canada, sent by his parents to give him a greater appreciation of North America, where there were substantial family assets that would one day be his responsibility. Writing from Government House in Ottawa, he starts an account of his travels with 'Dear Mummie' and ends, 'reams and shoals of love, Billie'. 'I had a proper set to on China last night,' he details, 'with the Christian Scientist editor of the *Ottawa Citizen*. He is very liberal, misinformed, prejudiced and incredibly woolly headed, but not a bad chap.' Later he turns to the people he has met. 'Do you know the Canadian Lady Scarborough, Lady Currie? She is a sweet. She is all fished up in her best clothes and her rings on every finger and she is just as nice as she can be. I thought she was a funny old bird at first, but when you get to know her a bit, she is fuller of sheer good nature and human kindness than you could imagine. Bobbie, I think, would listen for days.'

In 1929 Bill went to Germany and again sent back detailed political reports to his mother as if he were her eyes and ears. 'I am afraid that four weeks among them [the Germans] has destroyed any pleasant feelings for them that ten years of peace may have generated. You can't but respect them, but it is impossible to like them.'

Despite his travels, Bill had never quite blossomed in the way that was expected of him. Just as he had come to political maturity, his parents' once-shared vision was lost. Bill had tried to hold the middle ground between an increasingly right-wing mother and a more liberal father.

Bill's failure to fulfil all those early hopes his parents had invested in him might have been easier for him to bear if he had made a success of his personal life, getting out from under his mother's skirts and establishing his own happy home. Yet here too David Astor believes that his elder brother's difficult relationship with their mother affected his subsequent relationships with women. 'After our mother, we expected women to be entertaining, but we were also a bit frightened of being overwhelmed.' Melicent Hart, a friend of Bill's from wartime days in Cairo, who later used to accompany him to the theatre and ballet, feels, however, that rather than looking for a wife who was a carbon copy of his mother, he was seeking to marry her antithesis. 'He had his desperate craving for a wife and family of his own who would enable him to escape the clutches of his mother. I always knew when he had been with his mother because he used to twitch.'

At times this made him vulnerable to those who were only interested in his money. 'He was always looking for the right girl,' says another old friend, Joan Astley. 'We were good friends but we didn't have an affair. I don't think we even kissed. But I'm not sure if Bill didn't propose to me. He used to propose to everyone. Part of it was his problem with his mother – looking for an escape – and part of it was the war.' An unhappy decade-long pre-war romance with an American socialite Mary Stevens Baird, who was five years his senior, preceded Bill's first marriage at the comparatively late age of thirty-eight in June 1945 to the Honourable Sarah Norton, daughter of Lord Grantley. Friends recall how happy he was initially, especially when, in 1951, the couple had a son, named William Waldorf as was the family tradition. But Sarah fell in love with another man and the marriage ended in divorce in 1953. Visiting Bill at Cliveden in June of that year, his friend Maurice Collis, found him 'suffering'. Sarah's departure had been, Bill told him, 'a complete and shattering surprise'.

When one of her son's marriages ended in divorce, the outcome she had apparently sought, Nancy would suddenly change and become good friends with the women she had previously denigrated. James Fox saw his great-aunt in action: 'Her tactic was to strike at the exposed nerve, the one that only she could see with her uncanny instinct, and then to sting again before the victim had time to react. As they were ready to walk off, she would often wheedle and charm them into what would turn into enslaved, long-term friendships.'

What Nancy had conveyed to her children was her own dislike of sex and hatred of promiscuity. Over a family dinner she was once berating her sons about their matrimonial problems. Lord Gowrie, then in his early twenties, was there. 'She said, "I think you boys are very silly. You have perfectly good wives and yet you go jumping into bed with other people. It is not as if it is so wonderful. Sex is just like going to the lavatory." Then Jakie piped up: "A sort of Number Three then, Ma," and after that the phrase became a standing joke among the male Astors. "Oh, he's at Number Three again."' Jakie, like Bobbie, could tease her in a way that Bill, a witty speaker outside the family circle but quiet within it, could not.

Waldorf Astor's last words to his eldest son in 1952 had been 'look after Mother', which he repeated several times. Accordingly Bill had offered his mother the chance of staying on at Cliveden, but had insisted that, given the substantial running costs of the house and the large annuity she had been left in the will, she should pay her way. 'Won't go and won't pay,' Bobbie had predicted to Bill of their mother and he was right. She had rejected Bill's invitation – because, David says, she couldn't see why she should have to pay to live in her own home – and had decamped, resentfully, to her London home and her seaside retreat, Rest Harrow, at Sandwich in Kent.

On her regular visits back to the family seat, she would berate Bill for any small changes he had made while privately complaining to close friends that she had been thrown out. According to Joy Darby, 'Bill was always slightly apprehensive when Nancy was coming. She'd just ring and announce her arrival. And however hard he tried, when she got there she wasn't awfully nice to him.' When he had guests, she would delight in undermining him. 'At the end of one weekend,' says Joan Astley, 'Nancy took me for a walk round the garden and she began cutting armfuls of lilacs for me to take back to London. I didn't really want them but she said, "Oh don't worry, Bill hates anyone cutting his flowers," and turned it into a joke.'

If his relationship with his mother remained unresolved and diffi-cult, Bill had taken to running what was left of the family holding at Cliveden with uncertainty. Some visitors in the late 1950s, when Bill had restored the old tradition of open house entertaining, found it unaltered. Lord Longford, the Labour peer and Bill's contemporary from Oxford, thought the house and its routine little changed from the place he had visited thirty years earlier as a young man. Others detected subtler differences. 'Bill never really fitted in at Cliveden,' says Grey Gowrie, who witnessed both the last days of Nancy Astor's reign and the years in which her son held sway. 'It was a place that had been subject to this enormously powerful presence in Aunt Nancy, as I called her. She had quite literally ruled the place. Even at the tail-end of her reign, when I came in, she was very much at the helm. And after she had gone, it was still as if she was there.' Joyce Grenfell, the comedian and daughter of Nancy's youngest sister Nora, once described Cliveden as a great liner. When her aunt was not there, she remarked, it was as if the engines had been turned off.

With the removal of Nancy Astor from the house that she had made famous through her salons, there was an air, Lord Gowrie recalls, of 'the surrender of power'. It only seemed to add to Bill's profound unhappiness in that period. He had been torn between rejecting his mother's regime by ushering in his own style – remodelling the gardens, refurbishing the nursery floor, revising the guest list to exclude her old cronies and replacing them with artists and writers – and at the same time paying homage to Cliveden's recent, illustrious past. He had continued to invite politicians and world statesmen down for the weekend, and had succeeded in attracting big names, but without ever recreating that impression of making policy over his dining table – though as his son points out, 'he was more subtle than his mother, which was not difficult'. Again that air of walking in his parents' shadow, unable or unwilling to cast off their legacy, but incapable of matching it, went with him.

As head of the family, Bill Astor had had a difficult time not only with his mother but with his brothers as well. Some had kept away. David visited very rarely.

At Cliveden [Michael Astor wrote], my brother Bill, partly because of the difference in our temperaments, remained a stranger. His legitimate role as the eldest of the family, a role which he could outline in his own mind, was not one which I, viewing matters more empirically, was prepared to recognise. Separated by his view of himself as the heir-apparent, he stayed in my thoughts like a kind of mandarin, a cultivated official from another hemisphere who comprehended the mysteries of family institutions, of ritual and rite. The illusion was perhaps assisted by Bill's knowledge and affinity with the East where he had travelled extensively after leaving Oxford. His deductive intelligence, his kindness and his reasonable wish to assume responsibility, qualities and ambitions which I respect, remained unhappily for both of us concealed from my vision which at that time demanded from my friends a vivid, bold and innate expression of feeling. We were like two mariners cast off in an open boat, sharing little common language, making friendly faces in each other's direction, and each pulling in different ways. It was difficult being the eldest son. I did not, I regret, make the task easier.

With his younger brothers Bill could be schoolmasterly. With David there was simply a recognition that they were different and did their own things. Jakie worked closely with Bill on the racing stables, but after a row with Michael over the family's holiday home on Jura in Scotland, relationships were tense. 'Michael resented his brothers,' the current Lord Astor reflects, 'as David got the *Observer*, my father Cliveden, Jakie the horses. Michael used to complain he got nothing.'

Though Cliveden was often full of people, Bill was in 1959 an isolated, under-employed and lonely man, bursting with energy, intelligence and goodwill, but all of it unchannelled. 'I had the sense that he didn't have enough to fill his time,' says Joy Darby. 'He was always dreaming up some new project in the house or garden. Or painting.' He had lavished attention on the Cliveden stud. On his father's death it had been split between Bill and his younger brother, Jakie. Bill had had first pick of the filly foals, Jakie of brood mares.

It had started well. In 1953 his horse Ambiguity, wearing the Astor colours of light blue with a pink sash, had won the 175th Oaks at Epsom, beating Kerdeb, owned by the Aga Khan. But even here Bill had not emerged from under the shadow of his parents. The stud was never quite what it had been under Waldorf. Between 1907 and 1950 it had won 460 races and £500,000 in prize money, capturing the Oaks, the Two Thousand Guineas, the St Leger, but never the Derby. Bill had not made good this gap and in general his record in comparison to his father's was poor, though this was mainly because he had fewer horses.

Where Bill had carved out a distinctive role for himself, however, was in his charitable work. This was where he directed all that was best in him. It had started in a fairly conventional way: he had given his money, good name and time to an appeal for the Royal Naval Volunteer Reserve Club in the immediate post-war period. He had later become a patron and trustee of various other medical, hospital and housing charities like the Great Ormond Street Hospital for Sick Children Trust and the Peabody Trust. But with so much else in his life hidebound and blocked, Bill had struck out on his own. He was not satisfied with the conventional role of the great and the good in charities. He wanted a more hands-on role.

And so at Christmas of 1956, crushed by despair at the breakdown of his second marriage, he had set off in a Land-Rover with his chauffeur, George Chapman, an ex-commando, to assist those fleeing across the border into Austria to escape the Soviet clampdown on the Hungarian uprising. The western powers, wrapped up in Suez and anxious not to fall out with Moscow, had been full of words of condemnation for the Russians but had done little to stop them. So it had been left to individuals, latter-day Scarlet Pimpernels, to answer the plaintive radio appeals from Hungarians to help with the flood of refugees.

Jane Willoughby, Bill's niece, the daughter of his sister Wissie, had been amongst the first to go out to Austria in the autumn of 1956. When she returned briefly to England to raise funds for the relief work there, she had naturally turned to her wealthy uncle. He

had needed little persuading since he had already been reading letters
sent to Zara Gowrie, his old friend and tenant, by her aid worker
daughter Pamela Cooper, who was also out there. But Bill had
surprised Jane Willoughby by not only stumping up money, but
setting off for central Europe to lend a hand. He had spent the
Christmas of 1956 based at the Hotel Sacher in Vienna, travelling
each night to the border at Andau, where entire Hungarian families
were walking across the frozen flatlands of the Kis Alfold to reach
freedom.

He recounted his adventures in a letter to Joy Darby back at
Cliveden.

> I arrived at 2 p.m. At 4.30 started out for the frontier, went out in
> a howling gale of snow to the canal and was up all night hauling
> refugees across the canal in a collapsible canoe. I was alone on our
> side – a very brave young American bodies the canoe over – and
> when I hauled it I heard a whine and it was a mother and child –
> a dreadful job pulling them out, while holding the raft and a torch
> too! But as Chapman said, it was the most worthwhile Xmas of our
> lives. 80–100 got across. I had forgotten what real fatigue was and
> almost collapsed here on Xmas Day.
>
> The second time I went out, they left the American on the
> Hungarian side and so I had to paddle the canoe over myself to
> collect him. Like paddling thro' crème brûlée, the ice was so thick.
> I was scared as I touched the soil of Hungary, altho' the Hungarian
> guards usually fraternise and only shoot in the air pretending they
> are shooting at us.

Accustomed to living alone at Cliveden – a gilded cage, as David
Astor once called it – Bill had responded with great enthusiasm to
the camaraderie and opportunity to forget his own troubles offered
by the work with refugees. 'He became an enthusiast,' Pamela
Cooper later wrote, 'excited rather than daunted to come under fire
one night perhaps for the first time in his life. He declared it the
most worthwhile Christmas he had ever spent; it certainly made a
change from the splendid parties of Cliveden.'

'Bill and I had both, I think, gone to Hungary to escape from
unhappiness at home,' recalls Gloria, Lady Cottesloe. 'Like many
others there, we just hit it off. There was no sexual frisson at all,

which was unusual then because at that time men and women could hardly ever be friends without there being some sort of something. Bill had a gift for friendship, not just with women but with people of all backgrounds. In Austria, it really blossomed. He was one of the sweetest and most well-meaning men I have ever known.' In this wartime atmosphere of danger and not knowing what the next day may bring, Bill Astor had talked openly to her of his feelings of failure and the depression that had engulfed him. 'The one positive thing in his life, he said, was his son William,' says Lady Cottesloe. 'He had missed William's birthday party by coming out and felt very guilty about it.'

In Vienna Bill had made contact through Pamela Cooper and her husband Derek with Count Trapp, Prior of the Knights of Malta in Austria, and was one of the voices persuading the ancient association to use its buildings and resources to support the otherwise amateur effort at the border. This wealthy order, which enjoys the international status of a sovereign state, had developed from its early roots during the Crusades into a global charitable foundation.

Once back in England, he threw himself into fund-raising on both sides of the Atlantic. He flew to America, spoke up for the Hungarians on various chat shows, touched his American cousins for donations and persuaded Henry Ford II to donate a bus. He eventually raised over $100,000 in cash as well as various gifts in kind. In March 1957, in recognition of his efforts, he was awarded the Grand Cross of the Knights of Malta.

Inevitably there were those who poked fun at his pride in this official recognition – those who disparaged him politically were also to be heard murmuring that he hadn't done much on the border and that there were many more unsung heroes – but for Bill the Hungarian episode had been a fresh start. 'I think that expedition to Austria was literally the most valuable thing that ever happened to Bill as regards his happiness and moral strength,' David Astor later wrote to Pamela Cooper. 'It not only pulled him up at what he always said was his all time lowest point, it also gave him something to use as a lifeline.'

He never forgot the plight of those he had helped to escape communism and was a major donor when the Pestalozzi children's village was set up near Battle in East Sussex. This educational initiative, based on pioneering work in Switzerland, offered a safe place where refugee children from fifteen different ethnic groups, including some from Hungary, could start to rebuild their lives. Bill's trip to Austria had made him acutely conscious of the needs of refugees around the world. He had already shown an interest in the problems of the Chinese refugees in Hong Kong, and of some of the peoples of the Middle East following the post-war creation of the state of Israel. But buoyed up by his hands-on efforts with the Hungarians, Bill Astor had become ever more closely associated with the issue of displaced people. There were still 162,000 refugees in Europe, a million dispossessed Arabs in the Middle East, similar numbers of Chinese in Hong Kong, 10,000 White Russians without a home and victims of persecution dotted everywhere around the the world.

With a group of like-minded individuals, in the middle of 1958 he helped form what later became the British Refugee Council. It was to become his passion, the one area of his professional life where he could see the practical results of his own labours. He quickly became a skilled political lobbyist, fund-raiser and global ambassador for the cause.

That was not the limit of his charitable work – or his knack for innovation. After the birth of his son William he had set up the William Waldorf Astor Foundation with a bequest from his American assets of $500,000. The capital was to go into trust for his child – he later increased the sum considerably to cover all his children – while part of the interest generated, until the children reach adulthood, could be used to promote Anglo-American relations. The criteria were wide-ranging but allowed the brightest young British postgraduates to continue their studies for a time in the United States; Bill had urged the selection of those in less fashionable disciplines like nuclear physics. In addition to such public ventures, Bill Astor had, like his parents before him, dug deep into his own pocket for private and never publicised acts of charity. He could, of course, afford it, but the scale of his giving and his insistence that it should never be made public was something that Bronwen only slowly came to understand.

'He was the most generous man I ever knew,' says Melicent Hart. 'That people today remember him as some kind of degraded playboy is appalling. He was so unusual. I've met many rich people in my time and Bill was unlike any of them. He didn't exude that sureness of never having to worry about money. He understood that many – like me – didn't have a great deal of money.'

Bill's generosity, she says, stretched beyond cash. He lent her his London house in 1945 for her wedding and gave her his best guns when she went shooting at Cliveden. He not only helped her to pay for her son's education – at the same time as assisting at least four others – but took an interest in him, inviting him to Cliveden for weekends, embarking on schoolboy adventures with him, and even making sure that the kitchen served the lad's favourite chocolate pudding. Later, when Hart's colonial administrator father found himself retired and frustrated, Bill Astor again stepped in behind the scenes and arranged for him to be a part-time House of Commons clerk.

Another wartime friend, Joan Astley, has a similar tale to tell. 'He was one of the kindest, most sensitive men I have ever known. When my husband died leaving me with an eight-year-old son, Bill knew that I found parents' days at Eton an ordeal on my own, and so he would invite my son and me to stay at Cliveden for Eton's special days. He never failed to include us in every Fourth of June and St Andrew's Day. It was typical of a man who did not forget old friends.' On another occasion he took Astley's son Richard for a jaunt with his own son William on his Scottish island of Jura. 'We went on a great expedition across the island to stay in a primitive cottage for the night,' Richard remembers. 'He made wood fires to keep us warm and cooked our breakfast over them the next day. He did it all for our benefit – the simple pleasures that we might otherwise have missed out on. He made it all such fun. I'm a teacher now and I know how hard it can be with teenage boys to put them at their ease. But Bill had a special way about him, a special rapport with children. Even when you saw him at Cliveden, you were never in awe of him.'

Bill adored having children around at Cliveden. He had once handed over the house to his mother so that she could organise a children's party. Princess Anne and Prince Charles were among her guests and she soon banished the nannies and had the children – including Princess Anne in a pale blue frilly dress – following her example and rolling down a grassy bank near the main terrace.

Joy Darby, his secretary between 1954 and 1961, also experienced his generosity. A cottage on the estate, North Lodge, went with her post. 'I also had a garage but to get to it I had to walk down a leafy glade and it made me nervous at night. When I mentioned this to Bill, he straight away had a garage built for me.'

Meeting Bronwen, just as he was beginning to rediscover some purpose and self-belief, made Bill Astor feel that finally and belatedly his life was coming together. Yet already the storm that was later to engulf them both was gathering. 'Even those like the Astors,' wrote the family biographer, Lucy Kavaler, of the late 1950s, 'secure at the top of the social pyramid and rich, despite increased socialism, were not immune to the effect of a flock of angry young men holding an unflattering mirror to the faces of the rich.' Though the Astors were not quite so closely identified with the rest of the British upper classes, her general point is a valid one. Although the aristocracy had rediscovered a certain prestige in setting standards in Macmillan's crypto-Edwardian world, it was increasingly lampooned and accused of holding Britain back. Its powers were being steadily eroded along with its wealth and it was being set up as the Aunt Sally on whom the ills of the nation could be blamed.

In the Lords, from 1958, life peers began to join in the task of scrutinising the elected chamber. The last gasp of aristocratic political power, the advent in 1963 of Alec Douglas-Home as prime minister, was, in the words of social historian Anthony Sampson, more a farce than a drama. Bill's increased workload and his good fortune in love could not immunise him from an emerging and irresistible culture which mocked and despised his class. The angry young men playwrights of the late 1950s condemned the rigid social hierarchy of Britain and sought to bring it tumbling down. In *Queen* magazine the satirists declared 1959 'A Bad Year for Dodos' and attacked judges, generals, toffs and the Archbishop of Canterbury as virtually extinct species.

Bill Astor, with his romantic hankering after the old order and his paternalistic inclinations, could not help but be wary of the changes afoot, but he could not have suspected that one day he would be targeted by the radicals as a symbol of all that was wrong with the country.

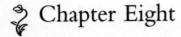 Chapter Eight

To live here [Cliveden] would be like living on the stage of the
Scala Theatre in Milan. Its beauty is purely scenic . . . There is a
ghastly unreality about it all.

Harold Nicolson, *Good Behaviour* (1955)

Bill Astor's decree nisi from his second wife – on the grounds of his
desertion – came through in June 1960, but it wasn't until the beginning of October that the decree absolute was granted, leaving him
free to marry again. Finally he and Bronwen were able to name the
day. She chose Saturday 14 October 1960, just two weeks later,
because it was her parents' wedding anniversary and in the forty-five
years since their marriage, they claimed, it had only rained twice on
the day.

The couple continued to keep their intentions secret from all but
a chosen few. 'Life has changed colour for me and I long to yell "I
love Bronwen and Bronwen loves me – for keeps" but I don't,' Bill
wrote to her in March 1960 in a missive that reveals the humour
they shared. 'Like the BVM [Blessed Virgin Mary] I wrap the secret
in my heart, though I must say I resemble her in no other way, nor
is my loving you as surprising as a Virgin Birth.'

Bronwen wanted to be able to work up to the last moment without
facing a barrage of questions about her dress and her new husband.
However, the amount of time they were spending together, Bill's
evident delight in her company, and Bronwen's occasional appearances at Cliveden – at one lunch, when Bill was detained elsewhere,
she was seated against her wishes at the head of the table by Mr Lee,
the long-serving and intuitive butler, who used the excuse that only
she knew how to operate the button that summoned the next course
– had all long before combined to create an air of expectation among
friends and relations which, of course, soon reached the ears of the

press, anxious as ever for news of 'our Bronwen'. By late August speculation about an impending marriage was appearing in print. The *Daily Sketch* accurately predicted an autumn wedding.

Bronwen was booked for the whole week before the wedding to do a show at Harvey Nichols with the Italian designer, Princess Irina Galitzine.* She wanted to honour the commitment but made an excuse and managed to get the Friday off. No one in the audience or backstage knew it, but at a low-key event on Thursday 12 October Bronwen Pugh gave a discreet swan song to the world of modelling. There was no announcement, no flowers, no farewells, no words of appreciation. She just picked up her bag and walked out on six years' hard slog.

For Bill, it was inconceivable that his wife should continue to have a career. It may have become socially acceptable for titled men to marry model girls in the late 1950s, but working wives were out of the question. And Bronwen left the catwalk with few regrets. She was at the summit of her profession, the best-known model of her day, and was getting out whilst she was still ahead, before age caught up with her and Mary Quant, Twiggy and Jean Shrimpton swept away the ageless, austere, aristocratic look of the 1950s that Bronwen had come to epitomise.

> If not strictly ladies [the fashion historian James Sherwood has written], then the models of the fifties were at least women. In the sixties, models became 'girls'. The enfant terrible of Paris, Yves Saint-Laurent, declared the Paris couture dead (again) and the focus of fashion moved to London – the epicentre of the youthquake. The new boutique culture of Mary Quant and Barbara Hulaniki's Biba was specifically targeted at the youth of swinging London. Before the sixties high fashion wasn't targeted at youth. The sixties saw the beginnings of fashion's enduring obsession with youth.

Grandeur and remoteness – Bronwen's trademarks – were the very last qualities associated with the childlike Twiggy.

Even Bronwen's agent only learnt of her plans a few days beforehand. Peter Hope-Lumley had been turning down bookings at her

---

* Cousin of Jean Dawnay's husband and later one of Jacqueline Onassis's favourite couturiers.

request for some time, but she had given him no reason. When finally she came clean, Hope-Lumley was both disappointed and delighted. He was losing one of his best clients. 'She stopped at the right time, when she was at the very top. She was never overtaken by the next generation of little dolly-birds in mini-skirts.'

On Friday 13 October, the couple released an engagement photograph to the press. It was taken by Norman Parkinson, a great favourite of the royal family, and showed Bronwen, seated and demure, staring straight ahead while Bill, standing behind her, seemed to surround her with his protection. It was accompanied by a simple news release saying that the couple were to marry. No date was given but the unspoken implication was that it would be in several weeks or months, certainly not the next day. Yet by the time most readers had digested the picture in their newspapers that Saturday – 'BACHELOR GIRL TO WED' is how the *Daily Mail* put it – Bronwen was no longer Miss Pugh but Viscountess Astor.

In the heart-searching that followed the death of Diana, Princess of Wales, in August 1997, it was assumed that the paparazzi, stalking their famous victim in search of a photograph, were a new phenomenon. But the night before her wedding Bronwen had to put herself in the hands of an ingenious taxi driver to shake off a determined press posse acting on a tip-off – probably from the registry office – that the next morning the papers' favourite model was marrying Lord Astor. She had dined with her parents at the Savoy but still had to collect her dress from a little-known designer in Chelsea – the only one able to fit it and make it in less than two weeks. To have asked Balmain to work on such a schedule would have been out of the question.

When the Pughs emerged onto the forecourt of the hotel, they were greeted by a bunch of reporters and photographers. To be followed to the dress designer's would give the game away, so Sir Alun – he had been knighted the previous year – bundled his wife and daughter into the back of a cab and the cabbie managed to shake off their pursuers in the late evening London traffic. It was a curious mixture of high drama and farce and, if she hadn't realised already, made the bride conscious that her wedding the next day was guaranteed to be a media circus. The episode also left the three of them, she recalls, 'with a feeling that we were out of our depth with what was happening'.

The pack had made the entirely logical assumption that, if there was indeed to be a marriage, it would be at Cliveden and so headed down there, assembling early on the Saturday morning at the Pheasant pub by the main gates. Bill and Bronwen had, however, chosen Hampstead for the civil part of their marriage. So Bronwen was able, accompanied only by her sister Gwyneth, with her husband Ron, and her parents (Ann was overseas), to slip almost unnoticed out of the family home at Pilgrims Lane into the registry office. She had already handed over her flat in Hyde Park Square to her old friend Christine Tidmarsh.

Bronwen wore a white ottoman silk dress coat with a bandeau by James Wedge to match, white shoes, gloves and bag. Where the two straps of the bandeau overlapped on her forehead, she pinned the brooch Bill had given her as a prelude to his proposal. She had no doubts. Even her reading of Teilhard de Chardin's *Le Milieu Divin* appeared to be endorsing her decision to marry; in the margin of her original copy she wrote simply 'Bill'. The passage read:

> Humanly speaking, the internal passivities of diminishment form the darkest element and the most despairingly useless years of our life. Some were waiting to pounce on us as we first awoke: natural failings, physical defects, intellectual or moral weaknesses, as a result of which the field of our activities, of our enjoyment, of our vision, has been pitilessly limited since birth. Others were lying in wait for us later on and appeared as suddenly and brutally as an accident, or as stealthily as an illness. All of us one day or another will come to realise, if we have not done so already, that one or other of these sources of disintegration has lodged itself in the very heart of our lives.

Bronwen was sure that she was being called to make good by her love the damage that had been done to Bill from that early denial of his mother's love through to an adult life where he believed himself unlovable. 'Bill thought he was a failure. My whole energy was now directed to boosting his confidence, telling him he was a success, anything to counteract that sense of failure and worthlessness.'

I feel you are a rock of strength [Bill had written to her during their secret engagement]. Rather varied foundation, but the end product is a rock. On which I build. Of course Don Quixote d'Astorga would willingly burn at the stake everyone who has ever made love to you, but the Sancho Panza reflects that if you had been a virgin of 30 the whole affair would never get off the ground. So I scrub the past and concentrate on my adoration of you and my dreams of the future. I am yours. All, head first: all in: completely.

At Upper Grosvenor Street the groom had been experiencing more than his share of last-minute nerves. Bill had woken in a panic and in desperation had gone round to see his friend and Mayfair neighbour Leo d'Erlanger, a financier involved in the early plans to build the Channel Tunnel. D'Erlanger managed to calm him down by taking him to his own parish church – run by the Jesuits at Farm Street – to say a quiet prayer. Bill later admitted to Bronwen that his fear of failing again had almost got the better of him.

Bill's youngest brother Jakie was his witness at the registry office. After the brief ceremony the wedding party drove down to Cliveden, where two very different crowds were waiting for them. There were photographers and reporters encamped at the gate, their numbers swelling throughout the morning to around sixty. And at the house a group of about fifty friends and family – a small gathering by Cliveden standards – had assembled. They had only been notified of the event the previous day. In his diary for 13 October, Maurice Collis wrote:

> Miss Thom, the secretary at Cliveden, rang up this morning to ask me to come up tomorrow and drink a glass of champagne with Lord Astor at 12. 'What is the occasion?' She said, 'I am not allowed to say.' 'Well, I have guessed.' 'Don't tell anybody.' However, I had not really guessed it for I did not know whether the occasion was to announce the engagement between Bill Astor and Bronwen Pugh or whether it was to be the marriage itself.

Such short notice meant that there were many notable absentees, including David Astor, who had been Bill's best man in 1945.

First there was a blessing in the family chapel, the green copper-domed Octagon Temple on a bluff over the Thames with biblical mosaics and stained-glass windows, where Bill's father and grand-father were buried. The short service was led by the vicar of Hitcham. Since Bill's first marriage had been in the Church of England and his second in the Church of Scotland – which took a more tolerant line on remarriage – a full Christian marriage ceremony third time round was out of the question. Both Bill and Bronwen wanted some religious element on this day: she because she was fast coming to believe, under Teilhard de Chardin's influence, that God was central to her great spiritual experience of fifteen months earlier and that He had therefore entrusted Bill and all his wounds to her care: Bill because his own Anglicanism had been rekindled as his love for Bronwen grew and he appreciated, albeit partially, what a profound part the spiritual played in her life.

After the service there was first of all a reception for the Cliveden staff. In what was for Bronwen a foretaste of the highly regimented and hierarchical world of the house, they assembled to raise a toast to their new mistress before going off to prepare and serve lunch in the dining room. 'At lunch there were some attempts at speeches,' Maurice Collis recorded rather grudgingly, 'old Lady Astor making one of them, and of course when she speaks it is always a success. She rolled off her stories. Photographs of the bride and bridegroom were handed around.' He also noted that he had heard that after Bill had informed his mother of his wedding plans, he had emerged from the room 'white'.

After lunch there were the uninvited guests to deal with. 'We had to do a photocall,' Bronwen recalls. 'We sent a message to the pub saying it was all right for them to come. It was an extraordinary sight to see all these people walking down the drive towards us.' At first it was simply bride and groom before the flash-bulbs, but then one of the reporters spotted Nancy. 'A tiny figure peeped round an eight foot hedge,' the *News Chronicle* reported.

Smoked out of her vantage point, dressed in a fur stole with a small netting hat perched on the crown of her head in memory of a bygone fashion, Nancy soon showed that she had lost none of her bluntness when dealing with the press. 'I do wish she'd take that hat off,' she announced, gesturing at Bronwen. 'Isn't it terrible? I can't think what made her wear it. It looks like an aircraft propeller.' With that she broke off and, playing to the gallery, marched up to Bill and told him to tell Bronwen to remove her hat. Pacified by her son, though the hat remained in place, she returned to the journalists. 'The wedding dress is nice,' she conceded. 'But Bronwen is not my cup of tea. I'm a social reformer and all that. I don't know if she is in favour of that sort of thing.' 'THE NEW LADY ASTOR (NOT MY TYPE SAYS NANCY)' was the *News Chronicle*'s headline. The press's concentration on the differences between the two Lady Astors prefaced what was to be a trial for Bronwen during her marriage.

For the most part it was Bronwen and not her famous mother-in-law who was the focus of the guests' attention. The *Daily Express* entitled its report 'MISTRESS OF CLIVEDEN' and had Bronwen, as polished and as superficial as ever when dealing with the press, gushing about 'my wonderful new husband' and how she had fallen for 'his gentleness and because he was sweet to me . . . and very handsome'. The real dynamic behind their relationship she kept to herself.

Among those of Bill's relatives who attended, she quickly made a good impression but most, aware of his recent unhappiness, were only too willing to believe the best. Phyllis Spender Clay, his cousin, wrote to Nancy Astor as soon as she had received her invitation: 'I've just had a wonderful invitation from Bill who asks us to come and see him follow in the steps of King Solomon, Bluebeard, Henry VIII and Lord Beatty. I do wish we could be with you and pray that he is really going to find happiness at last.' The last named, fifty-four-year-old Earl Beatty, had just married nineteen-year-old Diane Kirk, a model girl.

It was not the most unflattering parallel drawn about the day. That prize went to the *Daily News*: 'The new wife of Astor,' it reported, 'likes country life, cooking, flower arranging and interior decorating, much like the Duchess of Windsor.' The portrait it painted of Bronwen was an entirely false one, taking no account of her own professional success, but the comparison to a woman still regarded by most of the British public as a pariah was a curiously unkind one that sat uncomfortably with what was otherwise an overwhelmingly favourable write-up on Fleet Street.

Only a handful of Bronwen's friends were able to attend. Kenneth Armitage, Nicky Haslam and Christine Tidmarsh were there, but her old college friend Diana de Wilton was overseas. 'We were living in India at the time of her wedding,' she recalls, 'and I wanted to send a present but wasn't sure of the address or even how to address Bron now. So I wrote to her mother and she sent me a very sweet letter back. "Do keep in touch with Bron," it said, "I think she needs friends from her old days to remind her of ordinary life."'

Before settling down to her new life at Cliveden, Bronwen went off on honeymoon with Bill. It was an unconventional trip. The first week – at Bronwen's insistence – was a lazy time on the Greek island of Rhodes. It was planned as a chance to relax after all the frantic activity and cloak-and-dagger arrangements of the previous weeks and months, but Bronwen's inoculation went septic and for a while it looked as if she might have to fly back to London for medical treatment. Fortunately there was a gathering of the Knights of Malta on Rhodes at the time and Bill was able to find a good doctor through his contacts there.

Plenty of rest was prescribed, but no sooner was Bronwen showing signs of recovery than they set off for the Middle East, where Bill – who had recently succeeded Lady Elliott as chairman of the Standing Conference of British Organisations for Aid to Refugees, a body made up of representatives of fourteen aid agencies which had overseen World Refugee Year between June 1959 and May 1960 – had an official tour planned. Accompanied by Bill's old friends from Hungary, Major Derek Cooper and his wife Pamela, daughter-in-law of Zara Gowrie, and a tireless charity worker for various causes including the Save the Children Fund, the newly-weds visited Palestinian refugee camps in Beirut, Baalbek, Damascus and Jericho. Baalbek in particular made a lasting impression on Bronwen. 'The horror of the conditions there was so great that it was like being in a pressure capsule. It was as if the misery made a physical impact on me and almost overwhelmed me.'

To travel in the space of ten days from the catwalk at Harvey Nichols to destitute people in the desert of Syria was quite a culture shock for Bronwen. 'I had a very strong sense that being with Bill in his work, supporting and encouraging him, was what I was supposed to be doing. But I was always exhausted because it was all so new. Bill could sleep on the floor at anytime during the day, but I couldn't. And the conditions we saw were so appalling. Small rooms with three families, each with four or five children, divided by bits of cardboard, and no sanitation.'

Struggling to take it all in and make sense of it, and still not over her illness on Rhodes, Bronwen found the whole trip a mental and physical ordeal. Nothing in her life up to then had prepared her. Her upbringing had been sheltered and largely middle class, while her experience of travel was confined to European cities and the familiar world of couture houses. Suddenly she found herself witnessing extremes of poverty, destitution and despair at the same time as enjoying her honeymoon. She could be forgiven for thinking it was all a dream.

At one stage the heat, the exhaustion and her own confused and emotional state combined to precipitate a peculiar out-of-body experience. 'We were in the middle of the desert and we were visiting Bedouins. They had killed a sheep especially for us. It was like being on a film set. We were sitting in a vast tent, waiting for about an hour before the sheep was presented to us, cooked. By this time I had had all these cups of strong Arabic coffee and suddenly I just was not me. I was sitting there and I was inhabited by an Arab woman. I knew if I opened my mouth, I would start speaking Arabic. They put the sheep's eye on my plate. I was the honoured guest. I managed to pass it over to Bill. He could eat anything. Everything else was all going on around me. For ten minutes or so – I couldn't say how long it lasted – I wondered how I was ever going to get back into my own head. And then it just clicked back.'

The immediate causes of this curious episode are obvious, but the particular way in which Bronwen was affected by that combination of extremes is instructive. With hindsight she believes that this desert out-of-body turn fits in with the pattern of other seemingly inexplicable experiences she had been having since childhood, part of her own capacity to move beyond the here and now and on to a spiritual plane, especially at moments of strain or crisis or deep emotional pain.

There were more peaceful moments, staying at the Coopers' temporary home, an old quarantine centre at Ma'an in Jordan. Pamela

Cooper's twenty-year-old son, Grey Gowrie, was also there and found the image of Bronwen in the desert an inspiring one. It was not just her beauty that attracted the young man. He had also noticed some special quality in her and dedicated his 'Semi-Spiritual Poem' to her:

> Looking for Damascus
> we have flown over much dry land,
> and a few clouds wake
> our river memories.
>
> Somewhere underneath
> the Princess came
> with camels, no doubt, and eunuchs,
> looking for Damascus,
>
> a husband, fresh riches and a green garden
> all to herself. But these were
> the fabled, dusty
> days before aeroplanes.
>
> History has it
> no one was allowed to see her
> except black girls and the eunuch
> of longest standing,
>
> but does not say
> if she succeeded,
> whose tracks are patterns now
> in the dry land.
>
> Our Lebanese pilot
> has no use for them:
> since each in his own way
> finds out Damascus,
>
> maps and radar
> will lead him where
> St Paul needed visions
> as we do – only

ours are filigree and tug the eye
off re-enactment. The hot browns
and purples of the desert, the places where
all but flowers last a million years,

grant their peace and memory to humans
homing on Damascus. Clouds may
obscure our landing, but rumour goes
it's raining over there.

After a final trip to another heart-breaking refugee camp in Nazareth, the couple allowed themselves a little more time for more traditional tourist pursuits and travelled south to the ruined ancient city of Petra, carved out of red rock and approached, at the time, on horseback. It was a brief stop-over, marred when they were held up by bandits who snatched their wristwatches and various pieces of jewellery. Unwell and exhausted, Bronwen was anxious to get home.

Yet home was no longer a peaceful one-bedroom flat in Hyde Park Square, where she could collect her thoughts and energies before appearing in public. It was a stately home set in 450 acres, where the mistress was as much on display as its various paintings and Roman sarcophagi, and where the ghost of a past chatelaine, Nancy Astor, haunted every self-consciously grand nook and cranny of the Italianate classical building. Bronwen was under no illusions that with so many of Nancy's loyal staff still in place at Cliveden, not to mention her portrait by John Singer Sargent hanging on the main staircase, the new Lady Astor's every move would be noted and compared unfavourably to her predecessor. Inheriting her mother-in-law's old bedroom and 'boudoir' only increased the temptation to draw parallels.

Moreover, since he had moved back to the house in 1952 Bill had been in sole charge for all but the few short months of his second marriage and had made it, as far as he could in view of its accumulated traditions, his own. It now ran the way he wanted it to and was arranged as he had decided. While he was anxious to share it with Bronwen, it was not as if they were starting out afresh, setting up home together. She was giving up everything to do with her own life and slotting in to his, all the time conscious that he was not expecting her to change the regime he had fashioned. In terms of their home, at least, it was as if she were joining an already well-established firm. Even if she had harboured ambitions to make a splash, there was nothing in her background or adult life that could have prepared her for the task.

Her situation was not entirely dissimilar to Nancy Astor's when, in 1905, she first arrived as a new bride at Cliveden. She had found it an alien world after the relaxed routine of Mirador, the Langhorne ranch in Virginia. The house had felt, she later remarked, like a stronghold which belonged to someone else – the Astor family, her husband Waldorf or her father-in-law, even after he had moved out and given it to the couple as a wedding present. It took her a decade to consider it hers. She claimed ownership through remodelling and left her mark by removing the gloomiest quasi-ecclesiastical touches, replacing a Minton tiled floor in the main hall with stone flags, and adding cosy chintz to the main entertaining rooms.

If Bronwen wanted to follow her mother-in-law's example, she could likewise bide her time. In reality she had few ambitions to make Cliveden her stage. She had proved herself on a public platform already. The sense that her marriage to Bill was in some spiritual way preordained made her act in an oddly selfless way. She was content to let things be. While Bill was in control and on top form, she was happy to play the supporting but restricted role that he expected of her. It was more than just pragmatism or the discretion of a new, much younger third wife. 'When I first moved in, I never even unpacked my books. My clothes only filled a fraction of my cupboards. I might have moved a sofa round a little, put up new curtains, but that was it. Bill hated change. In the London house I didn't even touch an ashtray. At Cliveden my sitting room was already furnished. I was surrounded by so much that my own things felt unimportant. And I was still on this spiritual high, so it didn't really seem to matter. I just thought it would sink in gradually, that this was my anointed lot in life.'

It took some time for those around her to realise that she was not about to upset the apple cart. 'When she arrived,' remembers Joy Darby, 'some of the staff, especially the ones who had been there under Nancy Astor, made it difficult for her. Well, not so much difficult as didn't make it easy. Mr Lee, the butler, had a very superior manner with her and made it clear that she shouldn't interfere in the running of the house.' Intimidated by the staff and by the expectations of her, there was a great temptation simply to let them carry on. For Bronwen the task was to balance getting on with employees who knew far better than she how to make things run in accordance with her new husband's wishes with what was expected of Lady Astor – by Bill and his circle. 'I ask myself now why I didn't try and get help. Perhaps it was that Bill was enough or that it never occurred to me to ask.'

Inevitably there were occasions when she got it wrong. One maid left a few weeks after Bronwen arrived, saying that she couldn't work for a woman who knew so little about what was expected of her. One of Bronwen's duties was to discuss the menus for each day with Chef. 'Once, early on, I made the mistake of opening a fridge in the kitchen. Some of the staff had been complaining about the food they got and this fridge was full of old leftovers. Chef gave notice on the spot. Bill had to sort it out and then I went to apologise.' Thereafter she adopted a strict policy of non-intervention. 'If I was asked a question by Chef or the housekeeper, Mrs Ford, I would simply say "whatever you think". I was the second Mrs de Winter. I was always opening doors in the house and discovering rooms I had never seen before. It was only at the very end of my time there that I saw the servants' rooms.'

These were contained in one of the two wings that stretched out from either side of the main building. The smaller of these was kept shut for most of the year and only opened for guests on high days and holidays – Ascot Week, Christmas, family occasions. The larger, on the river side, housed the kitchens and the staff quarters. In the basement was the staff dining room and Mr Lee's sitting room. On the next level were the kitchens, along with offices for Bill's secretaries and the agent, Mr Wiseman. And then above that were the staff bedrooms and married quarters.

One evening, when Bill was hosting a Masonic dinner* and

---

* Alun Pugh was a Mason, so Bronwen took it for granted when she discovered that Bill was one too. In 1965 Bill founded a Cliveden Lodge.

Bronwen had to make herself scarce after joining the all-male group for drinks, she found herself a perch in the corridor that led from the main hall to the kitchens and watched the food in transit. 'I was horrified to realise that every meal depended on "Sailor". He was the odd job man and he had been shell-shocked in the First World War. He would carry these terribly heavy wooden trays, piled with dishes and plates and hot food and so on, from the kitchen to the dining room. I was sitting on the windowsill in the passage and watched the entire performance.'

Bronwen herself also felt that she was putting on a performance. It was as if she had found herself suddenly living some fairy story where a prince whisks his Cinderella off to his castle and they live happily ever after. But the books never explain how Cinderella copes with being a princess, with her insecurities about her own humble background and with the intimidating courtiers around her. Even if Bronwen had wanted to, it would have been hard to disguise how entirely foreign she found the whole Cliveden machine. Before taking up her window-seat vantage point, for instance, she had had to ask the staff's permission.

Some of the older staff, trained to expect a haughty indifference to the mechanics of how the house ran, regarded Bronwen's naïvety as tantamount to heresy; she should at least pretend she knew what to do. Most, though, warmed to the relaxed *ingénue* who was their new boss. Molly Thomsett, who worked there as a maid alongside her husband, describes life at Cliveden 'beginning again' when Bronwen arrived, though tellingly she adds: 'I always had the feeling that Lady Astor would have liked a smaller house.'

That was clearly out of the question for Bill, so Bronwen played the part as best she could. And, as she had shown on the catwalks when Balmain shaped her into his Garbo, she was adept at taking on a role as if it were made for her, while all the time keeping her real self and her feelings carefully under wraps. Even the redoubtable Mr Lee soon came to respect the new Lady Astor and what he took to be merely an instinctive sympathy for Cliveden and its rhythms. In March 1961, after a lifetime's service that stretched back to Bill's early childhood, he announced his retirement. 'He put his hand on Bill's shoulder,' Bronwen remembers, 'looked at me and said, "You're all right now, my Lord." I just cried.'

There were certain formalities to be gone through each day. First her maid would come into her bedroom with the breakfast tray and then lay out her clothes and put the toothpaste on her toothbrush. If the diary was busy with visits and guests, there might be as many as five outfits selected for her. Though in theory such service was a luxury, it further removed any sense of privacy for Bronwen. 'The first maid I had was terrifying. She had been with the Duchess of Roxburgh previously. She would put out the clothes I had to wear. No discussion. I had so few clothes anyway that she was mortified. An awful lot of those first three years seemed to be spent with dressmakers trying to put together a wardrobe. I had no dress sense at all. I had only put on what I was told as a model girl.'

Sometimes, before breakfast, she would drive with Bill down to Ilsley in Oxfordshire to watch trainer Richard Hern put the Astor racehorses through their paces. It was quite a performance because Taylor, the groom at Cliveden, would have to set off an hour before the couple with a horsebox and their riding horses so that when they arrived at Ilsley they could hack up to the gallops to watch the racehorses. It was several years before Bronwen could persuade Bill that she was just as happy to stay in the car or approach the gallops on foot. She had never had a passion for ponies; but she soon realised that Bill's horses, his racing friends and his trips to meetings were a sizeable part of his life. Like everything else, she tried loyally to take it on board. In case she was in any doubt about what was expected of her, on her bedside table when she arrived she found a copy of *Points of a Horse* by Captain Oates.

Though she dutifully read and digested it, theory and practice were not the same. Up at the stables at the main house, Taylor had been instructed to buy a horse for her. 'The first horse I had was called Moneybox and it was far too strong for me. It bolted on the way home and I nearly fell into the fountain. I wasn't at all a good rider. Bill gave me another horse where my feet almost touched the ground. But it was safe. I never got to the point of hunting or anything. Bill would hunt nearly every weekend during the winter, but he would say that it would spoil his hunting if I went out with him.' For Bronwen it was a blessed escape.

After breakfast the couple would go to their respective, adjoining offices. For Bronwen there would be household matters. 'I would go and see Chef practically every morning to discuss meals. I learnt from Bill how to put a menu together, how to think not just of hot and cold courses but also sweet and spicy courses, methods of cooking and the colours of the food – green peas, red beetroot and so on.' She even got to find it interesting, though there were still occasional gaffes: one evening in Ascot Week she suggested gazpacho for a starter, forgetting that after supper the Cliveden houseguests were going to a ball at nearby West Wycombe, home of the Dashwood family. 'We all smelt of garlic and couldn't dance with anyone but each other.'

The Cliveden routine was, despite all the post-war changes in Britain, still firmly rooted in Edwardian times. Guests – who were expected to dress for dinner – were summoned to eat in the Madame de Pompadour dining room by a gong. Afterwards they gathered round the fire, the ladies led out by Bronwen and the gentlemen following on later. Then there would be 'entertainment'. Maurice Collis, the writer whom Bill indulged over many years and who liked to play up his association with Lord Astor and Cliveden, paints a rather dated picture of the after-dinner jollity.

These parties were apt to be humdrum on occasion, as Bill held to the Victorian notion that charades, guessing games, songs at the piano, traditional in his father's and grandfather's time, were the way to entertain guests after dinner in the drawing room. There reigned an atmosphere of extreme respectability. I never heard even a risqué story. I shall not forget how shocked the guests were on one occasion when Bill, turning over the pages of a portfolio of Stanley Spencer's drawings, inadvertently displayed two scenes wherein the artist, prompted by one of the less acceptable forms of sexual deviation, depicted himself seated in the nude on a double earth-closet with a woman he was instructing in the transcendental significance of coprophilia. Bill had hurriedly to turn over the page. On such evenings the ladies would sit in groups gossiping about their children, their dogs and their horses. No drinks were served after dinner. Not till it was time to go did Bill fetch a glass or so of port or a watery tumbler of whisky. The butler or footmen never appeared with trays of glasses. Bronwen used to sit stitching a piece of embroidery.

Guests' every need was attended to by the butler and his sizeable staff. Those who travelled up to Cliveden by car would find that their vehicle had been taken into the garage, cleaned and filled up with petrol before being returned when it was time to leave. Kenneth Armitage, Bronwen's old friend from London, caused quite a scene when he refused to hand over the keys to his rusting Land-Rover. The house was constantly full of freshly cut flowers, grown in the glasshouses by Frank Copcutt, head gardener since Nancy Astor's time, and his team of assistants. When Bronwen insisted, he showed her how to make a table decoration, but all other flower arrangements simply appeared.

The master and his wife were treated with a mixture of reverence and indulgence. So when a fire broke out in the clock tower at the front of the house, no one thought to inform Bronwen what was happening. She only realised that there was a problem when she came down the main stairs and saw Mary, one of the head gardener's assistants, staring out of the window at the five fire engines that had been summoned. If there was a journey to make, Bronwen – who had previously taken such pride in being an independent woman able to drive herself in her own car – would be ferried by one of the chauffeurs who would have already undertaken a dummy run so as to be able to make an accurate estimate of the time needed. And even if they got back in the early hours, there was no question of her or Bill letting themselves into their own home with a key. A night watchman was on duty at all times.

Although as mistress of a great house, she was in theory in a position of authority, never had she felt so disempowered. It was as if everything simply happened around her and she could drift in or out at whim. Her physical presence was required but not her mental engagement. Even when she had been packed off to bed with a cold or bronchitis, a table would be laid in her room so that her husband and whatever guests were staying could join her, bed-jacket tied discreetly round her shoulders, as dinner was served in full splendour at the end of her bed.

The only post-war rent in the Cliveden fabric was the presence of the National Trust – or more specifically, their allotted slot, each Saturday in spring and summer between two and four-thirty, for showing visitors round the main entertaining rooms on the ground floor. Their guide was Mr Bramshot, Cliveden's resident carpenter, and Bronwen even tagged along occasionally in her early months there, so as to learn more of the history of the house to share with guests over dinner. Later she came to appreciate Bill's view that it was an intolerable intrusion on rooms that were in daily use by the Astors and their weekend visitors. Magazines and letters had to be picked up and put away, cushions plumped and roped off areas created in order to turn a domestic environment into a museum piece. Bill found it so irritating that he talked more than once of moving away.

Yet his own style was markedly more relaxed than that of his parents. And this in turn gave Bronwen the lead that she had been looking for. 'It was never intimidating there,' says Nicky Haslam. 'I remember turning up rather late for a formal dinner in the dining room and Bronwen wasn't in the least upset. She just made a joke of it. I think that was the point. Bill wanted to make it more relaxed than it had been in his mother's day and Bronwen did that for him.' According to Grey Gowrie, 'while Cliveden itself remained a stuffy place, once Bronwen was there, it cheered up. She and Bill were never stuffy people.'

Part of the change came because Bill encouraged Bronwen to invite down her friends and colleagues from the world of fashion, to inject the new blood of the fifties and sixties into his social world, which remained largely rooted in the immediate pre- and post-war generation. Some of them enjoyed every minute. 'I did so enjoy my visits to Cliveden,' the couturier Norman Hartnell wrote later. 'Bill so intelligent, elegant and gay, and you sometimes in your shabby mackintosh and mud-stained gum-boots and then you appearing later in all your Balmainian beauty of ruby velvet and your own beauty and radiance that permeated through all the rooms and galleries of your home.' It was not always an entirely comfortable mix. 'When I went to stay at Cliveden,' says Nicky Haslam, 'I was astonished at how Bronwen had overnight become a country lady, wearing a terrible mustard tweed suit and reading farming magazines.' Kenneth Armitage was another who sensed his old companion from London was drowning. 'Bronwen was gracious, seemed at home and would introduce you to everyone, but there never seemed to be any young people around and I just wasn't that interested in meeting old dowagers and politicians. I'd sit next to them on the sofa and find I had nothing at all to say.'

Just as Bronwen's former milieu, the fashion world, was embracing the freedoms and novelty of the sixties, she appeared to friends to be going in the opposite direction, back to the 1910s. One image recorded by Maurice Collis in his diary seemed to sum up both the scale of the transformation in Bronwen's life and the underlying strain this reinvention of herself was causing. She was sitting by the fire one evening working on a piece of tapestry of a peacock's tail which, she admitted, would take her five years to complete. 'She seems to get it out only on these occasions, when there are guests staying and after dinner. I said, it was as if she retreated into it as protection. "Ah," she said, "you know me too well."'

Her principal impact in her first years at Cliveden was in her efforts to carve out some time and space where she and Bill could enjoy the sort of privacy and family life she had known in her parents' home. For Bill, this was something totally foreign. He had grown up to regard Cliveden as akin to a hotel and felt happiest when he was surrounded by crowds of people. But on this point he gave way to Bronwen's gentle insistence.

She had the small bathroom on the landing outside her bedroom made into a kitchen. Each morning, when she and Bill got up, she would cook breakfast, which they would eat either in her palatial main room, overlooking the Thames, or, in the summer months, on the wide rectangular terrace outside her bedroom. Later, their children would come down the back stairs from the nursery to Bronwen's bedroom and join their parents for the first hour of the day. It was a small oasis of calm and normality which she defended fiercely and which Bill came to treasure. Somewhere there was an odd echo, he once pointed out, of the days when he and his brothers and sister came down the same stairs to their mother's or their father's bedroom for their daily dose of Christian Science.

Even in their haven, the traditions of Cliveden would intrude. The bacon that Bronwen cooked would be laid out ready for her with the rinds removed. During the day there might be guests for lunch, or Bill might have to travel to London for Refugee Council meetings or attendance at the House of Lords. Often Bronwen would accompany him and occasionally they would stay in the London house in Mayfair. On quieter days at Cliveden they managed to find time to take a picnic and seek out a secluded spot on the estate. Bill was a keen amateur painter. Canning's Oak,* with its outlook over the Thames, was a particular favourite. They also enjoyed boat trips up to Cookham or Boulters Lock.

Persuading Bill to relax and be satisfied with just her company took a great deal of effort on Bronwen's part. He had grown up with constant activity and a never-ending procession of guests, but she believed that, if she was to be the rock he needed, she had to find ways of encouraging him simply to enjoy being. Svetlana Lloyd recalls a conversation she once had with Bronwen during her time at Cliveden. 'She told me that she prided herself on being completely still and cultivating stillness and that Bill was like a moth twirling around her. He could never sit still in a chair for more than a moment. He seemed to me never to enjoy just one person, he always needed ten or a hundred to move between. It was as if he could never concentrate for a second before moving on. It made me feel very uncomfortable. But Bronwen would sit there and be very still, doing her embroidery, an oasis of stillness for him.'

Bill's restlessness would often carry him away. There would be work to inspect on the estate. Bill updated the rose garden with designer Sir Geoffrey Jellicoe to a pattern based on a Paul Klee abstract painting. He replanted the beech wood along the cliffs above the Thames. He regularly visited the Canadian Red Cross hospital, which had been in the grounds since the war. Or he would deal with paperwork in his office, fulfilling his ever expanding charitable responsibilities.

Bronwen, too, was in demand. The combination of her celebrity

---

* Named after the nineteenth-century Prime Minister George Canning, who had stayed at Cliveden and sat under the tree to enjoy the view.

and her wealthy new husband made her an obvious target for charity fund-raisers. Cliveden already had its established causes and Bronwen soon found herself wearing a hat, carrying a handbag, making small talk and acting as the local doyenne at fêtes for the St John's Ambulance and the Women's Institute. It wasn't an altogether unaccustomed role – she had done some ribbon-cutting during her heyday at the BBC – but proceedings then had focused on her celebrity; the social deference she encountered now was a very different matter.

She slowly introduced a few ideas of her own to Cliveden's charitable round of activities. Her links with the fashion world – save for a few personal friendships – had hardly survived the change in her life. In January 1961 she was back with Balmain at 44 rue François Premier, but where six months before she had been the star of the show as the new collection was unveiled, now she was one of his customers. Bill gave her an annual allowance of £2,000 to spend on herself (and later their children), which was by the standards of the time – her father earned the same amount as a county court judge – a huge sum. 'I was always fine with the pennies, but not so good with the pounds. Once things got over a certain point I lost all perspective. Bill once sent me to buy a carpet from a shop near the house in Upper Grosvenor Street. When I got back he asked how it had been. I said "Over £1000", but when he asked how much over, I didn't know. It could have been £1000 or it could have been £5000. It just didn't seem real to me.'

In October 1962 Bronwen used her long-standing connections with couturiers to stage a gala in aid of the St John Ambulance Brigade. A catwalk ran from Cliveden's main hall, through the drawing room and into the library and guests saw the latest designs by Norman Hartnell and Claude St Cyr. Bronwen resisted all efforts to persuade her to show one more time: she sat in the audience – alongside fellow organisers Lady Joubert and the Marchioness of Zetland; but she did agree to a photograph, taken by rising star David Bailey, with five other acclaimed beauties, including her Central contemporary, film star Virginia McKenna, and the new doyenne of the British catwalk, Jean Shrimpton. The *Daily Sketch*, in its lavish coverage of the event, wrote of 'the new Cliveden set'. Bill, conspicuously, was absent 'on business' and the experiment was not repeated.

The main activity of the house was entertaining. After the collapse of his second marriage, in his darkest days, Bill would often complain to Joy Darby that without a wife it was impossible to entertain as he would have wished. With Bronwen to show off, and a consequent new lease of life, plus the new-found sense of self-worth afforded by his work with refugees, Bill threw himself and his home into a ceaseless round of partying. There were dinner parties, working lunches, duck shoots on the Cliveden pond and pheasants in the woods in winter, Ascot Week parties in June; even on relatively mundane weekends there would be between fifteen and twenty people to dinner.

Nancy and Waldorf Astor's much-discussed salons had traditionally been made up of a smattering of famous figures from politics, academia and the arts, plus a few representatives of Nancy's extended family as well as what her sons sometimes called her charity cases, either fellow Christian Scientists or civic dignitaries from her Plymouth constituency. Bill and Bronwen's recipe was superficially quite similar. There were politicians like Lords Boyd and Boyd Carpenter, plus a sprinkling of senior civil servants and ambassadors. Sir Philip de Zulueta, the distinguished diplomat who went on to be private secretary to Harold Macmillan, was a regular. Bill liked people with ideas. The scientist, writer and later Labour cabinet minister C. P. Snow, the authors Dame Rebecca West, Enid Starkie and Freya Stark, the philosopher Isaiah Berlin, the artist Stanley Spencer and the radical clergyman Bishop Mervyn Stockwood (a maid who unpacked his bag mistook his vestments for his night shirt) were all on the guest list. And then there were those who shared Bill's interest in refugees plus some whom he was supporting either financially or psychologically with the pampering of a Cliveden weekend.

Bronwen had been given a blue folder by Bill's secretary. It contained various lists of names and telephone numbers – of couples, of single men, and of single women who were regular or potential houseguests. Then there were lists of men and women who could be asked to dinner to make up the numbers. Most lived close enough to be called at short notice should someone else drop out.

Bill's immediate family were not frequent visitors and only some of their names appeared on the lists. Bill was closest to Jakie, through their shared interest in racing, and set great store by his step-brother Bobbie Shaw, but with his other brothers he could be distant and over-bearing. 'Bronwen once told me,' David Astor says, 'how shocked she was when she saw Bill with us, his three brothers, having a lunch party discussion about a thing we had in common – our shares in a property in Scotland. She was amazed to find the attitude he adopted was so martinettish.'

Beneath the surface, however, the social cocktail had changed since Bill's parents' days. Certainly there were fewer politicians and fewer leading figures amongst those who did come to Cliveden. Bill shared his parents' great generosity, but perhaps not their discrimination. 'He had a foolish side to him,' says his old friend Joan Astley. 'You would meet some very strange types at Cliveden.' Ron Barry, Bronwen's brother-in-law who struck up a warm friendship with Bill, recalls that 'there would always be people whom I can only describe as freeloaders, happy to drink Bill's champagne and guzzle his petrol in their cars, but with little personal connection and often even less respect for their host. They just saw him as a meal ticket.' Bronwen's sister Ann, used to the lively rhythm of the diplomatic world, was disenchanted when she came to visit. 'The impression my husband and I got when we went to Cliveden was that the place was full of hangers-on. Looking around the table, they were all there because of what they could get out of it. It was not a very nice atmosphere.'

Casual observers of Bronwen on such occasions rarely noticed even a flicker of discomfort. She was, after all, adept at putting on a mask. Some of the most thoughtful, however, detected a degree of unease in her outwardly welcoming demeanour. 'Bronwen was never a great one, I sensed, for society people,' says Joan Astley. 'We got on well and I always thought it was because we knew what it was to work for a living. She always veered towards professional people.' Just occasionally she could find Bill's playful excesses too much. 'There was an episode during the time when we were at table which was a little out of the ordinary,' wrote Maurice Collis of a dinner party there.

Bronwen suddenly said: 'Where's Bill gone?' I looked and saw he was not in his place at the top of the table and supposed that he had been called away, as sometimes happens, to the telephone. But from what was being said by the women on his right and left it became clear that he had got under the table. He emerged soon afterwards by Bronwen's feet, having crawled the length of the table. The butler and footmen looked on with the expression of people laughing in rather a shame-faced way. Bill said when he got up from the floor that one of the two women by him had betted that he wouldn't do it. I thought that on the whole it did not go down too well.

This was an isolated incident. One of the things that had brought Bill and Bronwen together was a shared sense of humour. The innocent good fun of his parties, with their underlying primness, fitted well with a certain reserve noted by many of Bronwen's admirers in her model-girl days. If she ever looked concerned, it was perhaps that she saw more clearly than her husband that some of his guests were exploiting him. Or that, with some of the grand society figures that he invited, she was aware – or was made to feel aware – of the modesty of her background. She was conscious, too, of the mental comparisons being made between her, a model girl, and her mother-in-law and Bill's two previous upper-class wives. People would occasionally treat her as if she were some sort of ornament without a mind of her own whom Bill had picked up to decorate his house.

Most significant in her reserve, however, was her developing interest in religion. If Cliveden life gave expression to the outward-going side of her nature, in private she remained committed to developing a relationship with God through reading and prayer. After her initial discovery of Teilhard de Chardin Bronwen devoured each of his books as soon as it appeared in translation. Even in his earliest texts like *Le Milieu Divin*, written in 1927 in an attempt to temper his evolutionary theories with standard Catholic notions, Teilhard had been insisting that one loved God most effectively through living in and engaging with the world, not withdrawing from it. It was a notion that Bronwen was trying to live out at Cliveden. Teilhard taught her that God was everywhere and unavoidable in her marriage, her new home and all that went with them.

God, in all that is most living and incarnate in Him, is not far away
from us, altogether apart from the world we see, touch, hear, smell
and taste about us [Teilhard wrote in *Le Milieu Divin*]. Rather He
awaits us every instant in our action, in the work of the moment.
There is a sense in which He is at the tip of my pen, my spade, my
brush, my needle – of my heart and of my thought. By pressing
the stroke, the line, or the stitch, on which I am engaged, to its
ultimate natural finish, I shall lay hold of that last end towards which
my inner-most will tends. Like those formidable physical forces
which man contrives to discipline so as to make them perform
operations of prodigious delicacy, so the tremendous power of the
divine attraction is focused on our frail desires and microscopic
intents without breaking their point. It sur-animates; hence it neither
disturbs anything nor stifles anything. It sur-animates; hence it introduces a higher principle of unity into our spiritual life, the specific
effect of which is – depending upon the point of view one adopts
– either to make man's endeavour holy, or to give the Christian
life the full flavour of humanity.

Teilhard became Bronwen's secret ally in the world of Cliveden,
directing her back to the God-given source of strength and direction
that had been with her since her own dark night of the soul. When
the strain of acting the hostess, doing what was expected of her,
putting up with the occasional taunts of staff or guests who regarded
her as a parvenue, became too much, she would return to Teilhard
and his conviction that all life has a spiritual purpose. It was a question
of having sufficient belief in God to trust Him to guide your life, to
follow His will and to react to it.

Yet talking about religion was taboo: 'You didn't talk about God
with guests. Horses, people, anything, but not God. It would have
been considered very anti-social.' To reveal her passion for a still
little-known French Catholic priest in a house where, under Nancy
Astor, Catholics had been regarded as a heretical fifth column would
have been blasphemy. It would have been a rude shock for some of
Bill's old friends, who still regarded Bronwen as a beautiful plaything,
had she started outlining Teilhard's theories about God and evolution.
So, unwilling to risk embarrassing her husband and unsure of her
ability to explain what she had read, she simply bit her lip. There

was an element of one of the oldest of Christian notions at times of trial – offering one's difficulties up to God.

Occasionally there would be people who took sufficient interest in Bronwen to draw her out on the subject. Alec Douglas-Home, the future Prime Minister, and Lord Alexander of Tunis, the war hero, were two, but they were the exceptions. For the most part her burgeoning religious faith was her secret. It was as if she was still leading a double life, publicly striving to be the perfect wife and hostess in trying times and circumstances, while privately exploring a spiritual world that was far removed from polite society, politics and sport. The terrible irony of Teilhard's insistence that no division could or should be made between the 'within' and the 'without' was not lost on Bronwen. Circumstances simply meant that she had no choice but to live with the fudge.

Even with Bill, she had to tread carefully. He was obviously aware of her profound interest in religion and the energy she had channelled into it since her discovery of Teilhard and the connection he had made for her between her own spiritual insights and God. Yet he was worried that Teilhard was becoming for Bronwen what Mary Baker Eddy, the founder of Christian Science, had been for his mother – some sort of guru who inspired her to act in strange and unpredictable ways. In private Bill could travel part of the way along the road, even making such public commitments as seeking confirmation in the Church of England soon after their marriage. The couple were regular communicants at nearby Hitcham church. Yet this was just the surface of religion for Bronwen. She was embracing a much more radical and mystical credo that aspired to touch in a direct way every aspect of life.

Bill's religion was, by contrast, more traditional and ritualistic in its emphasis, heartfelt but less demanding than Teilhard's outlook. And he had inherited from his mother a certain, though much diluted, suspicion of Catholicism. It was only later in their marriage that he felt relaxed enough to allow and even encourage Bronwen to join other Teilhard devotees in the burgeoning network that had grown up in England after the publication of translations of his books.

Nancy Astor's missionary spirit about Christian Science had, in fairness, waned considerably in her dotage. If she was less dogmatic on this subject, though, she had become increasingly difficult about everything else. For Bronwen there was not only the problem of coping with her aggressive, intimidating and still famous mother-in-law, who regarded her as an empty-headed usurper, but also of mitigating the continuing upset Nancy caused Bill.

Regular guests at Cliveden came to admire Bronwen's tact in handling her mother-in-law's occasional forays from her homes in London and Kent to Cliveden. Marie-Louise de Zulueta remembers one weekend in particular. 'Old Lady Astor looked quite extraordinary in a long skirt, lace-up boots and a corduroy golfing cap, worn over one eye. Bronwen was so kind to her, but she did nothing but criticise and announce that she was never asked to stay – which was completely untrue. Bronwen always remained calm and unmoved by these goings-on, but it cannot have been easy for her.'

Nancy continued to treat Cliveden and Bill as if they were her property. 'Old Lady Astor announced that she wanted to see the children,' says Lady de Zulueta, 'so we went upstairs together. She then proceeded to grab my small son by the collar and, glowering at him, said, "What's your name?" "Francis de Zulueta," he replied – he was about four at the time. "What's yours?" She was delighted with this and announced firmly, "I like that boy – he's got guts." Later she climbed into bed with the children amidst squeals of delight!'

At mealtimes Nancy would often sit in Bronwen's place at the top of the table and issue directions to the staff. She could be very rude to other guests, particularly if they were Bronwen's friends. Christine Tidmarsh was ticked off publicly for wearing too much make-up. However, more often than not it was Bronwen who suggested that Nancy would sit at the top of the table. It mattered little to her where she sat and this was a way of placating her mother-in-law. Or she would seat an interesting man at the top of the table, opposite Bill, and put herself and Nancy on either side of the honoured male guest. It was a question of finding a compromise to avoid confrontations.

Maurice Collis attended a dinner at Cliveden on Boxing Day 1960, Bill and Bronwen's first Christmas together as a married couple. The Pughs were there, along with Grey Gowrie and Bill's friends

Lord Palmer, the biscuit heir, and his wife. Nancy Astor was also at the table,

> looking rather pale but as sharp as ever . . . This dinner party gave me the chance of observing how Bronwen was managing the job of being mistress of Cliveden. When it came to the moment the ladies should rise from the table, I watched to see how she was going to get her mother-in-law on to her feet. My experience on such occasions was either that Nancy called out across the table to her son that she wanted to get up and wondered why he didn't give the signal or, when asked to rise, refused to do so, saying she hadn't finished dinner. The way Bronwen managed it was half to rise from her seat and leaning across Lord Palmer fix the old lady with her eye, the expression on her face being respectful but firm. It was exactly the right way to go about it. The redoubtable Nancy got up without protest.

Bronwen recalls it as a rare painless victory. 'She would stand over me and needle me and try to find my weak spot, find a way of making me burst into tears by saying rude things, but usually she was wide of the mark. She'd criticise my appearance, but that meant nothing to me. It is what people do about models all the time. The only time she really got to me was when I was pregnant: "What do you think you're doing marrying my son? . . . You have no right to all this," and so on. Or she'd be whispering to someone about you and then the next minute would be delightful to your face. Usually I just laughed and she would laugh and then say she didn't understand me.'

Not getting a response was what irked Nancy Astor most. She had systematically worked her way through her daughters-in-law, finally reducing them all to such a state that they refused to allow her back into their homes. Cliveden was the only place she could still find a welcome. 'By Bronwen's time,' says David Astor, 'my mother had lost much of her attack. The first wave of daughters-in-law had had to deal with much more sting. Later she was still cruel, but it was like a record stuck in a groove. She would use phrases, likening a conversation with someone she considered dull to "fishing with a dead worm", but she began to use it about everyone. Her needling became stale and destructive, her behaviour seemed simply like bullying. The humour that used to redeem her had gone.'

Yet it would be a mistake to regard Nancy Astor as so reduced in these early years of the 1960s as to be unaware of her own impact. According to Freya Stark, who visited during this period, she was 'full of sparkle . . . she forgets everything (but I nearly do so); still I feel that her age has much more life in it than lots of people's youth, and there is something very touching in an ardent spirit where the body gets so frail.' James Fox, her great-nephew, presents a less benign picture:

> By the mid-1950s, things had changed for Nancy. She had lost her touch. She had begun to develop a monstrous streak in her behaviour. The wit and speed that had carried her into Parliament, through successive turbulent elections and public life for over twenty-five years as a politician, were disappearing, leaving a blunt weapon in their place. Like a damaged prize-fighter, the fearlessness, after all those years of holding her corner against a battery of male resentment, was giving way to cantankerousness.

There was still a furious energy but it was channelled into destructive things. Her son Jakie, taking her face in both hands, once said to her, 'The trouble with you, Mama, is that the engine works perfectly but the steering has gone.'

Nancy's bite may have been softened, but Bronwen touched two very sensitive nerves. Firstly she made it plain to Nancy that she knew she had had a negative effect on her son's life. Bronwen's aim was to give Bill the strength to break that destructive bond. Many years later, in her paper 'Of Psychological Aspects of Motherhood', Bronwen wrote:

> If we are afraid of the disapproval of our provider, our mother or mother substitute, we soon devise means of retaining their love by acceptable behaviour, by developing a false self that covers up the real self. We can see this sometimes in highly successful people in the world who have suddenly in middle-age found life meaningless. They have spent their whole life doing what they 'ought' to do to please their provider.

Secondly Nancy's other daughters-in-law were not installed at Clive-den. Bronwen could never reveal to her mother-in-law quite how ambiguous she felt about her inheritance via marriage, and so she became a focus of Nancy's still raw regret at having left her marital home in 1952. 'Don't think of me at Cliveden with the new ménage,' Nancy wrote to Waldorf's sister, Pauline Spender-Clay in 1961. 'Although I am perfectly delighted Bill is happy, it is agony going there and seeing someone sitting in the place where I sat for 150 years. I am quite ashamed of myself, but it really is.'

That sense of being exiled shaped her whole attitude to Bronwen, Bill and Cliveden. In July 1961 she wrote to Lord Brand, her sister Phyllis's second husband: 'I went to Cliveden for the weekend and had very great difficulty leaving. Some day I am going to turn Bill and his third wife out. I won't go on about that because it is very boring for you. I am sending this because I want to get it off my chest.' Her dissatisfaction was evidently a frequent subject of conversation with her circle.

At least she could take some pleasure in the fact that Cliveden's nursery – albeit remodelled by Bill – was once more resounding to the cries of small children. Bill's son by his first marriage, William, lived with his father and spent only a limited amount of time with his mother. He was nearly nine when he attended Bill and Bronwen's wedding. A press photograph of him at the time shows him standing with his famous grandmother. She is smiling benignly for the cameras down on the little boy, his fringe flopping into his eyes and his double-breasted coat seemingly too tight. He is resisting her advances, pulling his hand away as she reaches for it.

The marriage coincided with William's departure to prep school, the first step on the well-trodden family path to Eton; this might easily have turned him against his new stepmother, but the two quickly struck up a good rapport. Emily, Bill's daughter by his second marriage, spent time with her father only in the holidays, living most of the year with her mother. These arrangements could be more problematic but did not prevent Bronwen getting on well with her stepdaughter. 'She was tremendously kind to Bill's son by his first marriage, William,' says Marie-Louise de Zulueta, 'and to his young daughter Emily by his brief second marriage when she came to visit. They were so happy that I always felt that it was sad for Bill that he had not met and married Bronwen in the first place. He would have avoided a lot of unhappiness by doing so.'

Bill was determined to have children with Bronwen, brothers and
sisters for William and Emily, part of the new family he was building
at Cliveden. Initially his enthusiasm outstripped hers. 'I came from
a family where motherhood was little valued,' Bronwen says, 'and
therefore I didn't have strong feelings about it until I became a
mother. And then I couldn't wait to have six children.' Bill guessed
she was pregnant before she had even noticed. 'We were in New
York and I was tired and a bit irritable and he suddenly said, "You're
not pregnant, are you?" It hadn't occurred to me. But he was right.
I was six weeks.' Bill was over the moon, posting regular bulletins
to friends like Joy Darby. 'All goes well. Bronwen getting larger
visibly . . . Bronwen is huge and lovely. Triplets at least? I look
younger and younger – an illusion of course.'

On 1 December 1961 a baby girl, named Janet Elizabeth, was
born in her mother's bedroom at Cliveden. Medical staff at the Red
Cross Hospital in the grounds were on alert but, although it was a
long labour, Bronwen was able to have a home birth.

Norman Parkinson took the christening picture and Janet was
welcomed into the Church of England in the Astor family chapel
on 9 January, wearing the robe that had once been her father's.
Gavin Astor, Bill's cousin from the Hever Castle branch of the
family, and Lady Palmer* and Pamela Cooper were among the godparents.

Bronwen's long labour left her exhausted. Bill was convinced that
she was suffering from post-natal depression. Once again, at a time
of physical and mental stress, she had an unusual experience, this
time a vision. It was two days after Janet's birth. 'Bill had gone on
a shoot. I was lying in my bed and I suddenly saw these angels.
They were tiny and going up and down, as if on a ladder. It was
extraordinary. They were in brilliant colours and they were looking
at me and smiling a wonderfully merciful smile. They had brought
me a message. "You forgot that the dynamic of the universe is
self-sacrifice." I was appalled. They were right. It had been a difficult
labour and I had been afraid for my own life. If I'd put myself to
one side, I'm sure I would have relaxed more and the labour would

* An old friend of Bill's and wife of the biscuit millionaire.

have been easier.' Aware that Bill already thought she was not quite herself, she didn't mention the episode to him – or to anyone.

The issue of how Janet should be cared for plunged the couple into the only disagreement of their marriage. Nanny Green, who had been employed during William's childhood, had by now retired. 'She was a typical *Daily Telegraph* caricature of a nanny, her hair pulled back tightly in a bun and very fierce,' recalls Joy Darby. 'She was extremely protective of the nursery floor and most of the staff were frightened of her.' Bill's first instinct, keen as ever for things to be done as they always had been, was to ask her to come out of retirement. Bronwen was not convinced. She wanted to bring up her own baby. At the very least she wanted someone younger caring for her. But Bill insisted. Nanny Green, however, recognised the limitations of age and politely but firmly declined. And so Bronwen chose her own nanny. 'I was not happy with this at all, but there was no other way so far as Bill was concerned; being a wife was more important. In those days in that society you handed children over to nannies and saw them at breakfast and again at tea. At Cliveden I did it his way, but it upset me. It was the hardest thing. I lived with it but I regret it now. It damages your bonding, though bonding was not, as such, even acknowledged then.'

Though she was delighted with Margaret, the nanny, Bronwen looked forward to the one day a week when she was off and she could spend most of the time with her daughter. Even then a nursery footman would be hovering. And though many mothers would relish the prospect of never being disturbed by their children at night Bronwen felt that she was missing out on a part of motherhood in order to be, in her husband's terms, a good wife. It was an unenviable choice, but not one that she revealed to outsiders.

It was only when they were away from Cliveden, particularly on the Astors' Scottish estate, that Bronwen was able to have what she perceived as a normal family life with Bill and Janet. Her favourite time of the year was the four or five weeks in August and September when they went to Jura, a small, thinly populated island in the Inner Hebrides, where Nancy and Waldorf's sons shared the use of a large house. Meals would be taken round a big table with only a butler and a cook to assist them. There was deer-stalking around the island's twin peaks – the Paps of Jura – and day after day of fishing, about which Bronwen was passionate. She developed there into a good shot. All notions of being on display evaporated. A few friends would be invited to join them, but essentially this was Bronwen's time with her husband, baby daughter and two stepchildren.

'Bill took me up there before we were married and once I'd seen Jura, I knew I could survive Cliveden. I always wanted to go there on our own, before any guests would join us, but Bill was always reluctant until his last summer. All his life he had been surrounded by crowds of people and I think he worried whether we would have anything to say to each other – or rather whether we would have enough. And as soon as he relented and we got there, he found he loved it.'

Each spring they would set off for the United States, where Bill would spend several weeks consulting with the Astor trustees and his cousin Vincent, with whom he shared a passion for naval matters, about the English branch's investments and the gradual reduction of the Astor Manhattan property portfolio. The American Astors had slowly been changing the nature of their investments since the Second World War, moving into publishing with *Newsweek*, which they bought in 1937. In the late 1950s, shortly before his death, Vincent Astor had embarked on what has been dubbed 'the last great American Astor building project'. He had planned the $75 million forty-two-storey Astor Plaza on Park Avenue to rival the nearby Rockefeller Center, one American dynasty's legacy dwarfing another's. The land was owned by the English Astors, but the whole project went wrong from the start. Vincent feared it would be the death of him and sold out to Citibank as the headlines about 'DISASTER PLAZA' multiplied.

On their first trip there in March 1961 Bill was able to introduce his new bride to his American cousins – both Astors and Langhornes – and many friends at a dinner and dance at the former family hotel, the Astor in Times Square. Bronwen even gave a short speech and subsequently struck up a warm friendship with Brooke Astor, who had been left a widow when Vincent died in 1959. He had bequeathed her almost all of the American Astor fortune, an act of love tempered only by his determination to deny his half-brother Jack and his nephew William any inheritance. The bequest to Brooke was divided between $60 million for herself and $70 million for the Vincent Astor Foundation. When she met Bronwen, Brooke was in the process of turning the foundation into one of the most lavish funders of the arts in American history.

While she was very fond of her cousin-in-law Bill, Brooke was acutely aware of his weaknesses. 'Bill Astor was really overwhelmed by his mother,' she later wrote, 'and as I grew to know them over the years, I became more and more fascinated by Nancy and more and more sorry for Bill. He seemed to have very little of the Langhorne dash.' With Bronwen, however, Brooke had more in common. Both were third wives of Astor patriarchs. Both had taken on older men accustomed to living life in public, surrounded by hundreds of acquaintances but few friends. Both had worked hard to create a loving and private home life for their husbands, to build the sort of intimate, supportive marriage that had previously eluded them. And both were − though Bronwen did not know it at the time − destined to live out lengthy widowhoods defending the reputation of their dead husbands.

Following that first meeting, the link grew closer − Brooke was later godmother to Bill and Bronwen's second child − but perhaps what initially interested Brooke in Bill's new wife was her connection with Balmain. For she was a great fan of the French couturier, describing one of his creations that she had bought while in Paris as 'the most beautiful dress I have ever owned. It combined turquoise satin knots over the shoulders, a waist of dark green satin and an emerald green satin skirt so large that it took two maids to press it.'

Another new friend for Bronwen was Mary Phipps, the wife of Bill's Langhorne cousin Tommy. She was charged with taking Bronwen shopping. 'Bill used to ask me what I had bought and if I had not bought anything he would say, "What!" He expected me to buy things every day. I just didn't know what I was doing. Mary came along, and then she brought whole suitcases of clothes to my room from which I was then supposed to choose items. I grew to hate it. It was like being force-fed. Bill once took me to Winstons the jewellers. They pulled out all these drawers of wonderful jewellery and said try this on and try that on. When I showed no interest in having anything, he was furious. I couldn't cope with all the material stuff but he hated his generosity being refused.'

Despite such tensions, however, Svetlana Lloyd, by then living in New York with her new husband, found Bronwen 'undoubtedly very happy. I marvelled at how she coped with that sort of life – having to go out constantly to lunches and teas and dinners and speaking to all these much older people. It seemed very tedious to me, but she was radiant.' For Bronwen there was no mystery. She was, for the first time in her life, being looked after by Bill in every detail. 'I had never had so much attention.'

After New York, there would be a trip to Barbados and then to the Bahamas to stay with Ronnie Tree, the ex-husband of another cousin of Bill's, Nancy Lancaster.* Here Bill had various property interests. Each year he would buy a plot of land in either the Bahamas or on Barbados and build a house which he would later sell on.

The American trips also gave Bill an opportunity to extend his work for refugees. The trip in the spring of 1961, ostensibly to introduce Bronwen to his American family, also allowed him time to forge closer links between British refugee organisations and their American counterparts, particularly in view of the plight of 180,000 people displaced by the war in Algeria. As part of a transatlantic dynasty, Bill felt that his role was an appropriate one. He was also adept at getting donations out of wealthy people, including the Catholic Archbishop of New York, Cardinal Spellman. The refugee work also meant further trips to world hot spots. The couple returned to the Middle East; in Jordan they had an audience with the young King Hussein and in September 1962 they visited Israel. Bill also went to Hong Kong.

Bill Astor, encouraged by Bronwen, was becoming passionate and fulfilled once more by his work. But these serious interests coexisted with a healthy dose of play, the line between them blurred. Since he didn't need to work, Bill always maintained the air of an enthusiastic amateur. In May 1963 he wrote to Lord Shackleton on House of Lords business: 'really to have your Division on divorce on the Friday of Ascot Week is very difficult because clearly most of the peers who

---

* The daughter of Nancy Astor's oldest sister, Lizzie.

have sympathy for the Division are likely to be at the races. However, I will do my best ... The best moment would be 7 pm. which would allow one to get up from the races and go out after.'

The remark may have been made lightheartedly, but it places Bill Astor in a particular mindset and even period. The aristocratic philanthropist, the effective social conscience or dynamic reformer based in the House of Lords, such as Shaftesbury and Wilberforce, had been a feature of the nineteenth century. Such men had lived on in the twentieth century – the prison reformer and Astor family friend Lord Longford is the best example – but to increasingly little effect as their role was usurped by campaigning bodies and governments.

It was not only in the lavish scale of their daily round at Cliveden that Bill and Bronwen Astor were living ever more out of their time. Even their social life, amid though never at the heart of the well-born elite that prospered so ostentatiously in the Macmillan years, was built on sand. While fashion trends were undergoing a revolution, the age of deference towards one's social betters, of a ruling class based on birth and not merit, was on the wane. Bronwen may have retired as a model girl at the right moment before she became a victim of changing ideas, but marriage had landed her in a quasi-Edwardian world that had too little connection with contemporary Britain. The very proper parlour games of Cliveden, the deference between servants and their master and mistress, the traditional set-up of the house, all were increasingly out of step with what went on beyond the main gates.

In August 1960, two months before they were married, the Lady Chatterley trial overturned a thirty-two year ban on D. H. Lawrence's tale of an affair between the lady of the house and her gamekeeper. Within a year 2 million copies of the book had been sold in the UK. It was not that either Bronwen or Bill had any personal stake in censorship or even in the protection of certain social norms; but the debunking of such conventions had a profound impact on the upper-class world in which they moved.

Change and fresh ideas were in the air everywhere: John F. Kennedy was elected as US President in November 1960; in Britain Tony Crosland called for 'dynamism' on the left in a celebrated essay in *Encounter* magazine; and even Macmillan himself signalled the end of the cherished notion of the British empire with his 'wind of change' speech in South Africa. Institutions were suddenly the subject of scrutiny and the new weapon of satire. The aristocracy was just as much a target for the reformers and the comics as the Church of England, where the 'Honest to God' controversy, provoked by a book published in 1963 by Bishop John Robinson of Woolwich, unleashed a national debate about the need for a modern image of God. And the press that had previously fawned over Lords and Ladies was suddenly displaying a new-found sensationalism that began, many believed, in 1960, when the *News of the World* serialised the memoirs of the actress Diana Dors. She revealed in what was widely regarded at the time as shocking detail the voyeuristic tastes of her ex-husband Dennis Hamilton at their home on the Thames near Cliveden.

While Cliveden continued as it had for fifty years, elsewhere the start of the sixties saw a headlong rush to celebrate change and innovation. In 1961 the Soviet cosmonaut Yuri Gagarin became the first man in space. In the same year Russia also detonated the first H-bomb, while in July Dr Beeching began his radical carve-up of Britain's railways.

In Berlin that August barriers were going up, not coming down, as the Cold War intensified. It brought in its wake spy scandals like the discovery of Russian infiltration at Portland submarine base in Dorset and the Vassall affair, in which John Vassall, a naval clerk, handed information over to the Soviets, was caught and was imprisoned for eighteen years.

Heightened political tensions abroad were matched by those at home. The Liberal victory in the 1961 Orpington by-election threw the Macmillan cabinet into crisis. Labour overtook the Conservatives in the polls and stayed ahead for almost three years until their election victory in 1964. The satirists had a field day lampooning the Prime Minister. The advent of *That Was the Week That Was* on BBC television drew weekly audiences of 12 million as the nation began to see the absurdity of being ruled by, and expected to look up to, a government with a disproportionate number of hereditary noblemen – the Earl of Home as Foreign Secretary, the Earl of Cromer as Governor of the Bank of England, the Duke of Devonshire at the Commonwealth Office.

There is a sense of meaninglessness in the London of the time [wrote Emma Tennant of the early 1960s]. The struggle of the fifties to return to the thirties has on the whole been lost and there has come the two-car family and an abundance of machines. People are assured they live in an age of unequalled prosperity. But the class horror that is England is if anything more visible now that efforts are made to narrow the gap: people who canvass for the Tories at the election appear to bear no relation to those in estates, a word so carefully chosen for its gentility but serving only, in the end, to underline the difference between the background of the canvasser, his duck-shooting estate behind him, and themselves.

Twenty-five years later the British public woke up to the idea that the royal family was not the role model it had always been held up as and directed their anger at being deceived towards any and all of the Windsor clan; in those early years of the 1960s it was the British aristocracy who increasingly received similar rough treatment. Their unelected status as moral guardians of society was undermined by a series of scandals typified by the sordid headlines that surrounded the divorce of Margaret, Duchess of Argyll. As a group they were shown to be hypocrites of the first order. While Bill and Bronwen Astor had claimed no special virtues – indeed Bill was arguably not even a fully paid-up member of the British establishment – they were soon to feel the full glare of public scrutiny and judgement.

Chapter Nine

Like the medieval church, which outlawed then hunted lepers,
witches, Jews and prostitutes, the press promptly set itself up as
the protector of the Ordinary Decent Folk of England against
the licentious aristocracy and governing classes – or what
remained of them after the Second World War. Even the
most peripheral families felt the tremors and quaked.

Pamela Cooper, *A Cloud of Forgetting* (1993)

In the cycle of entertaining at Cliveden, the weekend of 8 and 9
July 1961 seemed routine. Bronwen, who was five months pregnant,
remembers the heat. On the Saturday it was seventy degrees and by
Sunday it was up to seventy-three.

The guest list was perhaps a little more glittering than usual. The
President of Pakistan, Field Marshal Ayub Khan, came with his
entourage as part of a three-day visit to London en route to Washington
to discuss with President John F. Kennedy the growing east–
west crisis over Berlin and the role of his own non-aligned movement
in reducing international tensions. Bill had met the Pakistani President
dent through his old friend, the playboy and racehorse-owner Prince
Aly Khan, who was head of Pakistan's UN delegation and a close
confidant of President Ayub Khan. Aly Khan had long believed that
Bill's potential as a diplomat for Britain on the world stage was being
wasted. He once wrote to their mutual friend Sir Gilbert Laithwaite,
then a senior civil servant at the Commonwealth Office and a former
British high commissioner to Pakistan, to urge greater use of Bill's
'exceptional qualities and qualifications'. So, although Aly Khan had
been tragically killed in a car crash in 1960, when the Pakistani
President was in Britain for the weekend in July 1961, it seemed
natural to accept an invitation from Lord Astor, about whom he had
heard so many good things.

The presence of such an important international statesman attracted over the weekend other friends of the Astors with an interest in world affairs. On the Saturday Earl Mountbatten, the Queen's cousin and the last Viceroy of imperial India, which included Pakistan, came to lunch with his daughter Lady Pamela and her husband, interior designer David Hicks. They were joined at the lunch table by Sir Gilbert Laithwaite, Lord Dalkeith, later the Duke of Buccleuch, and his wife, as well as Bill's aunt, Pauline Spender-Clay, and an eclectic mix of others who illustrate the extent of the Astors' entertaining circle. Bill had invited an old friend from the refugee world, the Polish Countess Sophie Moss and her two daughters. There was Captain Jenkinson, a racing contact, the artist Felix Kelly and the traveller and writer Derek Patmore. By the Saturday evening some of the lunch guests had left, to be replaced by the cartoonist, author and designer Sir Osbert Lancaster, the economist Sir Roy Harrod and his wife, and Bill's son's housemaster from Eton. Sunday brought the philanthropist Nubar Gulbenkian and his wife, and Sir John Wolfenden, author of a reforming report on decriminalising homosexuality in the 1950s, and his wife.

There, too, for the whole weekend were John and Valerie Profumo. Profumo was a longstanding colleague of Bill Astor. They had never been close but their association went back to the days in the 1930s when Profumo had been a ward chairman in Bill's East Fulham constituency. Subsequently he had been decorated for bravery in the Second World War, had entered government in 1952 and had risen to be Secretary of State for War under Harold Macmillan. He was a man tipped to go higher. His private life seemed equally blessed. The dark good looks he had inherited from a long line of noble Italian ancestors had attracted the actress Valerie Hobson, and in 1954 he had married the much-fêted star of *Kind Hearts and Coronets* and the West End production of *The King and I*.

The weekend away at Cliveden came at an opportune moment for Profumo, who was having a particularly tough time in Parliament with a group of opposition Labour MPs: the dour ex-sergeant-major George Wigg was baying for his blood after his decision to send 6,000 British troops to assist oil-rich Kuwait against the predatory advances of its neighbour Iraq had ended in farce, with ill-equipped soldiers fainting by the dozen in the desert heat.*

After dinner on the Saturday evening Bill and Bronwen took some of their guests for a stroll in the grounds to make the most of the balmy evening. Bill wanted to show the visitors a new bronze he had commissioned of his son William riding a dolphin which stood next to the swimming pool. The route took them across the front courtyard and past the high wall that separated off the swimming pool. Bill and John Profumo were walking ahead of the rest of the party.

When they opened the gate in the garden wall, they were greeted by four people. One of them was Stephen Ward, an osteopath who had the tenancy of Spring Cottage on the Cliveden estate in return for giving Bill regular treatments for his bad back. (A keen huntsman, in 1949 Bill had had a particularly bad fall and suffered backache ever after as a result.) As part of the deal, Ward – like others on the estate – was allowed by Bill to use the pool by prior arrangement. One of his party, a young woman called Christine Keeler, had just lost her swimsuit in a prank and, as Bill and Profumo entered, was hurriedly looking for a towel. By the time Bronwen, Valerie Profumo and the other Cliveden guests arrived, Keeler was covered up. A couple of the group from Cliveden then decided to take a dip to cool off on the stifling evening and borrowed costumes and towels from the pool house. Afterwards it was suggested that Ward and his party might like to come back to the main house for a drink.

Christine Keeler was subsequently to talk in newspaper interviews about a naked romp round the pool, with Bill and Profumo chasing her, of Bronwen arriving in a tiara and looking shocked (she was in fact wearing an ordinary evening dress), and of high jinks later on in Cliveden itself when Keeler climbed inside a suit of armour. Bill, in a submission later prepared for the enquiry that examined what

---

* On 30 June 1961 Profumo had sent British troops to protect Kuwait from General Kassem, leader of Iraq. However, because of tensions in the east, Profumo had not been able to muster sufficient forces to deter the Iraqis. British soldiers were needed first and foremost in Germany, and those sent to Kuwait were badly prepared. The debacle damaged Profumo's reputation, though Kassem's advances were ultimately rebuffed.

became known as the Profumo scandal, was adamant that when he entered the pool area, he found 'about six people, all of whom were either in bathing costumes or wrapped in towels, and at no moment did my wife and myself, or any other people in our party, see anyone without a bathing costume. According to Miss Keeler's account she went to the far end of the pool and put on a bathing costume, and this would tally with my recollection of some of those present being at the far end of the pool.' Bill was sure that 'no one saw any action to which anyone could take exception'.

And that was how the whole incident seemed to Bill and Bronwen that evening. They went back to the house with their own guests. Bronwen, who was finding the heat exhausting, retired early. Bill followed soon afterwards. While Keeler and some of the houseguests played with the armour, collected by Bill's grandfather, the host and hostess were fast asleep in their bed.

The next morning everything went like clockwork. After breakfast – taken downstairs in the main dining room when there were visitors at Cliveden – Bill found out what each of the guests wanted to do and then accompanied President Ayub Khan and his party on a trip to the Cliveden stud. Later Bronwen looked in on the swimming pool and saw Stephen Ward with some of his guests. There were also other families from the Cliveden estate present. John Profumo was having a swimming race with one of the Ward party, a man she later realised was Captain Yevgeny Ivanov, nominally a Soviet assistant naval attaché in London but also an officer in Soviet military intelligence.

Though she had been taking a dip almost daily in the hot weather when the pool was deserted, Bronwen felt uncomfortable in a swimming costume in front of so many people when she was pregnant, but Bill joined the throng for a short swim and then left to show President Khan the gardens. To Bronwen's untrained eye – she was still trying to find her feet in this her first summer at Cliveden – it all looked like innocent good fun, so she went back to the house to organise a game of croquet for other guests and thought no more about it.

Again Christine Keeler's version of events, as told to various newspapers in 1963, was much more colourful. She alleged that both Bill and President Ayub Khan had joined in a general frolic, with her and other girls sitting on their shoulders. Her claims came close to sparking a diplomatic incident when they appeared: the Pakistani government threatened to cancel their President's forthcoming state visit to Britain if he was not exonerated and an official apology issued.

Everyone left on the Sunday evening and life went on as normal at Cliveden. Bill did have momentary misgivings. On the Monday Joy Darby, whom Bill allowed to use the pool with her guests, turned up for work and found her boss in a bad mood. 'I remember the day after that weekend so well. I came into Bill's office and he was on the phone to Stephen saying, "You damn fool." Later on he told me that he was furious that Stephen had brought the girls and Ivanov up to the pool on the Sunday when he [Stephen] had known that Jack Profumo was there. A Soviet diplomat and the Minister of War together could be misunderstood and Bill thought Stephen was making mischief, but nothing more. Stephen knew very well that he was not to use the pool when there were guests in the house without getting Bill's permission first. Bill was upset all day.'

There had already been trouble with Ward over the pool, which was overlooked by the servants' quarters. A late-night swimming session for the guests at Spring Cottage had disturbed Mr Washington, the valet, who succeeded Mr Lee as butler. He had complained to Bill, who had taken the matter up with Ward.

Darby's memory is that in general her boss's patience with Stephen Ward was beginning to wear thin by this time. The swimming-pool incident came after pressure on Bill to break his links with Ward. Lady Grantley, the half-Hungarian spouse of Bill's first wife's brother, had had a heated disagreement with the osteopath one evening over dinner at Cliveden. Ward, Bill later wrote, 'attacked the Hungarians who had revolted against the communists and said that there was nothing to choose between them and Castro. Lady Grantley was very upset, as indeed was I, having been deeply concerned with the Hungarian problem. I got very angry and told him that if he felt like that he had better go and live somewhere else, and I went into the next room.'

Though Ward later apologised and explained that he simply opposed all violence, his left-wing views were a source of irritation to Bill. The episode prompted Lady Grantley, Bronwen recalls, to press Bill in person and later by letter to evict such an unsuitable tenant. Bronwen herself missed the incident because she was in bed with flu, but when she heard of it, it fed into an undercurrent of concern at her husband's link with Ward.

She had never met the osteopath before her arrival at Cliveden, but his name had been mentioned to her on the social circuit when she was a model girl. He was precisely the sort of man that she always sought to avoid: 'I remember once being at a party, and my hostess pointed Stephen out to me and said, "I'm not going to introduce you to that man there who knows my husband because I don't think he's up to any good." That was it, but it stuck in my mind that Stephen Ward was a person up to no good.'

Yet on first making his acquaintance at Cliveden, she was pleasantly surprised. Ward appeared respectable and mentioned in conversation many well-placed patients. 'Stephen came to dinner one night at Bill's suggestion because we were often short of a single man to make up numbers and I was amazed. He was perfectly charming, had good manners and a good appearance and so on. Then there was the row over Hungary and it made me think. By that time I had had one treatment with Stephen at Bill's suggestion and had felt that his conversation was very intrusive. He asked very personal questions. I had decided not to repeat the experience and that I didn't like him. But it was nothing then that I could point to.'

Bill had first met Ward in the early 1950s via his half-brother Bobbie Shaw. Bobbie recommended Ward as a good osteopath with a long list of satisfied clients who ranged from prime ministers (Winston Churchill and Anthony Eden) to film stars (Elizabeth Taylor and Danny Kaye). Ward was also a portrait artist of growing repute whose sitters had included the Duke of Edinburgh and Princess Margaret.

Though his political sympathies were a romantic mixture of socialism and egalitarianism, Ward was greatly impressed by titles and saw Bill as a means to gain a personal and professional entrée into such circles. He liked to hobnob with dukes and lords, and they in their turn found him amusing if occasionally slightly dangerous company. For he enjoyed a somewhat dubious reputation on account of his penchant for always having young female ingénues on his arm. They were of a very particular kind. According to Claus von Bülow, a socialite and party-goer and then personal assistant to Jean Paul Getty: 'Ward never got near a girl who didn't drop her "h"'s.'

Ward would pick his women up, sometimes literally, from the roadside or from seedy downbeat bars, and mould them, as Christine Keeler's QC Jeremy Hutchinson was to remark in 1963, 'like a perverted Professor Higgins'. Ward preferred to liken himself to the Pygmalion of Greek legend, breathing life into beautiful statues. His greatest 'creation' was a young woman called Valerie Mewes, whom he transformed into the young starlet Vicki Martin before she was killed in a car crash in 1956. Christine Keeler was another protégée.

This was another side of the Stephen Ward who had appeared so uncontroversial to Bronwen at that first dinner party. Von Bülow describes him as 'in some ways akin to a pimp', though his interest in the girls had nothing to do with money and centred on control, voyeurism and a peculiar delight, as Grey Gowrie puts it, 'in introducing the wrong side to the right side of the tracks'. He liked escorting young women like Keeler, brought up in a converted railway carriage in Wraysbury on the outskirts of London, to smart parties. He once even persuaded Bill Astor, who was always a soft touch when it came to a pretty girl, to allow him to bring another of his 'charges', sixteen-year-old Mandy Rice-Davies, up to a Cliveden dinner party, at which Pamela and Derek Cooper were present, to see if she could use her cutlery in the right order and not make a fool of herself (this was before Bill's marriage to Bronwen). Pamela Cooper's only comment in her memoir was that her husband afterwards confided 'that it seemed odd that Stephen should produce such mediocre fare'. Clearly Ward's reputation had gone before him.

However, whereas most men knew to regard Ward with detached amusement, Bill Astor let him become involved in his life. In 1956, after Pamela Cooper had turned down his offer of Spring Cottage, a quaint half-timbered riverside nook with a high-sloping turreted roof, elaborate chimneys, wooden pillars and a carved balustrade, Bill agreed to his then wife Philippa's suggestion that he let Ward use it for a peppercorn rent. In return the osteopath would be on hand each Saturday, after hunting, to give Bill and any of his guests a massage. Bill saw it as a perfectly harmless professional arrangement.

When, in 1957, Bill's second marriage had broken down and his entertaining at Cliveden was dramatically scaled down, he would occasionally drop in on Spring Cottage and find Ward, as ever, surrounded by attractive young women. It was a pleasant distraction for a lonely man in the period before he met Bronwen. 'It was with the benefit of hindsight a pity that he kept that company,' says Joan Astley, 'but I think he found Ward a kind of escape, wandering down to that cottage from time to time, sitting there like an old pasha surrounded by all those pretty girls. There was nothing bad or evil in that.'

Through his osteopathy practice and his work as an artist Ward also met highly respectable women, and on one occasion in the late 1950s he introduced one of these contacts to Bill Astor. She was unmarried, Bill was separated and lonely. A brief friendship flourished but soon afterwards the woman in question became engaged to someone else. It was a one-off. Ward's role in Bill's private life, later much exaggerated, was slight.

It did, however, give Ward a chance to work his way into Bill's world. He would invite himself to dinner up at Cliveden, where he could indulge his insatiable appetite for meeting famous people. 'I sat next to Lord Hailsham and discussed the future of commercial television,' he boasted in his diary for 1958. 'I played bridge after dinner with Lord and Lady Dartmouth. Duncan Sandys was a frequent visitor with his red dispatch boxes from his ministry . . .'

It seemed like harmless social climbing. Equally harmless were Bill's trips down to Spring Cottage. Mandy Rice-Davies now says: 'When I was down there nothing ever went on. All these ridiculous stories about orgies – I never saw one. I used to take my tapestry down there and stitch that. If Bill popped in, it would be for a cup of tea. Once or twice he took us for a walk in the grounds. That was it. Stephen always had pretty girls down there, but Bill never once made a pass at any of them.'

Only once did Bill have any misgivings about activities there, and this came in the summer of 1961, after the swimming-pool incident when Bronwen and others were urging him to reassess Ward. After he was 'pressed' to drop in for a drink after dinner, Bill arrived at the riverside cottage to find a scantily clad girl, Valarie Holman, doing a provocative dance to entertain Ward's other guests. Bill left soon afterwards and later recorded that 'I cannot help but note a resemblance between this meeting and the occasion on which Mr Profumo met Miss Keeler. In both cases Dr Ward engineered a meeting after dinner when one was mellowed by food and drink on a summer's night, in which one was suddenly confronted with a young lady scantily-dressed.' In the light of such a remark, the anger Joy Darby witnessed the day after the swimming-pool incident makes more sense. He was beginning to suspect that Stephen Ward was not quite so respectable and uncomplicated as he had at first imagined.

Other friends of Ward travelled a similar path and believe that the man they knew in the 1950s changed as the 1960s went on. He used drugs, consorted more frequently and more openly with prostitutes and developed a passion for the occult. However, he indulged these tastes in London. Anyone seeing him at Cliveden would perhaps believe him to be a little relaxed about his morals but certainly nothing more sinister. And with Bill Astor in particular he was anxious to keep up appearances: he needed his essentially quite prim and proper landlord to introduce him to his social circle.

Grey Gowrie, who was then an undergraduate at Oxford and would in the late 1950s and early 1960s come to Cliveden to see his grandmother at Parr's Cottage, reinforces the impression that the ambience at Spring Cottage in this earlier period was relaxed, appealing but uncontroversial. 'Stephen was good company. I used to go to parties at his cottage. They were jolly, not orgiastic. There was a bit of innocent malarkey, swimming in the Thames, but nothing more. Compared to my grandmother's or even Bill and Bronwen's there was a classlessness there. There would be picnics, cocktails, jokes that seemed risqué for the time but now would be very tame indeed. Certainly none of the girlfriends I took there were ever rudely propositioned or invited to orgies and neither was I.'

Bill certainly regarded Ward and the goings-on at Spring Cottage at this time as amusing but nothing more – as he told his cousin Hugh Astor, up on a visit from Hever: 'I remember driving to Cliveden once with Bill and he told me about Ward and the galaxy

Stop the traffic:
Bronwen pictured on
a Berlin street in 1956
by photographer
Charles Wilp.

Calendar girl: adopting a Marlene Dietrich pose, Bronwen was the face of the year on celebrated photographer Peter Clark's 1958 calendar.

Best Wishes for 1958 from Peter Clark

Artist's model: the painter and later avant garde film-maker, Donald Cammell, persuaded Bronwen to let him do her portrait in 1957.

Faces of the sixties: after her marriage, Bronwen did only one more assignment. She was photographed – seated far right, her dress disguising the fact that she was already pregnant with Janet – by the rising star David Bailey for *Vogue* in 1961 as one of the 'faces of the sixties'. Standing in the middle at the back is Virginia McKenna, the film star, and on the left, also standing, is Jean Shrimpton.

Domestic bliss: Bronwen and Bill celebrate the arrival of daughter Pauline in 1964 with this shot at Cliveden. Bill's children William and Emily (standing and seated left) are joined by the couple's elder daughter Janet.

Mistress of Cliveden: Bronwen at work in her 'boudoir', once the study of her formidable mother-in-law Nancy Astor.

Left: William Waldorf Astor, the third Viscount Astor of Cliveden.

Right: On the estate: Bill, an accomplished water-colourist, at work in the Water Garden at Cliveden.

Left: Taking a peep: Nancy Astor looks on in October 1960 as her son Bill presents his new bride Bronwen to the press. Nancy told reporters that Bronwen was 'not my type'.

Profumo scandal: Bill Astor's decision to let Spring Cottage (above) on the Cliveden estate to the society osteopath Stephen Ward set off a chain of events which were, in 1963, to condemn both Bill and Bronwen as players in the sex and spying affair that had gone down in history as the Profumo scandal. Such was its national and international impact that, with allegations of orgies at Cliveden making headlines, traffic came to a standstill as crowds gathered around the Old Bailey in central London in record numbers to witness the trial of Ward in July 1963 on vice charges (below).

Bronwen (far right), with Bill, her daughters and the Beatles at Cliveden in 1964 where they were filming scenes for *Help!*

Evangelist: Bronwen, recently widowed, gives a talk on Teilhard de Chardin at St Mary-le-Bow in Cheapside in the City of London in November 1968.

At peace: Bronwen relaxing at home today. The photographs were taken by Jane Bown, some forty years after the two had first worked together at the height of Bronwen's fame.

of young ladies he had around him. He said it in a way that made it clear it hadn't struck him as odd. Bill was a trusting man, naïve even. He liked youth and beauty. He was mildly flirtatious, but it was all entirely innocent on his part.'

If Bill had any deep-seated concerns about Ward it was to do with money. Though he was well-paid as an osteopath and his work as an artist was lucrative, Ward was perpetually short of funds. He was continually asking for loans. Bill was, as Bronwen puts it, 'someone who gave money to anyone who asked for it'. He never wanted any formal or public recognition. Yet he was growing fed up with Ward's demands – to the extent that when he lent Ward £500 to help out with a short-term financial crisis at his practice, he insisted that the osteopath must not only work off his debt by giving treatments to guests at Cliveden as usual, but also send detailed invoices to the Astor accountants to provide documentary evidence of his payment in kind.

In London Ward shared his flat in Wimpole Mews with a succession of young women, including Keeler and Rice-Davies. Though he did have sex with most of them, it was a rare occurrence. His real interest lay in pairing them off with wealthy and often influential men and watching while they seduced their escorts. Short-term cash-flow problems aside, he had no real need for money and any cash that changed hands after such encounters was a present for the girls. Ward was a pervert who liked watching the mating game from start to finish.

Ward's private activities were well-known to some members of the political and social establishment whose needs he and his cohorts often serviced. 'I remember one dinner party where all round the room were girls and men tied and gagged in various attitudes and they so remained during the entire meal,' the osteopath recounted in his diary. 'Suffering was an essential part of their enjoyment. No cruelty was done – I myself never saw any cruelty, though I certainly heard of it being practised . . .'

Bill Astor, however, did not figure in that louche London world frequented by Ward, according to Mandy Rice-Davies. 'Bill was never a part of the seedy night-life that Stephen liked. I never saw him in any of those clubs. I saw virtually everyone else who was someone, but never Bill. If he liked a touch of the demi-monde, his friendship with Stephen was enough.'

Quite why Bill did not ask himself more questions about Ward remains puzzling. Even if he lived in ignorance of his tenant's other life in London, it would have been relatively easy to find out about it. Yet Ward was bright and charming. There was a part of Bill that didn't quite fit in with the established way of doing things and the free spirit that he saw in Ward therefore appealed to him. Ward's subversion of social conventions would equally have brought a wry smile to Bill's face. Moreover Ward had deliberately set out to win Bill over at a time when he was most vulnerable, just as his second marriage ended. 'I think that Stephen Ward was three times as clever and artful as the ordinary person,' says Bill's younger brother David. 'I don't think Bill had any reason to be suspicious of him. My brother Bobbie was much more streetwise than Bill and as soon as he saw Stephen, Bobbie knew he was a bad boy. But he still fell under his influence.'

At one time Bobbie Shaw was suffering from a poisoned arm and in great pain. When David questioned him about it, Bobbie said that Ward was dealing with it and would be offended if he went to see a doctor. He wasn't prepared, David recalls, to incur Ward's disapproval. So David rang, put Ward in his place and sent Bobbie off to someone qualified to help him.

Bronwen feels that Ward did exert some sort of mental hold over Bill. Her spiritual antennae detected what she could only describe as an air of evil about him. She likened him to Rasputin in his dealings with Bill. Yet, however much she gently pressed her husband, and she did so with increasing frequency, Bill would not or could not finally break his ties with Ward. In one respect Bill's tolerance of Ward fitted in with a more general approach to the hordes of people he allowed to enjoy his hospitality even when he – and Bronwen – could see that they were spongers. 'Bill always saw the good in everybody and never the bad. Even if he saw bad, he would excuse it. It was part of the Christian Scientist in him from his upbringing. They have no Devil. He had no idea that there could be such a thing as evil.'

Moreover, there were those close to Bill who dismiss the suggestion that Ward was in some way a special friend of his. Bill saw him, they maintain, as just another hanger-on at the Cliveden court. 'He [Stephen Ward] presumed on Bill's generosity,' writes Pamela Cooper. 'Many of Bill's friends did the same – except that Stephen wasn't really a friend. Bill once asked me if I thought Stephen was a spy. I couldn't imagine he would have asked such a question about a friend.'

Cooper remarks that 'in his character, there was something not quite right about Stephen'. Women in particular quickly sensed that his interest in them was unhealthy. Lady Grantley had already taken a strong dislike to him. According to Joy Darby, he would call her on Fridays to find out who was coming to Cliveden that weekend in case they might want him to sketch them or give them a massage. 'I was always evasive about the weekend guests. He was always wanting to ingratiate himself. He was a sponger, but there was something more about him that made me uneasy.' Joan Astley once had a stiff neck when she was visiting 'and Bill insisted on Stephen Ward treating me. I really didn't want him to. I didn't care for the man. There was something untrustworthy about him.'

Yet the misgivings were not confined to women. Lord Longford, who in sixty years as a prison visitor has prided himself on always finding something good in the most unlovable of men and women, could find little to say in mitigation for Ward on the basis of their encounters at Cliveden. 'He had this way of trying to ingratiate himself with you. He kept offering to treat my shoulder but it was just a way of trying to get a hold on me.'

Yet most guests did not confront Bill with their unease. Frank Longford did not mention it to Bronwen either for fear that she and Ward were in cahoots. 'My impression was that Stephen Ward and Bronwen had turned up at Cliveden at the same time, that he must have produced her, as it were. It was only later that I realised I was mistaken.'

With so many names in the blue folder of potential Cliveden invitees, it was quite possible that occasional visitors like Lord Longford could have been ignorant of Ward's presence on the estate since the time of Bill's second wife. Longford was not alone in making an erroneous connection between Bronwen and the osteopath who knew both pretty young women and well-born older men. Ward's friend, the actress Maureen Swanson, had in the mid-1950s married the future Earl of Dudley, thirteen years her senior. It was a misapprehension that was later to cost Bronwen dear.

Any regular visitor or close observer of events at Cliveden as 1961 wore on, however, could not mistake the frostiness between Bronwen and Ward. 'I always felt the hair stand up on the back of my neck when he was in the room,' Bronwen maintains. 'I said to Bill that I did not want him coming to dinner any more. I knew nothing about his girls. The only time I would ever go anywhere near Spring Cottage was if I was out on the boat. I once had to drop in a message for Stephen as I was passing on a walk because he had no phone and Bill wanted him to give a guest a massage, but that was it. If I'd known about the girls, I would have said more. It was just him I disliked.'

Household records show that between 1960 and 1963 Ward joined the Astors for dinner just twice – Boxing Day 1960 and Saturday 30 December 1961. 'Once Bill had married Bronwen,' Grey Gowrie recalls, 'I never saw him at Ward's cottage and indeed Bill and Bronwen were scarcely ever mentioned. It was as if they lived in another world.' Yet Bronwen could not persuade Bill to evict Ward from the cottage, or even to stop him coming up to the house on a Saturday afternoon to treat guests. It was these minor perks of his tenancy that Ward's detractors later used to powerful effect against the Astors.

When he came up to the house to do his work, Ward would occasionally bring a girl, whom the staff were on strict orders to leave sitting in the main hall. 'I remember very distinctly coming down for dinner and seeing this girl sitting there,' says Bronwen. 'I had no idea who she was and just said, "Oh, hasn't anyone given you a drink?" She said she didn't want one. I thought no more about it and went into the drawing room to meet the guests. Later it turned out that that was Christine Keeler. She put it in her autobiography that we had had a chat.'

Given her antipathy to Ward, it is curious that she did not take a tougher line. After all, Bill was clearly devoted to her and increasingly Ward was treating her as if she were a rival for Bill's affection, a block on his access to financial support and social introductions. 'It all came down to confidence,' she explains now. 'I was not confident enough at Cliveden to be able to deal with the staff, to change the furniture, to insist on how I wanted to bring up my daughters. How could I say to Bill that I didn't want Stephen there at all, to get him out of the cottage? I agree anyone with the slightest bit of confidence who felt as I did would have done so right away. I was just completely out of my depth. So I let it continue.'

Bill Astor was, however, certainly aware of his wife's antipathy to Ward. He would have done well to listen to her. Shut out of Cliveden, Ward began to find pretexts to ask Bill over to his London flat. 'It was always at Stephen's request,' Bronwen says. 'Bill would never have gone round off his own bat. Stephen was always dreaming up some reason why he had to talk to Bill urgently. He was manoeuvring, manipulating. At the time we just didn't see it. It was only later that we managed to put it all together.' These occasional visits, undertaken by Bill reluctantly but innocently, were later to take on a more sinister line when it emerged that Keeler, Rice-Davies or other 'protégées' of Ward had been present.

It was eighteen months before either Bronwen or Bill Astor realised that one seemingly harmless weekend at Cliveden could ruin their good names. In Bronwen's case the shock was further delayed because Bill struggled for months to keep the full extent of the potential damage from her. 'We were happy. I was finding my feet running the house, getting on with a new butler. Throughout the whole affair our diaries would be full every day. We carried on as normal. Bill kept saying that it was a storm in a teacup and that was enough for me. Bill had no idea at that time of Stephen's double life or the extent of his depravity.'

A series of innocent episodes that occurred between the fatal weekend and the explosion in the press of the Profumo affair only served later to implicate the couple ever deeper in events. At the time, they were as nothing as Bronwen dealt with more pressing concerns – she had her first child in December and then an early miscarriage in November 1962; she worried increasingly about her mother, who had suffered the first of a series of strokes in the same year. While her father's career in the judiciary continued – he was chairing an enquiry into the Bahamas police that year – Bronwen's mother was increasingly incapacitated, with the burden falling disproportionately on Gwyneth, who was closest geographically to Hampstead and, while she was still a sub-editor, had fewer other responsibilities.

Bill was ever more closely involved in his work for refugees. Much of 1962 was spent trying to persuade the Conservative government to waive tax on a charity record produced by international recording stars like Bing Crosby, Maurice Chevalier and Ella Fitzgerald in aid of displaced people. Despite Bill's best efforts he failed. He also returned with Bronwen to the Middle East and to Austria, where 3,000 people had fled from Yugoslavia.★ From the floor of the House of Lords, and later in meetings with Chancellor Adenauer in Bonn, he took up the question of those who had missed out on compensation from the West German government following the war. Bill was busy and happy. Bronwen's sense of mission in regard to her marriage was being fulfilled.

At the start of August 1961, with Berlin soon to be divided by the wall and the Cold War reaching a new intensity, Ward sought to persuade Bill that his new friend Ivanov might be a useful conduit back to Moscow for the British government. Bill was sceptical but agreed to meet the two of them for lunch. Ward himself was evidently under pressure from the Soviet agent, who mistakenly believed that Bill, as a senior English peer, would have direct access to the Prime Minister.

Ivanov said little to impress Bill, but as a precaution, lest anything be made of the meeting by the Soviets, Bill decided on 2 August to write to the Foreign Office and offer an account of proceedings. He gave a brief description of the positions of Ward and Ivanov, offered no comment or endorsement himself but added Ward's address and suggested any further contact be made via the osteopath direct. A few days after he wrote the letter, he departed with Bronwen for

---

★ Since the end of the Second World War there had been a steady flow of political refugees, notably Croatians and Albanians, leaving Yugoslavia. In the early 1960s, when hopes of political liberalisation there were dashed, the tide of refugees increased, stopping only in 1966, when President Tito did introduce reform and open the country's borders.

Jura. That was the end of the matter as far as he was concerned.

By April 1962, however, coded references to John Profumo's liaison with Christine Keeler after their swimming-pool meeting at Cliveden and to her simultaneous affair with Ivanov began appearing in the press. According to Keeler, Ivanov had driven her home to London after the weekend at Cliveden and seduced her at the Wimpole Mews flat. Their affair, she said, was still going on when she was contacted by Profumo, who also had sex with her there.

It was either Keeler or Ward – or both of them separately – who started the rumours. Both liked to gossip, boast and embroider. Keeler may not immediately have realised the security implications of what she was saying, but Ward did. The Secretary of State for War and a Soviet spy sharing the same girl would give rise to some interesting pillow-talk which could pose a threat to national security.

Queen magazine, where Robin Douglas-Home, nephew of the Foreign Secretary, was an associate editor, started the ball rolling with a brief piece in its regular feature, 'Sentences I'd like to hear the end of.' It read: '. . . called in MI5 because every time the chauffeur-driven Zil drew up at her front door, out of the back door into a chauffeur-driven Humber slipped . . .'

Though Bill was far removed from the centre of political life and Fleet Street, he was close enough to hear the rumours about Profumo over his dinner table. Yet in October 1962, at the height of the Cuban missile crisis, he was once again playing along with Ward's fantasies about being some sort of international spy-master. After, as Bill later wrote, 'considerable persuasion', Ward brought Ivanov to lunch at Cliveden. Bill listened but 'refused to be a channel between him and the Foreign Office.' He suggested Ward contact officials there direct, but did agree to arrange another lunch to introduce Ivanov to the writer and journalist Lord 'Boofy' Arran. It took place at Cliveden on 27 October, just as the Cuban crisis ended. Arran was not impressed and took the suggestion no further.

To Bronwen – who was present at the lunch and aware of her husband's misgivings – the two Ward initiatives seemed harmless and doomed to failure. She might have been less willing than her husband to play Ward along, but respected Bill's interest in security matters, which went back to his wartime involvement with the navy. Yet neither of them could anticipate that the two episodes would later be used to suggest that Cliveden was at the centre of some MI5 entrapment plot aimed at persuading Ivanov to defect.

Much was made in the coverage of the Profumo scandal of the notion that Cliveden was used by Bill to seduce spies to the British cause. With hindsight it can be judged a foolish notion. The historian and espionage expert Nigel West writes:

> I have no knowledge of any connection he [Bill Astor] may have had with the Security Service, and the external evidence suggests there was none. If he knew Profumo was involved with Keeler, he did not report it to MI5. Keith Wagstaffe, who was Stephen Ward's case officer, has never mentioned any link to Astor and I doubt there was one. The MI5 operation to entrap Ivanov was the reason for Ward's recruitment, and I don't think there was any reason to involve Astor.

What links did exist between Ward and the security services were initiated by Ward himself, who fantasised about espionage, fuelled by his promises of information that he could not deliver and maintained by very junior operatives at MI5.

As autumn turned to one of the harshest winters on record, in front of Bronwen Bill was still laughing off whatever worries he may have had concerning the whole Profumo business. Ward began to be courted by MI5, but it was Christine Keeler who transformed corridors-of-power rumours into front-page news. She had got herself involved with a West Indian man, 'Lucky' Gordon, who rapidly became infatuated with her. She tired of him just as quickly and, when he wouldn't leave her alone, lured another West Indian, John Edgecombe, into protecting her. At the end of October 1962 there was a knife-fight between the two men at a Soho nightclub. Thereafter Keeler went into hiding and threatened Edgecombe with the police. On 14 December he turned up at Ward's flat in Wimpole Mews, where Keeler was visiting Rice-Davies. Convinced that she had Gordon inside, he shot at her. The police were called. Edgecombe was arrested and charged. (He was later found guilty of possessing a firearm with intent to endanger life, and jailed for seven years.)

Keeler was suddenly facing an appearance as a witness in court. She panicked and, in an attempt to save her own skin, started talking to the press about the Cliveden weekend and her two lovers, the Secretary of State for War and the Soviet spy. It was at this point that Bill Astor realised he had to take decisive action to protect his good name. 'Most people forget the time-gap between 1961, the weekend, and 1963, the scandal breaking,' says William Astor, Bill's son. 'Who could have imagined that after two years had gone by the story of the pool encounter would appear? I remember that we were all amazed by the series of unfolding events, most a total surprise, and powerless to do anything. Political crises have a momentum all of their own and all get swept along. I remember the hysteria at the time and it was remarkable that both my father and Bronwen kept family life reasonably normal.'

On 28 January 1963 Bill met Ward at the osteopath's solicitors to discuss Keeler's threats to go into print. Later the same day he saw his own lawyer to ensure that pressure was put on the *Sunday Pictorial* not to publish Keeler's 'exclusive'. Then he sat down with Ward and Profumo at Upper Grosvenor Street to discuss how best to tackle the problem.

He advised Profumo 'to see the Attorney General or Minister of Defence [his immediate government superior] that very day and put himself completely in their hands'. The following week he gave Ward £500, which he believed would go towards proving that Keeler was lying to reporters. She claimed there was a security angle to the story, since Ivanov had asked her to question Profumo about military secrets (she was never able to substantiate the claim). Bill was also contacted by Keeler, who revealed that she was considering leaving the country with Rice-Davies rather than face a court appearance. He counselled them not to go.

In each instance Bill left the onus with those who could potentially drag him down. He would have protected himself better had he contacted the Attorney-General directly about Profumo, avoided giving Ward the money, and refused to talk to the two young women. On all three counts, he was later judged to have compromised himself – being complicit in Profumo's deception of Parliament, funding Ward's cover-up and in league with two young

women of questionable morals in their flight from justice. His generosity, his loyalty to friends, an outmoded code of honour, a certain
guilelessness and his chivalrous weakness for a pretty girl in distress
were together his undoing.

That did not, however, become obvious until later. At the end
of February, convinced that he had done everything in his power
to minimise the risk of scandal, he set off with Bronwen for their
annual visit to United States and the Caribbean. While they were
away, however, events gathered rather than lost pace. Keeler linked
up with a former Labour MP, John Lewis, who held Ward responsible for the break-up of his marriage ten years earlier. Obsessed by
the idea of revenge on Ward, Lewis encouraged Keeler to talk to
the press about Ward's call-girl racket and put her in touch with
John Profumo's old enemy, George Wigg, who was close to Harold
Wilson and was a key figure in Wilson's election in February 1963
as Labour leader in succession to Hugh Gaitskell.

'It took me years to realise it,' Bronwen says, 'but there were plots
within plots. Lewis wanted to get at Stephen. Wigg wanted to get
at Jack. Bill and I got caught in the middle of the whole thing. It
might all have been smoothed over if it had not been for these two
men wanting to get their own back. Every time it calmed down
again, they would go and stir it up with the press and then Stephen
started doing the same thing.'

Keeler was due to appear at Edgecombe's arraignment on Thursday
14 March but, ignoring Bill's advice, fled the country. A few days
later Mandy Rice-Davies gave an interview to the *Daily Sketch* where
she boasted about her life with Ward and the unnamed 'top drawer'
people he knew. The whispering campaign against Profumo was
increasing each day and on Thursday 21 March George Wigg used
parliamentary privilege to raise on the floor of the Commons Christine Keeler's unpublished allegations about her simultaneous affairs
with him and a Soviet spy. The next day Profumo denied any impro-
priety in the Commons, mentioning in the course of his rebuttal the
weekend at Bill and Bronwen Astor's home. It made headlines. Like
it or not, they were being dragged into the scandal.

Even at this advanced stage Bronwen continued to accept uncriti-
cally her husband's assurances that all would be well. 'We were in

New York and the press began ringing up. When we moved on to the Bahamas, they were really chasing us, demanding a statement. Bill continued to protect me. He said it was just some problem with Stephen Ward. Naturally I believed him. It seemed like just another thing impinging on our private life. I'm wiser now, of course, but then I just didn't want to know. Maybe it was something in me but I felt that I couldn't be involved in everyone's life. I hardly knew Jack Profumo. So I held myself apart at first.'

While she felt sympathy for Profumo's wife – after the scandal she would meet Valerie Hobson regularly over lunch for mutual support – she could not believe that anyone would hold her and Bill responsible for policing the morals of people who came to stay with them. 'It wasn't a monastery. You invited people to stay. You gave them a room. If they went into someone else's room, what was I meant to do about it? It wasn't considered polite to mention it. When I once asked Bill, he just laughed and said don't interfere. I didn't have a clue about country house life.'

Profumo's threat to sue anyone who contradicted his version of events succeeded in silencing most of his doubters, but there followed a barrage of articles which alluded to, without actually mentioning, the affair. With a dispassionate eye from the other side of the Atlantic, *Time* magazine in March 1963 reported:

> On the island where the subject has long been taboo in polite society, sex has exploded into the national consciousness and national headlines. 'Are we going sex crazy?' asks the *Daily Herald*. 'Is chastity outmoded?' asks a school magazine for teenagers. 'Are virgins obsolete?' is the question posed by the solemn *New Statesman*. The answers vary but one thing is clear: Britain is bombarded with a barrage of frankness about sex.

The morality of government ministers and the whole ruling class in particular was being held up to scrutiny. If Profumo came to represent the first of these groups, Lord and Lady Astor, however mistakenly, were the sacrificial lambs for the second. Their names and pictures, alongside that of Cliveden, were everywhere in the press, though no specific allegations were made for fear of libel. The *Daily Express* was particularly damning. Bill heard via a friend that the *Express*'s owner,

Lord Beaverbrook, had instructed his editors to spare no blushes in nailing Lord Astor as 'a callous libertine' living out a sham of a marriage.

Beaverbrook had been close to Bill in the 1930s and 1940s, when his newspapers made a point of highlighting the work of the young MP for East Fulham. Beaverbrook had even colluded with Nancy and Waldorf Astor in covering up details of Bobbie Shaw's conviction for gay sex. However, in the fifties Beaverbrook had fallen out with the Astor family en masse because of his irrational hostility to David Astor and the *Observer*. Beaverbrook once accused David to his face of wanting 'to take my place on Fleet Street'. When the *Observer* ran a critical profile of the *Express* owner in 1951, Beaverbrook believed that his previous goodwill towards the family had been thrown back in his face. Thereafter he held any Astor – save perhaps Nancy – in public contempt. Since Bill had been a director of the *Observer*, a newspaper constantly attacked by the *Express* titles as pacifist, anti-semitic and anti-Catholic, he was, for Beaverbrook, an obvious target. The scandal gave him his chance.

The couple returned to Cliveden on 12 April to find the steady trickle of innuendo linking them with Profumo, Ward and Keeler now also mixing in with details percolating down from Edinburgh, where behind locked doors the Duke of Argyll was suing his Duchess for divorce in an infamous case of perverse romps. The Duke had named 200 co-respondents. As the social historian Christopher Booker puts it: 'a boundless fantasy emerged in which not only every member of the government but the entire upper class of England seemed to have been caught up in an orgy of model girls, perversions and fancy dress sexual frolics.'

Bill was stunned the day after he arrived home when he was asked to grant a police interview. When he heard from the officers about the full extent of Ward's activities and the assumptions that were being made about him on account of his friendship with the osteopath, he finally decided to do what Bronwen had been urging for two years – to ask Ward to vacate Spring Cottage. However, his tenant got in first, offering to leave. It may just have been intended as a gesture, for when Bill accepted at once, Ward was very taken aback. 'I had always believed,' Ward told his friend Warwick Charlton, 'that Bill wouldn't let me down. I thought he could do something to restore my good name. I thought he might hold a party at Cliveden, collect some notables, and have me down as a sort of gesture of solidarity. Imagine my shock when he at once asked me to let him have a letter vacating the cottage. I was absolutely flabbergasted. I then began to realise that the waves were coming aboard and soon I would be clinging to the mast.' Given the virtual ban that Bronwen had imposed on Ward at the dinner table, his high hopes of Bill were misplaced and a sign of how quickly he was losing touch with reality.

Bill did pay Ward £200 in lieu of improvements that had been carried out at the cottage during his tenancy and offered a guarantee for a further £1,500 to cover legal expenses but Ward felt betrayed. Increasingly isolated, he dwelt on the collapse of his friendship with Bill and concluded that it had all started to go wrong when Bronwen arrived. He began to blame her and hinted to friends that he had been behind her marriage to Bill, that he had groomed her as he had others and that, though she was no better than Keeler or Rice-Davies who liked to describe themselves as models, Bronwen now believed herself above him and had abandoned him. 'He made the whole thing up,' she says, 'because he was so upset, so angry and he dated his demise with Bill from the moment I walked through the door. I think he realised that I was going to break the mental hold he had on Bill.'

Ward began writing to and talking to anyone he could find who would listen. On 7 May he managed to arrange an interview with the Prime Minister's private secretary, T. J. Bligh: he complained of police interference in his osteopathy practice and threatened to sue, calling Profumo and Bill as witnesses. 'Both of them were closely involved in the truth of the incident,' he told Bligh. A few days later, on 19 May, Ward was sounding off to Henry Brooke, the Home Secretary, in a letter which alleged that it was 'through Lord Astor' that Christine Keeler had met Profumo. 'I intend to take the blame no longer,' he wrote. Bill was being presented as the prime mover in Profumo's affair rather than an innocent bystander.

Ward was clearly acting irrationally, striking out at everyone around him as he saw the pillars of his life – his practice, his popularity as an artist and his social life – crumbling under a determined assault from the police. At the start of May, just as he was sullying Bill's name within government circles, he was also writing to him, begging for money. 'Can you help me sort out some of my problems and save something from the ruin? Anyway I desperately need your help or I shall go completely under.' Generous even when his generosity might be used against him, Bill sent £200 – a considerable sum for the time, equivalent to around £2,000 today. He went one step further. Aware that Ward's practice was suffering, he suggested that Bronwen's mother, who was suffering a lot of pain after her stroke, should go for a treatment with Ward. 'He knew Stephen was hard up,' Bronwen says, 'but he still didn't believe the rumours about him. Do you think if he had known what sort of man Stephen really was, he would have sent his mother-in-law, who was a magistrate, to him?'

Bill consulted his lawyer, Bill Mitchell, an old friend with whom he had served in the Second World War. Since the Astors had done nothing illegal, and Profumo was still maintaining that there had been no wrong-doing on his part, Mitchell advised that they should continue with business as usual and offer no comment to any specific question about the scandal. At Ascot in June the couple was, William Hickey reported in his 'society column' in the *Daily Express*, looking 'urbane and relaxed'. Bill toasted Lester Piggott's triumph in the Gold Cup and headed back to Cliveden with Bronwen.

Bill's readiness to take his lawyer's advice was about more than simply adopting a posture. He was afraid that if he did tell all he knew he would implicate those he wanted to protect. Jack Profumo was an obvious example. At their meeting back in January, when Keeler was threatening to go to the press, Bill must have realised that Profumo was lying to his government colleagues about the nature of his involvement with the girl. If Bill were to make a statement, he would immediately be questioned about what he knew of Profumo's behaviour.

Then there was the question of how he himself had ended up with Ward on his estate – at the behest of his ex-wife. How could he involve her? And there was also the woman friend whom he had met in the late 1950s through Ward. She was now happily married and respectable. The last thing Bill wanted to do was drag her name through the papers. The police, in their interview with him, had thrown in a whole list of names, seeking out their connection with Ward. Bill had refused to comment on anyone.

'The only thing that Bill was guilty of in this whole ghastly business was having Stephen Ward on the estate,' says Bronwen, 'but Bill wouldn't explain how that came about. And it wasn't only his lawyer he consulted. He went on several occasions to see his bishop.'

Following his confirmation in the Church of England – a move which convinced the local Anglican bishop of his good faith and led to Bronwen being granted a dispensation, although she was the wife of a twice-divorced man, to receive communion – Bill had come increasingly to share his wife's need for spiritual advice. She derived hers from Teilhard de Chardin. He chose Gordon Savage, Bishop of Buckingham, and on many occasions discussed with him his dilemma over the unravelling Profumo scandal and how much to say. The bishop later recorded his impressions of these meetings.

'Perhaps sometimes too easily led, and certainly too modest to defend himself against mean criticism, but guileless, he was, as I understood him, straight as a die. You could bet your bottom dollar on what he said as being wholly true, wholly reliable, regardless always of personal cost to himself.' Bill's problem, though, was the potential personal cost to others if he spoke.

His purpose [in seeing the bishop, Savage wrote] was to seek strength in his personal resolve to tell the truth, the whole truth, to hold nothing back, regardless of consequences. I was struck again by his transparent honesty and simple determination. The consequences he most feared were not on himself but on his family and also on those whom he might need to incriminate through direct questioning, by the full answers he was expected to give. I remember so well him saying . . . 'You see, Bishop Gordon . . . if I answer fully and truthfully that question, think of the hurt the possible publicity will give to X or Y.'

There was pressure, too, from those in positions of power who feared that Bill might reveal their association with Ward. 'There were one or two politicians who had been to Stephen's parties and then to stay with us,' Bronwen recalls. 'They were pressing him to keep their names out of it.' However, the greatest influence on Bill in choosing the policy of silence was his bishop. Bill had decided to take the Christian course of turning the other cheek.

Buttressed by their mutual love and their knowledge that they had done nothing wrong, Bill and Bronwen simply carried on as usual. On 24 April they attended the marriage of Princess Alexandra to Angus Ogilvy. Though not a regular in royal circles, Bill's wide social world included the couple – and, through their shared passion for racehorses, the Queen herself, who met Bronwen when she visited the Cliveden stud.

On 25 May Maurice Collis was at dinner at Cliveden with Tony Keswick, a director of the Bank of England, and Sir Philip de Zulueta, the Prime Minister's private secretary and Bill's old friend. 'Bill seemed in excellent spirits,' Collis wrote in his diary. 'Bronwen was lively too. Altogether there was no sign that an atrocious storm was about to burst.' However, Collis adds a potentially revealing footnote about the presence around Cliveden of police dogs. 'Bill put it down to the rising value of his Renoirs, Matisses, Derains.'

For Bronwen Cliveden was beginning to feel like a prison. 'People started to cancel their invitations or just didn't turn up. They were taking sides without ever hearing our side. We were held responsible for this, that and the other. They would walk out of rooms when we walked into a party so we stopped going out as much. That started in the May. I had been a model girl, so everyone assumed I was in on Stephen's world. Nobody ever said it to my face, but the stories soon reached me.'

In public and in private they were inseparable. 'We never spoke about it but I had so much love and respect for Bill that I simply accepted that he did not want to talk about it because it made him depressed. I saw my job as to keep him amused, diverted and happy at home which I think I did very successfully. We were always laughing, making jokes. None of that had changed. In a funny way, though, I was much more worldly wise than Bill. I could see the false friends but it would not occur to me to upset him by talking to him about it. The few times that I tried, he just changed the subject. It would have been the best thing in the world to talk, but we didn't. And the tension just built up and built up inside him. I think he was terrified that I would leave him. It never occurred to me. People said to me later, "Why didn't you leave him when you heard the stories?" but it never occurred to me to believe them – or, even if they were true, to leave. I was there for a reason.'

The weight of allegations and insinuations against John Profumo reached crisis point on 5 June. He was pressed once more by government colleagues, who had received briefings on Ward's various conversations with and letters to ministers on Profumo's relationship with Keeler. Finally the Secretary of State resigned from the government and, he told a packed House of Commons, from Parliament, admitting that he had lied about his links with Keeler.

If Bill and Bronwen harboured any hopes that this might be an end to their suffering, they soon discovered it only increased the pressure. 'WHAT THE HELL IS GOING ON IN THIS COUNTRY?' the *Daily Mirror* asked the next morning. With Profumo now effectively off stage, the whole government – and especially the Prime Minister Harold Macmillan – was now under scrutiny over its handling of the affair. In the debate on Profumo's resignation on 17 June, one of Macmillan's own backbenchers, Nigel Birch, called for the Prime Minister's resignation.

As the ruling classes were everywhere accused of hypocrisy and double standards, Bill and Bronwen Astor became for the press and the public alike the epitome of a corrupt, amoral, self-serving elite who preached one thing to those who looked up to them and did another in the privacy of their homes and swimming pools. Committed to silence and carrying on as usual, the couple only accentuated the impression of casual indifference to all that was swirling around their heads.

There were, according to Christopher Booker, deep forces at play:

The Profumo affair was merely the focus and catalyst for the coming to a head of that revolution in the mood and character of English life that had begun to show itself late in the summer of 1955. It was the end of a trail which had its beginnings in those first grumblings of Henry Fairlie against the Establishment and Malcolm Muggeridge against the monarchy; a trail that had led on through the Angry Young Men and all the resentments sown by Suez, through the heyday of affluence through all the mounting impatience with convention, tradition and authority that had been marked by the teenage revolution and the CND and the New Morality, through the darkening landscape of security scandals and What's Wrong with Britain and the rising aggression and bitterness of the satirists, in ever more violent momentum. And now, in that wet and windy June, the climax had arrived. Not one ingredient was missing. With Profumo's admission of guilt, all the swelling tide of scorn and resentment for age, tradition and authority, all the poisonous fantasy of limitless corruption and decay into which it had ripened, were finally unleashed in their full fury.

The government's response was to deflect attention onto Ward, and so on 8 June the police, acting on the orders of the Home Secretary, arrested the osteopath and charged him with living off immoral earnings. Keeler and Rice-Davies and a number of Ward's other associates, including several prostitutes, were questioned and pressed to provide evidence that he was their pimp. No longer was it simply a question of spies or lying to Parliament; the affair became, according to The Times's editorial on 11 June, 'a moral issue' about the future direction of Britain.

'Profumo, Keeler, Rachman, Rice-Davies, Astor, Edgecombe, Gordon, Ward – they were like stopping places on a London bus,' wrote Ludovic Kennedy of these dramatic times. 'Other names too had been bandied about, those of peers and cabinet ministers lurking on the periphery. There had been tales of unspeakable orgies, of a sort of General Post of unbuttoning of trousers and lifting of skirts. Tremendous whipping parties were said to go on at a house in Mayfair; at one, I was told, a small grocer had had a heart attack and died.'

On 10 June Bronwen was sufficiently concerned by the turn of events to take up her journal, begun in 1959 but left almost untouched during the first hectic years at Cliveden. Her anger at Bill's treatment, her fear for their good names, her sense that greater forces were at play and that God had put her in this terrible situation for a reason shine through in her often passionate, sometimes half-formed private reactions to the turn of events.

The very reason I married Bill – no – one of the many – protection. Protection against the forces of evil which now, since the summer

of 1959, I know I exist to confront. July 8th 1961 the Profumos
came to stay the weekend . . . Tonight Bill and I cooked our dinner.
But B's back wicked from cutting his toenails. He saw Dr Bailey
as SW [Stephen Ward] is in prison. He [Bill] feels remorse as we
wonder what the future holds in accusations. But I refuse to recognise or see any fault in his generosity. One does not give with
strings attached. He is the victim of generosity and hospitality. Our
Cliveden world is being blown up in our faces, but we shall build
again. I feel perfectly calm and pray for those whose souls are given
over to the devil to use as he wishes in his destructive ways.

Such specific thoughts Bronwen kept to herself; she concentrated
on giving Bill her total support and attention. Watching horrified
from the sidelines as his name was associated with ever more disgrace-
ful goings-on, he didn't know where to turn. His lawyers continued
to advise silence and keeping to his daily routine. On 12 June,
however he wrote a short, friendly letter to his old friend Peter
Thorneycroft, the Minister of Defence and Profumo's immediate
superior, offering to help in any way he could in the internal investigation that the Prime Minister had set up under Lord Dilhorne, the
Lord Chancellor. Bill copied the letter to his mother's one-time
friend Harold Macmillan, though the links between the Prime Minister and the Astors had soured since the mid-1950s, with David Astor's
attack on Suez in the *Observer* and what Bill's son William describes
as 'the final nail in the coffin – the break-up of my father's marriage
to Philippa, his niece'.

If he had been in any doubt about how the political and social
establishment viewed his part in Profumo's demise, the curt, formal
acknowledgements that Bill received from both men's private secretaries made it plain he had already been judged and found guilty of
involvement with Ward's unpleasant activities. He was now effectively an outcast. When a copy of Bill's letter was passed to his old
friend and frequent guest at Cliveden Philip de Zulueta, now a senior
civil servant at Admiralty House, de Zulueta wrote straight back to
Macmillan's private secretary: 'Mr Bligh, I have *not* got in touch!'
(his emphasis). No one in official circles dared to have any contact
with Bill Astor.

Details of the scandal had spread around the world, and as far away as Washington Bill Astor's good standing was being questioned in official memoranda. J. Edgar Hoover, head of the FBI, was convinced that Soviet-funded call girls had been working to disgrace men like Profumo and Bill Astor, whom he perceived as having political power on account of his title and family connections. In an FBI memo on the scandal, names of those affected were listed: 'Lord Astor of England on whose Cliveden estate sex orgies reportedly occurred; it was here that Profumo first met Keeler; Douglas Fairbanks Jnr, movie actor; Earl Fenton, American screen writer; and many others also involved.'

On 17 June, in the middle of Cliveden's traditional Ascot Week round of parties and entertaining, Bronwen confided in her diary: 'Cliveden besieged. Press watched everything and tried to bribe staff for pictures of the swimming pool. Thursday it rained so we were spared too many. Only Hardings* refused to come to Ascot.' When Chief Inspector Samuel Herbert and DS John Burrows of the Metropolitan Police turned up at his front door on 19 June, just as those Ascot Week guests were leaving, Bill was in despair. They made it clear that they were attempting to find sufficient evidence to bring charges against him of allowing a brothel at Spring Cottage. He was near to collapse. 'I had the sense of Bill as a man who found he was in over his head,' says Lord Gowrie. 'He was not a person who thought ill of people or who was calculated in his behaviour, seeking his own best advantage, but he was not decisive. He listened to his lawyers and he wrung his hands. He had a flawed decency – like most of us. Bill's flaws simply became more obvious.'

Bronwen saw more to events than what lay on the surface. 'I felt as if we were in the eye of a storm of evil. It is like a hurricane and you just stand there and you bend and you have to hang on to your roots. It just grew and grew. I sensed the evil all around us as more and more people were sucked in. Bill never said a thing to me. He wouldn't speak about it. I just tried to be strong for him without ever really knowing what it was that he was worrying about at that time. I only found out later.'

---

* Field Marshal Lord (John) Harding was a war hero and royal servant – latterly commander-in-chief of the British Army on the Rhine.

Her own belief and self-confidence gave her the strength to support him, to offer him, as Teilhard advised, 'unconditional love'. It also helped her to see a pattern. 'As Bill began to collapse, I realised that was why I had been sent there. That was God's plan for me. I never felt abandoned by God. It was the opposite. I thought, Thank goodness I am here. No wonder I had to marry this man.'

Chapter Ten

I can't feign indifference, detachment or subtlety. I just adore you.

Bill Astor to Bronwen Pugh (1959)

Nowhere, it seemed, could Bill and Bronwen Astor escape the smears. On 25 June *Paris Match*, alongside a picture of the couple, compared Bill's behaviour to aristocratic reprobates of history. 'AUJOURD'HUI BILL – DANS LA BOUCHE D'UNE KEELER' ran the headline. The implication – that their marriage was merely a smokescreen – was plain.

On Friday 28 June Ward appeared in Marylebone Magistrates Court charged with a variety of violations of the Sexual Offences Act of 1956, including brothel-keeping, procuring, living on the earnings of prostitutes and abortion offences. Some 120 people crammed into a public gallery designed for thirty. Much was made in summarising the evidence before the magistrates (as the first part of the judicial process) of the £200 that Bill had given Ward to help Keeler and Rice-Davies to pay the rent on their Fulham flat.

Mandy Rice-Davies was called as a witness. She was questioned about the money and about her relationship with Lord Astor. Did she have to have sex with him in return for the £200? 'No,' she replied. 'But I did sleep with him later.' When it was pointed out that Lord Astor had denied any such involvement, she said, 'He would, wouldn't he?' The courtroom erupted into laughter and the phrase was splashed all over the next morning's newspapers. According to the *Daily Telegraph*, 'There was a gasp in the crowded courtroom when she named him.' Even in America, Rice-Davies's remarks made headlines. 'ASTOR IS MENTIONED AT WARD'S HEARING', said the *New York Times*.

Those four words struck such a chord because they seemed to

sum up the hypocrisy that underpinned the whole Profumo drama and the public's new suspicion about what their social betters were saying. Jack Profumo had lied so it was taken as read that in this matter Bill Astor was also lying. So celebrated did Rice-Davies's quip become that it is now to be found in *The Oxford Dictionary of Quotations*, with Bill Astor's adultery for ever taken as historical fact.

Still Bronwen was carrying on as usual with a busy diary. At the time of Rice-Davies's court appearance she and Bill were hosting a charity concert for 250 guests at Cliveden by guitarist Andres Segovia in aid of Lifeline, the international committee for aiding displaced persons in Germany. She had tried to respect his wish not to discuss the scandal but it was the only time she broke the taboo. 'I asked him if he had slept with Mandy Rice-Davies. He said no, but I will never forget the look of hurt on his face that I could even think it was true. I knew he was not lying. He had a particular way of behaving when he was lying. He'd stutter and avoid my eyes. I would have known.'

Soon afterwards she wrote in a great fury in her diary: 'Last Saturday it was said in court by Miss Mandy Rice-Davies that Bill had paid the rent on their flat and she had had intercourse with him. Pff! She has gone too far and has not reckoned with *me*! Supposed to have had an affair a few months after we were married?! Bill's lawyer denied it.'

Wives, received wisdom tells us, are always the last to know if their husbands are being unfaithful, but Bronwen's stout rebuttal of the claim is backed up by Bill's unofficial confessor, Bishop Gordon Savage, the one man to whom he spoke openly during the whole Profumo chapter. Without breaking the secrecy of the confessional, Savage later recorded his own angry reaction to Rice-Davies's claim: 'I was so sure from his words that this was not so. I am absolutely sure from everything he ever said that that was not the Bill I knew.'

Almost four decades after the event, it is hard to reach a definitive conclusion about the alleged liaison. Of the two people who would know, Bill Astor, who always denied it, is dead, but Rice-Davies stands by her claim to this day. 'Peter Rachman [her married boyfriend] had died and I was very upset and staying at Stephen's flat,' she says. 'I'd already tried to commit suicide. Bill came round. I had a record player in my bedroom. Stephen didn't have one. I had a new Ray Charles record. We went into the bedroom to play it. We talked about music. And that was it. It wasn't earth-shattering. It was just a congenial get-together. Bill's testosterone got slightly the better of him. It was the period when Bronwen was pregnant.'

Yet however plausible this sounds, the timescales simply do not add up. Rice-Davies has never named a specific day or even month when the incident took place, but Peter Rachman died on 29 November 1962. Bronwen was not at that time or at any time until after the Ward trial pregnant. Her miscarriage in early November 1962 came before Rachman's death and at the start of her pregnancy.

Why, though, would Rice-Davies have made such a mistake and still maintain her position almost forty years later? She knew Ward was innocent of the charges brought against him. She regarded him at the time and continues to regard him as a victim of injustice. She has moreover claimed ever after that she has a heavy heart about the damage the scandal did to Bill Astor. Yet her words gave the impression that Bill was an unfaithful husband and – in the light of the £200 he had given Ward to help with rent – that the osteopath may indeed have been charging for sexual favours.

Transcripts and eyewitness accounts of that day in Marylebone Magistrates Court suggest that Rice-Davies volunteered the piece of information about sleeping with Bill. She had no need to say anything about it – she wasn't answering a question, and it seemed, reporters in the courtroom recall, like a piece of bravado to shock the packed gallery to which she was playing. Yet, behind her show of confidence, eighteen-year-old Rice-Davies was a reluctant witness, her plans to escape to Spain to avoid the trial blocked when police arrested her, detained her in Holloway Prison on a minor motoring offence and confiscated her passport. During many hours of interview with the police, she had been told that Christine Keeler had revealed the liaison between Rice-Davies and Bill Astor, so she would have known that, in court, if she denied it, the prosecution had conflicting evidence. The next morning, when her remark about Bill made headlines – and indeed ever after – she could hardly go back on what she had said.

Yet, as her various accounts of the Profumo scandal over the years make plain, her memory is not infallible. *The Mandy Report*, her 1964 comic-style account of her rise to stardom, has Bill's picture on the front cover but makes no mention of his alleged infidelity with her. By 1980, however, she was giving a detailed version of the seduction that coincides with much of what she now describes. Yet in the same book she reports how in the early 1960s, when she was at Spring Cottage, Nancy Astor was driven around the Cliveden estate each day to 'keep a close watch on affairs, although officially the lady of the house was now Bill's wife, the model Bronwen Pugh'. Nancy Astor, as her own correspondence and Cliveden household records make plain, was an infrequent visitor and was certainly not escorted round the grounds as a moral watchdog.

Again, when Rice-Davies writes of how she would 'relax, chat, [have] tea or dinner at the house with the Astors' or 'have a dip in the pool', she is flying in the face of the evidence of carefully maintained household records. Save for the one meal she came to with Ward at the age of sixteen before Bill married Bronwen, she was never a guest for tea or dinner at Cliveden. And, like many others who have attempted in describing the Profumo scandal to make Cliveden sound racier than it was, Rice-Davies, writing in 1980, mistakenly linked Bronwen with Stephen Ward: 'Many of Stephen's girlfriends, including Bill Astor's wife, had met their husbands through Stephen.'

Rice-Davies can be forgiven for getting confused on this last point since the assumption, to Bronwen's horror, was in the summer of 1963 and for a long time thereafter fairly widespread. Maurice Collis reports in his diary a visit to the artist Feliks Topolski at the start of July 1963. 'He said that during a recent visit to Paris he had seen in the *Paris Soir* photos of the women Ward was supposed to have started in life by training them how to secure rich husbands. Among the girls was Bronwen. I said that Ward's hand in the Astor–Bronwen Pugh marriage was nil. I had seen its genesis and development with my own eyes.'

In the wake of Rice-Davies's allegation, Bill's friends began making their excuses and cancelling.

Geoffroi de Waldener★ showed his true colours [Bronwen wrote in her diary of a racing trip to Deauville in France], and would not

★ Baron Geoffroi de Waldener, French nobleman and racehorse-owner.

take him to the Jockey Club dinner under the pretext it would be embarrassing to Bill. But we must lead a normal life otherwise people will believe Bill to be lying like Jack. French don't see why the fuss, and believe Bill to have done all these things. Went to Grand Prix. Afterwards to Maxim's dance. Nigel Campbell* told me French attitude – a nightmare, and had to leave – cannot bear people believing these lies.

When they arrived back from Deauville, there were letters waiting for both Bill and Bronwen from his younger brother David, questioning Mandy Rice-Davies's account. 'Wrote adamantly that I, of all people, should and do know that Bill did *not* have an affair with this girl,' Bronwen recorded, 'that *I would know if he were lying* [her italics], and would not allow him to lie – (the truth would rebound 20 years later on William – "the sins of the father . . .")'

A couple of days later Maurice Collis went to dinner at Cliveden. He found Bill a changed man.

As I looked at his face, while we stood a moment in the outer hall, I was moved by the expression of suffering I saw there. There was a softness, even sweetness in his eyes, a look of gentle appeal which in all the years I had never seen before. I had a sudden inclination to embrace him, but only pressed his arm. He half closed his eyes and sighed: 'Yes, yes, the only thing is to keep up one's dignity, go on as before and not engage in any public slanging match with these women . . . I have to bear all this scandal without an opportunity of replying. Anyhow it is difficult to prove a negative, prove there is nothing, nothing in the stories invented about me by goodness knows whom.'

Over dinner that night Collis learnt that the press were now circling Cliveden in helicopters at all hours of the day in the hope of witnessing an orgy in the grounds, a romp by the swimming pool or suspicious comings and goings. Bronwen told him that she was now afraid to go outside. He went on:

Bronwen said, 'All this has been a test of friends. Some when asked to dinner or lunch have made excuses.' And she added laughing:

* Stockbroker and husband of famous model Barbara Goalen.

'There were some old friends who complained saying – we have come to you all these years, but you never once invited us to an orgy. After all I've been married to Bill since October 1960, nearly three years. Of course I would have noticed if he had been living the way scandal would have it. It was a great surprise to Bill when some of the people he thought his oldest and best friends doubted or even went against him in the crisis.'

Surprise is perhaps too gentle a word. Shock would have been more appropriate. On 10 July, Bronwen wrote in her diary that some friends had remained loyal. 'Over dinner I asked Charles Rutland★ whether we should go on to Gilbert Miller's dance. He would say as he is sensible, has been through hell over his mother-in-law and knows what looks right and proper. He advised me to go. Bill tired but so glad we went as after the first surprise everyone *so* nice. We whirled round the dance floor a couple of times with Reggie and Alice Winn† – then home.'

Cliveden was ever more under siege. One night the croquet hoops were stolen by what the Astors could only presume were souvenir hunters. On another occasion the head gardener was approached by reporters asking whether he could verify the fact that he had acted as a go-between, carrying money between the main house and the orgies going on at Ward's cottage. *Private Eye* went so far as to concoct a satirical spoof on the National Trust brochure about Cliveden, highlighting the best places to find people having sex. When Bill and Bronwen left the estate, their car was followed. One evening they were due to attend a concert at the Royal Festival Hall. They handed their tickets over to Bronwen's parents and sent Sir Alun and Lady Pugh in the Rolls-Royce with Chapman at the wheel. When the chauffeur opened the door outside the concert hall, the cameras immediately began clicking, only to fall silent when it became clear that the occupants of the car were not the Astors.

It was a rare victory and caused them much mirth. Those who saw Bill and Bronwen at this time sensed that Bill was close to breaking point. 'He was very low around the time of the trial,' says

★ Charles, tenth Duke of Rutland, son-in-law of Margaret, Duchess of Argyll.
† Daughter and son-in-law of Nancy Astor's sister Lizzie – Bill's cousins.

Ron Barry, Bronwen's brother-in-law. 'He kept blaming himself although I could never see what it was what he'd done wrong. "Nothing would have happened," he kept telling me, "if it hadn't been for me and now the government is at stake."'

It was Bronwen, however, who witnessed the full extent of his despair. 'There was one evening when Bill said that he couldn't stand it any more and that he was going to go to America. I was in tears. I didn't know what to do. Then my father telephoned. He and my mother came down straight away and stayed and persuaded Bill not to go. It would have looked so bad. It wasn't that he was in any way guilty but just that he was such a terribly nervous creature.'

It is significant that in extremis she turned to her own family and not to Bill's. Sir Alun Pugh in particular became a trusted adviser to the couple. 'Parents have been splendid,' Bronwen wrote in her diary. 'Father delights in telling members of the bar how Stephen Ward cured Mo's [mother's] fibrositis.' By contrast, with his own cousin, Hugh Astor, during this period, Bill presented a brave face. 'We never discussed the problem,' recalls Hugh. 'If I bumped into him it was Hail fellow well met.' Bill's mother, whose mental health was by now deteriorating fast, was deliberately kept in ignorance of the scandal by her butler, who would remove all references to Bill from her morning papers.

The one Astor who did try to help was Bill's younger brother David. 'I remember saying to one of my younger brothers,' recalls David Astor, 'shouldn't we do something to try and see Bill and help him? My brother said, "How do I know what Bill has been doing?" He wouldn't do it. I think I was the only one to see him and the reason for the other three [siblings] was not wanting to know.' This lack of instinctive trust, the time-honoured feeling that there was no smoke without fire, was mirrored on Bill's side by a reluctance even to agree to meet David. 'I had to force my way in because his lawyer was giving him the wrong advice. He told him to carry on going to race-meetings and the like as if nothing had happened. Really he should have given him good common-sense advice which would have been to show that he was upset by all his friends being involved in the Ward case. By smiling in public and saying nothing, it was as if he thought he could buy his way out of anything.'

David's plea fell on deaf ears. Bronwen, too, was pressed by friends to speak out but resisted. In a letter of reply she drafted at Cliveden to one such plea on 8 July, she wrote:

Bill will admit in due course that he should have taken Stephen's private life more seriously. Since our marriage Stephen rarely came to the house except to give treatments. Most of what went on was in London, it appears, and no-one here noticed anything unusual going on at the cottage. Bill's fault was to treat Stephen too lightly, and because he – Stephen – had been kind to Bill after Philippa's departure, dining with him, amusing him etc., Bill was not critical enough of his – Stephen's – own life.

In the end, however, she did not send the letter. She remained committed to the policy of silence.

On 22 July the Ward case moved to the Old Bailey. Two days later Mandy Rice-Davies was in the witness box repeating her evidence about Bill. Once again she was the star of the show, as Ludovic Kennedy wrote in his eyewitness account of proceedings. 'Astride her golden head sat a little rose-petalled hat, such as debutantes wear at garden parties . . . Her simple grey sleeveless dress accentuated the impression of modesty . . . until one looked at it closely. Then one saw that the slit down the front was only held together by a loose knot – when she walked one could see quite a long way up her leg . . .'

'Did you have intercourse with him?' Rice-Davies was asked by counsel after she had confirmed that Bill had once provided half the rent for the flat in Fulham which she shared with Christine Keeler.

'Not when he paid the money – two years later,' she replied.

At this stage the judge, Sir Archie Marshall, intervened. 'Where did you meet Lord Astor?' he asked.

'At Cliveden.'

'Did you ever see him at the flat?'

'No, but I know that Stephen brought Bill – Lord Astor – round to the flat.'

'Stephen Ward had taken Lord Astor round to Comeragh Road when you were out?' the judge recapped.

'Yes, sir.'

For Ludovic Kennedy, in the press gallery, the implication about

Bill was clear – that he was a regular client of Ward's girls but that somehow he had escaped being charged. Bill was not so much covered up by the establishment, Kennedy concluded, as not given a chance to clear his name.

Later, when questioned by counsel, Rice-Davies subtly altered her story about Bill. 'That was the first time I had intercourse with Lord Astor,' she said, as if there had been several subsequent occasions, a suggestion she has since denied. And she implied – again adding to what she now says – that Ward was in the flat and watching them.

'Was Ward at the flat on that occasion?' she was asked.

'Once.'

'When you had intercourse with Lord Astor?'

'It was quite normal for him to be in the flat.'

Again the judge stepped in. 'It was normal for Ward to be in the flat when you were having sexual intercourse with other men, was it?'

'Oh yes,' Rice-Davies replied, once again playing to the crowd, 'it's quite normal, isn't it. There's nothing wrong with it.'

The court laughed but the judge rebuked her. 'This is the third time you have gone on talking without reason for so doing.'

When Stephen Ward gave evidence, he rejected out of hand her claims about Bill. 'I deny that she had a relationship with Lord Astor,' he stated categorically. Although he had been happy to link Bill with the Profumo–Keeler liaison in his debriefings for civil servants and reporters, it is significant that he drew the line at this. Despite his despair and doubts about his friendship with Bill Astor, and his willingness to damage a friend who he felt had deserted him, Ward did not stoop to this accusation. But his words came too late. Listening to reports of court proceedings brought to their house in Upper Grosvenor Street by their legal representative, who had attended as an observer, the Astors could do nothing.

Yet it was clear to them, and to those close to them, that Bill was being placed in an impossible position by the conduct of the trial. The matter of the £200 cheque he had given Ward, allegedly for the flat where Rice-Davies and Keeler lived, was brought up in the context of the osteopath's trial for living off immoral earnings: the implication that Bill Astor frequented prostitutes was plain. Yet the charge was never made out loud and could therefore not be rebutted. The story that was told – Rice-Davies's account of her alleged one-off liaison with Bill – damaging as it was to his reputation and wounding to Bronwen, was presented as a simple act of friendship, not a business transaction.

Sir Alun Pugh, with his many years of experience of courtroom procedures and ploys, was convinced that Bill was cleverly being set up. 'The venom shown by the judge and the prosecution bewildered me. After the time when Bill's name was mentioned, it turned into a nightmare. I got the impression that there was personal rancour at the back of this concealed attack on Bill.' Sir Alun put it down to those grandees who had never forgiven Bill after the failure of his second marriage and pointed a finger particularly at the Prime Minister, Harold Macmillan, who he believed was allowing public prosecutors to act out his own grudge against Bill Astor.

Others had alternative theories. Bishop Gordon Savage, Bill's informal confessor, thought he detected a more global conspiracy. 'I see the whole scandal as being a gigantic plot to discredit the honoured name of Astor. The USSR at that time of the Cold War was always poised, ready to discredit a prominent member of this and other governments.' While the Soviets did occasionally express an interest in corrupting the British aristocracy, it is overstating matters to describe the name of Astor as 'honoured' in Britain, certainly among the upper classes. Yet it did undeniably have a global cachet and in Russia Nancy Astor's headline-grabbing visit in July 1931, when she was accompanied by George Bernard Shaw, was still remembered, if not with affection – she had attacked Stalin and his system remorselessly during a two-hour meeting with the Soviet leader – then as an indication that the Astors were formidable political players. However, Bill could scarcely be described as prominent in government circles, but Bishop Savage's confusion and willingness to see such a widescale conspiracy illustrates the effect the scandal had even on sceptics and may explain why so many of the Astors' friends simply stood back in bemusement at a time when the couple needed their support.

Bill had insisted on being up in London during the trial, Bronwen remembers, and was, contrary to all suggestions made at the time, willing to speak if called. He did not, however, force himself forward. 'That is why we were in London. Why be there unless there was a chance Bill would have to appear? The lawyers on both sides argued about what effect his evidence would have. Yes, he could have said that Stephen did not, to his knowledge, live off immoral earnings, but by that time he had concerns about Stephen's character which might have come out if he was cross-examined and damage Stephen.'

If Ward's lawyers had judged that Bill was too ambiguous a witness to help their client, the prosecution was thinking of calling him to get him to talk about his new-found doubts about his ex-tenant. But for them too there was the prospect of cross-examination by Ward's counsel, when Bill could have said some very positive things about the defendant. In the end Bill's non-appearance was the result of a decision taken by lawyers. He was caught in the middle of their crossfire.

Yet Bill's failure to speak up for Ward was much criticised as evidence of his own weakness of character. It was assumed he had refused to stand up and be counted. To the charges of sexual licence, hypocrisy and adultery that were already laid at his door was added the suggestion that he was a coward who had deserted a friend in need. 'I thought Bill Astor behaved rather shabbily towards Ward,' Ludovic Kennedy writes today, 'in not having anything to do with him after his arrest and trial. He could have appeared as a character witness at the trial. He could perhaps have attended in court anyway. He might have provided a car to take Ward to and fro each day. But as far as I can recall he did none of these things.'

In his summing-up of the evidence against Ward, the judge made much of the absence of Ward's influential friends in the witness box as a sign of the defendant's poor character. 'There may be many reasons why Ward has been abandoned in his extremity. You must not guess at them, but this is clear: if Stephen Ward was telling the truth in the witness-box, there are in this city many witnesses of high estate and low who could have come and testified support of his evidence.' Later, he returned to the point: 'Many witnesses who could have been called have not been called in connection with the defence. They could have enormously strengthened the case concerning the earnings of prostitution.'

Ludovic Kennedy felt that 'the judge was only echoing what was in all our minds. Where was Lord Astor? . . . They [Bill and other Ward associates] had issued statements and denials, but that was not enough. There could be little doubt that if they had taken the stand to strengthen Ward's evidence, they would have enormously strengthened the case for the defence.' About Bill in particular Kennedy was withering: 'For years, poor innocent, he [Ward] had deluded himself into thinking that Lord Astor and others were his friends; and now had come the shattering awakening. He was not their friend at all: he was the court jester, the grand eunuch, the private medicine-man whose usefulness was over.'

Yet Bronwen's analysis of Bill's dilemma regarding giving evidence either for or against Ward is backed up by a number of sources, including David Astor. 'Bill told me around the time of the trial that he had thought he knew Ward but now he wasn't so sure. He was very shocked by Ward's Russian connections and felt that he no longer knew what else he might be hiding.'

David, Jakie, Bill's lawyer Bill Mitchell and Bronwen's father had all attended a pre-trial meeting at Upper Grosvenor Street to discuss the question of Bill's appearance in the witness box.

> David was breathing fire and talked about the fight for the honour of the Astor family [Sir Alun later wrote]. He was begging Bill to go into the witness box and give evidence. Bill was quiet, almost lethargic. I got the impression he would only go into the witness box if he were lifted into it. It was a very confused discussion in which I took little part, other than bolstering up Bill, for I felt that there were factors and undercurrents of which I knew nothing. I felt confirmed in this when, in another of my talks with Bill, I asked him point blank why he would not give evidence. His reply was 'because it would involve another woman'. Then I left it.

Sir Alun, writing in 1968, was sure that the woman concerned was Bill's second wife Philippa, at whose suggestion Ward had first come to the Cliveden estate. It might equally well have been the woman who had been introduced to Bill by Ward following the collapse of his marriage to Philippa.

When privately questioned in August 1963 by a friendly journalist,

Kenneth Rose, over his non-appearance at court, Bill preferred to stick to the explanation about following lawyers' advice. 'I was never asked at any stage of the case by either side to be a witness. You see I had no specific evidence to give on any of the charges for which he was put up on trial. As far as I could see I knew nothing about any of the charges.' Since an implicit assumption was made in court about a connection between the £200 Bill gave Ward for rent and his subsequent alleged sex with Rice-Davies, Bill may have been being naïve here.

Bill had also taken advice from Sir Alun Pugh about the quality of the evidence against Ward. Sir Alun believed the osteopath would undoubtedly get off with or without Bill's intervention, but he had not taken into account the extent to which the jury would be influenced by the unremittingly hostile attitude of the judge and by the seeming ineptitude of Ward's own counsel. However, despite his bemusement at events in the high court, Sir Alun was convinced that no appeal court, less influenced by popular outrage, would uphold a verdict of guilty on Ward.

If he failed to make a public gesture, however, Bill had done the next best thing, Bronwen claims. He had paid part of Ward's costs. In the same conversation with the writer Kenneth Rose on 14 August 1963, quoted above and recorded in detail by Rose, Bill insisted that he had helped Ward considerably 'whenever he asked me to'. When Rose challenged him about Ward's trial costs, Bill went on: 'It is a fact that I spent over £2,000 on his defence and that was quite a large sum. In fact everything that he asked me to give, only it was most important that he was able to meet the costs of the defence and so I helped him in that way. I helped him considerably.'

However, he refused when pressed to confirm that he had actually paid out money for Ward's defence. A question mark remained in Rose's mind following the conversation: had Bill Astor given money or simply offered to underwrite the costs? Yet since Ward died before any lawyers' bill could be presented, Bill was never to find out if his former tenant had intended to take up his offer of financial support in his legal battle. The debt would have passed to Ward's estate and, like as not, died with him.

The night before the jury reached their verdict, 30 July, Stephen Ward, convinced that the trial was going to end badly for him, wrote a series of suicide notes; he gave a final interview to the *Daily Express* and inter alia once more claimed to have introduced Bronwen to Bill. 'Someone had to be sacrificed and it was me, but when the Establishment want blood, they get it.'

After the reporter left, he took an overdose of barbiturates. He was rushed to hospital and lingered on long enough for the judge to justify hearing the jury's verdict – guilty. The osteopath would, however, never serve a day in prison. He died on 3 August. Alongside the news of Ward's death, the following day's papers carried pictures of Bill and Bronwen smiling happily at the Goodwood meeting that was going on that week. It couldn't have created a worse impression of them, but it was a fake, taken before they had even heard that Ward was ill.

'Bronwen and I were staying with Mr and Mrs Paul Maze* in their cottage near Midhurst,' Bill later wrote. 'We went racing on the Wednesday and as we left the course we saw in the evening paper that Ward had taken an overdose of drugs and accordingly we decided not to go to the races any more, staying quietly with the Mazes on Thursday and coming home to Cliveden on the Friday [the day Ward died].'

Bill did issue a statement: 'Stephen Ward possessed remarkable gifts of healing which he exercised skilfully, conscientiously and generously. Those who were so fortunate as to have been treated by him will remember him with great gratitude. His readiness to help anyone in pain is the memory many will treasure.' Ludovic Kennedy was among those who were not impressed. It was, he wrote, 'an epitaph on Ward of quite staggering unsuitability, the sort of thing one would expect from a head of state on the death of a distinguished specialist'.

Writing to his friend Maurice Collis, Bill went further, repeating Judge Pugh's assessment: 'The sad thing is that he [Ward] would almost certainly have got off on appeal, as I gather the law is very doubtful. It has been so difficult to know how much to say and how

---

* Paul Maze, a French artist, often called 'the last of the Impressionists'.

much to keep quiet, but I think for the moment silence must still be golden.'

In her diary Bronwen lamented Ward's death. Though she had never wanted him at her dining table, she knew that with the osteopath off the scene, there would never be a chance to clear Bill's name in court. 'All week felt a terrible dread. Now no appeal, no show-down on the appalling partiality of the judge's summing up. Father staggered at the judge and his saying that his [Ward's] friends had deserted him. Press playing this up. But Bill has done nothing to reproach himself with as he waited each day to be called and was not.'

Immediately after Ward's death, Bill descended into a pit of remorse, blaming himself for everything that had happened. In particular, he feared the effects of the scandal on Bronwen. So self-critical was he that on 5 August she felt moved to write him a letter from Cliveden to the London house.

> Darling, All love and re-assurance. There is nothing we can do but wait for the Report[*] and let the Beaverbrook Press and all the rest of them do their damnedest. Father is vehement about Marshall's mud-slinging and can't wait for the start of the new law term and the judges' dinner to say so. Do not reproach yourself one jot. I do not reproach you one iota. *You* were let down.
>
> Long talk with Chiquita[†] – agrees with me some of your relations are mad. Nothing matters besides our love for each other and the children. Darling I adore you. Don't forget to smile. *All* my love.

Bill and Bronwen maintained their public silence. Those close to them, however, could not mistake the strain. Nancy Lancaster, Bill's cousin, wrote to Bronwen the day after Ward died. Bronwen replied on 6 August. 'I understand your desire to help and appreciate it fully. We are indeed in great need of help. If I appear to suffer unduly, it is because by thus entering into the complexities and tragedies of all concerned, I can in some way mitigate Bill's suffering which is very great. You realise you have in your midst a Welsh mystic.' It was a rare reference to her religious beliefs and the strength she derived

---

[*] Lord Denning's officially commissioned enquiry into the security aspects of the scandal.
[†] Bill's brother Jakie's first wife.

from her spiritual life and awareness of the close presence of God. It also sums up her position succinctly – suffering with and on behalf of Bill rather than in her own right.

Ward's death and their seeming indifference prompted a further round of attacks on Bill and Bronwen. Ward's sometime confidant, *News of the World* reporter Peter Earle, claimed on 4 August that Bill and Ward had been so close that Ward had found Bronwen and trained her up for Cliveden. It was of course untrue but in the hysteria of the time no one stopped to question the assertion.

With Profumo out of office and in hiding, and Ward now dead, the *Daily Express* concentrated its fire on the only player still at large, Bill:

> Everyone is still asking why Lord Astor did not – as the popular phrase goes – come forward in defence of his friend. That, I think, is unjust to Lord Astor. The truly puzzling question – which has gone unasked in all the excitement and tragedy of the last seven days – is why the viscount was given any choice in the matter at all. Why was he not brought into court as a witness for the prosecution? The prosecution said there was no evidence to show why Lord Astor's celebrated cheque was paid to Ward. If the Crown really wanted to know why, you'd think that the first person to ask was the man who signed it.

The ordeal was far from over. Kenneth Armitage met Bronwen in London at this time. 'We walked back to Upper Grosvenor Street and when we came in, Bill was sitting on the bottom stair with his head in his hands. It was such an image of misery that it has always stayed with me. He was clearly very upset and very confused. Bronwen comforted him and later explained to me that he was so used to groups of people that he couldn't bear the isolation that followed the Profumo scandal. No one would go to Cliveden. Everyone dropped them.'

Mulling over what had unfolded, Bill reached his own verdict in a letter to his lawyer in August 1963, days after Ward's death: 'I really do apologise for this awful mixture of stupidity, unwisdom and chance and misplaced kindness and heaven knows what all which produced this situation.'

Chapter Eleven

Bill is dead. The Cliveden period is over.

Maurice Collis, *Diaries* (1966)

At the end of 1963 an Austrian sociologist, Heinrich Blezinger, carried out a study on the British public's attitude to the Profumo scandal. Among other questions Blezinger, based at King's College, Cambridge, asked his respondents to name the principal players in the drama and identify them from photographs. In this poll Bill Astor came fifth equal with the Russian spy, Yevgeny Ivanov, trailing behind Christine Keeler, Stephen Ward, John Profumo and Mandy Rice-Davies. Though his active involvement in the whole affair was minimal, in the public's imagination, fed by newspaper headlines, establishment scapegoating, Mandy Rice-Davies's eye for an eye-catching yarn and Stephen Ward's lonely death, Bill was at the heart of the matter.

Some 60 per cent of those questioned recognised him from a picture, with smaller numbers able also to point out Bronwen. Just as in the 1930s Nancy Astor's Cliveden had been publicly but mistakenly labelled as the base of a pro-Nazi appeasement set by journalists, politicians and, trailing in their wake, the public, so now the house's name became a by-word for sexual licence and depravity. The difference now was that, as a National Trust property, the grounds were open daily for most of the year and Cliveden itself each Saturday to anyone who wanted to come and look for telltale signs of orgies in the main hall or naked lords swinging from the chandeliers in the Madame de Pompadour dining room.

Asked by Blezinger about the sexual morals of government ministers and aristocrats, only half felt that having a mistress was 'quite current' in the political establishment, but more than 80 per cent believed the upper classes guilty of such hypocrisy. Since Bill was the representative of the social elite among the principal Profumo players, the popular verdict on him and his behaviour was clear.

Far from being the extremely plush brothel of the public imagination, however, Cliveden was fast taking on the air of a mausoleum. 'The house was completely empty,' regular guest Maurice Collis lamented in his diary, 'the great hall without a soul and nobody coming or going. The silence and emptiness were somehow ominous.' The Astors had been largely abandoned by polite society. 'Once the scandal broke, many former guests deserted Cliveden but of course continued to dine out on the fact that they knew Bill and had been guests in his house,' says Joan Astley. 'They were very ready to blame him over Profumo.'

'It is hard to conceive the suffering and hurt they had to endure from men and women who had accepted their hospitality and whom they had thought of as friends,' Pamela Cooper wrote later of the treatment the Astors suffered. Even when they were out of the country Bill and Bronwen were hounded by those eager to judge them over the Profumo scandal. In October 1963 they attended a dinner while holidaying in Salzburg and found themselves rebuked by a fellow guest over Bill's failure to appear in Ward's defence at the trial. As ever, they chose not to respond.

In the silence created by Bill and Bronwen's determination to do the Christian thing and turn the other cheek, it was open season on Cliveden's master and mistress. Those who had once happily sipped their champagne were now ready to believe even the most lurid stories about them. In some versions Bill was addicted to kinky sex, with Bronwen dressing the part as a strict disciplinarian to satisfy him. In others, even Nancy Astor was colluding in the degradation of her one-time home. Rumour had it that she had invited a group of US senators to Cliveden. When she asked Bill whether the house would be free that night, he said that Stephen Ward and his girls would be there. Nancy suggested, it was said, that they combine the two groups. The Senate Foreign Relations Committee reported privately that it was the best party they had ever attended. There was not, of course, a shred of truth in the story but it did the rounds and caused much guffawing in gentlemen's clubs.

Some old friends rallied to the Astors. Peter Carrington, later a Conservative Foreign Secretary and a near neighbour of Cliveden, made a point of calling in to see Bill and Bronwen as a public gesture of solidarity. Zara, Lady Gowrie, was furious, her grandson Grey recalls, 'with the people she deemed "hypocrites and pharisees" who suddenly refused even to acknowledge Bill'. The extent to which the Astors were now regarded as pariahs can be judged by the fact that Zara Gowrie's brother-in-law and his wife wrote urging her to leave her cottage at Cliveden lest she be tainted by the unholy reputation the whole estate now enjoyed. Pamela Cooper, Zara Gowrie's daughter-in-law, reports that another member of her mother-in-law's family, Dermot McCalmont, 'during Royal Ascot Week, smugly announced that he had refused to shake hands with Bill and that many in the Royal Enclosure had also cut him dead'.

Such public gestures did not always betray double standards. Some old friends were clearly bemused and didn't know what to say or do. Writing from her home in Italy, Freya Stark commented to a friend: 'I have been glad not to see the papers. I would write to Bill but don't know quite how as I have no idea of what he is accused. Did he know of what was happening? I can believe one can let a sort of animal quickness that senses danger fade out of one's system if one doesn't keep it alert.' In others, though, Grey Gowrie believes, the rejection of the Astors had more to do with self-interest. 'People behaved exceptionally badly. Even those who had been happily bed-hopping and were known to be in their own circles went around with their noses in the air about Bill. They were frightened. They sensed it was the end of an era.'

Bill's crime was apparently to be caught – or at least in court it seemed that he had been caught – acting improperly. Others who had done what he was accused of – some of them the very people he remained silent to protect – feared guilt by association. It was as if Bill and Bronwen were contagious. If they broke all links with Cliveden, these fairweather friends calculated that perhaps their own double lives could go on undisturbed. A token sacrifice, however, was not enough. Those who threw Bill to the dogs refused to see – or didn't want to see – the broader changes afoot in Britain in the sixties.

Harold Macmillan had maintained the illusion that his pseudo-aristocratic regime was protecting Britain's position as a world power.

Yet in the wake of the scandal the Prime Minister himself appeared bemused by the turn of events and increasingly incapable of governing. The illusion had been shattered and Labour leapt to a 20 per cent lead in the polls. The economy was in decline, with enforced devaluation of the pound on the cards. In the wars that were soon to dominate the world stage in Vietnam and India, Britain was apparently unable to influence events.

> Stray hints that not everything on this traditionally somewhat staid and self-restrained island was any longer all it was assumed to be [writes the social historian Christopher Booker] had been reaching the outside world for two years – ever since, in the summer of 1963, the world had been amazed to learn in quick succession of the Profumo Affair and of the Great Train Robbery. The following year had seen the even more startling emergence of the Beatles, as the most celebrated show business phenomenon of the Sixties.

A new aristocracy was being established to replace the nobility who had been so derided and disgraced during the Argyll and Profumo scandals and the ensuing rush of revelations. The new role models in sixties Britain were pop singers, photographers, artists, decorators, writers, designers, magazine editors, people like Mick Jagger, Jean Shrimpton, Lord Snowdon, Mary Quant, David Bailey and David Hockney. It was a classless elite, some of them of humble birth – Bailey was the son of tailor from the East End of London – and some of them grand – Lord Snowdon had been educated at Eton.

If the reversal in their fortunes left many in Bill Astor's erstwhile social world feeling bemused and defensive, the sight of Mary Quant and Jean Shrimpton being so canonised by the press must have caused Bronwen a wry smile. Only five years before, working in the same industry, she had enjoyed similar treatment. The British media and public have always liked first to build up and then destroy their heroes and heroines. So 'our Bronwen', the Welsh girl who had beaten the French at their own couture game, was now, in some people's mind, little better than Christine Keeler or Mandy Rice-Davies.

In political circles, too, Bill Astor was a convenient scapegoat for the woes of the Conservative Party post-Profumo. Harold Macmillan

struggled on until October before resigning and handing over to the
Scottish aristocrat Alec Douglas-Home, who tried his best against
the tide of the times but lost the 1964 general election to Harold
Wilson's Labour Party. Though the Conservatives, after thirteen
years in power, were beset by other, more complex problems, the
scandal had become a rallying point against the ineptitude and hypocrisy of the outgoing regime. 'He [Macmillan] had a great resentment
against Bill and our family,' says David Astor. 'I think he must have
felt that Profumo was a fragile fellow, open to this mistake and that
Bill had put him together with Ward and Ward's world and that
had brought down his government. I don't think he ever forgave
Bill or me. He had to ask me to dinner at Downing Street and tried
to make out that he hardly knew me. But he had almost lived in
our home in my mother's day.'

Macmillan had initially hoped that the publication of the Denning
Report might have marked the end of the hysteria. Denning, a distinguished lawyer and later senior judicial figure as Master of the Rolls,
took evidence from a variety of sources, including Bill. His conclusion, published on 27 September 1963, was on the face of it a
complete vindication of Bill's reputation. 'Lord Astor had no sympathy with Stephen Ward's political views and made it clear to him,'
Denning wrote. Of Bill's various efforts to introduce Ward to the
Foreign Office, the report said these should not be seen 'in any way
as sponsoring his [Ward's] views'. Denning refuted any suggestion
that Bill had paid for Christine Keeler to abscond before the Edgecombe trial in March of 1963. And of the key weekend at the
Cliveden swimming pool, Denning concluded that it was 'of critical
importance' but that 'nothing improper' had happened at this 'light-
hearted, frolicsome bathing party'.

Denning rebutted claims that any significant breach of security
had occurred in the affair. He thereby let John Profumo, the British
government and the security services off lightly, while Stephen Ward,
to whose sexual habits Denning devoted much attention, was painted
as the villain. 'It is,' Denning concluded, 'better for the country . . .
that this unfortunate episode should be closed.' His report was
designed to do just that.

The Astors had set great store by the Denning Report and Bill was delighted when it appeared. He issued a brief comment to *The Times*. 'The Denning Report speaks for itself and I note and accept its conclusions and propose to take Lord Denning's advice and say nothing more whatsoever.' Yet despite the hullabaloo that surrounded the publication of the report – on the eve of its appearance, in unprecedented scenes, people queued round the block to claim their copy from Her Majesty's Stationery Office – it was soon being rubbished in the press and Parliament. The brief of the enquiry was deemed both narrow and unclear. Its access to key documents was questioned and Denning's role as effectively judge, jury, prosecution and defence counsel condemned. The document was, it was said, a whitewash aimed to serve the interests of Macmillan, his government and what was termed 'social order'. Denning's habit of describing Stephen Ward simply as 'Ward', while referring to others as Mr Profumo, Lord Astor and so on, merely added to the impression that he was working to a prearranged script determined by strict reference to an outdated social hierarchy.

It was only after the Denning Report had been so comprehensively dismissed that Bill finally realised that there would now be no respite for him. The Great Train Robbery, which took place on 8 August, just days after Ward's death, had given the couple a few days' peace, but the Profumo scandal and its players remained high on the newslist. Rice-Davies and Keeler in particular were always ready with another publicity stunt up their sleeves. Everywhere Bill found doors shut in his face. At the British embassy in Washington his former secretary Joy Darby was refused permission by her new boss, the ambassador David Ormsby-Gore, later Lord Harlech and a Macmillan relative by marriage, to allow Bill Astor on to the premises. 'Bill was visiting Washington early in 1964 and simply wanted to meet me there. The ambassador said we simply couldn't ask him to the embassy. There was even a question mark over my own future. They were anxious that the press would get hold of me and my connection to the whole business.' A man whose whole life had been lived in this public world, Bill was devastated by such censure.

The press, convinced that it was only a matter of time before they uncovered the sex ring at Cliveden, pursued the Astors with great determination. Soon after Ward's death *Daily Mail* and *Daily Express* reporters camped out at the house on Jura, disturbing the peace of the usual late-summer idyll for Bronwen. Bill even invited them for a drink in the local bar and had them laughing, but it cut no ice with editors back in London. They were convinced the Astors had a story to tell and kept them under constant surveillance.

The Profumo scandal cast a cloud over every other undertaking that Bill took up. In the autumn of 1963 he asked his friend Kenneth Rose if it would be possible to say something in his 'Albany' column in the *Sunday Telegraph* about various charitable initiatives. 'We had a big meeting,' Bill reported, 'at the Red Cross in London. We organise help in the event of any disasters. As a result of what happened in Yugoslavia, we were able to organise help immediately to relieve the terrible tragedy. Lady Limerick and myself published a communiqué on the work done but the press ignored it.' Anything with his name on was tainted.

The initiative of which he spoke to Rose was arguably the most important of Bill's public life. Certainly it ranks alongside his work in fashioning the British organisations supporting refugees into the British Refugee Council. In December 1963, Bronwen remembers, her husband woke up in the middle of the night bursting with a new idea – to get the various development agencies working with displaced people to cooperate in a public appeal each time there was an emergency situation. Previously they had acted in a piecemeal fashion. At his behest on 18 December 1963 a gathering of the great and the good of the British overseas aid charities took place in central London. Bill represented the refugee bodies, Lord Inchyra the Red Cross, Lady Alexandra 'Baba' Metcalfe Save the Children and others Oxfam, Inter-Church Aid (now Christian Aid), War on Want, the Foreign Office, the Colonial Office and the United Nations High Commissioner for Refugees. 'It was Bill who persuaded them to be there and to act together,' says Bronwen. 'He was very good at getting people to cooperate.'

The result was that the various agencies agreed to work as a team on a coordinated appeal to the British public each time a disaster occurred somewhere in the globe. The existing emergency committee of the refugee organisations was to be expanded into the Disasters' Emergency Committee (DEC) and staffed by Red Cross personnel.

Bill was keen to involve the broadcasters, with the idea that there could be one nationwide television and radio appeal to answer the crisis. It took two years to arrange, but once up and running it has remained the system for channelling aid to crisis points in the world ever since.

The meeting decided that Lord Inchyra would chair the new organisation and his deputy at the Red Cross, Sir Patrick Renniston, would also act as number two on the DEC. There was to be no public role for the founder, Bill Astor. How much this was due to his own unwillingness to risk damage to the fledgling organisation by his association with it and how much it was due to the reluctance of his colleagues to have a publicly disgraced man as a figurehead was not recorded in the minutes of that first meeting.

There were other charitable initiatives, too – again behind the scenes. Bill's long-standing interest in the east and his dismay at the turn of events in Tibet, where Chinese occupying forces had driven the country's spiritual leader, the Dalai Lama, into exile in 1959, led him to endow a centre for Tibetan studies at London's School of Oriental and African Studies. He was also instrumental in establishing a Central African Relief Committee.

Yet Bill could not escape his recent past. It haunted him at every turn. A Profumo industry was up and running. In November 1963 he was approached by Mandy Rice-Davies's agent, who offered him money to cooperate on a book project with her. A feature film made in Germany, *The Christine Keeler Story*, depicted several of the players, including Bill, around a swimming pool having sex and smoking dope. In the United States, in a novel called *Dr Cobb's Game* by Vernon Cassill, Cobb was a thinly disguised Ward and 'Bill Astor' was complicit in all the sex and spying. In each of these takes on the affair, Bronwen was either dismissed as if she were some upper-class wife who simply turned a blind eye to her husband's serial adultery in order to live in a big house, or else presented as a willing participant in the sexual high jinks.

Bill effectively withdrew from public life. He would occasionally speak in the House of Lords or attend private meetings on refugees, but when it came to fulfilling his previous role at the sort of charitable functions that had once loomed large in the Cliveden diary, he often abdicated in favour of Bronwen. Buttressed by what she knew was a strong marriage, even if others doubted it, as well as a spiritual mentor who taught her to place everything in God's hands, she was prepared to brave the quizzical, knowing stares and behind-the-hand whispers about her past.

> Our work appears to us, in the main, as a way of earning our daily bread [Teilhard had written]. But its essential virtue is on a higher level: through it we complete in ourselves the subject of divine union; and through it again, we somehow make to grow in stature the divine term of the One with whom we are united, Our Lord Jesus Christ. Hence whatever our role as men may be, whether we are artists, working-men or scholars, we can, if we are Christians, speed towards the object of our work as though towards an opening to the supreme fulfilment of our beings. Indeed, without exaggeration or excess in thought or expression – but simply by confronting the most fundamental truths of our faith and of experience – we are led to the following observation: God is inexhaustibly attainable in the totality of our action.

In December 1964 Bronwen acted as patron for a charitable gala performance of the musical *Robert and Elizabeth* at London's Lyric Theatre which aimed to raise funds for a hostel for Welsh girls who came to London. In April 1965 she opened the rally celebrating the golden jubilee of the Women's Institute and later that month moved beyond the traditional role of cutting ribbons to enter the national debate about the merits of natural childbirth, addressing a women's lunch and rejecting the conventional wisdom that hospitals were the only place to deliver a baby. Forceful, determined, opinionated, at ease with herself, she was not afraid to speak up.

She was by then, on the subject of childbirth at least, holding forth with some authority, since in April 1964 her second daughter Pauline Marian – after one of Bill's Astor aunts, Pauline Spender-Clay, and with an intentional religious reference in her second name – had been delivered in her bedroom at Cliveden. She had announced her pregnancy in the dark days immediately after Stephen Ward's death. 'We are bubbling over with happiness,' she told reporters, but many wondered out loud whether this was simply a desperate attempt to make a public show that her marriage, so brutally dissected and called into question by the whole scandal, was in good shape.

It was a no-win situation. A certain image of their partnership had now been established by Stephen Ward's lies and nothing was going to displace that. Bronwen's only course of action was to rise above the rumours and act as if she had not heard them. It was business as usual. Norman Parkinson took the christening picture and a small group of family and friends gathered in the chapel at Cliveden for the baptism. Brooke Astor, Bill's American cousin by marriage, was among the godparents as was the Queen Mother's nephew, Simon Bowes-Lyon, grandson of Pauline Spender-Clay.

The balance in Bill and Bronwen's marriage was shifting in the months after the Profumo scandal as he shrank back into himself and relinquished whole areas of their life to her while she was driven on and emboldened by anger at the injustice of what had happened to them. Bill brooded increasingly about the strain his low spirits and the whole episode had put on her and their marriage.

> My own darling [he wrote from the Bahamas, where he was saying in the spring of 1964 while Bronwen waited back at Cliveden for Pauline's arrival]. It was wonderful to hear your voice – even tho' it was over a bad line. I had been so mortally worried over you . . . and worried if you have trouble and fury at all this nonsense. That any friend of mine should have let us down in any way and pained you is agony to me. Also it is so hard to have to say nothing – and do nothing – so much harder than action. But I know that with your love and loyalty, our love will see all this nonsense through.

In the early years their home had been filled largely with Bill's friends, who shared his interests. As some of these people peeled away, it was Bronwen's smaller but more constant circle of family and friends who were, in the main, the couple's defenders. Bronwen's father, Sir Alun Pugh, grew ever closer to Bill. 'Saturday, Father came,' Bronwen wrote in her diary towards the end of 1963. 'Sunday G[wyneth] and Ron. Monday Father and Mo . . . So depressed were it not for *my* family.'

Around the house, Bill began to leave details to an increasingly confident Bronwen. 'I even managed to pluck up the courage to have an argument one day with Mr Washington, who had taken over from

Mr Lee as butler. It was about something so trivial that I can't remember it now, but Bill and William were leaning over the banisters listening to me and later cheered me for standing up for myself.'

In the early months of 1965, while in Nassau, the couple had been invited to dinner by their old friends Harold and Virginia Christie. Also there were the Beatles and Richard Lester, who was directing them in *Help!* While not entirely *au fait* with the scale of their celebrity, Bill realised from Bronwen's reaction that the four young men were regarded as exceptional and so, when they mentioned that they needed a backdrop that looked like Buckingham Palace, he suggested they come to film at Cliveden that summer.

When the fab four were in her house, Bronwen remembers, she felt like a teenager and wanted to tell them that she had all their records. Paul McCartney in particular made a strong impression. 'We were walking down the main stairs and he said, "What's that wonderful smell?" It was the time of the year when there were lilies from the glass houses everywhere in the house and so I said it was them. "No, not them," he replied, "it's you." It was fabulous.'

Nancy Astor died peacefully at the beginning of May 1964 at Grimsthorpe, her daughter Wissie's house in Lincolnshire. The final straw had been another suicide attempt by her beloved Bobbie in March. Just before she died, the sweetness had returned to her nature. She imagined herself back in the Virginia of her youth at Mirador, her father's house in the Blue Ridge Mountains, riding along red clay roads with her sisters and brothers. 'Am I dying or is it my birthday?' she had asked Jakie, surprised to be visited by so many of her children at once. 'A bit of both,' he gently informed her.

To the end, her visits to Cliveden had been tense and difficult times for Bronwen. In November 1963 Bronwen had confided to Maurice Collis that Nancy was 'all right for a short time, but if she stays the weekend I admit it's tiring. I had her entirely by myself last weekend when Bill was away.' After a post-Christmas dinner the same year Collis had walked along the terrace with Nancy.

She began talking away on her favourite topic – her having had to vacate Cliveden. 'I hate coming here. You can imagine after being chatelaine for forty years, it's not very pleasant to see the place you loved in other hands. I should have insisted on my husband leaving it to me for life. Though I don't like coming, still I feel I ought to come. Bill would be so upset if I didn't. It's not that I have anything against Bronwen. She is very gentle with me.'

It was as close as Nancy ever came to acknowledging Bronwen.

For Bill Nancy's death was both a release and a cause of additional suffering on top of all that he had endured during and after the scandal. His relationship with her remained unresolved to the end, as Bronwen's diary shows. 'On Friday his mother rang and he went into terrible depression. Said he must go to a psychiatrist in N York.' Despite a lifetime's efforts he felt he had never won her love. She had no emotional tenderness for him, he told Collis in June 1964. 'When he was young and loved her,' Collis recorded of the conversation, 'he suffered very much from the unkind things she said, but when he ceased to love her, he got to like her better.'

There was a memorial service in Westminster Abbey later in May. The Prime Minister, the whole cabinet, and a sizeable proportion of the Commons and Lords were there. As a mark of respect for a pioneering politician who never held office, it was an impressive turnout. For Bill and Bronwen, though, pride at the respect that Nancy had commanded was mixed with dread at having to face people who had disowned them.

Afterwards friends remarked that Bill never quite recovered from his mother's death. His health certainly got much worse but the downturn was caused by a combination of factors. Bronwen had not accompanied him on their annual trip to the States in the spring of 1964 because she was heavily pregnant with Pauline. While he was there, Bill had consulted his American doctor about the high blood pressure and weak heart that had afflicted him since childhood. The doctor changed his medication, but it proved a disastrous prescription when taken in conjunction with the tablets Bill's English doctors had given him. Coming on top of the strains and stresses of public disgrace, plus the loss of his mother, it left Bill lethargic. In September 1964 he suffered a mild heart attack.

The decline had been in progress for a while. In June 1964 he had written in reply to Joy Darby's letter of condolence about his mother's death: 'It has left us all a bit tired – on top of which my interior workings are playing up a bit . . . All is quiet and peaceful. We go to Jura and then to Venice and Florence – and I think take no part in the Election.' In September 1964, just before he suffered the attack, Freya Stark had written to a friend from her home at Asolo:

> the other arrivals are the Bill Astors, spending ten days at Cipriani's and sketching in my garden. He is such a poor little waif of a man. I sometimes feel it is just some rather expensive clothes walking round with no one in particular inside them. But she is rare and beautiful, and good, with lovely honest eyes which she never plays with. They are a rather touching couple, he always with a well-intentioned but silly value, and she quietly putting it right.

Bill was taken ill in Italy and flown back to England. In October, when he wrote to Joy Darby again, he described himself as an invalid. 'I am kept in bed most of the day but I get up a little bit. They say that there is no reason why I should not be as good as ever, but I am more worried whether I will get as good as ever during this hunting season.' His sense of humour had not deserted him. 'I think the effect of winning the Doncaster Handicap and the Newbury Autumn Cup two days running is what gave me the heart attack. Watching the Cesarewitch on television nearly gave me another.' His horse, Grey of Falloden, had won.

With Bill so obviously in distress, those who visited realised ever more forcibly the extent to which Bronwen was propping up this broken man. 'I think Bronwen was the best thing that ever happened to Bill,' says David Astor. 'She was marvellous, wholly wonderful. All his relatives owe her an endless debt because her steadiness and loyalty to Bill was absolute. She never varied and she never let him down.' Hugh Astor echoes the sentiments: 'The Profumo scandal ruined his health. It was down to Bronwen that he survived that period at all.' And William, Bill's son who lived with the couple when not at school, witnessed the ever deepening bond between his father and his stepmother. 'Bronwen did not have an easy time married to my father: first she had to overcome family suspicions, then the Profumo crisis, resulting in my father becoming a near invalid. But in those last two years of his life, he and Bronwen were very happy together.'

Bill would often spend mornings in bed; at other times he was so reduced that he was forced to use his father's electric bath chair to go round the grounds. Never had the age gap between the couple seemed so obvious, yet in the face of adversity they grew ever closer and more reliant on each other. With two young children, two stepchildren, an ailing husband and a hostile outside world only too ready to judge her poorly, Bronwen had much to keep her busy. She prided herself on running Cliveden as Bill would have and ensured that the informal, family air they had both established was maintained in the midst of the usual, though reduced, round of entertaining. She even joked to friends that occasionally she felt possessed by the authoritarian spirit of Nancy Astor. 'When I am late for dinner and come down the staircase to a group of guests waiting for me I shout at them, "Come on now," as if they had kept me waiting.'

Bill had high and low points in this period. On one occasion, when he had invited some Arab sheikhs to lunch to talk about horseracing, he was so exhausted that it was Bronwen who later accompanied them to the stud and read the pedigrees of the Astor horses out of a book. In January 1965 he followed doctors' advice on the need for warmth and took his wife on holiday to Marrakesh and in March they made their usual spring trip to the Bahamas. Cliveden, Bill suggested, made him nervy and irritable – a result, he speculated to Maurice Collis, of the continued presence, in spirit at least, of his mother.

In April 1965, when they returned to Cliveden, the extent to which the Profumo scandal still dominated Bill's thoughts can be judged by this conversation recorded by Maurice Collis.

Speaking of the Ward imbroglio he said (alluding to the charge that he had deserted Ward in his need): 'I paid for Ward's defence and when it seemed possible that the jury might find him guilty, I took the best legal opinion and on being advised that Ward would be acquitted on appeal, I was on the point of writing to reassure him on this point and to promise to pay counsel for the appeal, when the news came that he had made an end of himself. The charge that Ward was

living on the proceeds of prostitution was unsustainable. He was quite
incapable of carrying on a business of that kind; he was a casual happy-
go-lucky sort of chap.

In June he appeared in good spirits when Collis visited again, though
the recent death of the ardently loyal Zara Gowrie had saddened
him. In July he even attended the House of Lords to vote in favour
of the abolition of hanging. After his own recent experience of the
courts, he now had little faith that they could never make mistakes.
Bill suffered a relapse after the late summer visit to Jura. His weight
had fallen to eight and a half stone. He rallied briefly in October
and began planning a service in the family chapel to celebrate his
marriage to Bronwen.

In these last months his own interest in religion grew. At the time
of his confirmation in 1962 Bill had told his local bishop, Gordon
Savage: 'This is really my nailing my colours to the mast. I want to
be listed as those who are practising members of their church.' However, this became more than simply a matter of church attendance.
In October 1964 he wrote to Joy Darby: 'One of the monks at
Nashdom [Abbey, near Cliveden] has given me a course of reading
which is so deep and difficult that 20 minutes concentration on it
sends me to sleep for about an hour. All of which is just what the
doctors order, I suppose.'

Marvelling at his wife's strength and determination in the face of
their detractors, he began to pay more attention to her spiritual
interests. They would pray together each evening at the foot of their
bed. In December 1965, Bill wrote to a French friend of his admiration for 'Le bon Père Teilhard de Chardin'. She responded by being
more open about her beliefs at Cliveden, even giving friends copies
of Teilhard's writings as Christmas presents in 1965. 'I joined a Teilhard group in the middle of 1965. I had met one of the members,
Joanna Kelly, who was the governor at Holloway Prison in London.
The group met there to discuss Teilhard's writings which were just
appearing in Britain. There were similar groups growing up everywhere. I was told by the doctor that I needed to get out a bit. I was
looking after Bill constantly night and day. He was in bed most of the
time and incapacitated. It was agony. Being able to talk kept me going.'

Other members of the group knew who she was, but their discussions were private. If she talked about her life, she knew that there was no chance of anyone going to tell the papers. For the first time in her life she felt a kind of spiritual solidarity. Her own spiritual journey had been undertaken largely alone and through books. Even when she made the link with Christianity and began to attend Anglican services, she found no one who was willing to talk openly about the workings of the Holy Spirit or a personal experience of God. Yet the Holloway group was made up of Teilhardians who used the same language as she did and who were not ashamed to acknowledge God's role in their lives. Moreover most – like Teilhard himself – were Catholic and for the first time Bronwen appreciated the more powerful sense of community and open, unabashed spirituality in the Roman church compared to her own Anglican roots.

The friend she made at the group who was to have most influence subsequently on her life, however, was an Anglican. The Revd Michael Bruce was vicar of the Grosvenor Chapel in North Audley Street in central London, close to the Astors' London home. He would usually join her there for supper before they travelled to the group together; afterwards they would mull over some of the thoughts that the meeting had prompted in her.

The spiritual sustenance she derived from the group made her bolder at Cliveden. With Bill's agreement, she asked Dom Robert Petitpierre, an Anglican Benedictine monk at Nashdom and a friend of Michael Bruce, to exorcise the house. The pervasive sense of evil that she had written about in her diary during the Profumo scandal seemed to have taken root subsequently in their home. What she had not expected was that, as the evil forces were driven out by Dom Robert, they would, like other experiences in the past, leave their physical mark on her.

There were no specific manifestations about the house [Dom Robert wrote later of his work there, removing Bronwen's name to protect her anonymity], but there were a lot of accumulations from the past, much of them quite sticky, and so she considered the house needed cleansing. I exorcised and blessed the interior but I had neglected to warn the woman owner that the ceremony might make demands on one or other of us. At the end she felt so drained and

tired, indeed so completely exhausted, that she had to retire to bed
and stay there for almost an hour.

His account fails to mention that he advised Bronwen to cleanse
herself after the ordeal. Before going to bed, she had to bathe to
wash away the pollution that had, she sensed, poured over her. 'And
when I woke up afterwards, it was as if everything was immediately
different. I remember going downstairs for dinner as if I was floating
and asking Washington if he had noticed the change. He said, "No,"
of course.'

There was also an improvement in Bill. He joked with his brothers
that his mother's brooding presence had finally been removed, but
in private he acknowledged that his own health had improved following the exorcism. He felt well enough in October to attend a refugees'
conference in Amsterdam, but it left him exhausted. Kenneth Rose,
when he visited Cliveden at the end of the month, was both shocked
by Bill's physical decline and amazed by his mental vigour. 'Bill
appears like a man of seventy,* he is so haggard and worn. We
talk of his plans for a ten-day campaign next October in aid of
non-European refugees.'

He clearly had some inkling that his own end was not far off and
was putting his affairs in order, but the provisions of his will show
that he did not believe death to be imminent. That autumn he gave
a large collection of coins to the Ashmolean in Oxford plus some
early manuscripts to the Bodleian. They had been collected by his
grandfather and bequeathed to him because his father was not interested in them. He had been keeping them in Tate and Lyle boxes
in Upper Grosvenor Street.

In November he was admitted to the Middlesex Hospital because
of his heart flutters. He returned home for Christmas. At first he was
very weak, and Bronwen, remembering her vision of angels straight
after Janet's birth, tried a desperate remedy. 'I prayed that God would
take my energy, my life even, and give it to Bill. Of course it was
illogical to say to God, take my life, because I had two small children,
but I did, and the next morning Bill said that he felt absolutely
marvellous. "I know I'm getting better," he told me.' At the end of

---

* He was actually fifty-eight.

January 1966 he hosted a formal dinner where he played party games as of old with a mechanical parrot and then convinced Bronwen and his doctors that he was well enough to go to the Bahamas to avoid the worst of the British winter. The couple flew out to Nassau on 1 March.

On 6 March, as they were relaxing and apropos of nothing, Bill turned to Bronwen and told her that he had finally understood why it was that she had married him. 'He didn't say a great deal more – but that put me on a tremendous spiritual high. I felt so strong, so confident that now it was going to be all right.' Later she was to tell friends that in those last days Bill had been easier and gentler, that they had been some of the happiest times of their married life.

The next day the couple were invited to lunch at Harold and Virginia Christie's. Since Janet and Pauline were flying out with their nanny, Margaret, a couple of days later, Bronwen had shopping to do in Nassau and arranged to meet Bill at the Christies'. She arrived there to find he had collapsed. A doctor was called and came immediately. He thought it was a heart attack and at once gave Bill an injection which relieved the pain and soothed him. Then he took an electrocardiograph. 'He will be all right,' the doctor reassured Bronwen, but soon afterwards Bill said that he could not see her. He became very cold.

An ambulance was called and Bronwen accompanied Bill to hospital. Once he was settled in, she drove back to their house at Lyford Cay to collect bed-things for him. It was a two-hour round trip but she was not unduly concerned; as she was leaving the hospital, she had met, by chance, Milicent Fenwick, an American friend of Bill's from his Oxford days. Fenwick agreed to sit with Bill until Bronwen got back.

Before Bronwen returned to the hospital at 4.30, Fenwick had been asked to leave Bill's room and the doctors were battling to save his life. Bronwen was not allowed in. Finally a doctor came out to tell her, almost angrily, that they had not been able to save her husband. 'I went and stood at his bedside with Milicent. She was a Catholic and said we must say a prayer.'

There was no time for grieving. At once Bronwen was on the phone to Bill's brothers David and Jakie, who flew out immediately to join her. 'It is odd the things you remember. That Astor humour, even in such a dark moment, was still there. I said to Jakie, "Bill's left me," meaning he'd died, and Jakie replied, "Who for?" It shouldn't have been, but it was frightfully funny.'

Bill's doctor from New York came straight to Nassau to carry out a post mortem. He found that it was not a heart attack but an aneurysm, which explained why Bill's sight had been affected and why the doctors' frantic efforts to revive him had failed. After the post mortem Bronwen, Jakie and David accompanied Bill's body to Miami where, after a small funeral service, he was cremated. 'Again there was this odd mixture of laughing and crying. I had to choose an urn to carry his ashes, so I picked one that looked like the Gold Cup because it was a racing prize he never won.' The next day Bronwen and his brothers-in-law set off back to England, where Bill's remains were to be placed in the Cliveden chapel alongside his mother and father.

'In a strange way I was still on this spiritual high. I knew I wasn't behaving as people thought I should. Yes, he died and that was tragic for me and the children and I mourn him every day. But the day before he died he had understood why I had married him. So if God had directed me towards this unhappy man who believed he was unlovable, then I felt I had brought his soul into light. I had done what God wanted and at some time there would be something more. But I couldn't have explained that to Jakie or David. They had no idea about that side of me.'

The obituary writers produced bland tributes. *The Times*'s only judgement in a straight account of Bill's various posts and honours was to compare his racing record unfavourably with his father's. At least one of the Astors' friends felt that this was wholly inadequate. 'I was surprised, as were many others,' wrote Bishop Gordon Savage, 'to see that the obituary majored on certain events of the recent past, instead of providing a balanced picture of his outstanding contribution to his country and beyond.' He sent a short additional obituary, which was published, highlighting Bill's generosity and his work for charity. 'To those of us who knew him he was simply "one of us",' Savage wrote later, 'who happened also to be "a very good man", and who, with all his faults and failings and with all his brilliance was simply no worse than most of us, and certainly he himself in his modesty didn't regard himself as any better.'

The *Observer*, the paper Bill had once assumed he would edit, where he had been a director and where his brother David was in charge, managed only a sentence conveying details about the memorial service. David had commissioned a piece from Bill's old friend, the scientist, writer and politician C. P. Snow, but chose not to publish. The article lingered in detail on the events of the Profumo scandal. 'It was supposed to be an objective portrait, putting in what Bill's detractors said of him, repeating such irrelevancies as that he was unpopular at his private school fifty years ago and referring to the Ward case,' Maurice Collis recorded after being shown a draft. He was at Cliveden when it was given to Bronwen for her opinion. She 'read it and in her rather abrupt downright way said, "Throw it in the fire." One could not ascribe malice to Snow, only ineptitude.'

Such dilemmas illustrate how difficult even those close to Bill found it to respond to his death in public. In private, however, Bronwen was inundated with notes of sympathy which dwelt on the many aspects of his life that had been obscured by more recent events. Letters came from public figures like Sir Olaf Caroe, chairman of the Tibet Society, Asia expert and a member of the Standing Committee on Refugees:

> The best friends, I think, are those who came late in life and Bill was that to me. I have a great love for him, his sweetness, his gaiety in good and ill fortune, that sort of wistfulness one detected, that deep humanity, the knowledge that he could value weakness no less than strength. In all this there was nobility in its time-honoured sense. I don't think I have known any other man so intensely lovable. I have tried to write a brief bit on these lines for *The Times*. Whether they will publish it, one doesn't know. In it I have said that, as near as any contemporary, Bill fulfilled Santayana's picture of the sweet, just, boyish figure, so much so that it is hard to find in English the *mot juste* to describe him. He used to amuse me so much by pursuing with me his passion for mythical names of horses. This is just one of the thoughts to keep and treasure for a laugh when one remembers him. His work with refugees may be his monument, that and his

great and generous heart over aiding people and projects he judged
to be deserving. I knew from a talk we once had that things for
you will be far from easy.

Sir Isaiah Berlin, with whom Bill had worked on the Astor Foundation and the selection of young scholars to go to the States, was
another to write in praise of the many unsung acts of charity that
Bill had undertaken. 'I want to tell you – what indeed you know
already – that your husband was one of the kindest, most public-
spirited, human human-beings I ever knew.'

There were tributes, too, from those he had helped behind the
scenes. Joanna Kilmartin, the wife of one of David's colleagues at
the *Observer*, wrote:

> I don't know if he [Bill] ever told you – it would be typical of him
> if he had not – how tremendously generous he was both with his
> time and his financial help to my mother and to me when I was a
> child. He was the best and nicest person with children I have ever
> met and I still remember how I felt about him when he was an
> exalted adult and I was a lonely and probably impossible child. I
> can remember whole conversations we had out riding together
> almost verbatim – about religion, about Wagner, about reconciling
> me to family troubles. He was a marvellous and loyal confidant.
> There must be hundreds of people whom he has helped during his
> life who feel the same way.

And then there were those who realised what a difference Bronwen
had made to Bill. 'Even in your sadness,' Freya Stark wrote, 'there
must be great comfort for you, for you were able to give Bill the
true happiness of his life, something so deep and timeless I don't
believe he had ever known before. He was a good and true friend
and many people will miss him.' Bill's relative by marriage, Ronnie
Tree, echoed such sentiments. 'I know how sad you must be, but
at least you have one real comfort. You were a wonderful wife and
gave him what he had always needed and up to your advent never
had complete sympathy and understanding. You should be proud of
what you did and it must be a comfort when you need it.' Billy
Wallace, who at the time of Bronwen's engagement to Bill had
warned her against marrying a 'child-snatcher', wrote to say that he

had been wrong in his assessment of her late husband and she had been right.

Bronwen had already reached her own verdict on what had made her a widow with two small daughters at the age of thirty-five. 'We had been shut out from the world. Bill took it all on himself. That is why he died. He thought he had done this to everybody – brought down the government – but he also knew that he hadn't done anything. He just felt responsible.' It was an assessment shared by others. Bishop Gordon Savage, who gave the address at the subsequent memorial service, believed that Bill died 'mainly from a heart broken by the relentless and terrifying pressure of repeated callous misrepresentation; and by hounding by the media'. He was in effect an early victim of the press behaviour that was later to become all too common and would prompt calls for privacy laws. When John Smith, a Conservative MP and friend of the Astors, was appointed high steward of Maidenhead, in succession to Bill, his speech made headlines in the papers. It was, he said, 'deplorable that such a charitable man as Bill Astor was killed by a lack of charity in others. Maidenhead was good and fair to him but other people further afield were not. He minded dreadfully and it killed him.'

Bronwen, with hindsight, takes the analysis further. 'I don't want to say that Bill was some fantastic saint, but he had a genuine goodness and, as Charles Spencer said at his sister's [Princess Diana's] funeral, genuine goodness has this effect of stirring up the opposite and that is what I felt we were doing. The force of darkness that engulfed us was colossal.'

There was a memorial service for Bill on 24 March at St Margaret's Church, Westminster. The list of those who attended gives a snapshot of the areas of public life where Bill continued to be regarded with affection. The complete absence of mainstream politicians – save for Lord Carrington – equally reveals where Bill's reputation had been ruined and where there was to be no remorse. The American ambassador attended, as did Viscount Furness on behalf of the Sovereign Order of Malta, along with representatives of the many refugee bodies, charities and institutions that Bill had funded.

Bill had left, via his foundation, substantial trust funds for his children when they reached adulthood, along with various bequests to relatives and friends. Bronwen received £250,000, but to avoid death duties the money was in America. It was a large sum and made her, by contemporary standards, a millionaire. The extent of Bill's generosity raised some eyebrows even among those who were aware of the depth of his devotion to her. She also had the jewellery he had given her and the impressive collection of modernist paintings with which he had showered her each birthday and Christmas. Under a deed of gift he had drawn up several years earlier, she was also to receive some of his paintings by Derain, Renoir, Dufy and Stanley Spencer. However, since five years had not elapsed since the signing of the deed, Bronwen would have to pay huge death duties on the works. With her bequest tied up in America, she had to sell most of them to meet the tax bill.

The bulk of Bill's estate went, of course, to his son and heir William, who had been based at Cliveden throughout his father's marriage to Bronwen. Though the English Astors still had a sizeable fortune, it had been much reduced in Bill's lifetime and under his direction because his younger brothers had insisted – against Bill's advice – on selling off their property holdings in Manhattan so as to benefit from the capital, not just the interest. Bill had occasionally questioned the family's future at Cliveden because of the intrusion of National Trust visitors each Saturday, but his will makes it clear that he had assumed William would one day make the house his home because it provided Bronwen with Parr's Cottage, Zara Gowrie's old home on the estate, as a modest dower house. If he had imagined that William would move away from Cliveden, then he would not have seen the need to make plans for Bronwen to stay near the main house. In any case, he clearly assumed that his death would be some time ahead, since Parr's Cottage was suitable for a middle-aged widow, but entirely inappropriate for a young mother with two small children.

At the time of Bill's death William was only fourteen and therefore could exert no control over his own destiny or that of Cliveden. It was a matter for a group of trustees, including Bill's brother Jakie, but excluding Bronwen. They tried to handle a difficult and sensitive situation tactfully and deal with various outsiders like Lord Mountbatten, who were anxious to make their views known. 'Mountbatten rang me,' David Astor recalls. 'He said, "I am ringing you up as godfather of your nephew [William] and as a close friend of his mother. It is your moral duty to see that his mother is treated decently and is respected as William's mother." He did the same to Jakie.'

Mountbatten's fear appears to have been that William might somehow carry on living at Cliveden with Bronwen, his step-mother. Yet the legal situation made any such suggestion foolish. On the death of his father Bill's son became the responsibility of his mother. The only question then was whether Bill's first wife, since remarried and divorced, should move to Cliveden to be with him, or whether William should go to her. Either way Bronwen would have to leave and she accepted her fate calmly. Her attitude to the place and its ways had always been ambiguous, though during the second half of her marriage she had felt more able to cope with running the house. The trustees took the view that, in changing economic and social times, the huge cost of the upkeep of Cliveden could no longer be justified.* Whether its recent notoriety affected their judgement can only be a matter of speculation. William and his mother found a more modest new home at Wantage. 'It would have been very difficult for me to stay at Cliveden,' William now reflects, 'as my father had not handed over enough to save his estate from substantial death duties. However, even if that had not been the case, I don't think any of my uncles wanted me to stay on as I don't think Cliveden was a happy place for them and they could not imagine any one else being happy there. To them it was a house haunted by their mother. My father with Bronwen had finally laid that ghost to rest. To me it was home and I hated moving but there was really no alternative.'

Bronwen was aware of William's distress at leaving Cliveden but was powerless to do anything to change the decision. Her main concern in the months following Bill's death was that the closeness that he had been so keen to foster between his four children from

---

* Cliveden was handed back to the National Trust. Under the terms of Waldorf Astor's original bequest in 1942 it had to be used to promote Anglo-American understanding and so it became a British base for the American Stanford University for several years. In 1984 this condition was by-passed and Cliveden is now run as a luxury hotel, with William, Bill's son, on the board of directors.

three different marriages should not be lost during the upheaval. When she raised the question, her fears were brushed aside. At first she imagined it was thoughtlessness in the midst of a greater crisis, but gradually she detected a more sinister attitude. It was as if she was being hurried out of her marital home and doors closed behind her. She was informed by letter of the date by which the Astor trustees expected her to vacate the premises. When she contacted Mountbatten to request a meeting to express her concerns about the four children, he refused point blank to speak to her. 'I was told by others that henceforth it would be better if Janet and Pauline were brought up to regard William and Emily as their cousins, not their brother and sister.' The question mark that had hung over her marriage in the public's mind since Stephen Ward had told lies about his role in introducing her to Bill was now, it seemed, being extended to cover her children, the younger of whom was not even two when she lost her father.

Certainly, it seems the trustees were not quite sure how to handle her. Her manner of coping with her grief, her religious enthusiasms and her determination to go her own sweet way regardless of the conventions of the society into which she had been introduced by her marriage must have puzzled them. When people tried to include her – by inviting her to parties, dinners or country weekends – she invariably declined, unable to face a world which at that time simply made her feel uncomfortable. She knew, too, that at such events she would be introduced to suitable men. There was an assumption that she would soon be looking for another wealthy husband. Nothing could have been further from her thoughts.

The author Kenneth Rose sums up best the uncertainties of this time among all concerned in his recollection of a lunch at Cliveden in March 1966. He was startled when David Astor, another guest, took him aside and suggested walking to the chapel to see Bill's ashes. David began by questioning how Bronwen was coping and expressing disquiet at her overtly religious attitude to Bill's death. 'Her friends will think her very strange,' he remarked to Rose. 'He said it was time she cut away from Cliveden, centred her life on her own children, and above all left William to become part of his mother Sally's life rather than her own. She had, he said, lost Bill and lost his son.' Rose recalls thinking this a harsh attitude on the part of a brother-in-law.

Yet during her last months at Cliveden, between Bill's death and the date on which she had been told to move into Parr's Cottage (1 August 1966), Bronwen was determined to maintain the house's traditions, whatever toll grief and disharmony had taken. Maurice Collis, who visited on 12 March, found her tearful, 'thinner and somewhat worn'. Her parents, as ever, offered strong practical and emotional support, but her mother had in 1965 suffered a third and more debilitating stroke and the Pughs had left Hampstead in the autumn of that year and moved down to an old rectory in Dunsfold, Surrey, which they shared with their daughter Gwyneth and her husband. The following April Sir Alun had a mild heart attack.

Bronwen made sure that the Ascot Week celebrations took place as usual for the final time and then she decided that she would have one last party to say goodbye to the place at the start of August. She invited her close family, Bill's siblings and a small number of friends and arranged a huge firework display as a last farewell. 'The party was marvellous. All Bill's brothers were there. I was happy to leave the house, but the end had come so suddenly. It was shattering.'

In these last days at Cliveden, Bronwen was near to collapse, spending several days confined to bed, still unable to grasp what had happened and beyond coping with the upheaval of packing up such a vast home. With the help of Jean Redclyffe-Maud,★ Bronwen gathered together those items of furniture she would need to furnish a new home and moved out temporarily to Parr's Cottage. With the help of her brother-in-law Ron Barry, she had found Tuesley Manor, which stood in thirteen acres near Godalming in Surrey. It was close enough to visit her parents daily and, though modest in comparison with Cliveden, was sufficiently large and secluded to enable her to bring up her family in peace, out of the public gaze and away from society. After various building works had been completed, she took possession in March 1967, leaving the Cliveden estate before some

---

★ The wife of one of the Oxford academics who had befriended both Bronwen and Bill as a result of their support for students through the Astor Foundation.

3,000 items of what had been her home went under the hammer in a vast public auction.

In all the frenzy and change that followed Bill's death, it was only her belief that God was with her that sustained her. She continued with the Teilhard group at Holloway Prison. 'It was the one thing that I could hang on to on the spiritual side. Everything else was so awful.' And she began to talk much more openly of her beliefs, no longer embarrassed to bring up a taboo subject. Before she left Cliveden, she invited Dom Robert Petitpierre back to exorcise Spring Cottage. After Ward had vacated it, the next tenant had committed suicide there. Conscious of the profound effect his previous efforts had had on Bronwen, Dom Robert insisted that this time she leave him to carry out the ritual on his own.

Bill's family and friends assumed that Bronwen's interest in religion was simply her way of coping with grief. To those who had known nothing of her spiritual life before Bill's death, her reliance on God came as a surprise, but even those who had recognised or been told of her interest in spiritual matters long before linked her fervour with a need to explain away the tragedy that had overtaken her. 'My impression was that she was very disturbed by the whole Profumo business,' Kenneth Armitage says, 'and found in her religion a kind of appeasement that obliterated, purified and made good the whole episode.' Her sister Ann puts it more bluntly. 'My impression of Bronwen is that her life has been so unsatisfactory that she is constantly searching for something to put it right and she cannot just accept life as it is. She has got to have something else.'

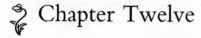 Chapter Twelve

> Conversion is like stepping across the chimney piece out of a
> Looking-Glass world, where everything is an absurd caricature,
> into the real world God made; and then begins the delicious
> process of exploring it limitlessly.
>
> Evelyn Waugh

Tuesley Manor may have been small by the standards of Cliveden,
but it was picturesque and ancient. The pretty, many-gabled house
dated back to the eleventh century and was one of the first hundred
manors mentioned in the Domesday Book. With its country cottage
windows, moss-encrusted red-tiled roof and mellow ochre-coloured
Bargate stone, it was as far removed from the classicism of Bronwen's
marital home as was possible. In place of the self-conscious grandeur,
scale and clinical Italianate lines of the mansion on the Thames,
Tuesley Manor was rambling and vernacular in style and modest in
size, with eight bedrooms. There was a walled garden, a tennis court,
dovecote and lawns sweeping down to a stream with woods beyond.

Despite its charms, Bronwen regarded Tuesley as a pragmatic
choice. 'I've always felt hemmed in here, not by houses but by the
sides of the valley. If I had my choice I'd live on the top of a
mountain. It's the Celt in me.' Yet after a decade in the public eye,
Tuesley did at least afford somewhere off the beaten track where
Bronwen would not have to worry about being constantly on show.

She did not, however, abandon everything of her life at Cliveden
at one fell swoop. Many of the trappings took years to fade away.
It was only in the mid-1980s, for instance, that she abandoned the
habit of dressing for dinner – or at least changing her clothes. It was
a form of grieving, continuing to act as if Bill were there even though
time and place had moved on.

Her attitude in this period to her recent past was, to some extent, ambiguous. Some of those who had judged her so cruelly during her time at Cliveden were no doubt confident that she would revert to type, abandon the conventions of upper-class country or society life and fall back into the middle-class ways of her upbringing. There was a large part of Bronwen that craved the anonymity and consequent freedom of just such a return. This was, as it were, the 'Bronwen' side of her. Set against this was what might be described in shorthand as her 'Lady Astor' side. Here it was not so much that she delighted in her title, but rather that she continued to act with the authority and confidence that she had slowly developed through running Cliveden and running it well. For one thing, she was aware of what her critics amongst Bill's old friends thought of her and a part of her did not want to give them the satisfaction of believing they were right.

And then there were the Astors – and her feeling, after Bill's death, that she and especially her daughters were being treated like second-class members of the family. She did not want her children to be looked upon as the poor relations of the clan, unable to live up to their siblings and cousins because some people believed that their mother simply didn't know the right way to behave.

So at Tuesley she started off with a domestic set-up that mirrored that of Cliveden in miniature. Her lady's maid stayed on until she reached retirement age. There was a butler cum chauffeur cum footman who lived in the flat next to the walled garden, Margaret, the nanny to help with her young daughters, and a cook and gardener who were married and lived in a small cottage just up the valley. She continued to run the London house in Upper Grosvenor Street just as Bill had and while there would entertain those 'society' friends who had remained loyal through all the turmoil of recent years.

There, too, she would attend to an ever greater burden of charitable commitments. Those who had worked most closely with Bill and knew him well were anxious that she should step into his shoes. She had been overwhelmed with requests to take over from Bill in various capacities at many charities. She tried to respond positively to them all. In October 1966 she went to open a new centre at the Pestalozzi village for refugee children on the south coast near Hastings. She chaired the Refugee Circle, a group of medium-sized chari-

ties working with displaced people. And in April 1967 she raised
£40,000 in the States to establish in Bill's name a fund to educate
young Arab refugees. She took over as head of the William Waldorf
Astor Foundation, which spent part of the interest on Bill's children's
trust funds to foster Anglo-American relations. There were regular
dinners with a bevy of heads of Oxbridge colleges – Isaiah Berlin,
William Hayter and John Redclyffe-Maud – to decide which students
wanting to travel to the States were suitable recipients for grants.
She enjoyed being in such academic company, but felt aware of the
paucity of her own formal education. 'I was inundated with requests
almost as soon as Bill died. Within a month I was chairman of the
Refugee Circle. Within two months I was chairman of the Astor
Foundation. People were turning up thinking I could turn on the
tap of Bill's money. I tried to answer them, to say yes as Bill would
have, to carry on, but I was just overwhelmed. It gave me no time
to deal with what was a terrible grief.'

The ceaseless round of charitable activities also kept her name in
the news. In September 1968 it was reported in most of the papers
that she had coopted her old model friend Svetlana Lloyd to help
organise a ball at the Café Royal in central London to raise funds for
refugees. The next year she opened an exhibition of photographs of
displaced Palestinians on behalf of the Council for the Advancement
of Arab–British Understanding and a picture of her at the launch
with long hair tucked into a beret appeared in most of the nationals.

It was as if, in these first years after Bill's death, she was being
pulled in two directions. The tension – between self-definition as
Bronwen or as Lady Astor – continued for many years. When her
stepson William married Annabel Sheffield in 1976, she announced
through the columns of *The Times* that henceforth she wanted to be
known simply as Mrs Astor. Her publicly stated reason – that there
were too many Lady Astors around (Bill's two previous wives were
still alive, there were Lady Astors among Bill's Hever cousins and
her brother Jakie had been knighted) – made good sense but masked
a deeper confusion about her place in the world. 'The real reason
was that I had found the status of the title had crept into my soul
and status is not a good thing for the soul. So I knew I had to do
away with it. It was like a spiritual exercise and it took me years

thereafter to feel calm about it. I was evangelical about being called Mrs Astor, which I slowly came to realise showed that I still had a problem with it. When, about ten years ago, I stopped caring what people called me, I knew that I had come through.'

The instinct to retreat from the world in those early years after Bill's death was a powerful one. Though she accepted his loss as God's will – albeit expressed with awful timing – she was still in a state of shock and reeling from the train of events that it had started. They had known each other for only seven years, been married for just over five. She had anticipated so much more time with Bill when they could have shared the things that each had held back – she her religious beliefs and her reasons for marrying him, something he had glimpsed on the eve of his death, and he his suffering after the Profumo scandal – about which he had kept silent, even to his wife. Now all that had to be left unsaid, unexplored, beyond reach. On the scandal and all it entailed, she followed Bill's policy of maintaining silence in public. In private, too, it was years before she felt able to answer her daughters' questions. They grew up hearing from others about their father's disgrace, but it was not mentioned at home, just as, during Bronwen's youth, her own father's First World War experiences were a taboo subject.

However, with her removal from Cliveden, one of the greatest sources of tension in her life – between her constantly developing spiritual convictions and the antipathy which any form of open, acknowledged religious enthusiasm had prompted in the circles in which she had mixed with Bill – disappeared. Potentially, now at last the spiritual and the material could be one. She was a wealthy widow, determined to prove her mettle by bringing up her daughters in a manner befitting Bill's children but, in theory, in other areas she could make her own social norms.

However, there were still obstacles to embracing openly a lifestyle in line with her religious beliefs. An eight-bedroomed house in thirteen acres and a legacy of £250,000 hardly fitted in with a policy of rejecting worldly goods. The way through the dilemma, she believed, was to work out why God had given her this fortune and what He wanted her to do with it. There were certainly plenty of people writing to her with suggestions. The Teilhard Society touched her for a large donation; other charities followed suit. 'I did feel preyed upon. They assumed I had far more than I did and there was an element of people taking advantage. My secretary still says that to me today when people write asking for money and I reply, "Of course I know it, but what's gone is gone." You do what feels right at the time and then never look back.'

Teilhard de Chardin wrote of 'Christian perfection through human endeavour' and described God as revealing Himself 'by the exact fulfilment of the least of our tasks'. Bronwen could then be both active – living and working in the world – but contemplative in directing all her energies, both practical and spiritual, towards God. The only question was what that work should be. Once again she waited for a sign.

Certainly she could now talk about her beliefs openly without fear of upsetting anyone who mattered. Many simply wrote her off as having gone mad on religion, but few people said it to her face and those who did found that she paid them no attention. In June 1968, for instance, she accepted an invitation to introduce a series of readings from Teilhard de Chardin's writings for the 'Ten to Eight' slot on BBC Radio. She hailed him as 'one of the greatest prophets, certainly in the twentieth century'. Yet her openness about her high regard for the French Jesuit could backfire. The *Daily Express* greeted her enthusiasm with the headline: 'LADY ASTOR BRANCHES OUT WITH A NEW CULT'. She did not let such reactions put her off. In November of the same year she took Teilhard as her theme when she gave one of a series of lunchtime talks at St Mary-le-Bow in Cheapside in the City of London.

It was to encourage this new-found candour that both Dom Robert Petitpierre and the Revd Michael Bruce suggested she accompany them to an inter-church conference in the Swiss university town of Fribourg in September 1967, organised by the International League for Apostolic Faith and Order, a small ecumenical group of which they were both leading members. It might seem like an odd invitation since Bronwen had hitherto shown no interest at all in church functions, but both priests had witnessed her growing interest in Christianity as well as her desire to develop that interest, and felt that the experience of sharing with other believers would be the next step on her journey. She was exhausted and needed a holiday and so on the evening of Sunday 3 September she found herself at the Salesianum, the main hall in Fribourg, with sixty-one other delegates, two thirds of them clerics.

There were representatives of the Vatican's Secretariat of Unity, of the pan-Protestant World Council of Churches and of the Lutheran Federation, along with people whose life's work had been to promote inter-church understanding. And Bronwen. Or rather Lady Astor. 'I remember looking down the list of delegates and seeing Bron's name,' says Flora Glendon-Hill, one of the sixty-one, 'and thinking, "What's she doing here? It's hardly her style." And then seeing her in one of the meetings. She didn't say very much, but she was young and beautiful and you noticed her.'

The period from the early 1960s to the mid-1970s was a time of enormous change, revitalisation and liberalisation within the main-stream Christian churches. New thinking and radical theologians – clerical and lay – caused ripples not only within their own denomi-nations but in the wider world as well. Religion emerged from its cloisters and became a topic of heated debate on television chat shows, newspaper columns and amongst the public at large. One fruit of this new climate was a rejuvenated ecumenical movement, which aimed to rediscover the common roots and purpose of the churches, put aside historical divisions, promote inter-communion and ultimately reunite them under one set of principles and one leadership. After centuries of mutual suspicion, the new spirit of openness to other denominations was at precisely this point adding new momentum and passion to the lives of many Christians.

The International League for Apostolic Faith and Order (ILAFO) was one of the forerunners of this new ecumenical tide, founded in 1951 under the auspices of the Anglican Bishop of Oxford. Michael Bruce was a leading light from the start, along with Robert Petitpierre and Eric Hayman, an Anglican layman and spiritual writer. Initially the organisation had been closed to Catholics, but with the reforming Second Vatican Council, which transformed the Church of Rome between 1962 and 1965, the hopes for ecumenical progress grew and ILAFO itself was changing. At the Fribourg gathering, for the first time in its history, there would be a Catholic speaker – the London-based Jesuit, Father Thomas Corbishley – and Catholic delegates like Flora Glendon-Hill, a lay woman who was principal of a pioneering residential unit for maladjusted boys.

The Second Vatican Council had paved the way for such participation by Catholics. One of its key statements, *Nostra Aetate*, insisted that different denominations once more treat each other as brothers and sisters. In March 1966 the Pope and the Archbishop of Canterbury had met in Rome for the first time since the Reformation and everywhere there were high hopes of real progress. Conferences, gatherings, prayer meetings, hitherto almost unknown or restricted to those who had been ordained plus a few token pillars of the parish, were now taking place almost week by week in Europe and North America to promote active participation by the laity.

The conference at Fribourg fitted into this new pattern. Nothing in her previous experience of organised religion had prepared Bronwen for what greeted her there. She was used to the simple, unfussy Sunday morning liturgies of Hitcham parish church, a world where religion knew its place and that place was once a week in a church. Only at her Teilhard meetings at Holloway Prison had she encountered either church-goers from outside Anglicanism or the concept of exploring belief as a group. Her own rapprochement with Christianity had been achieved largely alone, in private and via books. When she had spoken about religion at Cliveden, she had been misunderstood and treated as if she was slightly crazy. Suddenly she now found herself amongst a group of people with similar experiences, outlooks and knowledge. They spoke her language without embarrassment and didn't look at her askance. It was as if she had come home.

Her attendance at the gathering was reported in the news columns of *The Times*, where her movements were still followed though she had now left the newspaper tag 'our Bronwen' far behind. Yet this was the antithesis of the court and social page and her life as the chatelaine of Cliveden. Perhaps that was why, with her characteristic enthusiasm and openness to new ideas and experiences, she embraced it.

Each lunchtime there would be a eucharist organised by one of the traditions. People talked openly about how God worked in their lives. They pooled new ideas on religious practice and communal living, on how to reconcile one's beliefs with the world around. Through her friends Bronwen met others, like Corbishley and Glendon Hill, and heard of a scheme to set up some kind of residential ecumenical centre in Britain which would be a testing ground and an inspiration for a whole variety of new ideas. Then there was Robert (Bob) Balkam, an American Catholic who represented the Gustave Weigel Society, a small ecumenical group in the States. Balkam was also a leading member of the charismatic renewal movement which, in these heady days, had substantial overlap with interchurch initiatives; charismatic styles and forms of worship seemed to offer ecumenists the best way to celebrate their common beliefs together. Balkam was keen to foster charismatic renewal in Britain and saw the plans for an ecumenical centre as the perfect vehicle.

Charismatic renewal had been spreading rapidly through the States in the 1960s. The style of worship was relaxed, welcoming and informal; contemporary songs of love about Jesus replaced stiff old hymns, guitars the organ. Emotions were let out rather than kept shut in, denominational distinctions smoothed over rather than highlighted. Central to the developing movement was the idea that just as Jesus had empowered His disciples after His resurrection by bringing down the Holy Spirit on each of them at Pentecost, individual believers could be born again in the Spirit and receive similar gifts or charisms, described in the writings of St Paul. These included talking in tongues, where the Spirit would put unintelligible words in people's mouths; interpretation – being able to translate these outpourings; prophecy, either verbal, or by writing out words that the Spirit had put in your head; and healing.

Despite the New Testament endorsement for such charisms, many mainstream churchmen and churchwomen who observed these early charismatic gatherings, including some at Fribourg, found such outward signs of inner graces hard to accept. Some manifestations – particularly the sight of a room full of people babbling in a strange language – were seen as either profoundly misguided or a symbol of a collective madness. Bronwen, however, took what Bob Balkam told her in her stride. 'I recognised it at once as the same sort of experience of the Holy Spirit that I had had.'

Though she spent only a week at Fribourg, Bronwen returned with a new vision. The conference had ended with the formation of a new body, the International Ecumenical Fellowship, with Bruce as chairman and Glendon-Hill as organising secretary, and a promise to meet again in twelve months' time. Initially Bronwen was on the fringes of the largely British-based core group of this new organisation, but she was soon invited over to lunch at the home run by Glendon-Hill in Crawley with nurse Mary Tanner (a third partner, Jean Bennett, had recently died). She developed a close friendship with the two women and became interested in their plans for a centre to give IEF's dream practical expression. Glendon-Hill explained in detail the basic idea behind it. 'The question we were asking,' she says, 'was how could Christians learn to love each other across the denominations unless they got to know each other, and how could they get to know each other unless they had somewhere to meet.' She had seen how life in a community setting had healed and empowered previously damaged boys and was convinced that the same principles could be applied to a fractured Christianity.

There was also a personal drive to Glendon-Hill and Tanner's plans. After the death of Bennett, both had realised that their health could no longer deal with the strain of caring for maladjusted boys. They were in the process of running down the home, with the last charge leaving in July 1969. Thereafter they were looking for a property which could double as a house for them and a centre to promote their own religious plans. They had involved an Anglican vicar, John Burley, and his wife Elsa in the scheme and hoped that Burley – who had attended the Fribourg conference and was honorary secretary of the Society of St Wilibrord, an Anglican-Catholic group – would act as warden at their new venture. The Jesuit Tom Corbishley had also, since Fribourg, become an enthusiastic backer of the scheme and there was the suggestion that Bob Balkam might come over from the States with his family and help with the place.

Bronwen became involved in the project and was part of a close-knit group of activists. Following the sudden death of Michael Bruce at the start of 1968, she joined Glendon-Hill and Elsa Burley on a British IEF organising committee. She had already begun to give financial assistance to her new friends from Fribourg. In the autumn

of 1967 she had funded out of the Astor Foundation a trip to the
States for Bruce; here he met up with Bob Balkam and toured
Boston, San Francisco, Kansas, New York and Washington, promoting ecumenism and the IEF. In the aftermath of Bruce's death she
offered to help with the costs of purchasing a property for the proposed centre, but – rather like Bill in his response to the plight of
the Hungarian refugees in 1956 – she also wanted to roll up her
sleeves and get involved in a practical way. The most logical thing
appeared to be to sell Tuesley and move nearer to the new residential
centre when it was found. It would be, she convinced herself, a way
of recreating in a spiritual context the busy world of Cliveden which
she was missing in the peace of Tuesley. Only this time she would
not be greeting society people; the skills she had learnt as mistress of
a great house – hospitality, entertaining, management, friendship –
would be directed towards those who shared her religious convictions.

The search for a suitable property went on throughout 1968.
Eventually Glendon-Hill and Tanner hit upon Effingham Park, a
large Victorian mansion between East Grinstead and Gatwick Air-
port. They would put up £20,000 of the purchase price, with Bronwen giving a mortgage for the remaining £50,000.

Until now, Bronwen's involvement with the group she had met
at Fribourg had been something which she had kept largely to herself.
Her financial support – in 1968 she had sponsored a conference at
Arden House, near New York, on Teilhard de Chardin – had been
discreet. Now, however, she had to consult the Astor family accountants, who expressed some concern about the extent of her financial
commitment in a property she would not even own. Glendon-Hill
to this day vigorously denies that Bronwen was taken advantage of.
'Bron once told me,' she recalls, 'that people would often invite her
to places not because they were interested in her, but because they
knew she was wealthy. I think with us there quickly developed a
bond of trust and she knew that was not the case. We were offering
her friendship at a time when she was lonely. There were no invitations on her mantelshelf and she was struggling to hold on to her
faith in the face of others' slander and lies about her.' Moreover, she
points out, the £50,000 was eventually repaid in full.

With her grief still so close to the surface and her own ideas about her role so confused, Bronwen was, however, undoubtedly vulnerable. Having kept her spiritual side so closely under wraps at Cliveden, she had now, following Fribourg, swung in the opposite direction and the rush of enthusiasm, coupled with the freedom that wealth had given her in those first years of widowhood, meant that in any scheme she ran the risk of being exploited.

When she visited Effingham Park, her heart sank at the gloomy premises, yet she remained convinced that this was what God had mapped out for her and so buried her doubts. She and her daughters would, it was planned, move into one of the lodges in the grounds. More worldly concerns, however, saved them from their fate. It was not until three years after Bill's death that the extent of the death duties she would have to pay on the various valuable paintings he had left her was finally settled with the Inland Revenue. With rates at 80 per cent and the lawyers and accountants unable to find any way round the liability, she had to dispose of many of the canvases. There was a heart-breaking irony in being forced to sell Bill's presents to her in order to pay the duty he had incurred on the gifts. It also meant that she had to reappraise her financial commitments. Moving out of Tuesley so soon after refurbishing it, plus the loan for Effing-ham, began to appear, in her new circumstances, extravagances she could not easily afford.

There had also been worrying signs that the idealistic experiment in communal living to which she had committed herself so rapidly might not transfer well into action. Bob Balkam had come over from the States in the summer of 1969 with his wife, Lauren, and six children to join Glendon-Hill and Tanner at Effingham but the living arrangements had not been a success. Eventually it was Bronwen who sorted out his accommodation by purchasing a house for him in Godalming, though his day-to-day involvement with the planned community remained a key part of the vision.

Father Tom Corbishley blessed the new chapel at Effingham in September 1969, but by the start of 1970 the rebuilding plans were in chaos. Matters came to a head when Glendon-Hill suffered a heart attack in February of that year, while staying with John and Elsa Burley at their vicarage at Clacton-on-Sea. She was confined to bed for four months, and spent a further eight recuperating, during which time she took the decision to sell Effingham and repay Bronwen.

The others involved in the plans, however, were reluctant to let their dream go. Bronwen, too, remained committed and so in the summer of 1970, recast in smaller dimensions, the community found a new home at The Quarry, a smallish house in seven acres that adjoined Tuesley Manor's land. Bronwen bought the property outright. On 18 August 1970 the deed creating the Community of Christ the King was signed. Its aims were to 'advance the Christian religion by promoting and advancing the unity of Christians, particularly by fostering and developing spiritual ecumenism and the study of the prayer and worship of the diverse Christian traditions as found in the existing Christian churches and denominations'.

The trustees were Bronwen, Flora Glendon-Hill, Mary Tanner and Elsa Burley, but the shift from Effingham to Tuesley had also meant a shift in leadership. The Burleys had been appointed to a parish in Essex and played only a supervisory role. Despite Bronwen's offer to buy her a house in Godalming, Flora Glendon-Hill chose to live with the Burleys and likewise was sidelined, as was the IEF which, though it regarded the Tuesley community as part of its support network, was nowhere mentioned in the founding trust deed. Glendon-Hill and Elsa Burley became part of an outer circle who kept a watchful eye on the community. At its core were Bronwen, Bob and Lauren Balkam and Mary Tanner, who moved into a flat above a garage which adjoined The Quarry. The garage itself was then converted into a chapel.

In late 1969, just as the Effingham plans were beginning to collapse, Bronwen had gone public about the extent and depth of her faith when she decided to convert to Catholicism. Her move was, in one sense, a logical one. Many of those she mixed with – like the Balkams and Flora Glendon-Hill – were Catholics. Through her interest in Teilhard – another Catholic – she had begun to move in Catholic circles. The key influence was Father Tom Corbishley, whose base at Farm Street Church in Mayfair was close to her London house. Yet he certainly did not represent mainstream Catholic opinion and indeed in the late sixties and early seventies was a lone voice trying to push his church in Britain forward ecumenically via various inter-church bodies he had founded with Michael Bruce.

If Catholicism then might prove an unwelcoming climate for Bronwen's own particular ideas, she could also have reflected that she had friends like Bruce and Robert Petitpierre, who had been content to remain within the Anglican fold. There it was possible to believe in the real presence of Christ in the eucharist – normally associated as a Catholic idea – without having to join the Church of Rome. It was precisely this sort of middle-of-the-road Anglicanism that the Pughs had embraced once they turned their backs on the Welsh chapel.

There was also the problem of being committed to promoting inter-church understanding at the same time as changing denomin-ations. Since Fribourg a good deal of Bronwen's energy and money had been directed towards the IEF and its ambition to reverse the divisions of the Reformation. Yet by deciding to go over to Rome she appeared to be indicating that she considered one church closer to Christ's vision than another. Obviously most Christians working in the same field came with a historic association to one denomin-ation, but to change in mid-stream potentially discredited Bronwen as an ecumenical figure. 'I have always said to colleagues who discuss converting,' says Flora Glendon-Hill, 'that you should stick to the church of your baptism unless in conscience you cannot. I think Bronwen had reached that point.'

It was not a mortal blow to Bronwen's ecumenical standing. The depth of personal conviction behind her decision to convert was plain to anyone who spoke to her. And many devout ecumenists have at certain points had to nail their denominational colours to the mast. In the 1990s, for instance, Cardinal Basil Hume accepted large numbers of Anglican converts into his church following General Synod's decision to ordain women priests without breaking his own profound and long-standing commitment to church unity.

The most obvious reason for Bronwen's conversion was the scarc-ity of Anglican eucharistic celebrations. 'I needed daily bread. My life was so hectic at the time and I would be running round London looking for a communion service and there would never be one in Anglican churches when I wanted it. Often I'd end up in Farm

Street, where there were masses every half hour. I'd sit and watch. Here, I thought, was an organisation which understood the need for daily food in a spiritual sense.' When she discussed this with Tom Corbishley, she suggested that she should perhaps convert. He agreed instantly and said she would not need to take any instruction. He could vouch for her good faith and knowledge of God and His purpose in her life. It would be a formality. So she did.

Conversion is usually the culmination of a long-running internal, spiritual battle. For some people it can follow years of agonising. In Bronwen's own mind, however, the real conversion had come a long time ago – first in 1959, when her profound mystical experience of a divine being had given her a whole new perspective on her world, her career, and her personal life, and thereafter in her discovery of Teilhard de Chardin and her long struggle to apply his Christian thought, which she knew at once encapsulated and gave order to her own spiritual insights and her life. That struggle was still going on and her conversion to Catholicism was one part of it, a stepping stone rather than a destination.

While she took no instruction in the faith – something she was later to regret when she began writing and publishing and occasionally got into hot water because her theology was not always up to scratch – it would be wrong to imagine that her coming over to Rome was simply a whim. Bronwen remains deeply Catholic in her devotion to the sacraments, the Virgin Mary and the mass. Through her observations at various ecumenical conferences, she had come to see in the Catholic mass a mirror of her own journey.

She opted to wait until the Feast of the Annunciation of Our Lord, 25 March 1970, formally to be received into the church. News of her conversion inevitably reached the press, for whom she continued to be a newsworthy figure. Photographers and reporters waited outside the service at Farm Street and her picture – solemn and unsmiling in a conch-like hat – was in the papers the following day. Much was made of the recent death of her husband, the implication being that she was seeking in the moral certainties of Catholicism a solace for her grief. As ever when she made the headlines, only a part of the story was being told.

Bob Balkam was her sponsor. 'In retrospect,' he says, 'reflecting on her long interest in Teilhard and ecumenism, it didn't come as a great surprise. I was never aware of any particular struggle she had with it.' Other friends were equally unshocked. 'I was not surprised in that I knew that she had this Welsh mysticism, this being aware of an unseen world,' says Svetlana Lloyd. 'She had bent my ear about Teilhard de Chardin many times and he was Catholic.' Even Michael Brown, the vicar from the local Anglican church at Godalming, was there, invited into the sanctuary by Tom Corbishley in what was a forward-looking and innovatory gesture for the time.

'I was struck by what a public act of humility Bron's conversion was,' recalls Flora Glendon-Hill. 'During the service she had to walk the length of the aisle to have her confession heard in a confessional and she did it gracefully with great composure and dignity. I admired her for her courage in front of all those people who may well have been bemused by her decision.'

David Astor attended, along with other members of his extended family, as a gesture of support. Jakie could not make it but sent along two Catholic friends, the rising Tory politicians Hugh Fraser and Norman St John Stevas, sure that Bronwen would hit it off with them. Such an assumption betrays his view of Catholics as an odd, inward-looking sect. Indeed Jakie probably knew better, since his first wife had been a Spanish Catholic, but the Astors were, by public repute at least, anti-Catholic on account of their mother's profound and vocal suspicion of the Church of Rome. She had refused to speak to her regular houseguest Lord Longford for many months after he converted in 1940, cutting him dead at a Buckingham Palace garden party.

In general, however, Nancy's sons, cousins and grandchildren regarded Bronwen's decision as a personal one to be respected. On this occasion, it was the Pughs who caused her more grief. Sir Alun attended her reception, but Kathleen and Gwyneth refused to come.

In 1968, just two years previously, Pope Paul VI, otherwise a modern and liberal-minded pontiff, had published his much-debated, traditionalist and ultimately largely ignored encyclical *Humanae vitae*, banning artificial contraception. It had revived all sorts of age-old prejudices about Catholicism. 'Gwyneth said I was putting too much strain on my girls,' Bronwen recalls, 'that they would not be able to use contraception and that I would blight their lives. She thought of Catholicism as a monolithic structure of rules which you have to obey.'

Her daughters were not received into the Catholic Church with Bronwen, but Gwyneth suspected that they would soon follow her lead. Bronwen for her part knew that Gwyneth's view of Catholicism was two-dimensional and unjust. Moreover, it seriously under-estimated her own role both in interpreting her new faith and, as a mother, in guiding her daughters. Though in her attendance at the sacraments Bronwen was and remains fiercely Catholic, she has never been a slave to papal dictates, especially on such questions as sexual behaviour. When she joined the church she brought with her a long-standing independence of thought and, though initially she tried hard to curtail it and has never been one to flout the Pope's authority in public, she soon met many other Catholics who regarded the teachings of Rome with respect but not as compulsory if, in good conscience, they disagreed.

Gwyneth's disapproval – almost the first time in their adult lives that the two sisters had not supported each other – was a deep disappointment. Bronwen might have tried to reassure her sister over her fears for the girls, but by inclination the Pughs avoided confrontations or difficult discussions. Everyone was left to their choices which, however much they might appear misguided, were to be respected. So Bronwen simply accepted Gwyneth's coolness which grew even stronger the following year when, after attending both Anglican and Catholic services each Sunday with their mother and talking matters over with the nuns at a neighbouring convent, Bronwen's daughters both decided to become Catholics.

Kathleen Pugh did not live to see her granddaughters join the Catholic Church which was such anathema to her. She died soon after Bronwen's conversion, at the age of seventy-six. During her last years she had suffered increasingly following a series of strokes. Towards the end she was bedridden and unable to look after herself, relying heavily on Gwyneth and her husband Ron. Through their shared delight in the girls, Bronwen had discovered a way of com-municating with her mother, but the alienation she had felt since her childhood never went away. She mourned Kathleen Pugh's passing, but it was not the devastating blow it might have been.

Her father, however, was inconsolable. He effectively gave up on life and eighteen months later, in November 1972 at the age of seventy-eight, followed his wife to the grave. 'He was the backbone of my life,' says Bronwen. 'I was shattered. When my mother died, he just lost interest in living. He faded away gradually. He had a slight stroke, went to a London clinic and decided to die. He had been suffering from a detached retina and was in danger of going blind. He had chosen to undergo an operation to save his sight, but his heart gave out.' In the space of five years Bronwen had lost the two men who had been the centre of her world and had given it definition – first Bill, and now the father she had adored, whose approval she had sought since childhood and whose Welshness was one of the keys to her own self-image. When Gwyneth and her husband decided to sell up and move out of the home they had shared with the Pughs, finally settling in a farmhouse in Northumberland, Bronwen felt as bereft and abandoned as she had during her wartime days at Dolgellau. In the fledgling community at Tuesley, however, another extended family was at hand.

Shortly after she had purchased The Quarry and while building works were being carried out there in the autumn of 1970, Bronwen attended another IEF meeting at Salamanca in Spain. An unusual ingredient in the mix of such gatherings was a thirty-five-strong delegation of American Pentecostalists, led by David Duplessis. Their style of worship was charismatic, and enthusiastic. 'They scared the pants off the rest of us,' Flora Glendon-Hill recalls. 'This was the Franco era in Spain, when public gatherings by groups larger than four was forbidden and here were these people spilling out onto the Plaza Major, laying hands on all and sundry, asking them if they were saved. In the evenings they would have open-ended prayer sessions lasting up to four hours.'

Bronwen recalls that it went further. 'They were even laying their hands on donkeys. That really worried some people, but I thought it displayed their total sincerity, their respect for the whole of creation. I have always had a very inclusive view of creation, that flowers and plants and animals matter just as much as us. I think if I hadn't become a Catholic just before going to Salamanca, I would have ended up a Pentecostal.'

Glendon-Hill found such displays of emotion alienating. So did Tom Corbishley, who also was at Salamanca. And so did the majority of Catholics, who were wary of charismatic renewal. Only Bob Balkam shared Bronwen's enthusiasm, though there were, she soon discovered, some major figures within the Catholic Church who were in favour. Cardinal Leon-Joseph Suenens, a Belgian prelate with great influence in Rome, and Archbishop Helder Camara of Recife, a hero of the Brazilian church for his defiant attitude to that country's corrupt military regime, were both vocal supporters. But they were a minority. The attitude of many Catholics – both liberals and conservatives – is best summed up by the charismatic writer René Laurentin. 'The traditionalists fear destructive innovations, the establishment of a charismatic hierarchy, new "ecumenical confusions" and the manipulation of these naive groups by political leftists. The progressives on the contrary fear that the mysticism of the charismatics may lead to a dispersal of forces, or enable conservative clerics to gain control again or even become the Trojan horse of traditionalism.'

Just as the Community of Christ the King was coming into being, Bronwen's growing enthusiasm for the Pentecostal style of worship was to have a decisive influence on events at Tuesley. It served ultimately to separate her from more cautious voices like Glendon-Hill and Corbishley and draw her ever closer into a tight-knit quartet with the Balkams and Mary Tanner.

The Quarry had been converted to sleep up to ten people and was ready for use in January 1971. There was also a cottage alongside. If the set-up sounded to outsiders – including some of Bronwen's long-standing circle – like some sort of odd religious cult which had swallowed up their friend and her fortune, there was at least the comfort of knowing that it had the blessing of sober officials from within the Catholic, Anglican, Orthodox and Methodist churches. The community was inaugurated on 31 January by the local church dignitaries, including Bishop Michael Bowen of Arundel and Brighton. A future Archbishop of Southwark, one of only four metropolitan sees in the English Catholic Church, Bowen welcomed the pioneering initiative to establish a new style of lay community.

'Bowen saw the possibilities of community,' said Father Richard
Frost, the curate in the local parish of Godalming, who quickly
became involved in the venture. 'He gave the thrust that oversaw
the whole thing his support and patronage and he liked Bronwen.
He is an upper-class Guards officer and so there was much in common
in their backgrounds. He knew he was taking a risk, but he was
prepared to do so because he saw in her something extraordinary
and was very committed to ecumenism, which was one of the bases
of the community. It was only when he saw how the principle was
being lived out that he grew concerned.'

What the Catholic authorities looked for from the start was some
kind of leadership that reflected their own hierarchical structures and
which was underpinned with rules and regulations. 'Bronwen and
some of the others had brilliant ideas, but there was no one at the
rudder and Bronwen did not want to be that person,' says Father
Emmanuel Sullivan, an American priest who worked in the field of
ecumenism in Britain and kept an informal eye on Tuesley on behalf
of Bishop Bowen. Yet the concept of leadership was foreign to the
utopian pioneers of the Community of Christ the King. In setting
up something along lay lines, they did not want simply to imitate
the hierarchical model of the modern clerical world. Instead they
looked back to the early Christian communities of the Acts of the
Apostles. There was to be no one in charge. All were equal, all were
charged with embodying in their lives, words and actions the message
of Christ, and concepts of social status and money were to be abandoned. It was as much a product of its times and of the anti-
institutional instincts of its founders as it was of spiritual ideals. 'It
may have been naive,' Bronwen now says, 'but we were starting
blind. We would not conform to what others expected of us. We
wanted to do it our way and were carried along at first by enormous
enthusiasm.'

The ecumenical vision that had first inspired Glendon-Hill and
Burley became just one of three potentially conflicting strands that
operated within the community. Many of the individuals who initially
came to Tuesley were linked to the IEF and were determined to foster
better inter-church understanding by living and praying together.

At the same time, though, the community was committed to charismatic renewal through the Balkams and Mary Tanner. Before she met Bronwen, Tanner had shown signs of a capacity for locution – dictating thoughts and ideas when in a trance-like state which another (in this case Flora Glendon-Hill) had written down. These writings were accepted at Tuesley as the outpourings of the Holy Spirit through Tanner and had helped to inspire the setting up of the Community of Christ the King.

Bronwen was convinced of the authenticity of Tanner's gift but outsiders saw it as another sign that something bizarre was going on at Tuesley. Locution and automatic writing to this day carries the stigma of occultist and spiritualist experiments of the twenties and thirties. Georgie Hyde-Lees, wife of W. B. Yeats, for instance, had produced hundreds of pages of spirit-communications, many of them in mirror writing, in an effort to wean her husband off his obsession with both Maud Gonne and her daughter Iseult and to convince him of her own special powers.

The third strand in the community was its open-door policy, which both Bronwen and the Balkams insisted upon. For Bronwen it mirrored both Bill Astor's open-handed approach when it came to charity and her own subsequent belief that anyone who turned up at her door was sent by the Holy Spirit. To turn them away was to turn Christ away, but it meant that there was little or no attempt to discern whether visitors were interested in the ideals of the community or whether they were simply freeloading.

As Glendon-Hill and Corbishley's reactions at Salamanca had shown, ecumenical pioneers were not necessarily the same as charismatic ground-breakers. Moreover to offer as a community a warm welcome to all and sundry ran the risk of diluting an already weakened core vision. The latter complication was caused by Bronwen herself, but in the clash between inter-church and renewal ideas she was effectively caught in the middle, one of the old guard as regards IEF, albeit a somewhat compromised ecumenist in some eyes since her own conversion to Catholicism, but also an enthusiast for charismatic worship.

Once every three months there would be an IEF weekend of prayer and reflection at The Quarry. In the interim various IEF figures would come down and visit the community or send along people who they thought might benefit from staying there for a few weeks or months. The centrepiece of the Community of Christ the King, however, was its regular Friday evening charismatic prayer meeting, promoted largely via the fledgling charismatic network initiated by Bob Balkam.

The meetings quickly filled up, with people travelling great distances to attend. James More-Molyneux, a neighbour of Bronwen's, is just one of those who feel that their lives were changed by attending the prayer meetings at Tuesley. He had never been to such a gathering before and arrived having just heard that a dear friend's wife had been diagnosed with cancer. He got there a few minutes early and spoke to Bronwen about the sad news. 'The prayer meeting was held in a comfortable, panelled room with a log fire. About ten of us sat round in a semi-circle and the meeting commenced with a recorded talk by a Cardinal Suenens. After a pause someone asked for a certain hymn which we sang and this was followed by a deep silence, a Bible reading, a prayer. Then it happened . . . Bronwen said: "James has two people he wants us to pray for." Bronwen was sitting across the room from me, seven or eight paces away. What happened next was as sudden as it was fleeting in duration. It is not easy to describe – at the time, as Bronwen was speaking, it felt as though a swarm of bees was coming from Bronwen, straight for my forehead. Not real bees, of course, but energy, perhaps electricity: as Bronwen explained some days later, it was in fact the Holy Spirit that I was experiencing. Although the experience lasted but a moment, the effect was permanent. From that instant, I had enhanced compassion and felt led to visit sick people in hospital. I was able to meditate and felt the need to do so and I had an understanding of the nature of God.'

More-Molyneux's testimony cannot be lightly discounted as that of one in the first flush of idealism. He is the business brain behind the Loseley ice-cream and yoghurt empire, which he developed on his family's dilapidated and struggling estate after the Second World War. An eminently sane, logical man, he witnessed the Holy Spirit working through Bronwen.

The full range of charismatic gifts was on show. 'We praised God in tongues routinely at the prayer meeting,' Bronwen recalls. 'We would sing in tongues and people would go on babbling away. It's the sort of thing I did as a child. It's certainly childlike, a childlike stance of the heart, an attitude of openness. You would practise it in your own private prayer time, walking round the garden or something. It cuts out the mind so you are not thinking when you are doing it.'

She also discovered that she had what she believed to be the gift of healing. 'One of the young boys who was living in one of the cottages complained that he had an ulcer. I asked him where it hurt. It is there in St Paul about the gifts and fruits of the Holy Spirit and among them is the gift of healing, so I put my hand on his stomach and started praying to myself when suddenly he said, "Take your hand off, it's burning." I was amazed. I still am. I'm not sure if the ulcer went away. All I knew was that this heat was coming out of my hand and he got better.'

Bronwen tried to use this gift on subsequent occasions and later integrated it into her professional life as a therapist. 'It sounds odd, I know, but it is really very orthodox. One of the things that we were encouraged to do in the community was to read and study our Bibles. There wasn't much knowledge of the theology of the Holy Spirit at the time and we were working to develop it.' It was at this stage that she began to make good her own lack of knowledge of the scriptures, taking Bible study courses in Godalming with a largely Baptist group, at the nearby Catholic seminary of Wonersh and also in London, where Emilu Astor, wife of Bill's cousin Hugh and an evangelical Christian, ran classes.

As well as looking to biblical inspiration the founders of the community at Tuesley also believed that they were in line with the teaching of the landmark Second Vatican Council. Much of what happened at Tuesley is described in the key Vatican II document, *The Constitution of the Church*. Section twelve, for instance, reads:

> It is not only through the sacraments and official ministries that the Holy Spirit sanctifies and leads the People of God and enriches it with virtues. Granting His gifts 'to each one of us as He chooses' (I Cor 12:11), He also distributes special graces among the faithful

of every rank, by which He makes them able and willing to under-take various tasks or services advantageous for the renewal and up-building of the Church, according to the words of the Apostle: 'To each is given the manifestation of the Spirit for a useful purpose' (I Cor 12:7). These charisms, whether they be the more unusual or the more simple and widely diffused, are to be received with thanksgiving and consolation, for they are exceedingly suitable and useful for the needs of the Church. At the same time, extraordinary gifts are not to be rashly sought after, nor are the fruits of apostolic labour to be presumptuously expected. In any case, judgement as to their genuineness and proper use belongs to those who preside in the Church, upon whom especially falls the obligation not to extinguish the Spirit but to test all things and hold fast to that which is good.

There was such an air of excitement and novelty in the Friday prayer meetings that those who came along would want to stay – at first for the weekend and later for longer periods. The overnighters could be accommodated in The Quarry and its cottages, though often there was an overspill on to the sofas in the drawing room at Tuesley Manor. Longer-term visitors would stay at the Balkams' house, then move on to Bronwen's attic floor, and back to a spare room in The Quarry. There would be a communal meal at the weekends and, as the resident community grew, there would be group meetings and commonly agreed practices – silence during the day, taking a turn at chores in the garden, or helping in the house.

Since it was made up of lay people, not clerics, the community was never intended as the sole focus of members' lives. In theory they would continue with their outside jobs, bringing that experience of practical living in the world back to the spiritual life of the com-munity. Indeed the ties that bound those who were sent along by the IEF, those who turned up at random and those who stayed on after the charismatic prayer meetings were deliberately kept informal so that people could spend time at work and with their families. And plans for a more communal style of living – ploughing up the main lawn at The Quarry to plant vegetables, in a gesture later immortalised by BBC TV's *The Good Life* – never got off the ground.

There were those for whom the community did great things,

people in the midst of religious crises who in the relaxed and cushioned world of The Quarry could rediscover their direction. One man who came to stay for several months later went on to be an orthodox bishop. Others, particularly those who simply heard about the community by word of mouth and turned up at Bronwen's door, left feeling uplifted by the experience of living with others who had chosen something that was beyond conventional boundaries.

During the community's four years, some 250 people came, stayed for anything up to six months and then moved on. The tension between the ecumenical and charismatic components might have been overcome but for the increasing and ultimately overpowering influx of outsiders. The presence of these drifters, who had only the vaguest interest in religion but were keen, in the idealistic early seventies, to be part of an alternative experiment, caused the spiritual focus of the community to unravel. And then social services heard of Tuesley and the community's belief that Christ was at their door: single mothers, battered wives, anyone whose needs were beyond social services' budget was sent along. Some embraced the ideals of the community but most saw it as eccentric but a gift horse.

Bronwen and the Balkams began to come under pressure from all sides to curb their hospitality to such arrivals. 'I said to Bronwen more than once, "You can't do this business of taking people in," especially with extremely disturbed people,' says Flora Glendon-Hill. 'At the very least I asked her to consult with another trustee or a priest so that there could be some sort of vetting or assessment if the community actually had anything to offer that person. But Bronwen wouldn't agree and so she ended up letting in some angels of darkness. She knew it was risky, but she was determined to take the risk.'

Occasionally there were bust-ups and the group collectively would have to step in and move members round from one community house to another to avoid personality clashes. Yet the community had developed such a momentum that there was seldom a moment to take stock and recognise the warning signs. In a practical sense, basing the community on The Quarry suited her: she could live her previous 'Lady Astor' life with her daughters on one side of the garden fence, and give expression to her spiritual and charitable enthusiasms on the other.

Very quickly, however, it became clear that she could not maintain this distinction. Increasingly her lifestyle – dressing for dinner, breaks in London, outside friends, staff – caused dissension. In the heady forum of the community, which housed an increasing number of damaged, idealistic people, Bronwen found herself accused of playing the lady of the manor despite the commitment to equality. She was challenged to drop the trappings of her former life at Cliveden, but refused on the grounds that she had to bring up her daughters as her late husband would have wished. 'I think there was a lot of envy, but then envy was something that I did not understand until quite recently. So I never dealt with it.'

The more sober voices slowly withdrew. Members of an Anglican healing community at Burswood, for instance, distanced themselves,* while in the Godalming area the community itself began to get a bad name. When the cult horror film *The Exorcist* was shown in 1973, some pointed at Tuesley and began to mutter darkly that there were similarly odd goings-on up at the manor. There were also severe difficulties with the ecclesiastical authorities, which had initially given the experiment a warm welcome. A stand-off developed with the local Catholic parish of St Edmund's in Godalming and its priest, Father John McSheehy. Father Richard Frost, the young, forward-thinking curate, tried to bring the two sides together.

It was a sign of how far the ecumenical dream had been replaced by a more narrowly Catholic Pentecostal one that Bronwen and her colleagues, in Father Frost's judgement, thought that the community could strengthen the local parish. Father McSheehy, a man of traditional tastes – 'a no-nonsense ex-chemistry master with a basic outlook', as one parishioner puts it – suspected instead that they wanted to take over. 'It had started badly,' Richard Frost remembered, 'because Bronwen had been received into the church by the Jesuits at Farm Street and then just turned up at the local church. Father McSheehy felt that the Jesuits could at least have written him a letter out of courtesy, informing him. Everything that

---

* The local Anglican vicar, Michael Brown, his wife and two Anglican neighbours of Bronwen's, Geoffrey and Valerie Makin, had for most of the duration of the community met with her regularly as a gesture of support on behalf of their church.

Bronwen did thereafter, and everything that the community did, got up his nose. When I arrived in 1971 the community and Father McSheehy were at daggers drawn, although on a personal level his relationship with Bronwen was never hostile.'

When late in 1971 Bronwen asked for permission to have the Blessed Sacrament reserved at Tuesley's chapel, with communion services when a priest was present, Father McSheehy was concerned. It took seventeen years for the local bishop to give his permission, and he only did so then because there was a Poor Clare nun living as a hermit on Bronwen's land. 'I prayed for it every day for seventeen years,' Bronwen says. 'It was a great exercise in learning patience and perseverance.'

As part of his mediating role, Richard Frost spent time with the community and soon came to see that, for all its idealism and enthusiasm, there were severe problems. 'There were some elements within the group who were experimenting spiritually and otherwise. Most, if not all, of this was, I'm sure, going on behind Bronwen's back and without her knowledge at other properties than her home. It attracted young priests from Arundel and Brighton diocese, who were so disillusioned with the pace of reform in the Catholic Church that they were on their way out of the priesthood. They came down, stayed, let their hair down and did things they had no permission to do both pastorally and personally. So there were unsuitable liaisons, healing services, even exorcisms.'

There was even occasionally inter-communion. Again Father Frost was clear that this happened without the knowledge of Bronwen or the trustees, since the deed setting up the community made it clear that such a practice was not permissible under its auspices. The Catholic Church does not allow those from other churches to partake of the bread and wine in its communion services since they are not members of its flock and do not subscribe to its doctrine of transubstantiation (i.e. the belief that the bread and wine have become Christ's body and blood). Even those Anglicans who accept transubstantiation are not admitted to Catholic communion.

Father Emmanuel Sullivan watched the problems developing at Tuesley when he spent the occasional weekend there. 'I got the sense that Bronwen did not always know what was going on in other properties than her own home. There were some very dodgy things pastorally and individually going on behind her back.' There was also, Father Frost observed, an absence of common sense: 'Bronwen deliberately held herself open, often I think against her own deeply held instincts, because she believed this was the way to a higher life.'

With ever greater numbers of drifters turning up and the four founders beginning to take different positions on policy and on personal conduct, the community was coming apart at the seams. 'If you arrived there,' says Father Sullivan, who later helped to found a similar residential community at Hengrave Hall, 'you were instantly considered a member of the community. I thought this was a bad way to build a community. People were happy to go and share the general vision if it meant they were given a home and a share of Bronwen's wealth. It was very much a come and go community.'

Father Frost's attempts to mediate with first the local parish and ultimately the local bishop were not successful. When nuns from the nearby Ladywell Convent, run by the Franciscans of the Divine Motherhood, started getting involved with the community's activities, the Mother Superior wrote to complain to the bishop. Michael Bowen had been contacted by journalists, some of them members of the Godalming parish, who were anxious to expose a story of conflict and experimentation at the home of a woman well-known to the press. There was also the question of young priests and seminarians exceeding their authority and breaking their commitment to chastity in some of the properties around Tuesley. Despite his continuing goodwill towards Bronwen, Bishop Bowen felt obliged to withdraw his support. 'I couldn't make anyone see sense,' Father Frost recalls. 'It wasn't unlike a Waco situation and the sensible, restraining voices were all walking away. The Balkams saw themselves as the salvation of the church and the world. They regarded Bronwen as the provider but as far as I could see they did not respect her spiritual insights.'

Father Frost's involvement contributed to him suffering a nervous breakdown but his judgement on Bob Balkam is harsh. As one of the leaders of the community, Balkam organised international ecumenical charismatic conferences – at Roehampton in 1972, Guildford in 1973, both paid for in part by the Astor Foundation – and set up the National Service Committee for Catholic Charismatic Renewal in England and Wales, which continues to this day. 'I got the impression,' says Emmanuel Sullivan in a more measured appraisal, 'that rather like Bronwen and indeed others involved in that community, Bob was casting about for a commitment at this time.'

Those of Bronwen's friends who still visited her were alarmed at what they saw. All semblance of a division between her life at the manor and her activities at The Quarry had gone. 'We were all frightfully worried about this religious thing and the strange people who turned up,' says the normally relaxed Christine Tidmarsh. 'Bronwen can be very naive. She has always been a bit unworldly. You warn her, she laughs it off and then she is terribly surprised when something terrible happens.' Svetlana Lloyd was equally unimpressed. 'I couldn't bear it. Some of the people could be perceived to be spongers. Of course she would not hear of it.'

Towards the end of 1973 the rumours and unhappiness in the community had reached such a pitch that Flora Glendon-Hill called a special meeting of the trustees of the community, attended by Bob and Lauren Balkam and several priests who had been close to the project. She confronted them with detailed evidence of individual misconduct that threatened the reputations of all those involved. Certain new rules and regulations would have to be put into effect, she said, if the community was to survive. Her proposal was carried, but several of those present were unhappy and could not in conscience sign up. The Balkams were among those who resigned.

It was effectively the end of the experiment. Bronwen did not have the energy or will to fight to save it. 'It cost me a great deal of money but I thought that was why I had the money. I don't regret it at all, except that it was very hard on my girls. I can see now that I got my priorities wrong on occasion. Thank goodness it all came to an end before I did the children any more damage. There was not much normality here until it all fizzled out and I became a more normal mother. In London we lived a very normal life, but at Tuesley I had no boundaries. I would treat everyone as part of the family.'

Moreover, the interest of the press in the community was beginning to alarm her. When reporters approached her with questions about rumours of misconduct, she feared that the whole Profumo nightmare was about to start up again. The outward similarities were there – a big house owned by an Astor where there were persistent tales of odd goings-on, some of a sexual nature, which might compromise a powerful establishment in the form, this time round, of the mainstream Anglican and Catholic churches. And in Bronwen's mind, too, the parallels suddenly appeared all too obvious. Like Bill with Ward, she had given her money and trust to others who shared her property, if not her home, and about whose backgrounds and activities, she came to realise, she knew very little. She now risked seeing her name dragged through the press on account of what others had been doing behind her back but apparently with her blessing.

She took the decision in early 1974: the community had to come to an end. Already people were beginning to drift away. The Balkams moved out of their house, which was sold. The remaining members of the community slowly dispersed. Mary Tanner remained at her flat in the Quarry for several more years and for another nine the weekly prayer meetings continued, in more restrained although still charismatic form, until they became absorbed into the local parish. Bronwen subsequently rented out The Quarry as a small do-it-yourself residential retreat centre to well-established church groups before finally, in the early 1990s, selling it.

With the benefit of hindsight she occasionally uses such words as 'barmy' and 'shenanigans' to describe the four years of the community. Yet she remains close friends with most of the principal figures involved. Several of those who passed through her doors still write to her and testify to the beneficial effect their stay had on them.

Moreover, in her view the experiment, whatever its shortcomings, was ahead of its time and prophetic. She has no desire to disown it and regrets that it did not usher in other more enduring attempts to foster an authentically New Testament community spirit among lay Catholics. The Community of Christ the King, though in theory ecumenical, was increasingly the advocate of the charismatic, Pentecostalist message in the English Catholic Church. A quarter of a century on, it is now plain that the message got through – there is a flourishing charismatic network and even charismatic bishops – but the messengers were shot down in the process.

For the Catholic authorities, however, the experiment came at a difficult time. Enthusiasm for the new opportunities presented by the Second Vatican Council had led to all sorts of schemes and ideas, many of which only served to stoke up further expectations of reform. When that failed to materialise, many radicals departed in anger and frustration. Those who stayed on had to steady the ship and redirect their energies into less ambitious channels.

In such a climate the Community of Christ the King became just another worrying example of excessive zeal. After some initial enthusiasm priests and bishops offered little support in tackling its problems; they sought to make it more structured and to control its lay members, with Bronwen as a latter-day Mother Superior. It was not a role she was about to take on.

'This was an age of charismatic communities,' says Father Emmanuel Sullivan. 'There were experiments everywhere. Community was suddenly such an attractive thing, but it was a bit like people setting out for the Antarctic with only a cardigan. Making an enduring community can be a tough business and Bronwen was just too laid back. Her style is to start things up, to have a vision and then to wait for others to pick it up and go with it. At Tuesley, it never got beyond an armchair community.'

Bronwen's personal reputation in Catholic Church circles was damaged not as a result of the collapse of the community – which many clergy must have greeted with a huge sigh of relief – but rather because of the unorthodox goings-on in its midst. It took her many years to live down the idea that she was either dangerous or misguided. And amongst those in society who had always regarded her with suspicion, edited highlights of spiritual and sexual experimentation by those living in her properties swapped over dinner tables merely confirmed the verdict that she lacked judgement and was probably unbalanced.

According to some of those more closely involved, however, such often ill-informed views are wide of the mark. 'Bronwen had and has a very profound spiritual life and works hard to foster it with fidelity and perseverance,' says Flora Glendon-Hill. 'It is in that context that the years of the community must be seen. For Bronwen they were years of imbalance, of turbulence as she tried to find a practical way of living out her contemplative life. Such periods are not unusual in those who give themselves to prayer and are often – as in her case – followed by a new maturity and fruitfulness.'

Chapter Thirteen

> If there were a spiritual journey, it would be only a quarter-
> inch long, though many miles deep. It would be a swerve into
> rhythm with your deeper nature and presence.
>
> Father John O'Donohue, *Anam Cara:*
> *Spiritual Wisdom from the Celtic World* (1997)

There was no neat ending to the saga of the Community of Christ the King and Bronwen did not seek one. Though the format may have failed, she continued to believe in its aims and so some of what had gone on at Tuesley Manor up to 1974 continued once the other key players had departed. The clear biblical imperative to feed the hungry, clothe the naked and house the homeless remained at the heart of her attempts to live out her contemplative, spiritual life in the world.

People continued to turn up at the door for years afterwards. Her trust may have been dented by what had happened in the community, but she tried, whenever possible, to accommodate the requests that were made of her. In the cottages and The Quarry she housed over the years many who were troubled – recovering drug addicts, lost ecologists, even an exiled and penniless Ethiopian ambassador and his entire family. And she continued in public to defend the practice, rebutting a *Times* article in a letter to the paper in July 1984, in which she defended her policy of taking homeless people into her home and pointing out that there were benefits for both sides in such an arrangement.

It caused a minor stir in the diary columns and sighs of exasperation from her friends and family, who feared she had not learnt the lessons of her experiment, and predicted that she would be labelled a soft touch and deluged. Such prophesies turned out to be wide of the mark: the trickle of callers did not noticeably increase, and she avoided the indignity suffered a decade later by the writer Germaine Greer who, when she made a similar revelation in a national newspaper, was tricked by a tabloid journalist into giving him a bed for the night before he lampooned her some days later in print.

Bronwen's luck − or the protection of a guardian angel − held however vulnerable she made herself, though there were inevitably reverses. In October 1987 she ended up in court and in the news when a Canadian she had housed out of the goodness of her heart ran up a £2,000 phone bill and refused to reimburse her. Bronwen was open-hearted, but she was not completely unworldly. She received the court's backing in requiring him to pay her back at £5 a week.

When her daughters were away pursuing their education in 1985, Bronwen had made the decision to reduce her live-in domestic staff to just a single housekeeper. Though on the one hand she still craved constant company at home, her more introspective, Celtic side was demanding solitude, or at least an uncluttered household. There would always be people around in the cottages and up at The Quarry, but in the manor itself she had resolved to be alone. It was at this point that a young, very disturbed man arrived, clad from head to toe in rubber, claiming that the nuns at nearby Ladywell had told him Lady Astor could offer him a roof over his head in one of her cottages. She gave him a meal, listened as sympathetically as she could, but when she suggested he should look for a job, he got up angrily, strode out of the door and was never seen again.

Until 1992, when her son-in-law suggested that it was unwise, Bronwen always left her back door unlocked. By contemporary standards this has to be considered reckless, but it followed on logically from placing one's trust in God. If she was under His protection, she believed that extended to all aspects of her life. Tempering that fundamental − and fundamentalist − belief with a little worldly scepticism took years, as the pendulum gently swung back towards a middle ground where she could live out her faith in a measured, pragmatic way − which included putting on the bolt at night.

She was learning discernment. Her instinct remained to welcome all visitors, but she accepted that she had to question whether she was in fact the best person to help those who sought her assistance.

During the days of the community, she had often been urged to use some judgement in sifting the new arrivals but she had resisted the pressure. They were all sent by the Holy Spirit and she had to respond, she said. The collapse of that experiment meant that she had to start reappraising this viewpoint. As her friend the Carthusian monk Dom Bruno puts it: 'Some of us have to be handled roughly by the Lord before we will listen to Him.'

At first she relied on the instincts which had previously been held in abeyance. Common sense was usually enough. So, for example, when a member of the enclosed Carthusian Charterhouse at Parkminster in Sussex was slowly dying in a nearby hospital, she had no hesitation in allowing his family to use the cottage attached to The Quarry so that they could visit him daily. Her gesture was deeply appreciated by the family and the Carthusian community and initiated a long friendship with Dom Bruno at Parkminster, who became an informal spiritual and theological adviser to Bronwen. He helped her to build bridges with the Catholic hierarchy and kept her theology within orthodox boundaries. 'I quickly realised that, though she did not have a trained mind, she was remarkably intelligent and had much to say,' he says. 'She was the first person, for instance, to show me in a sensible, objective way how much women had suffered at the hands of the church. She was at that time struggling to turn a devout life into something practical and noble. There was a spiritual atmosphere around her that could never be captured by a camera or even in writing, but I was sure it was there. It was and is a genuine longing to be guided by the Holy Spirit in all she does. This is not always understood by people of a more timid disposition.'

As the link with Parkminster grew and matured, Bronwen took in several more members of the order who had decided that the religious life was not for them. Earning their keep as gardeners at Tuesley and living in one of her cottages, they eased their way back into the world. But Bronwen was not content with simply being an informal haven for those in trouble. Neither was she ready to settle down to a quiet life in the country. That restlessness and drive that had dominated her life made her search for some other more effective way of giving expression to her faith.

She sought to give practical help to individuals in need. Her housekeeper in this period, Verena Parrish, was a case in point. She had worked as a cleaner at the nearby Catholic seminary at Wonersh. She had little formal education, could not read or write and was regarded as delinquent by her employers. When after many years of faithful service she threw a tantrum, she was sent away and put in the care of the nuns at Ladywell, in the next valley to Tuesley Manor. They arranged for a psychiatric bed for Verena, but asked Bronwen to look after her until it became available. Within hours of Verena's arrival Bronwen was convinced that there was nothing wrong mentally with her guest. The tantrum, she discovered, had followed the death of a close friend and Verena's inability to express her feelings about her loss. Bronwen told the nuns to cancel the psychiatric referral, gave Verena a home at Tuesley, employed her as a housekeeper and, over the following eight years, taught her to read and write. It was only when Verena reached retirement age that she left to live in sheltered accommodation.

But Bronwen's enthusiasm sometimes let her down. In 1978 a nun who had not fitted into life at the nearby convent at Ladywell asked her if she might set up as a hermit in the woods on Tuesley's land. Bronwen immediately said yes. James More-Molyneux provided a wooden hut which he had designed for victims of the Algerian earthquake, but the young woman was severely disturbed and her solitary life only made her problems worse. Six difficult months later she ended up in a psychiatric hospital.

This did not stop Bronwen from subsequently taking in a number of hermits – one of them lived at Tuesley for seven years – but she now finally realised that she might have to select her lodgers more carefully and began to think about getting some sort of training.

Her commitment to charismatic renewal remained strong. One scheme that had never got off the ground during the days of the community was to open a coffee bar in Godalming in order to spread the Christian message in the town. The concept now became a project in its own right. The leading light was Alan Craig, who had been converted to Christianity by just such a place. He put up his £10,000 redundancy payment in February 1979 to buy the Pinocchio restaurant in Crown Court in Godalming and thereafter enlisted Bronwen's support as a trustee and occasional washer-up. The venture was supported by voluntary donations and backed by a prayer group of which Bronwen was a part and which met once a month at Tuesley Manor until 1997. A lawyer came along and offered his services, then a bank manager, an estate agent and an accountant. The local Council of Churches gave its support and The Cellar, as the coffee bar became known, thrives to this day.

While her daughters were growing up, Bronwen had decided not to attend religious conferences at weekends in order to spend more time with them, but in early 1983, as they were now away studying, she went off, for the first time in a decade, to a large charismatic gathering at La Sainte Union College in Southampton. There she met the main speaker Ruth Heflin, a flamboyant Jerusalem-based American charismatic Christian. They hit it off at once. After being told who Bronwen was, Heflin asked if she could arrange a meeting with Margaret Thatcher. Bronwen explained that it wasn't quite that simple because she did not know her, but agreed instead to take Heflin to meet some of Bill's old contacts at the Palace of Westminster. At this and subsequent meetings the two women discussed the possibility of organising a prayer and praise gathering to rouse the British out of their apathy. Bronwen was inspired and excited and came up with a typically theatrical idea. She hired the 10,000-seat Royal Albert Hall, where she had once trained, for the meeting. Heflin spoke, while her friend New York Rabbi Shlomo Carlebak sang.

On a sweltering day in July 1983, following a poor publicity campaign, only 3,000 people attended. A collection was taken to defer the costs but part of it was stolen and Bronwen ended up with a substantial bill. Such a grand gesture inevitably revived interest in her in the press. Future *Daily Express* editor Rosie Boycott was despatched to interview Bronwen as *Woman* magazine's 'Woman of the Week'. The resulting piece made great play of her more unusual religious convictions. Old friends who did not share Bronwen's enthusiasm for Christianity once again dismissed her as a religious eccentric. 'I have never been any good at getting together committees or a structure,' she now admits. 'Ruth and I just got carried away with our thoughts but it could have been organised so much better.'

Within the church, though effectively rooted in charismatic-style worship and a profound attachment to the sacraments, she has continued to be open to – and often ahead of – new trends. The late 1990s, for instance, have seen a resurgence in interest in Celtic Christianity. Bronwen had long found in its mystical insights a reflection of her own spiritual life. 'The Celtic mind,' writes the poet, theologian and expert on mysticism Father John O'Donohue, 'was neither discursive nor systematic. Yet in their lyrical speculation, the Celts brought the sublime unity of life and experience to expression.' The parallel with Teilhard's 'coextensive with the without, there is a within' is strong.

At the funeral of Father Tom Corbishley, who died in 1981, Bronwen met Tom Burns, editor of the Catholic weekly, the *Tablet*. He invited her to join the magazine's monthly, almost exclusively male, dining society, Tablet Table, where religious, ethical and moral dilemmas were debated by leading Catholics. She remained a regular for many years. She spoke on several occasions about her own mystical experiences at meetings of the Wrekin Trust, a secular organisation which aimed to bring together scientists and mystics. She remained an active member of the Teilhard de Chardin Society and travelled to international seminars.

In 1969 she had become involved in the Alistair Hardy Centre at Oxford University. Hardy, a distinguished marine biologist and former professor of zoology at the university, had on his retirement that year asked via the columns of *The Times* for anyone who had had profound religious experiences to come and share them with his new centre. The aim was to try to narrow the gap between God and Darwinism and its twentieth-century scientific legacy. Hardy wanted, he wrote, 'to make natural history more fertile by linking it to a new kind of natural theology'.

Bronwen wrote in response at Father Richard Frost's suggestion, met Hardy and slowly, over a number of years, became involved with his centre. Though they apparently came from different ends of the spectrum – she an ex-model and society hostess who was a devout Christian, and he an academic who had spent a lifetime working in a secular discipline which in theory left little room for religious belief – Bronwen and Hardy shared substantial common ground. His own journey to God mirrored her experiences of the divine as a young girl. He once described in a lecture how he 'came to feel the experience of God through the beauty and joys of nature. From very early days I was a keen naturalist and, when out on country walks by myself looking for beetles and butterflies, I would sometimes feel a presence which seemed partly outside myself and curiously partly within myself.'

Hardy died in May 1985 but his centre – known since 1995 as the Religious Experience Research Centre at Westminster College, Oxford – continues to grow in influence. Bronwen has been variously a patron, a trustee and, for several years, chairman of the society of friends. Her involvement, though, was not as a worker at the coal face and hence did not satisfy her yearning to bring together in a practical sense her own interests in God and science.

In the spring of 1983 she was attending a conference organised by the popular Franciscan preacher and Teilhard scholar Father Eric Doyle, when she heard a talk linking Christianity with psychotherapy. A light went on inside her head. It all fitted together. As a child she had wanted to be a fireman and rescue people. In her marriage to Bill she had been, she felt, sent by God to rescue a lost soul who believed himself to be unlovable. The community was another mission of rescue, with charismatic gifts offering the prospect of healing. After its collapse she had trained with the Citizen's Advice Bureaux, but had found she was hopeless at giving practical advice and filling out forms on behalf of clients because she spent hours talking to them in an effort to try to understand why they had got into a fix in the first place. And for years her reading had touched on psychological insights into the human consciousness. So here now she glimpsed a chance to turn that abiding interest into a career and, at the same time, make informed judgements on those who came to her door for help.

She arranged to meet the speaker, Brian Scott-McCarthy, and in the autumn of 1983 enrolled on a four-year training course run by the Association for Group and Individual Psychotherapy in north London. At first it was a struggle and she wondered if she had made the wrong choice or left it too late to seek an academic qualification. In her early fifties, she was after all a very mature student.

'Training was so difficult because I came with all this spiritual stuff and here was all this psychological jargon and a different way of looking at things. I just could not get the two together. It took me about two years before it clicked. Then I realised that the analyst was Jesus himself and the psychotherapist is just the channel. I made the link between the two. Jesus is the supreme analyst, always knowing what is in a person's unconscious, let alone conscious mind. Therefore the gift of the Holy Spirit is the gift of His own mind. To tune into the Holy Spirit in a spirit of silent prayer while listening to a patient is to tune into their deepest unconscious.'

The link that she made between God, charismatic gifts of the Holy Spirit and the role of the analyst was not a traditional one. Indeed psychotherapy is often regarded as a rival of, if not a replacement for, religion in the late twentieth century. Whereas in the past those with troubles would have consulted their priest in the confessional, or prayed to their God for guidance, today they go into therapy or analysis.

Yet there is a substantial overlap between the two disciplines. Sigmund Freud, father figure of the modern therapy culture, was, it is true, fundamentally scornful of religion's claims. Belief in God, he argued, was a neurotic response to 'the crushing power of nature', an illusion conjured up to deal with fear of dying. Carl Jung (1875–1961), Freud's most influential disciple, was, however, a profoundly religious man. He rejected the Freudian evaluation of God and put forward in its place in *Modern Man in Search of a Soul* the theory that the deity was part of the reality of the cosmos, which he referred to as the 'pleroma'. Jung in particular identified spiritual forces for good and evil within the world. 'How can I be substantial if I fail to cast a shadow?' he asked. 'I must have a dark side also if I am to be whole; and inasmuch as I become conscious of my shadow, I also remember that I am a human being like any other. The shadow belongs to the light as the evil belongs to the good and vice versa.' Jung believed that we all have an inner voice that we can hear anywhere. 'In each of us there is imprinted an image of God or rather God-image.' It was a phrase he had borrowed from the early church fathers and which he used repeatedly.

For Bronwen there was also the attraction of a close connection between Jung and her own guru, Teilhard de Chardin. Though the two never met, they were contemporaries, shared an independence of thought that often shocked their superiors, and knew and admired each other's work. 'Both priest and psychiatrist were explorers,' the poet, writer and Teilhard expert Neville Braybrooke has written; 'explorers of the within and the without of man and the links between the two. Their explorations began on immense and simple lines, and for both there was one decisive question to which everything led up.' This was how humankind was related to something infinite. Both men in their way rejected the suffocating institutionalised religion of their upbringing in the search for an answer, but Teilhard remained within the fold of Catholicism as an unorthodox and occasionally persecuted priest while Jung operated from outside. The parallels can be taken further. Indeed Jung's concluding sentiment in his 1954 book on the Old Testament figure of Job could have come from Teilhard's pen. 'No man is ever more than his own limited ego before the One who dwells in him, whose form has no knowable boundaries, who encompasses him on all sides, fathomless as the abyss of the earth and vast as the sky.'

An added attraction of Jung for Bronwen was his belief in the conjunction of opposites – masculine and feminine, the conscious and the unconscious internal and external, body, mind and spirit. In her own spiritual life, and particularly in her experience of the community, there had been a parallel belief. The Community of Christ the King looked forward to the advent of the Kingdom of God on earth, a time when, the Bible foretold, there would be the conjunction of opposites when, as the Book of Isaiah puts it, the lion will lie down with the lamb.

Bronwen's training, however, was eclectic, including elements of Freud with Jung, Klein and Abraham Maslow who developed his methods by studying those in good mental health. When she began practising she combined all this with the gift of healing which she brought from her own background in charismatic Christianity. So when she sees patients, they lie on a couch and she sits on one side of them on a chair as Freud recommended. While they are talking, she prays silently as she listens. Since they are facing in the other direction, they do not notice. Sometimes, she believes, the Holy Spirit puts words into her mouth to enable her to respond to what she hears. At the same time she relies on her own insights and training.

Although she stresses that such 'God-given' interjections are not always necessarily accurate and have to be tested by the rational mind, they nevertheless form an important and unusual part of her therapeutic method. 'I tell patients I have a spiritual dimension and I say that I will work with whatever spiritual dimension they have.'

Yet that continuing legacy of charismatic renewal in Bronwen's work does, undoubtedly, make her stand apart from secular therapists. In bringing together the spiritual and psychological in her own distinct method of practising, she has in her work – as in her life – found a synthesis of different and often disparate elements. Charismatic renewal, she once wrote, 'opens up the individual to levels of the unconscious which enable interaction with other human beings of a profoundly creative kind. From a Christian point of view, the listening, loving and helping is enabled and made possible through participating in an almost literal fashion in the ministry of Christ Himself.'

Bronwen's success in applying the insights she learnt in the heady years of the community to a career in psychotherapy impressed those who worked with her in the early 1970s. 'I believe that she finally found personal resolution when she settled down to study and develop a career in her own right as a psychotherapist,' says Flora Glendon-Hill. 'It's one of her best characteristics. She is persistent. When she feels there is something right – as she had in the community – then she follows it through until it works out or it collapses. She can be so determined she's like a twenty-ton tank.'

She practises at home for two days each week and for a couple of years worked at the Priory Clinic in Roehampton, south-west London, a rehabilitation centre popular with troubled celebrities and alcoholic footballers. Her professional reputation continues to grow and her unusual methods and background lead to invitations to speak at a whole array of different conferences. Soon after the death of the Princess of Wales, for instance, she was one of the keynote speakers at a gathering of therapists who were exploring ways to cope with the outpouring of grief their patients were experiencing. Given the parallels between her own history and that of Princess Diana, her insights were valuable. Both married older, titled men from famous but dysfunctional families; both were celebrated beauties who faced the glare of the media and experienced its whims; and both became enveloped in a long-running, front-page scandal.

Another reason for the interest in Bronwen's work as a psychotherapist within the profession had been her characteristic willingness to explore and experiment with alternative therapies usually regarded as beyond the pale. Since 1988 she has included rebirthing in her practice. In a technical sense, rebirthing means experiencing the physical and emotional trauma of your birth – some practitioners require their patients to sit in hot baths as if in the womb – but it is used more widely to describe the process by which breathing can be manipulated to trigger emotional releases. Bronwen's involvement in the field sprang from her interest in the power of breathing. 'I believe it is the key to everything. If I have a headache, I breathe. When Jesus gave the apostles the Holy Spirit He breathed on them and they breathed It in.'

The technique Bronwen uses for rebirthing works on the opposite principle to hyperventilation, when people over-exhale. In rebirthing she encourages patients to breathe in more than they breathe out. She sits beside them on the couch. Sometimes they experience pins and needles and numbness but it is not always painful. 'They are faced with their deepest fears and anxieties which are perinatal – i.e. traumas before and after the birth. It doesn't always work immediately. Some people have five or more rebirths before they start letting go. Even if you have had a perfectly nice birth, there is still the trauma of coming from the womb and your first breath.'

In these sessions Bronwen's own Christian background is more obvious. While she sits alongside the patient, she holds rosary beads and prays. Often she will lay hands where the patient feels pain, just as she learnt to do as part of the charismatic gift of healing.

Rebirthing is often dismissed by mainstream psychiatry, but Bronwen believes that it has a place in therapy. In her profession such views remain controversial, but she manages to push at boundaries without severing her links with the establishment.

She has similarly stopped short of breaking all ties with the society in which she once moved with Bill. She has, as she puts it, 'gone her own sweet way', but when it came to her daughters' upbringing she guided them along the well-worn paths. Both attended public schools – though Bronwen sent them to what had until recently been only boys' schools to study for their 'A' levels.

Again in line with what she believed Bill would have wished, in 1981 she threw a lavish old-fashioned coming-out ball for Janet and Pauline at Upper Grosvenor Street. There was another, more poignant, less well-advertised aspect to the evening. The lease was soon to run out on what had been Bill's town house since 1935 and she could not afford to renew it. The party was also a goodbye to one of the last remaining parts of her former life.

In the middle 1980s, as part of her training as a psychotherapist, she underwent six years of therapy herself. Up to that point, she had kept her grief and anger to herself, crying on her own, switching it off in public and often in private, too, with her children. Truby King babies, as she points out, are trained to cry on their own. Through her prayer life she had struggled to understand what had happened to her twenty years before, but there remained a residual sense of injustice that some people held her partly to blame for Bill's demise and that the unproven allegations at the time of Stephen Ward's trial had left a lingering distaste about what went on at Cliveden in the 1960s.

Bronwen detected what she took to be snubs everywhere. When, in the early 1970s, she applied to be a magistrate, she was turned down. Invitations did not come, old friends of Bill lost contact. She now realises that they may simply have been put off by her religious enthusiasms, unaware of their existence at Cliveden and unsure how to approach them at Tuesley. Yet before she went into therapy, she could not view these events objectively. She continued to feel judged and as a consequence hid herself away.

Initially the prospect of six years' analysis seemed a heavy price to pay for a career. It meant breaking her own vow of silence on the subject of Profumo and letting down barriers that she had spent two decades erecting, but she came to realise that finally she had the chance to confront with another her own confusions and pain. It was timely, for in the mid-1980s, building up to the twenty-fifth anniversary of the scandal in 1988, there was renewed interest in its central players. In 1984 *The Last Temptation*, a *roman-à-clef* by David Mure, an ex-naval intelligence colleague of Bill's, started the rot with its thinly veiled portrait of Lord Bill Asterisk, who was very keen on being whipped by prostitutes.

When various non-fiction writers subsequently began work on new interpretations of events in 1963, Bronwen felt sufficiently strengthened by her therapy to offer them limited help, including two personal interviews. She was bitterly disappointed to find in the resulting volumes the same old stories being told about her and her husband. In *An Affair of State: The Profumo Case and the Framing of Stephen Ward* by Phillip Knightley and Caroline Kennedy (1987), Bill is accused of having arranged Christine Keeler's flight overseas at the time of the Edgecombe trial which precipitated the Profumo allegations. Lord Denning, in his original investigation, had been given written and financial documents by Bill to show that this could not have been the case, yet the authors simply ignored these and indicted Bill.

Anthony Summers, giving the whole Profumo affair the gloss of a transatlantic spy scandal, concluded his best-seller *Honeytrap* (1987) with a description of Bronwen surrounded by books on religion – as if she were some latterday Miss Havisham and such reading matter were proof of her unreliability. He added:

> a woman who met Lady Astor through her Christian Centre says: 'on the first night I stayed at Cliveden, I was put into a room with a four-poster bed. There was a picture, a photograph of a bloke with strange eyes, on the dressing table. It was so strange that I got up and put it in the drawer. In the morning Bronwen told me that the picture was of the osteopath Stephen Ward and she always kept it there.'

There is an easy explanation for this tale. The woman concerned had come not to Cliveden but to Tuesley, claiming to be homeless. 'I let her stay in the spare room which has a four-poster bed and the next morning she told me about the picture that had disturbed her. It was a portrait by Stephen of Stanley Spencer who did have big starey eyes. Stephen was a very fine artist, but it was not of him, just by him.' Bronwen has since given the picture to her stepson William.

Yet by concocting the tale, Summers once again made the link between Ward and Bronwen. His misguided book was, however, not the hardest thing to bear. Michael Caton-Jones's 1988 film *Scandal*, starring John Hurt as Ward, Ian McKellen as Profumo, Leslie Phillips as Bill and Joanne Whalley-Kilmer and Bridget Fonda as Keeler and Rice-Davies was a box-office hit and attracted endless acres of newsprint. It portrayed Ward and Keeler in particular as the victims of the affair, and took the by now traditional track that Bill was a rich and randy fool who was complicit in all Ward's actions but who abandoned him in his hour of need.

Bill's son William offered to take his stepmother to see the film at a big cinema in Leicester Square and then on to dinner. 'We thought we ought to go and see what they were saying,' Bronwen recalls, 'and we knew that no one else would understand how we were feeling except for each other.' Watching it made Bronwen boil with anger. It appalled her that the same old misrepresentations were being made to a new generation about her husband. Her firm belief that, at some point in the future, she would have the chance to put the record straight after all the years of silence suddenly appeared a pipe-dream. 'I had thought I could go to the end if necessary, but in 1988 I got really down. I thought that there was no help anywhere, that I'd had it now. I just couldn't cope any more. That was my lowest ebb.'

Soon after seeing the film, she accepted a lunch invitation from Bill's old friend the Labour peer Lord Longford, who had written to express his sympathy at the unhappy memories the film must be awakening. She tried to explain to him why the film had had such a devastating effect on her, why she was still so angry twenty-five years after the event. Like many of her other friends, Longford was kindly but underestimated the depth of her upset. 'I felt unsupported but that only makes me feel angry. People kept saying, "Why can't you put this Profumo thing behind you? Let it go?" I can't let it go. It was a crucifixion experience and I still have not reached resurrection. I hope I reach it before I die.'

In particular she felt abandoned by her church. When she turned to clerics for support, they seemed frightened off by her anger. In desperation, she booked herself on a trip to the unofficial Catholic shrine of Medjugorje in Bosnia-Hercegovina in what was then Yugo-slavia. She had read reports of visions of the Virgin Mary many times over the previous four years.

Her personal breakthrough came on the final day. 'It was the last mass I went to before coming home. The preacher was an American Franciscan who was part of the community there. And he said, "Never forget you have been given the Holy Spirit and nothing outside you is stronger than what you have received within." And I just thought, Eureka! Why did I forget that? It put me straight back on track. I didn't really need to have gone anywhere to hear it. My local priest might have said it.'

In reality, the trough of 1988 took time to even out, but as Bronwen's career took off and she was able, encouraged in therapy and sustained in prayer, to live with herself and the contradictions and tensions of her life, she found a greater sense of peace. The joy of seeing her daughters married and mothers themselves eased the transition.

Bronwen's older sister Ann attended both weddings. After years of living separate lives with little contact the two have once more grown closer, while recognising their very different outlooks on life. In 1981, when Ann's husband Sir Reginald Hibbert was British ambassador in Paris, the couple invited Bronwen to a dinner to celebrate the work of Pierre Balmain. The couturier was reunited with his old muse and to mark the occasion she wore one of the dresses he had created for her and which had lain in the back of her wardrobe for over twenty years.

Gwyneth, however, did not live to see Janet and Pauline reach adulthood. In 1977, soon after she moved to Northumberland with her husband Ron, she died peacefully while sitting in front of the television. She had been born with a hole in the heart which, like Bill's heart condition, went undetected for many years and, at the age of fifty-two, her heart gave out. Bronwen was devastated. She had lost the person who had been closest to her throughout her life, the sister in whom she had confided, with whom she had shared her triumphs and setbacks, and to whom alone she had felt able to talk candidly about God when she feared no one else would listen. There was inevitably a powerful sense of abandonment – first Bill, then her mother, her father and now Gwyneth. As her own children grew up, friends would ask her about remarriage. At the time of Bill's death many people assumed it would only be a short period before she found a new husband, but they had misjudged her. Her sense of unfinished business with regard to the destruction of Bill's reputation in the Profumo scandal and her assumption of the burden of responsibility for one day challenging that injustice made it hard to find room for another man in her life when her late husband was still so much there in her mind and heart. After he had been so betrayed in life and death, to marry another would have been potentially another betrayal. While she resisted the impulse to canonise him in the process of striving for his rehabilitation, she met no one else who was such a compatible companion.

There were undoubtedly men who admired her from a distance, but most found her intimidating while the twists and turns of her life in widowhood have been too difficult for most to follow. Only one man proposed – a Nigerian prince whom she agreed to entertain at Tuesley on behalf of another charity. 'He was deadly serious even though he was half my age. I think he thought he was doing me a favour, that a woman shouldn't live alone. He couldn't understand why I turned him down.'

Though she admits occasionally to finding celibacy and the solitary life hard to bear, she is convinced that it is part of God's plan for her. Just as she regarded those who turned up at her front door seeking her help as sent by the Holy Spirit, she believes that if God had wanted her to remarry He would have sent along the right, available man. Instead she sees His design for her as being able to fashion her own life in line with the freedom she has achieved and the openings now available to women that were denied to her mother's generation.

If the suggestions that she should remarry were prompted either by fears that she was lonely or that she needed a man to take charge of her at times muddled financial affairs, then those who made them were misjudging both the independence Bronwen had learnt from childhood and her contemplative side which relishes solitude but which, with God present and active in her life, means she never feels alone.

Postscript
Tuesley Manor, Surrey, 1999

Three score years and ten, according to the Bible, is what most of us can expect from life. Science may have pushed back the threshold for a fortunate few in recent times, but with the onset of the seventies careers are usually winding down, interests being ruthlessly pruned and new projects rejected after a 'good innings'.

Bronwen Astor, however, is too sophisticated a Christian to take the Bible literally on this point. Indeed she delights in proving it wrong. In her seventieth year she seems to take on more and more. It is as if her life has finally got into gear at a time when others are disengaging, and she is determined not to waste a moment.

This might appear an odd judgement on one whose life up to now has, by conventional standards, been a success – she rose to the top of one of the most publicised professions in the world, married a wealthy man who, it is clear from his letters, loved her passionately, had two daughters – from which even the drama of the Profumo scandal and the false insinuations made about her cannot detract. Yet Bronwen Astor is merely amused by memories of her time as a model girl. She shows no sign of hankering after the Cliveden lifestyle. They were just the unimportant outer trappings of various parts of her past. Now she is driven on by her beliefs; after years of struggle she has resolved the long-standing tensions and conflicting loyalties that shaped her story and has found a new sureness of purpose.

There is her work as a psychotherapist – two days a week with patients, plus one afternoon either organising the Emmaus Christian Counselling Centre in nearby Guildford, a task she took on three years ago when the founder died, or involved with the Guildford Centre of Psychotherapy. Moreover, she is currently developing plans to run retreats at the small conference centre and chapel fashioned from some outbuildings at Tuesley after she had sold The Quarry.

Then there are her charitable activities – with the British Teilhard Association, as a patron of a marriage guidance charity and of the Catholic Bible School, with the Alistair Hardy Society at Oxford University and a host of smaller organisations that recall Bill Astor's interests and legacy. She favours local organisations, following her late husband's lead in dealing first with what was on his doorstep and only then moving on to embrace a wider world of need. She is, for instance, very active in her local parish as a eucharistic minister and reader.

In the gaps that are left in her diary she still attends conferences on the spiritual and psychological themes that so fascinate her and is an active member of groups like the Scientific and Medical Network, whose local branch meets at her home and which is dedicated to deepening understanding in science and medicine by fostering both rational analysis as well as 'intuitive insights'.

It is, of course, these 'intuitive insights' that appeal to this unconventional woman. This means, Bronwen explains, that people who work in the mainstream take a serious but open-minded look at alternative ideas. As a psychotherapist, she is mainstream, but her rebirthing work is, for many of her professional colleagues, out of bounds.

Bronwen is, as one astute observer of her life put it, 'a brave adventurer, not one to do the usual thing and dismiss things she doesn't at first grasp, but someone who follows them through out onto the frontier of religion and science and tries to find where they connect'. Like all explorers she may take the wrong path on occasion, diving down caverns of knowledge and not always returning with pearls. Some have doubted her sanity – 'she's wonderful, but some of the things she says and does are batty' was a reaction I came across more than once in her casual acquaintances.

Her choices may be wrong, but there is still that overarching sense that she is being guided by the Holy Spirit – guided to Bill Astor, to Catholicism, to the Community of Christ the King. Disasters disguise a greater purpose which she may not even understand at the time. For example, she believes that the community pointed to a model of religious organisation regulated by collective responsibility which will, if only because of the dearth of vocations, become more the norm in the church in the next century.

Forums like the Scientific and Medical Network nourish Bronwen's intellectual and contemplative side. Her prayer life remains the linchpin of her day. She is convinced that there is no need to rush about searching for God. He will find you.

But that other part of her – fun-loving, jolly-hockey-sticks, give-it-a-go Bronwen who conquered the fashion world through sheer determination – is still there. She regularly heads off in her sports car to go salmon-fishing in Scotland; she is also a keen wind-surfer. A couple of years ago she had Tuesley's swimming pool covered over so that she could use it every day during the summer months. And she is devoted to her grandchildren.

Behind all the key events of Bronwen's life lies an inner struggle to reconcile her beliefs with her worldly circumstances. At Balmain and at Cliveden the spiritual was shut out; later, in the community at Tuesley, the material became a source of friction. Today the two live, as far as is possible, in a pragmatic harmony, and this has given her a new energy.

On the table beside a sofa in her drawing room is evidence of the mix which has characterised and continues to shape her life. Fashion magazines mingle with society glossies, Christie's catalogues with the *Tablet*, the Catholic weekly. And as she sits talking of future plans, she is surrounded by reminders of all those different and diverse parts that have finally come together to make her life whole. Most of the furniture was brought from Cliveden. Bill's books – a history of Tibet catches my eye over her shoulder – are lined up on the shelves behind her. *Points of the Horse* is there somewhere too.

During her first six months at Tuesley there used to be a strong smell of cedarwood incense in this room whenever she walked in. She assumed that it was just the scent of the new bookshelves, and found it comforting. Only later did she read *The Swan in the Evening*, an autobiographical fragment by Rosamond Lehmann about the death of her daughter, which described a similar smell. According to Lehmann it was a sign of her daughter's presence and Bronwen was convinced that the scent she had noticed in her drawing room was Bill keeping watch over her.

On the opposite wall is a library that charts her own literary journey from Ouspensky, through the classics once prescribed by Mortimer Wheeler, and on to Teilhard and more recent religious and psychological tomes. Everywhere there are flowers and pictures. The valuable canvases may all have been sold or passed on to the next generation, but there are Bill's watercolours from around the Cliveden estate, the photographs of their engagement, of their marriage, of the proud parents with their infant children. And then there are the more recent additions – shots of her daughters growing up, her grandchildren, even a postcard of the Dalai Lama – propped up on the mantelshelf above the big open fireplace.

Yet this is no mausoleum; it does not celebrate a life that is over. There is certainly something otherworldly about Tuesley Manor, but that is more to do with its special atmosphere, which recalls something I usually associate with churches or monasteries. It is as if Bronwen's inner peace envelops the place. This is, I know intuitively, a house of God, albeit not in the conventional sense of austerity and apartness. Bronwen lives in the world, within its constraints.

Part of Tuesley's charm springs from the world she has created here, encompassing not only the small practical things – growing vegetables, making bread – but also the spiritual, and the integration of mind, body and spirit. By working over many years to bring these three together, she has managed to heal the confused young woman who hid behind the Garboesque beauty of Balmain's catwalk, to heal in her husband a man who believed himself unlovable, and latterly, as a psychotherapist, to heal those who come to seek her professional advice.

One of the things she has learnt in achieving this integration of the spiritual and the material is patience. It has taken time for the tensions in her life to resolve themselves – seventeen years before she could have the Blessed Sacrament reserved at Tuesley's Chapel; twenty-five before she could begin to talk about the impact of Profumo; almost her whole adult life before she found some common ground with her eldest sister. And that patience extends also to her spiritual life. According to Jacques Maritain, the celebrated Catholic philosopher, many people of goodwill would become 'persons of noble soul' if only they would not panic and try to resolve the painful conflicting loyalties of their lives too prematurely. We need to live with tensions, to go through that dark night of the soul revealed so memorably by the mystic John of the Cross, and wait until God works the transformation within us. Bronwen's own dark night took place back in 1959; the transformation process carried her through the scandal of the sixties, the experiments of the seventies and the learning of the eighties, and only now is she reaping the rewards.

As our conversation ranges across grandchildren, gardening and God, I am struck once again by one of her most disarming characteristics. Although we live in a society where open talk of God is often seen as a sign of oddness, she continually mentions Him as if He is someone she meets every day – which, in a sense, is true.

I once invited her to lunch with an old model-girl friend and all was going swimmingly until Bronwen's erstwhile colleague, lulled into a false sense of security by chat of clothes and couturiers, asked, 'And you're not still doing all that religion business, are you?' She had no doubt heard the rumours about the community at Tuesley but clearly believed that this had been some kind of illness and that Bronwen, who now appeared so 'normal', must be cured. And Bronwen came back, with a charming smile and that rippling laugh, to affirm her belief in God.

After all those years of pretending to be a material girl, she undoubtedly takes a residual pleasure in being so blunt and seeing her questioner so disconcerted. Yet for Bronwen it goes much deeper. For her it is unembarrassing to affirm an active relationship with her Creator and certainly not the mark of a religious maniac. Fifty years ago her attitude would have been commonplace. Today, in a secular society, it sounds so foreign to our ears that it continues to set her apart and invite ill-considered judgements.

A decade ago I used to edit a Catholic newspaper. Whenever I was asked about it at the time and subsequently, I would always qualify my brief account with '. . . but I'm not very religious', which is not precisely true. I'm certainly interested in religion, but I didn't want to sound unusual or out of step with the world around me, so I played it down and pandered to accepted norms. The biblical equivalent would be, I suppose, St Peter denying Jesus three times before the cock crowed.

Bronwen refuses to play such games and could never be accused of betrayal. It is a privilege for which she has worked and waited for many years, and though she may have refined her missionary zeal in recent years as the two threads in her life have achieved a natural equilibrium, still she never ducks a direct question. The lazy write her off as eccentric or crazy, but the truth is much harder to square with our stereotypes. If her talk of God belongs in a cultural sense to the past, then her fierce determination to explore that belief, to live it out actively in contemporary society and follow scientific and psychological developments, is positively modern and forward-looking.

That most anti-religious of figures, Nietzsche, once wrote: 'Life is lived forwards and understood backwards. The important thing about the Last Supper was the very thing not known about it at the time. The true meaning of the meal was only understood – could only be understood – in the context of what was to come.' As a summary of Bronwen's life, it fits neatly. It was only when she first discovered Teilhard de Chardin and, later, Catholic Christianity, that she began to see a pattern in her own life stretching back through the night when she thought she was dying, back in 1959, to that first perception of something other at the age of seven in a Hampstead garden. She now likens her life to a very modest version of the Way of the Cross, in imitation of Christ's suffering, but does so with the benefit of hindsight. Similarly she now sees Bill's – and therefore her own – suffering at the time of the Profumo scandal as a crucifixion. Her own subsequent life has been a search for a personal resurrection.

To define oneself, as she does, as a mystic may seem by contemporary standards either breath-takingly arrogant or utter folly. The word 'mystic' can mean so many things. Bronwen is not claiming to be a seer of the future or – in the traditional Catholic sense – someone like the classic mystic Teresa of Avila, who was open to extraordinary experiences that cast new light on the Christian mystery. Bronwen physically experienced God's overwhelming love just once. For Teresa of Avila it was a regular event.

Research carried out by the Alistair Hardy Centre shows that 60 per cent of the population will at some time in their lives have an experience that is beyond the five senses. All these might be labelled mystical. However, only 10 per cent of these people ever talk publicly about such experiences. The rest fear that they will be regarded as mad. Bronwen no longer has that fear. She describes her mystical experience in terms that echo those used by celebrated mystics down the ages, but she is also a mystic in the Teilhardian and – although it is an odd word to use in the context – workaday sense. She lives in a constant awareness of the close presence of God, is sure that she has experienced Him and is determined to give that essentially contemplative and spiritual experience some form of practical expression in her life.

It is her self-diagnosis as a mystic that sets her apart. I use the word 'self-diagnosis' not to distance myself from the claim, but rather to emphasise that I can never reach a full and final verdict about its truth. Only God can judge and only Bronwen can know in any definitive way if she is sincere. I believe her to be so. Everything I have seen her do, everything I have discovered about her past, has increased my belief in her sincerity. I started off liking her and being fascinated by a life story that has gone through so many different and diverse chapters. I conclude with all these feelings intact, but with admiration too and not a little envy of her self-assurance about her relationship with God.

Source Notes

Chapter One

John Davies, *A History of Wales* (London 1993).

D. Hywel Davies, *The Welsh Nationalist Party 1925–1945* (Cardiff 1983).

Notes on the Pugh and Goodyear family trees compiled by Sir Reginald Hibbert.

The Medical Register from the British Medical Association Library.

Welsh Guards' archive.

Correspondence of Alun Pugh in the Plaid Cymru archive at the National Library of Wales.

Papers in Bronwen Astor's private archive.

Archive of the Honourable Society of the Inner Temple.

Gertrud Mander, 'Truby King, the Forgotten Prophet', *British Journal of Psychotherapy*, 1996, 13 (1).

Bronwen Astor, 'Of Psychological Aspects of Motherhood', in *The Chichester Roundel* (Chichester 1990).

Chapter Two

Letters of Bronwen and Gwyneth Pugh to their parents in Bronwen Astor's private archive.

Gertrud Mander, 'Truby King, the Forgotten Prophet'.

Chapter Three

Documents provided by Central School of Speech and Drama from their archive.

Pierre Balmain, *My Years and Seasons* (London 1965)

Charles Castle, *Model Girl* (London 1977).

Jean Dawnay, *Model Girl* (London 1956).

P. D. Ouspensky, *The Fourth Way* (New York 1957).

Alan Bullock and R. B. Woodings (ed.), *The Fontana Biographical Companion to Modern Thought* (London 1983).

Chapter Four

Jean Dawnay, *Model Girl*.

Marie-France Pochna, *Christian Dior: The Man Who Made the World Look New* (New York 1996).

Christopher Booker, *The Neophiliacs* (London 1969).

Obituary of Bunny Roger by Nicky Haslam in the *Guardian*, 16 May 1997.

David Bailey, *Models Close-Up* (London 1998).

Charles Castle, *Model Girl*.

BBC television archives.

Chapter Five

Pierre Balmain, *My Years and Seasons*.

Pierre Balmain: 40 Années de Création à la Musée de la Mode et du Costume (Paris 1985).

Ginette Spanier, *It Isn't All Mink* (London 1959).

Michael Gross, *Model: The Ugly Business of Beautiful Women* (London 1995).

Jean-Noël Laiut, *Cover-Girls and Supermodels 1945–1965* (Paris 1994).

Chapter Six

Bronwen Astor's private archive – correspondence with Bill Astor.

BBC television archives.

Ginette Spanier, *It Isn't All Mink*.

Bronwen Astor, 'Of Psychological Aspects of Motherhood'.

Catherine Lucas, *The Times*, 23 May 1997.

Harvey Egan SJ, *Christian Mysticism* (New York 1984).

(ed. E. Allison Peers) *Collected Works of Teresa of Avila* (London 1946).

Shirley du Boulay, *Teresa of Avila* (London 1991).

Mary and Ellen Lukas, *Teilhard* (London 1977).

Pamela Cooper, *A Cloud of Forgetting* (London 1993).

Maurice Collis, *Diaries 1949–1969* (London 1977).

Chapter Seven

Michael Astor, *Tribal Feeling* (London 1963).

Viscount Astor's archive of his father's papers including letters and draft of his submission to the Denning Inquiry.

Virginia Cowles, *The Astors* (London 1979).

Richard Cockett, *David Astor and the Observer* (London 1991).

John Grigg, *Nancy Astor* (London 1980).

Christopher Sykes, *Nancy: The Life of Nancy Astor* (London 1972).

Lucy Kavaler, *The Astors* (London 1966).

Derek Wilson, *The Astors* (London 1993).

James Fox, *The Langhorne Sisters* (London 1999).

Hansard reports of Bill Astor's speeches in the House of Lords.

Maurice Collis, *Diaries*.

Nancy Astor's archive at Reading University – her correspondence with relatives and letters to her from her son Bill.

Letters to Joy Darby from Bill Astor.

Pamela Cooper, *A Cloud of Forgetting*.

Christopher Booker, *The Neophiliacs*.

Chapter Eight

Bronwen Astor's private archive – correspondence, household diaries from Cliveden, files on guest lists and her personal diary.

Interview given by Bronwen Astor to Olga Macdonald of the National Trust, 5 October 1994.

James Sherwood's introduction to David Bailey, *Models Close-Up*.

Maurice Collis, *Diaries*.

Nancy Astor's archive at Reading University – her correspondence with relatives.

Pamela Cooper, *A Cloud of Forgetting*.

Freya Stark, *Letters 1952–9 and 1960–80*, edited by Caroline Moorehead (London 1982).

Bronwen Astor, 'Of Psychological Aspects of Motherhood'.

Letters to Joy Darby from Bill Astor.

Derek Wilson, *The Astors*.

Brooke Astor, *Footprints* (London 1980).

Viscount Astor's archive of his father's papers, including letters and draft of his submission to the Denning Inquiry.

Christopher Booker, *The Neophiliacs*.

Emma Tennant, *Girlitude: A Portrait of the 50s and 60s* (London 1999).

Chapter Nine

Pamela Cooper, *A Cloud of Forgetting*.

Bronwen Astor's private archive – household diaries from Cliveden and her personal diary.

Christine Keeler, *Scandal* (London 1989).

Viscount Astor's archive of his father's papers, including letters and draft of his submission to the Denning Inquiry.

Phillip Knightley and Caroline Kennedy, *An Affair of State: The Profumo Case and the Framing of Stephen Ward* (London 1987).

Anthony Summers and Stephen Dorril, *Honeytrap* (London 1987).

Ludovic Kennedy, *The Trial of Stephen Ward* (London 1964).

Derek Wilson, *The Astors*.

Christopher Booker, *The Neophiliacs*.

David Thurlow, *Profumo: The Hate Factor* (London 1992).

Government papers concerning the Profumo scandal (1962–3) in the Public Records Office.

Bishop Gordon Savage's written recollections in Bronwen Astor's private archive.

Maurice Collis, *Diaries*.

Chapter Ten

Bronwen Astor's private archive – correspondence with Bill Astor and her personal diary.

Bishop Gordon Savage's written recollections in Bronwen Astor's private archive.

Mandy Rice-Davies, *The Mandy Report* (London 1964).

Mandy Rice-Davies with Shirley Flack, *Mandy* (London 1980).

Maurice Collis, *Diaries*.

Sir Alun Pugh's written recollections in Bronwen Astor's private archive.

Ludovic Kennedy, *The Trial of Stephen Ward*.

Viscount Astor's archive of his father's papers, including letters and draft of his submission to the Denning Inquiry.

Chapter Eleven

Maurice Collis, *Diaries*.
Pamela Cooper, *A Cloud of Forgetting*.
Christopher Booker, *The Neophiliacs*.
Lord Denning, *Report on the Profumo Scandal* (London 1963).
Lord Denning, *Family Story* (London 1981).
Archive of the Disasters' Emergency Committee.
Bronwen Astor's private archive – correspondence with Bill Astor and her personal diary.
James Fox, *The Langhorne Sisters*.
Letters to Joy Darby from Bill Astor.
Freya Stark, *Letters*.
Bishop Gordon Savage's written recollections in Bronwen Astor's private archive.
Dom Robert Petitpierre, *Exorcising Devils* (London 1976).

Chapter Twelve

Papers in Flora Glendon-Hill's private archive.
Austin Flannery (ed.), *Documents of the Second Vatican Council* (London 1975).
Thomas Corbishley, *The Spirituality of Teilhard de Chardin* (London 1971).
René Laurentin, *Pentecostal Catholics* (London 1974).
Brenda Maddox, *George's Ghosts* (London 1999).
Bronwen Astor's private archive – papers and correspondence.
James More-Molyneux, *The Loseley Challenge* (London 1995).

Chapter Thirteen

John O'Donohue, *Anam Cara: Spiritual Wisdom from the Celtic World* (London 1997).
Audio archive of the Wrekin Trust.

Index

Younger Brother, Younger Son

A Memoir

Colin Clark

'As exhilarating as a drive in a Bristol 401 . . . breezy and bracing and a bit dodgy round the bends.'

HELEN OSBORNE, *Sunday Telegraph*

Living in the shadow of an illustrious father, the art historian Kenneth Clark, and a formidable elder brother, Colin Clark, author of the acclaimed *The Prince, the Showgirl and Me*, has always derived great pleasure from simply being able to observe. In this delightfully engaging and informal memoir he writes with wit and affection about his extraordinary family and upbringing, his work and friendship with Laurence Olivier and Vivien Leigh, his life as a film-maker, his passion for cars, and the many loves in his life. Throughout there are entertaining vignettes of artists at work and 'monsters' at play. Anecdotes abound about his brother Alan, of course, as well as Henry Moore, the Queen Mother, Margot Fonteyn, Nöel Coward, Prince Charles, Rudolf Nureyev, Goldie Hawn and many more.

'Hilarious anecdotes and sharp portraits abound . . . exquisitely judged . . . Neither his brother Alan nor his father Kenneth would have been able to write a book like this – generous, reflective, witty and elegant.'

CHRISTOPHER SILVESTER, *Sunday Times*

'Unremittingly fresh, amusing and understated . . . This is quite the nicest memoir of room-serviced Bohemia since *The Moon's a Balloon* by David Niven.'

FREDERIC RAPHAEL, *Times Literary Supplement*

0-00-638824-8

Gerald Durrell

The Authorised Biography

Douglas Botting

'Douglas Botting is to be congratulated on *Gerald Durrell*. He has done a magnificent job in telling the complex story of a complex person, wrinkles and all.'

DAVID BELLAMY, *Literary Review*

When Gerald Durrell died in 1995, at the age of seventy, he left behind an extraordinary legacy. As a pioneer animal conservationist, television personality and much-loved writer who inspired generations of readers with books like *My Family and Other Animals*, *The Bafut Beagles*, *A Zoo in My Luggage* and *The Amateur Naturalist*, he packed a dozen lives into a single lifetime. Charismatic, passionate and above all dedicated to his crusade on behalf of animals and endangered species, he was founder of one of the world's leading zoos and of the Jersey Wildlife Preservation Trust, now renamed the Durrell Wildlife Conservation Trust in his honour.

'Brilliant.' DESMOND MORRIS

'Douglas Botting's biography is as large in spirit as the subject himself and opens the mind to many crucial concerns.'

DAVID HUGHES, *Sunday Telegraph*

'A monumental biography.'

ANTHONY HOLDEN, *Sunday Express*

'Botting's admiration and affection for his subject are infectious.' *Sunday Times*

'An absorbing, hugely appealing story.' *New Scientist*

0-00-638730-6

The Prince, the Showgirl and Me

The Colin Clark Diaries

Colin Clark

'Hurrah. Another Clark diary. Fruity, lascivious, apple-cart upturning, this has all the elements we have come to expect from the Clark school of diarifying . . . quite wondrously and toe-curlingly frank . . .'   JOANNA PITMAN, *The Times*

In 1956, the 23-year-old Colin Clark, younger son of Sir Kenneth, got his first job working as a humble 'gofer' on the film of *The Prince and the Showgirl* – the film that united Britain's foremost classical actor, Sir Laurence Olivier (who was also directing), with Hollywood's most glamorous sex symbol, Marilyn Monroe (on honeymoon with her new husband, the playwright Arthur Miller). The resulting confusions and complications are deliciously exposed in Colin Clark's first-hand record of the time.

'This is a wildly funny book . . . vastly better than the film it chronicles.'   SHERIDAN MORLEY, *Sunday Times*

'Sheer delight . . . a diarist who is as sharp, funny and irreverent as his older brother Alan.'

CHARLES SPENCER, *Sunday Telegraph*

'My favourite book of the year'   JOAN COLLINS

'Extraordinarily compulsive reading . . . a fascinating document.'   NIGEL WILLIAMS, *Mail on Sunday*

0 00 638710 1